POETRY & POSTERITY

E D N A LONGLEY

◆

Poetry &
Posterity

BLOODAXE BOOKS

ISBN: 1 85224 434 8 hardback edition
      1 85224 435 6 paperback edition

First published 2000 by
Bloodaxe Books Ltd,
Highgreen,
Tarset,
Northumberland NE48 1RP.

Bloodaxe Books Ltd acknowledges
the financial assistance of Northern Arts.

Cover printing by J. Thomson Colour Printers Ltd, Glasgow.

Printed in Great Britain by
Cromwell Press Ltd, Trowbridge, Wiltshire.

In memoriam
PADDY DEVLIN

Poetry, which is written while no one is looking, is meant to be looked at for all time –

KENNETH KOCH, 'My Olivetti Speaks'

CONTENTS

Preface: A Note on Posterity

Posterity is an unfashionable concept nowadays. Other words beginning with 'post' have reduced its popularity and challenged its authority. According to some literary theorists, we live in a post-posterity era. The future, like the past, has become a thing of the past so that we inhabit a postmodern continuum, cruise the interpretation highway, log on to an infinite set of rewritings and rereadings which can never be printed out. Similarly, virtual money is bad metaphorical news for the evaluative *caveat* 'Posterity has not printed its banknotes yet'. But few writers or artists behave as if such fluid conditions prevailed. And even those who espouse an aesthetic of the disposable would not deny their artwork its fifteen minutes of fame. Posterity, the chance of art communicating across time, is invoked whenever you fail to shred the poem, wipe the videotape, omit the formaldehyde. Art has the last laugh on works that (like Duchamp's urinal) laugh at art. Nor are all readers yet so diffused into cyberspace or locked into sectional 'interpretive communities', that they have ceased to be that still more unfashionable concept – a human being. As such, we can probably empathise, for instance, with W.H. Auden's effort to 'imagine a faultless love/ Or the life to come'. In doing so, we recognise that 'In Praise of Limestone' (see pp.167-77) has set some of its own sights on posterity. This poem is also relevant because it proposes the terms in which it might be understood, the grounds on which it might be valued. But most poets find ways of advertising their poetic landscapes to unknown readers.

Since the idea of posterity is inseparable from the idea of value, both ideas have come under fire together. In *Contingencies of Value* Barbara Herrnstein Smith uses the volatile reception of Shakespeare's *Sonnets* to argue that, because all readings are historically contingent, 'the properties of literary works' will never constitute the basis of any 'true' evaluation: 'those properties are *themselves* among the variables of literary value'. Thus when David Hume observed ...that ' "the same Homer who pleased at Athens and Rome two thousand years ago is still admired at Paris and London", we have reason to wonder if it is indeed quite the "same" Homer'.[1] Yet Smith may attribute too much agency to institutional forces, too little to literature's own devices. If, as has been said, a poem reads its readers, it encodes the parameters of its own interpretation.

This does not mean that poets can (consciously) control every nuance or anticipate all posterity's angles, though it is an academic fallacy that they always assume such authority. In his elegy for Yeats, Auden voices trade-wisdom: 'The words of a dead man/Are modified in the guts of the living'. But even as critical language changes, or favours qualities that interest a particular age or culture, there are things that it would be ridiculous to say about the *Iliad*. 'Homer' at this millennium is surely a little more 'the same' than the proverbial 'same' axe with its series of new heads and handles.

This book is often concerned with audience: with cultural and ideological 'variables' that influence the reading as well as writing of poems. Yet my aim is to clear one or two obstacles in the critical way, or stake out some critical territory, rather than relativise all reception. Smith says that 'with respect to value, everything is always in motion with respect to everything else', but the comparative value of value-judgments is also at issue – not just neutral relations between the variables.[2] Patterns emerge in the responses to Shakespeare's *Sonnets* that illuminate "the poems themselves". And when (in our role as posterity) we argue about value – as we go on doing, whatever our canonical criteria – we end up appealing to some diagram of "the poem itself". That this can never be definitive need not disqualify it as a working hypothesis which takes the argument further.

To claim that a poem or body of poetry will last ('So long lives this, and this gives life to thee') is the most extreme way to claim that it is good. Yet this rhetorical trope has roots in real desire. The model posterity poem is, of course, Horace's *Odes*, III, 33, the self-advertisement placed at the end of what he then saw as his finished lyric achievement:

Exegi monumentum aere perennius
regalique situ pyramidum altius,
quod non imber edax, non Aquilo impotens
possit diruere aut innumerabilis
annorum series et fuga temporum.
Non omnis moriar, multaque pars mei
vitabit Libitinam: usque ego postera
crescam laude recens, dum Capitolium
scandet cum tacita virgine pontifex...

(I have completed a monument, more lasting than bronze and loftier than the majestic plan for the pyramids, which neither corrosive rain nor raging wind can bring down, nor the infinite series of years nor centuries passing. I shall not wholly die: a large part of me will elude Libitina [the goddess of death]: I shall go on being renewed in the praise of posterity so long as the chief priest climbs the Capitol with a silent Vestal.)

Whereas at one level, Horace may inadvertently put a term to his
fame (if the 'dum' clause is to be taken literally); at another, he pits
his poetry's strengths against more powerful forces than human
institutions. Horace's *Odes* have thus far survived material hazard;
and since poets still revise and dispute 'Exegi monumentum' (which
condenses other aspects of his influence), the *Odes'* posterity as
tradition or intertextuality continues.

But more absolute survival remains at stake. All posterity poems
dwell on the tension between 'monument' on the one hand; time,
history and Nature powerfully allied on the other. Richard Wilbur
wrote 'To the Etruscan Poets' – an elegy for all the world's lost
lyrics – because he 'began to be burdened by the thought of how
it would be to have committed all of your best ideas, all of your
best sounds and movements, to a language now utterly dead':

> Dream fluently, still brothers, who when young
> Took with your mother's milk the mother tongue.
>
> In which pure matrix, joining word and mind,
> You strove to leave some line of verse behind
>
> Like a fresh track across a field of snow,
> Not reckoning that all could melt and go.

Modernity and its metaphysics have strengthened Libitina's hand.
Louis MacNeice begins 'Memoranda to Horace' with a blunt advers-
ative asyndeton: '*Aere perennius?* Dissolving dialects'. Although the
speaker later decides ' "More lasting than bronze" will do', he has
exposed the poem-as-monument to textual as well as historical
instability. The second stanza of Derek Mahon's 'Heraclitus on
Rivers' takes MacNeice's entropic vista to a logical and incontro-
vertible conclusion:

> You will tell me that you have executed
> A monument more lasting than bronze;
> But even bronze is perishable.
> Your best poem, you know the one I mean,
> The very language in which the poem
> Was written, and the idea of language,
> All these things will pass away in time.

Yet the idea of value persists this side of universal dissolution ('Your
best poem, you know the one I mean'). Philip Larkin takes a more
middle-distance view in 'An Arundel Tomb', a reflexive medita-
tion on posterity. Contemplating the 'earl and countess [lying] in
stone', the speaker notices, and notices himself noticing, a feature
that moves a modern spectator: 'His hand withdrawn, holding her
hand'. The reflection that this was originally 'just a detail friends

would see:/A sculptor's sweet commissioned grace/ Thrown off in helping to prolong/ The Latin names around the base' leads him to consider the meanings that the monument may have lost or found in the course of its survival into 'an unarmorial age':

> They would not guess how early in
> Their supine stationary voyage
> The air would turn to soundless damage,
> Turn the old tenantry away;
> How soon succeeding eyes begin
> To look, not read. Rigidly they
>
> Persisted, linked, through lengths and breadths
> Of time. Snow fell, undated. Light
> Each summer thronged the glass. A bright
> Litter of birdcalls strewed the same
> Bone-riddled ground. And up the paths
> The endless altered people came,
>
> Washing at their identity...

'Soundless damage' (imber edax) consists in the incapacity of 'the endless altered people' (innumerabilis/annorum series) to 'read' the tomb's full text, not merely to decipher 'The Latin names around the base'. Looking, not reading implies an erosion of complexity – 'contingencies of value'. Yet it also suggests a survival of the essential (meaning, not 'identity') rather than the accidental: 'a trough/ Of smoke in slow, suspended skeins/Above their scrap of history,/ Only an attitude remains'. As for the poem's own 'attitude', this depends on how we understand its intricately ambiguous last stanza:

> Time has transfigured them into
> Untruth. The stone fidelity
> They hardly meant has come to be
> Their final blazon, and to prove
> Our almost-instinct almost true:
> What will survive of us is love.

One interpretation is that untruth to history ('lie in stone') may be truth to art. Similarly, Larkin's armorial stylisation of industrial modernity ('slow, suspended skeins'), if partly parodic, implies that his poem, with its own conventions and formalities, will also transmit some kind of 'meaning' to the future. What he 'hardly meant' will not have wholly lost touch with what he (like the tomb's sculptor rather than its occupants) may have meant to mean. Indeed, poet and sculptor collaborate in a continuing 'blazon'. Perhaps the ultimate ambiguity is that Larkin cannot quite bring himself to fulfil the poem's logic with: 'What will survive of us is art'.

Poets who place form in the foreground of their enterprise are more likely to sustain the monumental analogy, however vestigially or self-ironically. But perhaps other poets dare not speak the name of a desire so fundamental to desire itself. Yeats, who shadows Horace in these modern posterity-poems, renewed the rhetoric of poetic durability by attaching architectural and sculptural symbols to his own achievement. Yeats's rhetoric as monument-maker is inversely proportional to the instability that his poetry negotiates: modernity, Irish and European wars, the disappearance of his cultural world, "modernist" challenges to his aesthetic that have brought 'dissolving dialects' into the heart of the citadel (see pp.216-17). These conditions sum up the assault to which the twentieth century has subjected poetry as 'monument' – a prominently self-referential word amid the turbulence of *The Tower* (1928). Only art, initially defined in 'Sailing to Byzantium' as 'Monuments of un-ageing intellect', alleviates a fear that enduring value, and the idea of value, have disappeared from the public world:

Come let us mock at the great
That had such burdens on the mind
And toiled so hard and late
To leave some monument behind,
Nor thought of the levelling wind.

Yet Yeats, too, must admit the possibility of 'dissolving dialects', of art-levelling wind, of people who might 'look, not read' or simply not be out there. His dialogue-poem 'The Man and the Echo' (1938) identifies the communication-gap between poet and reader with that between humanity and the universe. This implies that the stakes for poetry figure those for people. 'Echo' repeats the last phrases of the dialectically negative and positive creeds/ poems that 'Man' utters: 'Lie down and die', and 'Into the night'. The levelling repetition might be neutral or proleptic of posterity as a black hole. Ominously, as Warwick Gould has shown,[3] Yeats's instinct for revision, together with a range of contingencies, always deferred his projected 'definitive edition', his monumental book.

'Exegi monumentum' activates imagery of pyramids, tombs, statues and graveyards: 'Forms a stark Egyptian thought,/ Forms that gentler Phidias wrought', to quote Yeats's 'Under Ben Bulben'. When Larkin excludes history (he does not ignore it), love and death survive as the inextricable object of art on 'the same/ Bone-riddled ground'. If lyric poetry seems especially obsessed with posterity, this is owing to its complex interchange between self and artefact (in which the male self may invest more than the female). The poetic 'body' hopefully metamorphoses into inorganic permanence. In

my essay 'Larkin, Decadence and the Lyric Poem' I argue that
narcissism conditions Larkin's commitment to perfection of the
work. 'Non omnis moriar', says Horace. 'Once out of nature I shall
never take/ My bodily form from any natural thing,/ But such a form
as Grecian goldsmiths make', says Yeats in 'Sailing to Byzantium'.
Yet there is an opposing wariness of such iconic fixity, of the
artistic risks involved in ordering your own tomb. MacNeice's 'To
Posterity' begins: 'When the books have all seized up like the books
in graveyards'. Here petrifaction, rather than flux or dissolution,
symbolises inaccessible meanings. Robert Graves's satirical 'To
Evoke Posterity' represents posterity itself as a tomb, a death-mask,
a Medusa to which no poet or public man should defer:

> To evoke posterity
> Is to weep on your own grave,
> Ventriloquising for the unborn:
> 'Would you were present in flesh, hero!
> What wreaths and junketings!'

> And the punishment is fixed:
> To be found fully ancestral,
> To be cast in bronze for a city square,
> To dribble green in times of rain
> And stain the pedestal.

> Spiders in the spread beard;
> A life proverbial
> On clergy lips a-cackle;
> Eponymous institutes,
> Their luckless architecture...

> Alive, you have abhorred
> The crowds on holiday
> Jostling and whistling – yet would you air
> Your death-mask smoothly lidded,
> Along the promenade?

As applied to poetry, this parable suggests that conscious care for
posthumous fame detaches poets from the life of their own art.
(MacNeice makes a related point when he says that if poets do
their 'duty by the present moment, posterity can look after itself'.)[4]
Graves's imagery of (significantly 'bronze') statuary, institutes,
church and state equates posterity with the bourgeoisie. To evoke
posterity, in his lexicon, is to connive at pressures that would
defuse or engross poetry by tempting it to exchange its arrogant
freedom for a lesser vanity.

Graves does not mean that posterity does not exist. In character-
istic style, he warns that poetry must never seek popularity through
compromise but survive on its own terms by creating its own

audience. The next poem in his *Collected Poems* portrays his ideal posterity as the 'honest housewife' who will 'sort them out': the personification of sound value-judgments. And, of course, Graves's rhetoric says what, for Auden, all poets' criticism says: 'Read me. Don't read the other fellows'.[5] Posterity may be too assiduously courted whenever we catch poets prolonging a pose in the mirror of history – for instance, writing a letter with an eye not to the recipient, the messy moment, the point at issue, but to an eventual archive. Donald Hall distinguishes between 'true' and 'petty' ambition:

> True ambition in a poet seeks fame in the old sense, to make words that live for ever. If even to entertain such ambition reveals monstrous egotism, let me argue that the common alternative is petty egotism that spends itself in small competitiveness, that measures its success by quantity of publication, by blurbs on jackets, by small achievement: to be the best poet in the workshop, to be published by Knopf, to win the Pulitzer or the Nobel…The grander goal is to be as good as Dante.[6]

Yet the two kinds of ambition are not mutually exclusive and may be interdependent. Some of Yeats's letters involve a fascinating balancing-act between present and future audiences. There are extra-poetic worries too. Contemporary poets disposed to censor imperfections of the life will have noted the fallout from Larkin's uncleared attic – though what did he *intend*? But Ted Hughes's *Birthday Letters* shows, I think, that it is equally possible to make a stain worse by rubbing. In any case, the publication further illustrates the desire to reach, evoke, control posterity. But if Hughes's attempt proves counter-productive, this will be down to imperfections of the art.

'Exegi monumentum' finally speaks for more than personal or even artistic ambition. There are collective aspects to its insistence on poetry as communication, poetry as survival. On the first count, it covers Wilfred Owen's wish that his 'elegies' should go on refusing to console. On the second, it articulates the deepest impulse behind all human creativity and religion. It is no accident that love and death, tombs and statues, should dominate posterity poems. And while Yeats's running, losing battle with 'tatters in [his] mortal dress' is again paradigmatic; equally so is a war-poet's ever-impending deadline or Raymond Carver's resort to poetry rather than prose as he wrote against the dying of the light. In 'Through the Boughs', Carver sets up rhythmic cross-currents between a mimesis of time moving fast, and effects (observing the birds, addressing another person) that suggest the poet's mind at work on the world and thereby resisting the temporal flow:

Down below the window, on the deck, some ragged-looking
birds gather at the feeder. The same birds, I think,
that come every day to eat and quarrel. *Time was, time was,*
they cry and strike at each other. It's nearly time, yes.
The sky stays dark all day, the wind is from the west and
won't stop blowing…Give me your hand for a time. Hold on
to mine. That's right, yes. Squeeze hard. Time was we
thought we had time on our side. *Time was, time was,*
those ragged birds cry.

'Those ragged birds', as much as Yeats's golden singer, still speak
for the poet. Again, Frank O'Hara's habit of writing poems *in
medias res* does not really substitute process for product, flesh for
monument. His 'I do this, I do that' poems dramatise an obsessive
desire to preserve and transmit 'what is passing', to pit love
against death by making poetry permeate the whole of life. Here
communication and survival are indistinguishable. Comparing
O'Hara's poetry to New York skyscrapers, John Ashbery calls it
'modest and monumental'.[7] Donald Allen, editor of O'Hara's
Collected Poems, also uses an architectural metaphor, calling the
book a 'splendid palace'.[8] In 'Having a Coke with You' O'Hara as
lover says:

> it is hard to believe when I'm with you that there can be anything as still
> as solemn as unpleasantly definitive as statuary when right in front of it
> in the warm New York 4 o'clock light we are drifting back and forth
> between each other like a tree breathing through its spectacles
>
> and the portrait show seems to have no faces in it at all, just paint
> you suddenly wonder why in the world anyone ever did them
>   I look
> at you and I would rather look at you than all the portraits in the world…
>
> and the fact that you move so beautifully more or less takes care of
>   Futurism

But this is an old trope if in vividly fresh guise. Although the
speaker says of the artists mocked by the dead posterity of their
art, 'it seems they were all cheated of some marvellous experience',
he continues and ends with the *pleasantly* definitive: 'which is not
going to go wasted on me which is why I'm telling you about it'.
'You' is posterity (Futurism) as well as the loved one.

Yeats's testamentary disposition of his poetry in 'Under Ben
Bulben' contains an anti-monumental clause: 'No marble, no con-
ventional phrase'. In fact, this clears the way for a proper pyramid.
Posterity is asked to receive his complete works as their art itself
both admits and resists mortality: '*Cast a cold eye/ On life, on
death*'. Important to the final graveyard scene, as to the whole poem,
is the validating presence of tradition and form: 'An ancestor was

rector there...By the road an ancient cross...On limestone quarried near the spot...these words are cut'. Yeats's careful exterior decoration seems remote from 'the warm New York 4 o'clock light' or 'ragged birds crying'. Or is it? Monuments, of course, take many forms. But they do *take form*. Graves's main point is that a premature eye on posterity wrenches poetry out of the proper shape wherein and whereby it should reach posterity: 'their luckless architecture'. Horace rests his claim to fame on a formal achievement: 'princeps Aeolium carmen ad Italos/ deduxisse modos' (first to have based Italian poetry on Greek measures). In 'Personism: A Manifesto' O'Hara asserts, if only to break, the link between the formal and religious impulses: 'I don't believe in god, so I don't have to make elaborately sounded structures'. Yet he does not rule out found as opposed to pre-ordained shape ('You just go on your nerve'), and he reintroduces form by the back door: 'As for measure and other technical apparatus, that's just common sense: if you're going to buy a pair of pants you want them to be tight enough so that everyone will want to go to bed with you.'[9] Form as perpetual seduction contrasts (tonally as well) with Yeats's belief in form as preservative: 'all that is personal soon rots; it must be packed in ice or salt...Ancient salt is best packing.'[10] But whether form is a come-on or saves poems from going off, some kind of patterning remains integral to their traffic with posterity, as when accent and assonance create the memorable rising/falling cadence of 'when I try to imagine a faultless love/ Or the life to come', or when Carver's seemingly prosaic poem broods on its refrain. Kenneth Koch uses the same metaphor as O'Hara when he says of his own writing:

> The music has to be there...the pull of a phrase or a line is the only true sign that something worthwhile may be beginning. Whether it's in quatrains, couplets, blank verse, ottava rima, or free verse doesn't matter at all in that respect. It's like the difference between being attracted to someone at court or in a bowling alley. Along the way one may say something memorable.[11]

Poetry's oral origins suggest the interdependence of pattern and memory rather than an amnesiac affinity with hypertextual flux. While saying that a poet can take or leave rhyme (though not rhythm), Paul Muldoon calls it 'one of the crucial means by which, from an early age, we find shapes in the world'.[12] Those mechanisms of tradition which MacNeice calls 'repetition-devices' may be survival mechanisms.

Who would want to go to bed with a Language poem? A masochist, possibly. In the words of Geoff Ward: 'The...Language position...contemporary with the arguments of literary theory is

that the various kinds of linguistic dishevelment and terroristic
circuit breaking available to poetry belong to, as well as pointing
up, social/linguistic reality as a site of incessant contestation and
contradiction.'[13] The hostility of some 'literary theory' to any kind
of formal measure or pleasure or closure may be more than just
another neo-Poundian outbreak. It could mark intensifying splits
in the audience for poetry as compared with the broader horizons
that Louis MacNeice (as I suggest in an essay on 'MacNeice as
Critic') could still – just – keep in view. Certainly, the academic
and the poetry-reviewer less often speak the same language or
engage the same constituency, as Sean O'Brien complains in *The
Deregulated Muse*: 'it is of limited use to me to read criticism writ-
ten in the interior code of a class or professional cadre...Much of
my reading in recent years has been done in the context of working
as a reviewer for magazines and newspapers.'[14] In fact academics
who write even on contemporary poets, even if not openly hostile,
are not necessarily interested in 'poetry' or poetry criticism. (Hence
Larkin's more pessimistic view of 'Posterity' as Jake Balokowsky –
no 'honest housewife' he.) Peter McDonald in *Mistaken Identities:
Poetry and Northern Ireland* (1997) has attacked a complementary
derivative from theory: 'identity-discourse'. To prove his point,
along comes Peter Childs's *The Twentieth Century in Poetry* (1999),
whose last chapter is headed 'Anti- and Post-Colonial Writing:
Northern Irish and Black British Poets', and begins: 'This chapter
is concerned with identity, or, more specifically, with fractured,
heterogeneous, and hybrid identities.'[15] 'Linguistic dishevelment'
denotes a narrow view of poetry's potential effects; 'fractured...
identities' a narrow view of its possible origins. In 'The Millennial
Muse' I suggest that the conditions which gave us the plural noun
'poetries' make it harder for poetry to reach posterity. Poetries
reaching posterities seems unlikely.

Yet to indulge in terminal gloom ('The last poem has been writ-
ten') as to adopt a cheery Dunkirk spirit ('All those plucky little
poems!') might magnify rather than identify problems. Geoffrey
Hill's inaptly named sequence *The Triumph of Love* (1998) berates
contemporary poetic and critical decadence from an insulated
bunker somewhere on Parnassus: 'What remains? You may well ask.
Construction/or deconstruction? There is some poor/mimicry of
choice, whether you build or destroy'. Sven Birkerts's apocalyptic
The Gutenberg Elegies (1994) cries woe more eloquently and per-
suasively, as in his chapter 'The Death of Literature':

> The value of literature survives, as W.H. Auden said of poetry, 'In the
> valley of its saying where executives/Would never want to tamper' –

but it is a value that fewer and fewer people feel they cannot live without
... Literature – serious fiction and poetry and the discourse that has
always accompanied them and helped make them a way of talking about
important and difficult aspects of our universal experience – all of lit-
erature now occupies the place marked out by Auden as the estate of
poetry. Which is to say: It is not extinct, it has its partisans, it makes
its small noise, but does so as the big parade of the rest of the world
goes clattering by.[16]

Thirty-five years earlier, MacNeice's 'To Posterity' had spotted the
same tendency:

> When books have all seized up like the books in graveyards
> And reading and even speaking have been replaced
> By other, less difficult, media, we wonder if you
> Will find in flowers and fruit the same colour and taste
> They held for us for whom they were framed in words,
> And will your grass be green, your sky be blue,
> Or will your birds be always wingless birds?

Did MacNeice believe that, sooner rather than later, poetry would
have no posterity? Is 'To Posterity' prophecy or critique? In 'Louis
MacNeice's Posterity' Peter McDonald comments: 'the poem's
carefully pitched question is not presuming on an answer. "To
Posterity" may be speaking up for words, but it is also a poem
that has taken the measure of time's way with words, and knows
the odds against which, as a poem, it is operating.' The main focus
of McDonald's article is how MacNeice's own posterity, variously
'operating' (as the poem itself does) in the work of other poets,
lengthens the odds. McDonald raises the stakes when he concludes
that MacNeice's poetry may even, in some cases, be 'one of the
indispensable conditions for their poetry's existence'.[17] The academic
emphasis on Oedipal anxiety, on rupture, on Homer's blank con-
tingency misses the excitement, let alone significance, of posterity
as tradition and reinvention. Besides begetting a posterity for itself,
'To Posterity' may modify in its guts Yeats's 'The Fascination of
What's Difficult' and Keats's 'viewless wings of poesy'. But MacNeice
(like Yeats in 'The Man and the Echo') also equates poetic posterity
with human communication in the broadest sense. Here 'books'
(literature, poetry) and speech (language) belong to the same cog-
nitive system. MacNeice suggests two main ways in which humanity
would be impoverished if it scrapped this system, if 'we' and 'you'
ceased to communicate. First, the substitute media would be 'less
difficult'. Second, to lose language in its spoken and written forms
would be to lose a mediation between human beings and the phe-
nomenal world that creates as well as heightens experience: 'will
your grass be green, your sky be blue?'

MacNeice does not take a naively referential or representational view of language and literary language. But neither does he deny the intercourse between language and life, the cultural accretions of language, that constitute the ground of poetry. In 'Edward Thomas and Ecocentrism' I argue that Thomas conceives poetry ecologically; in 'Louis MacNeice as Critic', that MacNeice conceives poetry communally. But the distinction is not hard and fast. For both, poetry has a special capacity to make or elicit connections (including disconnections) that locate us in a 'difficult' earthly environment. When 'To Posterity' highlights its own connective tissue, as in the rhyme words/birds, this symbolises other possible reciprocities. Theoretically, the rhyme might be an arbitrary chime; artistically, it epitomises how poets take the chances that language gives them. MacNeice advances his argument through irregularities as well as repetition-devices. The phrase 'other, less difficult, media' occupies the 'speech' end of the poetic spectrum. It thus manifests the links between speaking, reading and writing, while interjecting a suitably difficult rhythm into the poem's longest line. 'Difficult' is also the only trisyllable in a poem that accents monosyllables as if to flaunt its 'beat'. In the last three lines a movement towards strict iambic pentameter, together with the concluding rhyme, carries an epigrammatic as well as visionary charge. Rhetorically designed to sting 'posterity', this effect may assist the poem's (and poetry's) survival in that direction.

The odds against which a poem operates include the noise of history as well as the silences of oblivion and dissolution. Literary history can be noisy too. Thus the study of reputations and readerships helps us to make more sense of the poetic 'stock-market' as captured, for instance, by Donald Hall speaking (in 1992) of modern American poets: 'Lately, after a decade of swoon, Frost's stock has ascended again; Benét has disappeared from the board. Meanwhile, Eliot remains under attack, Pound is an obsession or an anathema, Cummings dwindles, H.D.'s reputation rises, and Stevens is deified.' Of course, revolutions of taste are essential (if taste genuinely leads them). As Hall puts it: 'Excellent plain-speaking late twentieth century American poets will look boring for a while – as Dylan Thomas struts back from the grave.'[18] Yet bad taste can sometimes make poetry happen. In 'The Poetics of Celt and Saxon' I consider how Celticism, set in motion by Macpherson's *Ossian*, has inspired good and bad poems as well as problematic cultural and political ideology. The Ossianic phenomenon also illustrates the uses of Ireland as a vantage-point from which to think about poetry and audience. This is because Irish poets' awareness of multiple audiences, multiple traditions, both inside and outside the country, complicates horizons of expectation; while, at the same time, "Ireland" may loom too large for some readers, too small for others. In 'Pastoral Theologies' I argue that Irish Nature or country poetry can be misread by Anglo-American criticism. Meanwhile, the critical 'posterity' of Irish poetry in Ireland itself remains subject to historical convulsions. But my overall point, in several essays, is that the current over-emphasis on ethnic or national identities obscures the actively inter-national, inter-cultural aesthetic dialectics that shaped modern poetry in English.

Perhaps 'identity-discourse' has especially reductive effects on poetry because poetry itself has been reduced to a 'subculture' – as Dana Gioia calls it in *Can Poetry Matter?* Building on previous epitaphs for the art, Gioia argues that poetry, which once 'mattered to the entire educated [American] community', has 'lost the confidence that it speaks to and for the general culture', and thus ceased to be 'part of the mainstream of artistic and intellectual life'.[19] Yet in the US 'general culture' and 'mainstream' have also lost confidence. And even if we think that things are better hereabouts (risky, since posterity tends to be America), Gioia reminds us that poetry once mattered greatly not only as a social but as an intellectual presence. The more it is pushed to the literary margins (displaced by fiction, biography and theory to name but a few), the more literature itself is marginalised or blurred into culture, the more "culture" subdivides, the less ambition most poets display.

Fredric Jameson thinks it 'a non-Hegelian and moralising position' either to 'deplore or celebrate "an end of art" identified with the end of literature, the canon, or reading as such'.[20] Yet, to view poetry ecologically: should it not be practised and valued as an irreplaceable mode of cognition, one that creates meanings central to human culture, meanings unavailable elsewhere? Hence all the exegesis it attracts. Although poetry's primitive holistic functions – religious, philosophical, political, therapeutic, medicinal, festive – have been usurped, this need not shut down the holistic awareness that warrants all its 'ambition' and fuels the self-belief that Gioia finds lacking. If language is the 'matrix joining world and mind' (Wilbur), and poetry the most concentrated arrangement of language, poetry can potentially model 'world and mind' in their most complex structural interrelations. It also concentrates language as critique. Concentration, manifested as a 'music' (Koch) that overrides arguments about "free" or "traditional" verse, is the meta-formal quality that distinguishes the genre, allowing a poem to say several contrapuntal or contradictory things at once. The objection to a reductive practice and theory of poetry is that it makes culture or politics or the psyche a one-dimensional and hence simplistic and ephemeral criterion. *Birthday Letters*, overblown in its psychological aspect, has been received in this way. Hughes's consciously Freudian psycho-drama may actually tell posterity less about the psyche than Philip Larkin discloses in poems that also visit other points of the compass, and whose primary ambition is to be poems.

If poetry retrospectively appears prophetic, this is because it looks in more than one direction or in unexpected directions. Comparing a poet's cognitive processes with those of the researching scholar, Robert Frost says: 'The poet's instinct is to shun or shed more knowledge than he can swing or sing.'[21] Posterity catches up on poetry as poetry swings into the future. For example, I argue that the interrelations modelled by Edward Thomas's poems prefigure environmental thinking. Glimpses of new politics and metaphysics emerge from his meditation on the English countryside in several overlapping contexts: massive social upheaval, the Great War, traditions of rural writing, his own psychological problems. This also means that Thomas's brand of 'elegy', like Wilfred Owen's, keeps on conveying to posterity what posterity has lost. Here cultural memory depends on poetry being memorable. My last essay focuses on Northern Irish poetry at a historical moment that tests poetry's cognitive concentration. Drawing images from many sources, filtering history through various narrative meshes, changing the formal or generic angle, ultimately theorising the moment as no other medium can, this poetry may appear prescient to posterity. It may even be what survives of all the 'war and argument',[22] or at least until books seize up. Perhaps poetry is always elegy, for us and for itself. An anagram allows me to conclude: Posterity – it's poetry.

'The Business of the Earth': Edward Thomas and Ecocentrism

1

Modernism and Marxism fetishise the city, but in different ways. The one neglects 'Nature poetry' as having refused a cognitive and aesthetic revolution; the other criticises 'pastoral' as repressing the exploitation not only of urban workers in the present but also of rural workers in the past. For example, the unreal city of *The Waste Land* – which collapses historical cities into a spatial mosaic refracted through 'the simultaneity of the ambient' – does not meet the political demands that Raymond Williams (in *The Country and the City*) sees cities as making on the literary imagination. To Williams, T.S. Eliot's urban impressions appear 'as relentless and as conventional as pastoral...neo-urban imagery, of the same literary kind as the isolated neo-pastoral...[mediating] a general despair in the isolated observer'.[1] Ultimately he diagnoses a continuing, and perhaps necessary, conflict between modernist urban myth-making (best represented by the related but distinct consciousness-streams of *Ulysses*) and the collectivist 'social ideas and movements' also produced by the modern city. This dialectical model, with its 1930s aura, still excludes most twentieth-century rural writing in the British Isles. Although Williams finds among the texts of that tradition occasional resistance to an 'elegiac, neo-pastoral mode', nonetheless: 'The underlying pattern is...clear. A critique of a whole dimension of modern life, and with it many necessary general questions, was expressed but also reduced to a convention, which took the form of a detailed version of a part-imagined, part-observed rural England... [a] strange formation in which observation, myth, record and half-history are... deeply entwined.'[2]

These remarks follow an analysis of Edward Thomas's poetry, in which Williams discerns a few unpastoral sparks, but which he accuses of falling back on 'inexpressible alienation'. Thomas has often been squeezed by a pincer-movement of modernist and Marxist preconceptions – not that this has put off his many common readers. I want to change the perceptual ground by looking at his 'alienation' in the light of contemporary environmental theory: an approach that also reinserts him into the Edwardian period. Formerly

I have suggested that various factors prevented Thomas (1878-1917) from becoming a poet of 1900 and made him a poet of 1914. But the late twentieth century may both re-open some of Thomas's Edwardian contexts and link his 'critique of a whole dimension of modern life' (Williams) with issues now on the global political agenda. Perhaps Edward Thomas is a poet of the year 2000. Perhaps his symbolic 'warning' looks farther ahead than Wilfred Owen's, just as it had a deeper hinterland. His sonnet 'February Afternoon', which thrice repeats the phrase 'a thousand years', suggests how readily Thomas himself could think in terms of millennia, although the cumulative effect is hardly millenarian:

> Men heard this roar of parleying starlings, saw,
> A thousand years ago, even as now,
> Black rooks with white gulls following the plough
> So that the first are last until a caw
> Commands that last are first again, – a law
> Which was of old when one, like me, dreamed how
> A thousand years might dust lie on his brow
> Yet thus would birds do between hedge and shaw.

> Time swims before me, making as a day
> A thousand years, while the broad ploughland oak
> Roars mill-like and men strike and bear the stroke
> Of war as ever, audacious or resigned,
> And God still sits aloft in the array
> That we have wrought him, stone-deaf and stone-blind.[3]

Williams finds here 'a tension between [a] sense of timelessness and the sense of war in which, in a different sense "Time swims before me"'.[4] But 'February Afternoon' (to be discussed later) may, in fact, introduce a third perspective whereby human actors and constructs share in a larger earthly drama. This perspective defines Thomas's ecocentric sense of history.

In her book *Environmentalism and Political Theory: Toward an Ecocentric Approach* (1992) Robyn Eckersley sums up ecocentrism as follows: 'Ecocentrism is based on a...philosophy of *internal relatedness,* according to which all organisms are not simply inter-related with their environment but also constituted by those very environmental interrelationships.' Ecocentrism perceives the world as 'an intrinsically dynamic interconnected web...in which there are no absolutely discrete entities and no absolute dividing lines between...the animate and the inanimate, or the human and the nonhuman'.[5] Or, as Edward Thomas put it more musically and monosyllabically in 1915:

There's nothing like the sun as the year dies,
Kind as it can be, this world being made so,
To stones and men and beasts and birds and flies,
To all things that it touches except snow,
Whether on mountain side or street of town...

The irony that touches the levelling third line, with its regular monosyllabic iambics, denies humanity a primary or Promethean role in 'this world' and its making. I will argue, first, that Edward Thomas is a prophet of ecocentrism (cognate terms are biocentrism and geocentrism) not only conceptually but also in terms of poetic structure; and, second, that to read his poetry (and prose) in this light is to vindicate its Green politics/poetics against criticism from precisely those theoretical quarters which, for Eckersley, fall short of an ecocentric vision. Thus she finds that the 'orthodox eco-Marxist approach turned out to be the most active kind of discrimination against the nonhuman world'. This is because of its anthropocentric 'focus on the relations of production at the expense of the forces of production, and its uncritical acceptance of industrial technology and instrumental reason'.[6] Eckersley also analyses revisionist forms of eco-Marxism as modified by humanism and eco-socialism. While she discovers more common ground here with the ecocentric perspective, her conclusion is that anthropocentrism keeps sneaking back in, whether as a benign domestication of Nature or the recruitment of Green politics for an anti-capitalist agenda. Ultimately, the need for a paradigm-shift that would re-orient humanity's relation to the rest of Nature, is not accepted even by the most heretical Marxist thinkers.

Some of Eckersley's arguments have a literary-critical counter-part in Jonathan Bate's innovative *Romantic Ecology* (1991) and a geographic counterpart in Anne Buttimer's *Geography and the Human Spirit* (1993). Bate says in his introduction:

> The 1960s gave us an idealist reading of Romanticism which was implicitly bourgeois in its privileging of the individual imagination; the 1980s gave us a post-Althusserian Marxist critique of Romanticism. The first of these readings assumed that the human mind is superior to nature; the second assumed that the economy of human society is more important than...the economy of nature. It is precisely these asumptions that are now being questioned by green politics.[7]

In arguing that 'there is not an opposition but a continuity between [Wordsworth's] 'love of nature' and his revolutionary politics', Bate several times relies on the insights of Edward Thomas. However, he limits Thomas's ecocentric radicalism, his metaphysical and political leaps beyond Wordsworth, by highlighting only his 'localism' and concern with place-names. These emphases should be construed as strands of a larger web which amounts to more than 'connecting the self to the environment'.[8] Also, no writer more profoundly tested the Romantic poets' legacy to modernity than did Thomas in his criticism and poetry – even testing it to destruction. One problem with Bate's tentatively proposed 'ecocriticism' might be the soft streak in English readings of the English 'Nature' tradition. Here a merely personal subjectivity is the anthropocentrism that keeps sneaking back in. Nor should *every* Nature or country poem be identified with Green revolution – or all versified Green propaganda with poetry. Such traps were latent and occasionally articulated in a 'Green' issue of *Poetry Review* that appeared in 1990. Yet something more is required than the editor's reassurance that poets 'have remained animists...[exploring] the mini-Gaia of our daily life' or a reviewer's dismissal of 'telling one another how much we care in the worn-out words of greenspeak and sociobabble'.[9] The absent element might be historical and critical feeling for where (and how) poetry has pioneered Green themes. Otherwise it will lack the means to carry these themes further.

In her introduction to *Geography and the Human Spirit* Anne Buttimer calls for freedom from academic and ideological 'Faustian frames...which are no longer appropriate for the challenge of understanding humanity and earth'. She also states (and her findings stem from the International Dialogue Project 1978-1988): 'Proclamations about the meaning of humanness...make little sense geographically until they are orchestrated with the more basic nature of dwelling... Neither humanism nor geography can be regarded as an autonomous field of enquiry...The common concern is terrestial dwelling; *humanus* literally means "earth dweller".'[10] Earth, man and home are crucial and interactive terms in the poetry that Edward Thomas wrote from his particular 'temporal, geographic and cultural setting' (Buttimer's phrase). By persistently asking what it means to be an 'inhabitant of earth' ('The Other'), he anticipates the eco-humanism for which various theorists are arguing today. In 'The New Year' he takes a fresh look at the sphinx's riddle, at man the earth-dweller:

> Fifty yards off, I could not tell how much
> Of the strange tripod was a man. His body,
> Bowed horizontal, was supported equally
> By legs at one end, by a rake at the other:
> Thus he rested, far less like a man than
> His wheel-barrow in profile was like a pig.

Thomas's historical position and cultural co-ordinates place him at a nodal point in relation to current ecological issues and their intellectual repercussions. 'Mainly Welsh' but brought up in London, he moved physically and imaginatively from city to country, from metropolis to region, border and rural parish, from built to natural environments. He walked all over the south of England at a time when its suburbanisation, behind which lay agricultural depression, marked a new frontier, and perhaps limit, of the Industrial Revolution. The rapid transformation of rural southern England had no counterpart in any other European country. Thomas saw himself as a product of the London suburbs which had mushroomed without being conceptualised or imagined. One of his personae speaks of 'belonging to no class or race and having no traditions' and calls people of the suburbs 'a muddy, confused, hesitating mass'.[11] This is not just alienation that might have been voiced at any time since industrialisation or since the always-lost golden age. It belongs specifically and oppositionally to Edwardian England. Jose Harris, in *Private Lives, Public Spirit: Britain 1870-1914* (1993) emphasises how between 1871 and 1881 'the population of the most heavily urbanised counties increased by 75 per cent – the fastest decade of urban growth for the whole of the nineteenth century'. Consequently, the 'prolonged building boom of the 1870s and 1880s encircled all towns and cities with the middle- and working-class red or yellow brick suburbs, which remain the most enduring physical monument of the late Victorian age'.[12] Thomas's irritation with the title of Edward Marsh's 'Georgian' anthologies ('Not a few of these [poets] had attained their qualities under Victoria and Edward') might have extended to his own posthumous periodisation in such terms.[13]

Edward Thomas's career as a writer, including its poetic climax from December 1914 until his death, coincides with the trajectory traced by Samuel Hynes in *The Edwardian Turn of Mind*: 'to think of Edwardian England as a peaceful, opulent world before the flood is to misread the age and to misunderstand the changes that were dramatised by the First World War'. At the same time, Hynes exhibits a certain (possibly American, metropolitan and postmodernist) impatience with those who failed to swim with the tide of massive social upheaval. For example, he criticises C.F.G. Masterman's literary rural nostalgia – such as his regard for W.H. Davies's *Autobiography of a Super-Tramp* (also promoted by Thomas) – and Masterman's 'problem of accepting the idea of a twentieth-century, urban, industrial England'.[14] This was not necessarily a cultural or imaginative accommodation that could be made overnight. The 'shock of the new', as an aesthetic thrill, may bypass culture-shocks which literature needs time to absorb.

The 1930s, when English society had supposedly got used to the city, saw a back-to-Nature movement as striking as that of the 1900s – Louis MacNeice's 'hiking cockney lovers' in *Autumn Journal*. The scenario detailed by *Private Lives, Public Spirit* makes more room for Masterman's hankerings and for Thomas's disquiet with the suburbs. Throughout her study Harris stresses, not a Victorian national solidarity beginning to crumble after near-defeat in the Boer war, but a more volcanic and variegated historical, temporal and spatial picture. She concludes by underlining 'the varying pace of time, the idiosyncrasy of local habits and the frequent conjunction of quite dissimilar or contradictory social structures', and continues:

> Yet my overall point – that the true watershed came at the beginning [1870] rather than the end of the period...can be supported on many levels. The shift to a "modern" demographic structure began in the 1870s, and in the eyes of many contemporaries was already alarmingly advanced by 1914. The structural and qualitative transformation of cities did not come with with the Industrial Revolution but with the arrival of public utilities and municipal socialism after 1867...It was not the early nineteenth-century factory system, but the onset of mass-production and the retailing and financial revolutions of the 1880s that created the distinctive class, status, and consumer groups that were to characterise British society for much of the twentieth century.[15]

As a reviewer for the *Daily Chronicle* (from 1901) and the *Morning Post* (this was also the period when mass-newspapers proliferated) and in his other literary criticism, Thomas was explicit about contemporary instabilities and the challenges they posed to poetry in particular. In 1905, reviewing a book by the feminist Frances Power Cobbe, he describes the present as 'an age of doubt and balancing and testing – of distrusting the old and not very confidently expecting the new'. In the same year, reviewing new verse, he rebukes both literary Arcadianism and Arcadian literariness:

> [A] country life is neither more easy nor more simple than a city life. If it were, the world would now be ruled by the brewers, bankers, and journalists who are taking the place of hops in Kent. And just as, in thinking about life, we cry out for a return to Nature and her beneficent simplicity, so we are apt to cry out for a return to simplicity in literature ...A critic has lately spoken of *Tom Jones* and *Pendennis* as unrolling 'the infinite variety of human nature before us', and has compared Mr Meredith most unfavourably with them. They are simpler, and they do not disturb. Nothing could be more false than this attitude. If it were also strong, it might endanger much that is most characteristic of our age...Here, before us, are many views which would seem to have been inspired by a cunning search for simplicity. These men are trying to write as if there were no such thing as a Tube, Grape Nuts, love of

Nature, a Fabian Society, A Bill for the reform of the Marriage Laws; nor do they show that they are in possession of any grace or virtue which can be set up against those wonders of our age.[16]

Evidently, however, this is no straightforward hurrah for modernity. Thomas's allusions to economic and demographic change and to 'wonders of our age' are as ironical as 'cunning search for simplicity'. As for the political reformism also glanced at: his disagreements with his progressively minded father (a Liberal Party activist) and his reaction to the Bedales intelligentsia suggest dissidence from its ethos, if not its aims. Bedales was the progressive school in Hampshire near which Thomas and his family lived from December 1906. While Helen Thomas, who taught in the kindergarten, was inspired by the school's staff, she records: '[Edward] frankly did not like them, and to them he was an enigma – a solitary wandering creature…who had no political beliefs or social theories, and who was not impressed by the school or its ideals…they could not like him or rope him in at all.'[17]

Helen Thomas may take her husband's lack of politics too literally; but there might be good warrant for a writer not being impressed by any school and its ideals: Samuel Hynes quotes Beatrice Webb's admission 'without apparent regret, that she was "poetry-blind"'.[18] Yet Thomas then faced the task of developing a literary mode, and perhaps an alternative politics, which would at once interpret what was happening to Kent, remember that Grape Nuts could not be uninvented, and go beyond the false simplicities of poets such as those under review. It has to be said that it took him nearly ten more years, in the course of which his own 'love of Nature' (there is self-irony in the review, too) still perpetrated cunning simplicities: 'But at morning twilight I see the moon low in the west like a broken and dinted shield of silver hanging long forgotten outside the tent of a great knight in a wood…'[19] Thomas himself mocked 'my soarings & flutterings'[20] over *The South Country* (1909) from which that sentence comes. Yet some parts of the book organise his perceptions in a way that would eventually help to re-charge the 'Nature poem', while other chapters involve literary-critical, sociological, and ecological thinking that tends in the same direction. The literary-critical dimension matters: the Green movement does not always acknowledge its literary debts. Thomas returned to origins (early English and Welsh transactions with Nature); read, not only all Nature poetry up to its Romantic apotheosis, but also the entire tradition of 'country books' culminating in Richard Jefferies and W.H. Hudson; and asked questions about the meaning of this literature in irretrievably complex times.[21] His study *Richard Jefferies* (1909) charts Jefferies's discontent 'to some purpose...with modernity' and hard-won holistic awareness of 'the diverse life of the world, in man, in beast, in tree, in earth and sky, and sea, and stars'.[22] Thomas looked for contemporary works 'which really show, in verse or prose, the inseparableness of Nature and Man' and approved a modern 'diminution of man's importance in the landscape'. At the same time, he savaged the 'chattering' Nature-trash he received for review, and (prefiguring *Romantic Ecology*) regretted the scientific and literary specialisation that seemed to 'make impossible a grand concerted advance like that which accompanied the French Revolution'.[23]

On the sociological front, Thomas's prose abounds in semi-documentary portraits of obsolescent, displaced or potentially displaced country people. These figures flesh out Jose Harris's representation of 'a society in which rootlessness was endemic and in which people felt themselves to be living in many different layers of historic time'. What Harris terms 'a lurking grief at the memory of a lost domain' is, of course, partly Thomas's own grief colouring the canvas. But he does not merely foist his feelings on to real casualties of 'the 1880s when, alone among European countries, Britain chose not to protect home producers against American wheat, with a consequent collapse of archaic rural communities, an explosion of migration to great cities...'.[24] His father's more upwardly mobile migration from Wales enabled Thomas to connect an autobiographical deracination with the wider forces whereby the countryman was 'sinking before the *Daily Mail* like a savage before pox or whisky'.[25] Childhood holidays in Wales and Wiltshire had indelibly, if precariously, reconstituted the lost domain. A central trope in *The South Country*, as in Thomas's other prose, is a passage from country to city; then, usually by a second generation, from city to country in an attempted retrieval of loss. This reflexive narrative occupies chapter six, 'A Return to Nature', which concludes with a last glimpse of 'the man [from] Caermarthenshire', back once more in London 'ill-dressed' and 'thin', amid a pathetic march of the unemployed: 'Comfortable clerks and others of the servile realised that here were the unemployed about whom the newspapers had said this and that...and they repeated the word "Socialism" and smiled at the bare legs of the son of man and the yellow boots of the orator.'[26]

Stan Smith stresses 'A Return to Nature' in his interesting analysis (in *Edward Thomas*, 1986) of Thomas's situation as 'a superfluous man': a term that Thomas himself borrowed from Turgenev. But while Smith highlights the depopulation of the countryside, arguing that some of the natural beauties of Thomas's England depended on dereliction and that Thomas was responsibly aware of this, he may point his sense of superfluousness too much towards class, too little towards the lost domain with its cultural as well as aesthetic pull. For example, he identifies 'the crisis of a generation', which Thomas's writings enact, as 'the dilemma of a middle-class liberal individualism under strain, faced with the prospect of its own redundancy in the changed world of a new era, and struggling, with remarkable intensity and integrity, to understand the flux in which it is to go down'.[27] Firstly, it is not clear that the Edwardian period was such a bad time for middle-class liberalism. Secondly, even if there never has been a golden age but only 'an *imaginary* plenitude, a utopian land of lost content which is precisely nowhere',[28] Harris's study suggests that Thomas internalised a 'crisis' which can be seen as major historical watershed – not only in the context of England. What Smith perceives as Thomas's symptomatic political paralysis, his deadlock between resignation and revolution, may be a search for other parameters in addition to class-politics. His ultimate discovery of those parameters coincided with his discovery of distinctive poetic forms, and with the impact of the war on his existing sense of crisis.

Thomas's prose is undeniably romantic about 'children of earth', about men 'five generations thick', about the innocence or earth-motherhood of rural women.[29] Yet his empathy with the London unemployed, which includes their pre-London history, questions whether socialism is the only answer, and whether even rural poverty might not have harboured valuable communal and local meanings now dispersed. (This is not the same as claiming 'organicism' for any community: the clearances in the Soviet Union were to prove as socially disastrous as those in the Scottish highlands.) Similarly, he says of gipsies: 'They belong to the little roads that are dying out'.[30] One aspect of Thomas's thought, his inner western rather than southern landscape, understands depopulation, change, obsolescence, dereliction, though not with a consoling nuance: Cornwall's 'deserted mines are frozen cries of despair, as if they had perished in conflict with the waste'. On a longer time-scale the mines consort with 'cromlech, camp, circle, hut and tumulus of the unwritten years...a silent Bedlam of history, a senseless cemetery or museum, amidst which we walk as animals must do when they see those valleys full of skeletons where their kind are said to go punctually to die.' Yet the very intensity of this reaction suggests that Thomas sees the current transformations as uniquely ominous for man. The peril is exemplified by the situation of an old man, living in a London suburb where once his father farmed, and mourning the final loss of elm trees which 'had come unconsciously to be part of the real religion of men in that neighbourhood...and helped to build and keep firm that sanctuary of beauty to which we must be able to retire if we are to be more than eaters and drinkers and newspaper readers'.[31] Today's deep ecologists would endorse that inter-connectedness, rephrased in 'The Chalk Pit': 'imperfect friends, we men/ And trees since time began; and nevertheless/ Between us still we breed a mystery'. In a prose passage linked with the poem Thomas recognises (as he does elsewhere) that man has always acted upon Nature; yet he displays an ambivalence that foreshadows current debate as to whether the human impact has escalated into 'a new order of assault'. Thomas says: 'It is sometimes consoling to remember how much of the English countryside is due to men by chance or design...among the works of men that rapidly become works of Nature, and can be admired without misanthropy, are the chalk and marl pits'.[32]

Thomas's prose-writings criticise 'the parochialism of humanity' with respect to larger evolutionary processes. This critique, which chimes with the Green stress on the short-termism of our species, comes to a head in *The South Country* where he exclaims: 'How little do we know of the business of the earth, not to speak of the universe; of time, not to speak of eternity.'[33] Or, as Edward O. Wilson puts it in *The Diversity of Life* (1992): 'The biosphere... remains obscure.'[34] 'Earth', in Thomas's poetry, is not only a spatial but a temporal domain. Although (or because) he was a historian himself by academic training, *The South Country* attacks the tunnel vision of orthodox historians, comparing them to 'a child planting flowers severed from their stalks and roots, expecting them to grow'.[35] This covers not only 'the unwritten years' but also the excluded species and ignorance of how our own has survived. Similarly, Wilson observes:

> Humanity is part of nature...The human heritage does not go back only for the conventionally recognised 8,000 years or so of recorded history, but for at least 2 million years...Across thousands of generations, the emergence of culture must have been profoundly influenced by simultaneous events in genetic evolution...[and] genetic evolution by the kinds of selection arising within culture. Only in the last moment of human history has the delusion arisen that people can flourish apart from the rest of the living world.[36]

Thomas castigates that delusion when he says 'We are not merely twentieth-century Londoners or Kentish men or Welshmen' or appeals for a holistic approach to human and natural history. This would show us 'in animals, in plants…what life is, how our own is related to theirs…in fact, our position, responsibilities and debts among the other inhabitants of the earth'.[37] 'Digging' is both an eco-historical poem (like 'February Afternoon') and a symbolic model for eco-historical research:

> What matter makes my spade for tears or mirth,
> Letting down two clay pipes into the earth?
> The one I smoked, the other a soldier
> Of Blenheim, Ramillies, and Malplaquet
> Perhaps. The dead man's immortality
> Lies represented lightly with my own,
> A yard or two nearer the living air
> Than bones of ancients who, amazed to see
> Almighty God erect the mastodon,
> Once laughed, or wept, in this same light of day.

Thomas's eco-history provides a tough and agnostic basis for his ecocentric philosophy. He anticipated (by 80 years) Andrew Dobson's *précis*: 'The science of ecology teaches us that we are part of a system that stretches back into an unfathomable past and reaches forward into an incalculable future…'[38] Thomas says in the chapter of *The South Country* called 'History and the Parish': 'In some places history has wrought like an earthquake, in others like an ant or mole; everywhere, permanently; so that if we but knew or cared, every swelling of the grass, every wavering line of hedge or path or road were an inscription, brief as an epitaph, in many languages and characters. But most of us know only a few of these unspoken languages of the past…'[39] The text of the earth remains to be read, and not all its inscriptions are human. In 'November' the speaker notices that

> the prettiest thing on ground are the paths
> With morning and evening hobnails dinted,
> With foot and wing-tip overprinted
> Or separately charactered,
> Of little beast and little bird.

2

It is often claimed that any such long-term view is merely a device for discouraging political action and protest. Here I want to bring together Thomas's historical situation and his ecocentrism, at their wartime crisis-point, as a preliminary to exploring some of their structural and epistemological consequences in his poetry. Just as Raymond Williams sees 'February Afternoon' as simply opposing

a sense of timelessness to a sense of war, so Robert Wells has crit-
icised Thomas for being philosophically 'unable to protest; not
against the destruction of [English rural] culture nor against the
mass slaughter of the men who embodied the culture'.[40] It all
depends on what you mean by 'protest'. In 'In Memoriam (Easter,
1915)' Thomas does not minimise a catastrophe when, rather than
comparing the dead to flowers, or ridiculing that comparison, he
points to a socio-ecological alteration:

> The flowers left thick at nightfall in the wood
> This Eastertide call into mind the men,
> Now far from home, who, with their sweethearts, should,
> Have gathered them and will do never again.

Similarly, 'February Afternoon' and 'Digging' are not really say-
ing: it will be or was 'all the same in a thousand years' or several
thousand years. Both poems are partly framed as ironical questions
to *human* powers-that-be – political and religious – in the context
of an ecosystem to which they belong and from which they might
learn. Anger works through perspectives such as 'The dead man's
immortality/Lies represented lightly with my own', with the
ambiguity of 'immortality' (as in 'Haymaking', quoted below) and
the oxymoronic pun on 'represented lightly'. Here, you might say,
war-recruits achieve solidarity beyond the parochialism of the con-
temporary. Also, 'living air' and 'light of day' seem ecological
accusations. They contrast with the (self-sponsored) reduction of
the human element to dead 'matter' and the doubt as to whom it
matters in another sense. Indeed 'the living air', the biosphere,
questions the binary opposition of 'tears or mirth'. One sign of
such questioning is that 'Digging', the first poem that Thomas wrote
after his enlistment, revises a poem with the same title written
three months earlier. 'Digging' [I] ends:

> It is enough
> To smell, to crumble the dark earth,
> While the robin sings over again
> Sad songs of Autumn mirth.

'Digging' [II] picks up on the final rhyme, given more emphasis
and irony by a rhyming couplet: 'What matter makes my spade
for tears or mirth,/ Letting down two clay pipes into the earth?'
The rhyme scheme from poem to poem thus runs: earth/mirth/
mirth/earth. 'Earth' the key word in common, and the enclosing
term of the chiasmus, shifts in meaning from soil, *humus*, to more
global suggestions. The disturbing archaeology, or eco-history, of
'Digging' [II] upsets the harmony above ground in 'Digging' [I].

Here the robin's song ideally integrates what the later poem digs deeper to perceive as a recurrent split in (or owing to) human consciousness: we laugh or weep without making sense of the alternation. It may also be significant that the initial couplet provides the only full rhyme in 'Digging' [II], whose rhythms are closer to the speech, than to the 'song', end of Thomas's spectrum.

'February Afternoon' also enquires into the oppositional habits, the adversarial politics, that produce wars in which 'men' can only be 'audacious or resigned'. The sonnet incorporates a political bird-fable in its use of a starlings' parliament, perhaps its imagery of gulls led by rooks. But if the natural world is competitive, too, it seems better regulated. Men who plough (or dig) contribute to the system they alter. Men at war become unable to see or hear what the animal or vegetable creation might be suggesting. This blindness and deafness is totalised in a patriarchal Judaeo-Christian God 'aloft', transcendental, out of touch with the earth: 'And God still sits aloft in the array/That we have wrought him...' 'Array...wrought' hits at religious and perhaps literary forms whose detached artifice denies the substance that a genuine 'humanus' might have put there. ('Almighty God' in 'Digging' [II] is a similar construct on the part of our inability to read the evolutionary environment in which we have survived the mastodon.) When 'the broad ploughland oak/ Roars mill-like' with starlings, it is both an emblem of earth at war and a reminder of older earthly 'laws'. Thomas's historical sense in the poem functions in the same microcosmic way as his spatial sense. If he uses millennia to get into focus one day in 1916, one day in 1916 also focuses millennia.

Thomas's eco-history is equal to interpreting briefer time-spans and individual lifespans. 'Man and Dog' and 'A Private' complement one another as concentrations of Thomas's earlier rural biographies, which themseves culminated in several articles about rural and urban England preparing or unprepared for war: 'I shall write down, as nearly as possible, what I saw and heard, hoping not to offend too much those who had ready-made notions as to how an Imperial people should or would behave in time of war, of such a war...'[41] Robert Wells cites 'Man and Dog' when he faults Thomas for merely elegising a culture, thereby assenting in its 'general will to die'. This suggests that Wells, rather than Thomas, has succumbed to fatalism and 'shows little sense of the common tragedy in which Europe was caught by the war'.[42] England was a window for Thomas, not an insular limit, and 'elegy' is a wide-ranging genre, not an invariably passive lament:

> ' 'Twill some getting.' 'Sir, I think 'twill so.'
> The old man stared up at the mistletoe
> That hung too high in the poplar's nest for plunder
> Of any climber, though not for kissing under:
> Then he went on against the north-east wind –
> Straight but lame, leaning on a staff new-skinned,
> Carrying a brolly, flag-basket, and old coat, –
> Towards Alton, ten miles off. And he had not
> Done less from Chilgrove where he pulled up docks...

At certain historical junctures the artist's most useful action may be to point the camera. But there is analysis and criticism in this subtly blended elegy. As the speaker attends to oral history stemming from the last third of the nineteenth century, we learn in a seemingly incidental phrase that the man's 'sons, three sons, were fighting'. This information takes its place in a shifting history of hard work, hardship and environmental change. Industrial casual labour has encroached on farm-labouring, itself grown casual, and the old man, too, has been a soldier:

> His mind was running on the work he had done
> Since he left Christchurch in the New Forest, one
> Spring in the 'seventies, – navvying on dock and line
> From Southampton to Newcastle-on-Tyne.
> In 'seventy-four a year of soldiering
> With the Berkshires, – hoeing and harvesting
> In half the shires where corn and couch will grow.

If the close of the poem moves with an autumnal rhythm, it simultaneously condemns the exploitative ethic that has led to the war and the man's obsolescence:

> 'Many a man sleeps worse tonight
> Than I shall.' 'In the trenches.' 'Yes, that's right.
> But they'll be out of that – I hope they be –
> This weather, marching after the enemy.'
> 'And so I hope. Good luck.' And there I nodded
> 'Good-night. You keep straight on.' Stiffly he plodded;
> And at his heels the crisp leaves scurried fast,
> And the leaf-coloured robin watched. They passed,
> The robin till next day, the man for good,
> Together in the twilight of the wood.

This counterpoints the histories of man, robin and trees. All the life in the poem belongs in different but interconnected ways to what is always 'passing', to the business of the earth. However, there is an implied question about the accelerating human impact on natural systems and cycles. The old man's relationship to the earth, on balance – and *in* balance – positive, is becoming a thing of the past. On the other hand, within the politics of this scenario, the non-human creation is shown to resist subjugation: mistletoe plays hard to get; couch-grass grows with corn; the man can skin a staff but has been lamed by a fall from a tree; the robin appears noncommittal; the leaves 'scurry' as if speeding a departure. Meanwhile, humanity's self-destructive tendencies are accelerating too: 'shires' have become regiments. Thus the poem's valedictory vista disturbingly implicates all its readers ('the man for good'). According to eco-history, human endings matter but are not all that matter. And the business of the earth takes a long-term view: in a diary entry quoted below, Thomas implies that ruins are good news for jackdaws as a species. As 'The Mountain Chapel' reminds us: 'When gods were young/This wind was old.'

The old man's passing, individually if not culturally, might be seen as a fitting evolutionary return to the earth (compare the death of Lok in William Golding's *The Inheritors*). But this does not apply to the swifter recycling implied by 'Digging' [II] or grimly encapsulated in Thomas's lines: 'when the war began/To turn young men to dung' ('Gone, Gone Again'). The death of 'A Private' covers the intolerable plight of the old man's sons:

This ploughman dead in battle slept out of doors
Many a frozen night, and merrily
Answered staid drinkers, good bedmen, and all bores:
'At Mrs Greenland's Hawthorn Bush,' said he,
'I slept.' None knew which bush. Above the town,
Beyond 'The Drover', a hundred spot the down
   In Wiltshire. And where now at last he sleeps
More sound in France – that, too, he secret keeps.

The war has prematurely violated the ploughman/private's bonds with 'Mrs Greenland' – a joke that anticipates Gaia. And his riddle about where he sleeps, together with the poem's own ironic, riddling play on 'privacy' and secrecy, further accuses human agencies of usurping earth-mysteries. When Thomas himself got to the Front (in January 1917), it was not incongruous that his 'War Diary' should have intermingled Nature notes and battle log, thus conveying a whole environment under bombardment. The second-last entry (7 April) reads: 'A cold bright day of continuous shelling... Larks, partridges, hedgesparrows, magpies by O[bservation] P[ost]. A great burst in red brick building in N. Vitasse stood up like a birch tree or a fountain. Back at 7.30 in peace. Then at 8.30 a continuous roar of artillery.' An earlier entry also brings together birds and people in a senseless cemetery, a Bedlam of history: 'Sordid ruin of Estaminet with carpenter's shop over it in Rue Jeanne d'Arc – wet, mortar, litter, almanacs, bottles, broken glass, damp beds, dirty paper, knife, crucifix, statuette, old chairs...The shelling must have slaughtered many jackdaws but has made home for many more.'[43] Such impressions, for which Thomas's poetry and prose were prepared, destabilise the supposed opposition between 'Nature poet' and 'war poet'.

3

Thomas's poems are usually spoken by a first-person singular, and both text and author are, of course, inescapably human, inescapably 'cultured'. Nonetheless, his procedures do much to renew the root-meaning of *humanus*: to reinforce 'the inseparableness of Nature and Man', to diminish 'man's importance in the landscape', and to subvert anthropocentric authority. Thus David Gervais in *Literary Englands* (1993) misses a crucial point when he says, 'the typical Thomas poem takes place outside human settlement', or exclaims: 'How different it is from the England of the novelists! There are no steam trains [wrong] or ocean liners, telephones or suffragettes, garden cities or Labour MPs.'[44] In fact, most of Thomas's poems allude to settlement in one way or another; but his margins are, rather, a subversive locus from which to criticise 'the England of the novelists' and examine earthly tenancies. 'Up in the Wind', the first poem he wrote in December 1914, includes the lines:

> Her cockney accent
> Made her and the house seem wilder by calling up –
> Only to be subdued at once by wildness –
> The idea of London there in that forest parlour...

Keeping Jefferies's *After London* in his sights, Thomas strategically deflects 'the roar of towns/And their brief multitude' ('Roads'). Yet, as we have seen, he does not suppress what John Barrell (in his study of English painting 1730-1840) terms 'the dark side of the landscape' – the condition of rural England further darkened by war.[45]

Contemporary theory of landscape-painting argues that landscape is never 'natural', being always viewed through cultural lenses even before its reproduction; that its 'prospects' may be complicit with imperialism; and that the forward movement of the colonising eye, in the words of W.J.T. Mitchell's introduction to *Landscape and Power* (1994), 'is not confined to the external, foreign fields toward which the empire directs itself; it is typically accompanied by a renewed interest in the re-presentation of the home landscape, the "nature" of the imperial centre'.[46] Thomas was an anti-imperialist: he desired to rescue 'the home landscape', too, from 'Great Britain, the British Empire, Britons, Britishers, and the English-speaking world' and from a centralising metropolis.[47] But the imperialism against which he fought aesthetically was the imperialism of the human, rather than the capitalist, gaze (though the former begets the latter). His poem 'The Watchers' contrasts a carter 'Watching the water press in swathes about his horse's chest' with 'one [who] watches, too,/ In the room for visitors/ That has no fire, but a view/ And many cases of stuffed fish, vermin, and kingfishers'. That such a detached, prospecting eye implicates a death-dealing human imperium is central to the poem's critique of aestheticism, of art insulated from the pressure and fire of the non-human creation.

'Haymaking' and 'The Brook' indicate Thomas's awareness and wariness of the visual-arts landscape tradition. These poems, both in couplets, were written close together during the month of Thomas's enlistment. His poetry of July 1915 (it includes 'The Word', 'A Dream', 'Aspens', 'The Mill-Water', 'Digging' [II] and 'Two Houses') constitutes an extraordinarily intense meditation on history, memory, human dwellings, natural forces, language, survival. In 'The Word', a couplet poem that prefigures the others, 'a pure thrush word', 'an empty thingless name', proves more potent in the listener's consciousness than 'names of the mighty men/ That fought and lost or won in the old wars'. 'Haymaking' and 'The Brook' elaborate this tension in that they speak as from the end and from the beginning of history respectively, although the distinction is not absolute. The scene in 'Haymaking' is very deliberately a scene: one that underlines the specific – radical and demotic – varieties of pastoral to which it subscribes:

> The men leaned on their rakes, about to begin,
> But still. And all were silent. All was old,
> This morning time, with a great age untold,
> Older than Clare and Cobbett, Morland and Crome,
> Than, at the field's far edge, the farmer's home,
> A white house crouched at the foot of a great tree.

Although this freeze-frame suggests the rural English spirit of which Thomas had earlier wished to make 'a graven image', 'Haymaking' is also self-referentially conscious of frames within frames; and, like most other poems quoted in this essay, moves between 'different layers of historical time' (Harris). 'Under the heavens that know not what years be' Thomas lays out a vista of beginnings (the moment when agriculture starts), long eco-history (the 'great tree'), literary and artistic traditions (agriculture becomes culture), and possible endings. Indeed, the poem ends by enclosing itself, its pitch to posterity, within a receding and ambiguous wartime frame:

'The men, the beasts, the trees, the implements/ Uttered even what they will in times far hence −/ All of us gone out of the reach of change −/ Immortal in a picture of an old grange'. If 'Haymaking' ultimately stresses the visual, its collective earthly 'utterance' also depends on other kinds of sense-impression ('shrill shrieked…The swift', 'the scent of woodbine and hay new-mown').

Similarly, 'The Brook', written two days later, starts with the speaker 'watching a child/Chiefly that paddled', then takes in bird-song and 'a scent like honeycomb/From mugwort dull'. Yet 'The Brook' dramatises, rather than assumes, the primal epistemology of 'gathering sight and sound', and the speaker's peaceable sensory kingdom of birds, flowers and insects is allied to the 'motion, and the voices, of the stream' as well as to the focal, perhaps final, still-ness of 'Haymaking'. As this fresh scene edges the human presence, human culture, to its margin, it collapses the 'old' traditions whose evolution and construction is symbolised by 'Haymaking': a butter-fly behaves 'as if I were the last of men/ And he the first of insects to have earth/And sun together and to know their worth'. The poem ends with the speaker taken out of history, or history taken out of the speaker. A problematic configuration of living man, long-dead man, child, horse, trees and bird suggests that we have not begun to 'utter', that we lack a language for first ecological principles:

A grey flycatcher silent on a fence
And I sat as if we had been there since
The horseman and the horse lying beneath
The fir-tree-covered barrow on the heath,
The horseman and the horse with silver shoes
Galloped the downs last. All that I could lose,
I lost. And then the child's voice raised the dead.
'No one's been here before' was what she said
And what I felt, yet never should have found
A word for, while I gathered sight and sound.

Several of Thomas's poems establish a working relation between the 'natural' and the 'human', in which the senses, together or separately, constitute the basis for an 'interconnected web' (Eckers-ley). 'Digging' [I] begins: 'Today I think/ Only with scents'. In this present-tense scenario an inseparable 'Nature and Man' eco-logically co-operate as 'a bonfire burns/ The dead, the waste, the dangerous,/And all to sweetness turns'. Elsewhere, the 'Otherness' of species and natural phenomena resists control or translation. The rain is not always 'Windless and light,/ Half a kiss, half a tear,/ Saying good-night' ('Sowing'). Or, if the pathetic fallacy is inevitable, Thomas imprints Nature not only with human unhappiness but with human extinctions. In 'Rain' the speaker has 'no love which this wild rain/Has not dissolved except the love of death'. 'The Mill-Water' ends with 'water falling/ Changelessly calling,/ Where once men had a work-place and a home'. Here local economic change brings the 'Bedlam of history' into focus. The voices assigned to water and wind often appear adverse or inaccessible to consciousness. Similarly, if birdsong and human language converge in 'March' ('Something they knew – I also, while they sang'), they diverge in 'If I were to Own' (the thrush sings 'proverbs untranslatable'). Sometimes, as in 'The Word', concentration on natural sounds is correlated with a salutary loss of human memory that downgrades anthropocentric history: 'I have forgot...names of the mighty men'. Thomas's protagonist, however, frequently fails to translate, construe or utter the earthly text that matters more than those ironically lost 'mighty men', or he finds that his eye fails him. In 'Birds' Nests' winter-trees expose what he has missed, but this does not mitigate the failure: 'Since there's no need of eyes to see them with'. Chastened and educated, he goes on to discover natural micro-systems 'deep-hid'. In the paradoxically named 'First Known When Lost' bearings have to be revised after a woodman fells a copse: 'And now I see as I look/ That the small winding brook,/ A tributary's tributary rises there'. To 'see as I look' humbles the prospecting human eye, and true observation, the possession of 'eyes to see them with', socialises the 'isolated observer' (Williams) as an inhabitant of earth. John Barrell's essay 'Being is Perceiving' contrasts John Clare's subjectivity, constituted by a 'complex manifold of simultaneous impressions', with James Thomson's 'subject...which needed to announce itself as autonomous, as freeing itself from the determination of the objects it perceived'.[48]

Thomas's syntax, more sophisticated than Clare's, takes the reader on destabilising mystery tours that give the 'complex manifold' or interconnected web dimensions in time as well as space. As in 'Thaw', his syntactical manoeuvres, allied to changes of angle and vantage-point, help to alter power-relations between the human element and other perceivers:

Over the land freckled with snow half-thawed
The speculating rooks at their nests cawed
And saw from elm-tops, delicate as flower of grass,
What we below could not see, Winter pass.

'The Path' plays on the constrictions of human sight, human engineering, and, indeed, literary pastoral, as it lures the reader along unbeaten tracks:

> the eye
> Has but the road, the wood that overhangs
> And underyawns it, and the path that looks
> As if it led on to some legendary
> Or fancied place where men have wished to go
> And stay; till, sudden, it ends where the wood ends.

'Fifty Faggots' is a temporal microcosm in which seasonal change interacts with less predictable environmental forces, largely set in motion by human beings. The poem begins with a statement about visual, tangible present-tense presence: 'There they stand, on their ends, the fifty faggots', but then introduces history: 'That once were underwood of hazel and ash/ In Jenny Pinks's copse'. Further variables will determine relations between present and future as they affect

> a thicket fancy alone
> Can creep through with the mouse and wren. Next Spring
> A blackbird or a robin will nest there,
> Accustomed to them, thinking they will remain
> Whatever is for ever to a bird:
> This Spring it is too late; the swift has come...

Although bird and animal habitats have been influenced by human actions, the speaker/author is equally subject to the incalculable: 'Before they are done/The war will have ended, many other things/ Have ended, maybe, that I can no more/ Foresee or more control than robin and wren'. In the course of the poem, too, the same (or almost the same) object is consigned to a corresponding range of linguistic variables: faggots/underwood/thicket.

Foresight and control are also problematic when it comes to more elaborate edifices. Settlement, in Thomas's poetry, hovers on the verge of dissolution, the *unheimlich*: 'Where once men had a work-place and a home'. The rare 'Manor Farm', conjuring 'a season of bliss unchangeable', is far out-numbered by precariously placed or ominous dwellings. Thomas's 'houses' include: 'that forest parlour', 'A white house crouched at the foot of a great tree', 'road and inn, the sum/Of what's not forest', 'the woodman's cot/ By the ivied trees', 'Chapel and gravestones, old and few', the 'fir-tree-covered barrow on the heath'. It is striking how many houses are situated close to the mystery of men and trees, with trees as the dominant presence. Ideally, this situation should foster the reciprocities latent in the human/animal words 'crouched' and 'foot' applied to house and tree in 'Haymaking'. But 'The Barn' begins: 'They should never have built a barn there, at all −/ Drip, drip, drip! − under that elm tree'. The barn undergoes what, from the viewpoint of agribusiness, would be degradation: 'Built to keep corn for rats and men./ Now there's fowls in the roof, pigs on the floor'. ('Rats and men' seems pointed.) From a more holistic angle, the barn's decline has restored it biodegradably to Nature. First, 'Starlings used to sit there with bubbling throats':

> But now they cannot find a place,
> Among all those holes, for a nest any more.
> It's the turn of lesser things, I suppose.
> Once I fancied 'twas starlings they built it for.

Thomas's forest-fixation does not only reflect the tree-covered Hampshire hangers or mourn obsolescent wood-trades like charcoal-burning or, with pre-Freudian intuition, imply the wilderness of the individual unconscious. Ultimately it symbolises an evolution-ary and eco-historical perspective (the unconscious of the species, perhaps) within which all human settlements and systems appear vulnerable. 'The Green Roads' outlines this perspective in a sym-bolic diagram that layers the life-spans of different species and their members:

> The green roads that end in the forest
> Are strewn with white goose feathers this June,
>
> Like marks left behind by some one gone to the forest
> To show his track. But he has never come back.
>
> Down each green road a cottage looks at the forest.
> Round one the nettle towers; two are bathed in flowers.
>
> An old man along the green road to the forest
> Strays from one, from another a child alone.

The diagram includes an 'old' thrush, 'young' trees, a dead oak that 'saw the ages pass in the forest', and the poet-historian's accurate, foreboding footnote: 'all things forget the forest/ Excepting perhaps me...' Yet, as in 'The Mill-Water' and 'Tall Nettles', Thomas may partly relish the power-reversal whereby nettles come to 'tower', 'reign' or 'cover up'. In 'The Green Roads' the cottages, with subtextual anxiety, 'look at' the forest. In 'House and Man' the trees 'look upon' a house 'from every side'. On Thomas's time-scales, this isolated wood-dweller, paranoid about 'forest silence and forest murmur', represents more than 'an image of poverty'[49] or the disappearance of rural England: 'One hour: as dim he and his house now look/As a reflection in a rippling brook...' Rather than the human eye controlling prospects, the natural world disconcertingly 'looks' at our incursions (Ted Hughes takes up this idea) and forgets them. In 'The Long Small Room', one of

Thomas's last poems, the house metaphor overtly merges into earth-dwelling. An earlier poem, 'The Other', arrives at a brief moment of poise in which the divided protagonist internalises 'one star, one lamp, one peace/Held on an everlasting lease' and feels himself to be 'An old inhabitant of earth'. But 'The Long Small Room' is spoken retrospectively by a less secure lease-holder, who feels no better equipped than other natural phenomena to make sense of his environment:

> When I look back, I am like moon, sparrow and mouse
> That witnessed what they could never understand
> Or alter or prevent in the dark house.
> One thing remains the same – this my right hand
>
> Crawling crab-like over the clean white page...

Here the activity of writing figures at a distance from the possibility of deciphering or controlling the earthly text. 'Crab-like' further subverts the anthropocentric arrogance of *homo faber* as author and artist. Thomas's doubts about human constructs extend to the architectural model of the artist (a contrast with some of Yeats's emphases). It is not only 'superfluous men', to quote Stan Smith, who 'do not own [the house] or share in its significances'.[50] Man, in a more generic sense, may be superfluous. And 'ownership' here has to do with deeper eco-nomics. However, in other poems the earth offers its own kind of access to 'significances'. Raymond Williams gets it exactly wrong when he praises the opening lines of 'Swedes' ('They have taken the gable from the roof of clay/ On the long swede pile. They have let in the sun/ To the white and gold and purple of curled fronds/ Unsunned'), but objects to a comparison between this revelation and 'going down into an Egyptian tomb'.[51] The point is that the artifacts bearing witness to the pharaoh's glory – 'God and monkey, chariot and throne and vase,/ Blue pottery, alabaster, and gold' – are deathly, unnatural, unrenewable. Like the voyeuristic art associated with the 'watcher' in the inn, they contrast with what an ecocentric aesthetic might have to offer:

> But dreamless long-dead Amen-hotep lies.
> This is a dream of Winter, sweet as Spring.

The post-Darwinian as well as pre-Christian conjunction, 'God and monkey', satirises the link between art and the transcendental, immortalising claims of religion. The trenches did not make Thomas less atheistic: 'Rubin...believes in God and tackles me about atheism – thinks marvellous escapes are ordained. But I say so are the marvellous escapes of certain telegraph posts, houses, etc.'[52]

Yet Thomas does not entirely give up on the capacity of human-
ity to 'build' as well as 'see': to mediate or inhabit the environment
in more ecocentric ways. The interconnected webs of his poetry
are sometimes reflexively adduced as evidence that the earth cannot
dispense with the spider of human consciousness. Thus in 'Roads'
'The hill road wet with rain/ In the sun would not gleam/ Like a
winding stream/ If we trod it not again.' Only imagination can
establish the interconnections of metaphor or creep through some
thickets. Similarly, 'The Thrush' updates Keats's nightingale by
probing the bird's limitations in the cognitive business of 'reading',
'knowing', naming, and remembering: 'Or is all your lore/ Not to
call November November,/ And April April...But I know the months
all,/ And their sweet names...' This replies dialectically to the 'pure
thrush word' by valuing the human mind's interconnections with
'All that's ahead and behind', its unique ability to write the common
eco-history. Thomas applies the word 'roar' to any unmediated noise
– whether of towns, machines, trees, or artillery. 'Good-night', a rare
effort to connect explicitly with manmade London, is plotted in terms
of changing sounds, and moves in a (historical as well as geograph-
ical) direction opposite to the usual Thomas trajectory: from skylarks
'over the down', to 'suburb nightingales' to a city-centre 'noise of
man, beast, and machine' which submerges birdsong/poetry. But
the urban sounds include streets made 'homely' by the echo of his
childhood in 'the call of children...Sweet as the voice of nightingale
or lark', and the poem itself creates a fleeting community: 'homeless,
I am not lost...it is All Friends' Night, a traveller's good night'.
This provisional accommodation neither surrenders to nor evades the
built environment. It still insists that the contemporary London
suburbs and streets are the 'strangest thing in the world'[53] because
they have yet to be imagined as earth-dwellings, their roar assimi-
lated, even if the poem's own naming begins the process.

Thomas's versions of the artist involve not the builder or maker
but the listener, the observer, the nomad, the receiver of signals
from the environment, the apprentice to natural language, the
vehicle of human language: 'Will you...Choose me,/ You English
words?' ('Words'). Obviously this receptivity, too, is a strategic
construct, though the poetry does not impute invariable success to
its self-images. In 'Aspens' Thomas explores his ecological aesthetic,
defining it as a voice intermediary between earth and human beings:

> All day and night, save winter, every weather,
> Above the inn, the smithy, and the shop,
> The aspens at the cross-roads talk together
> Of rain, until their last leaves fall from the top.

> Out of the blacksmith's cavern comes the ringing
> Of hammer, shoe, and anvil; out of the inn
> The clink, the hum, the roar, the random singing –
> The sounds that for these fifty years have been.

Stan Smith emphasises 'dereliction' and the speaker's own 'redundancy like that threatening the blacksmith';[54] but Thomas again seems to move from a particular historical context to a longer eco-historical perspective, one that includes literary history. The 'inn, the smithy, and the shop' represent three perennial kinds of man-made 'house': society, manufacture, commerce. The poem erases these houses in what might be night, war, or a proleptic absence:

> The whisper of the aspens is not drowned,
> And over lightless pane and footless road,
> Empty as sky, with every other sound
> Not ceasing, calls their ghosts from their abode,
>
> A silent smithy, a silent inn, nor fails
> In the bare moonlight or the thick-furred gloom,
> In tempest or the night of nightingales,
> To turn the cross-roads to a ghostly room.

Yet this also suggests that the sounds associated with the trees (talk, whisper, call) are more durable, mindful and meaningful than the mechanistic noise of the smithy or the sub-linguistic and 'random' sounds attached to the social inn. The poem's own aspen-imitative music obliquely disparages the chime of 'ringing'/'random singing', which implies an incoherent or simplistic relation between society and expression. Once more a third force has entered the arena and its urgent if disregarded 'talk of rain' combines longer historical perspectives (the smithy is also a 'cavern') with a deeper aesthetic. 'Aspens' was written in 1915, so 'these fifty years' begin in 1865 and denote not old England but the modern 'cross-roads': the period of unprecedented change and now of war. Yet this half-century is itself a blip:

> And it would be the same were no house near.
> Over all sorts of weather, men, and times,
> Aspens must shake their leaves and men may hear
> But need not listen, more than to my rhymes.

Evidently Thomas is making Cassandra-like claims for his own 'marginal' poetry. 'Aspens' aligns it with the tree rather than the house; declares its grief more than personal; and insists on a necessary reciprocity between poetry and earth. Inseparable from 'all sorts of weather', the aspens – traditionally the tree with tongues – also symbolise earth's concern that mankind should tune in to its transmissions:

> Whatever wind blows, while they and I have leaves
> We cannot other than an aspen be
> That ceaselessly, unreasonably grieves,
> Or so men think who like a different tree.

4

Ecology, like economy, derives from the Greek *oikos*, home. 'Home' is a keyword in Thomas's meditation upon England (as England in his meditation on home): a much-canvassed topic, to which David Gervais has made the most recent contribution. Gervais stresses the 'partial, private' and provisional nature of Thomas's England; criticises any attempt to recruit his poetry for a pure elixir of Englishness; and says: 'We rarely find [Hardy's] *shared* meaning in the rural life Thomas writes about...Thomas did not come to his England from a position sufficiently *inside and of it* to think of it as more than special and local. He was reticent when it came to investing it with any significance beyond itself (as later readers have been tempted to do).'[55] Hardy's kind of 'shared meaning', may still be accessible in 'the inn, the smithy, and the shop', but the aspen-poet listens to disturbing winds that have already made Hardy's world still more precarious. (Hardy greatly valued Thomas's poetry.) If Thomas sought and found Englishness most persuasively in particulars, localities and momentary epiphanies, this in itself de-constructs the totalising, centralising propensities that 'Great Britain' was beginning to assume in the Edwardian era, and which were eventually to culminate in the Thatcherite project. Commentators such as John Lucas in *England and Englishness* (1990), who main-tain that 'rootedness is always something wished on others',[56] un-wittingly testify to the success of that century-long hegemonic trend. Thomas's local emphases, including his interest in dialect and folksong, can also be seen as intelligently conservationist. Jose Harris writes: '[an] intense and variegated local and provincial cul-ture was still a major strand in British social life between 1870 and 1914... [although] the late Victorian period saw a subterranean shift in the balance of social life away from the locality to the metropolis and the nation. The elements in this shift were complex and only partly visible to contemporaries...'[57] Evidently, they were visible to Edward Thomas, and he looked for countervailing elements in communities further from the metropolis. Hence his alertness to the literature of 'intimate reality' inspired by Ireland as contrasted with Britannia – 'a frigid personification'.[58] *Beautiful Wales* (1905) devotes half a page of its first chapter to reciting the names of places visited, and attributes extreme and holistic local loyalties to some of the people met. Of course, as *Beautiful Wales* indicates, the suburbs had reached Wales too, though change was slower there. Thomas's Anglo-Welshness may or may not have involved 'contradictions'.[59] It certainly gave him insights that dramatised the intricate conflict, throughout the British Isles, between modernisation and traditional kinds of communal self-understanding: a conflict that is not quite over yet. I have already argued that, for Thomas, 'shared meaning' requires participation in a wider web than the social nexus Gervais finds lacking in his work.

Thomas wrote three poems called 'Home', and two of them are unhappy. The first (February 1915) begins: 'Not the end: but there's nothing more', and turns on an unresolved tension between utopian or Arcadian possibility ('That land,/My home, I have never seen') and the 'fear [that] my happiness there,/ Or my pain, might be dreams of return/ Here, to these things that were'. On its social level, this parable sticks with the present while registering the lost domain. The third in the series, written (March 1916) after his enlistment, has a more exclusively cultural focus. The title is given in inverted commas, and the poem concerns a walk taken by three soldiers over 'untrodden snow' in the 'strange' countryside around their training camp, a landscape prophetic of foreign fields:

> The word 'home' raised a smile in us all three,
> And one repeated it, smiling just so
> That all knew what he meant and none would say.
> Between three counties far apart that lay
> We were divided and looked strangely each
> At the other, and we knew we were not friends
> But fellows in a union that ends
> With the necessity for it, as it ought...

In this poem of division and estrangement 'shared meaning' is precluded, because the meaning shared is that 'home' means different things, different places, different perceptions. The men have been constrained into a military, and perhaps national, 'union' that overrides local particularisms. Thomas's poetry is shaped by the antinomies: familiar/strange; known/unknown or unknowable; solitude/society. These antinomies raise overlapping questions about psychic, cultural and ecological belonging which are most affirmatively answered in the second 'Home' poem (April 1915). Here, to quote Robyn Eckersley, the various 'organisms' are harmoniously 'constituted by environmental interrelationships', while psychology and culture also achieve equilibrium:

Often I had gone this way before:
But now it seemed I never could be
And never had been anywhere else;
'Twas home; one nationality
We had, I and the birds that sang,
One memory.

They welcomed me. I had come back
That eve somehow from somewhere far:
The April mist, the chill, the calm,
Meant the same thing familiar
And pleasant to us, and strange too,
Yet with no bar.

The extension of 'nationality', historical 'memory' and shared meaning to birds is a subversive stroke in 1915. It sharpens the similar transferrals, in Thomas's prose, of socio-political vocabulary to 'this commonwealth of things that live in the sun, the air, the earth, the sea, now and through all time'. That phrase occurs in his meditation on 'the business of the earth' and on the reality that the 'rumour of much toil and scheming and triumph may never reach the stars…We know not by what we survive'.[60] The poem ends by including in its local ecosystem a labourer who 'went along, his tread/ Slow, half with weariness, half with ease'. The rhythm of his work joins the atmosphere of the evening in an implied model for the poem's ecological aesthetic: 'from his shed/ The sound of sawing rounded all/ That silence said'. This holistic construction of 'Home' partly endorses, partly qualifies, Thomas's wartime redefinition of "England" as 'a system of vast circumferences circling round the minute neighbouring points of home'.[61] Its ecosystem is not necessarily a national microcosm but cognitively self-sufficient. Thus the centrifugal implications converge on those of 'Home' in quotation marks. "England", as well as "Great Britain", has to be broken down. However, Thomas's originality in re-imagining the 'knowable community' is to fuse ecology and sociality, to unite environmental and local or regional priorities against the metropolis. Yet, as a poet concerned about the condition of England, Thomas sometimes insinuates that its 'system of vast circumferences' becomes the interconnected web of his own poems, which might have various local meanings. In the camp, talking to fellow-recruits about England, he was pleased to find: 'There isn't a man I don't share some part with'.[62]

Thomas's poetry destabilises authority, perception and time in a spirit often regarded as peculiar to modernist aesthetics. It does so with precise reference to environmental and epistemological issues latent in his immediate historical context. And it exhibits a kind of historical imagination usually precluded by the premises of American and Irish modernism. His antinomial landscape is also compounded of presence and absence: not a matter of theoretical protocols but of lost domains, senseless cemeteries and human departures – the 'flowers left thick at nightfall', 'two clay pipes', 'a ghostly room'. Stan Smith has shown that the 'ghost is one of the commonest tropes in Thomas's poetry'.[63] But absence in Thomas not only laments or prophesies loss, but marks what ought to be there. The poet returns from the margin, 'comes back...from somewhere far', with meanings for community.

Thomas is as occupied with meaning and language as modernist writing is supposed to be, and often more disturbingly. 'I read the sign. Which way shall I go?' says 'The Signpost', one of his first poems, and the poetry that follows reads many ambiguous natural and cultural signs that may be missed by contemporary theorists (Robyn Eckersley attacks 'The Failed Promise of Critical Theory' from an ecocentric viewpoint).[64] Indeed, Thomas's interest in language pivots on relations between Nature and culture: not just the anthropocentric question as to whether culture seeks to 'naturalise' itself for suspect political reasons, but the ecocentric question as to whether human languages remain in touch with their environmental origins. 'The Combe' begins: 'The Combe was ever dark, ancient and dark./Its mouth is stopped with bramble, thorn, and briar'. If this suggests the impenetrability of some earth-languages, the poem goes on to find the combe's stopped mouth less dismaying than an ecological violence that bears on England at war, not only with Germany but with itself: 'But far more ancient and dark/ The Combe looks since they killed the badger there,/ Dug him out and gave him to the hounds,/ That most ancient Briton of English beasts'. Thomas's humanising language for the badger (which invokes Celtic rather than imperial Britain) tries to heal a split in home and in natural man. In 'Words' Thomas celebrates the English language for being 'as dear/As the earth which you prove/That we love'. Language, too, has a long eco-history, being 'As our hills are, old'. Similarly, the elusive 'Lob' represents one language's evolutionary fitness in speech and writing: 'Calling the wild cherry tree the merry tree'. In this positive linguistic scenario, it is not that 'word' exactly or referentially reproduces 'thing', but that the associations of words, in an ecological sense, testify to the development of language (and literature) as a function of bodily, sensory, local and earthly existence. The likeness/difference of bird-language is not just a sentimentality on Thomas's part. Humanity has kept itself in the text through language. And our ability to ensure that language is 'Worn new/Again and again' ('Words') depends on recognising the 'lost homes' it harbours. But the dark alternative is that man's textual inscriptions may wear thin or lose touch. Two of Thomas's first poems, 'March' and 'Old Man', written on consecutive days, stand in an antinomial symbolic relation to one another. In 'March' Thomas identifies his own artistic release with thrushes imposing their song after bad weather has 'kept them quiet as the primroses' and postponed spring: 'So they could keep off silence/ And night, they cared not what they sang or screamed'. At the end of 'March' there is a sense that the linked vocal efforts of poet and birds have been productive. 'Old Man' begins by holding the human and non-human creation in a precarious intertextual balance:

Old Man, or Lad's-love, – in the name there's nothing
To one that knows not Lad's-love, or Old Man,
The hoar-green feathery herb, almost a tree,
Growing with rosemary and lavender.
Even to one that knows it well, the names
Half-decorate, half-perplex, the thing it is:
At least, what that is clings not to the names
In spite of time. And yet I like the names.

Certainly this does not subscribe to a correspondence theory of language, or suggest that any single verbal formula can get at 'the thing it is'. However, the contradictory names of the plant, and the speaker's liking for them, belong to a history of proximate if not shared meanings. In contrast, the end of the poem unravels the interconnected web ('I have mislaid the key. I sniff the spray/ And think of nothing; I see and I hear nothing') to open up a vista devoid of human presence, history, memory, meaning and language: 'Only an avenue, dark, nameless, without end'. Non-human creatures can cope with nameless things, or speak 'thing-less names', but not mankind. This ultimate or original absence is not the silence and night that Thomas sometimes welcomes as an earthly *requiescat*. Neither is it an abstract gesture towards philo-sophical relativism. It forebodes the premature encroachment of 'nothingness' if we 'mislay the key' to the domain, if we cease desiring to be 'not a transitory member of a parochial species, but a citizen of the Earth'.[65]

The Poetics of Celt and Saxon

The Celtic Twilight still lingers in the vicinity of poetry. Palely loitering, impalpable but imperishable, it blurs the creative and critical sightlines between Ireland and elsewhere – especially England, since Saxon Daylight is always its implied literary opposite. For instance, Tom Paulin has called Ted Hughes 'a domineering Anglo-Saxon Protestant drawn to a relaxed Catholic Celticism'.[1] I will return to these rather confused stereotypes, and ask whether Hughes and Seamus Heaney (to whom Paulin seemingly alludes) have themselves subscribed to a Saxon/Celt duality or double act. Michael Parker may not wholly misread the poets' own signals when he writes of the young Heaney: 'Perhaps after twenty-three years of intense exposure and devotion to Irish Catholicism, the "primeval" feel of Hughes's world appealed to the Oisin in him, with its ancient landscapes and its magical beasts, like the old Celtic gods, defiant and doomed.'[2] Yet St Patrick, who believed that he had routed Oisín, would be surprised by Parker's conflation of Catholicism with 'old Celtic gods' – as would W.B. Yeats and the clerics who called him a heretic. In Shaw's *John Bull's Other Island* Father Dempsey rebukes Broadbent, the Saxon Celtophile: 'When people talk to you about Fin McCool and the like, take no notice of them. It's all idle stories and superstition.' The poetics of Celt and Saxon, especially in their critical (call it 'ethno-critical') mode, are also hard to suppress. I will illustrate this by first reviewing some historical sources and contemporary symptoms of Celt/Saxonism, and by noting its appeal to John Hewitt (1907-1987) in the dualistic environment of Northern Ireland.

1

At Lubitavish on the slopes of Tievebullagh in the Glens of Antrim stands a megalithic circle known as Ossian's Grave. The stones pre-date the Fianna and their legend, but John Hewitt's poem 'Ossian's Grave, Lubitavish, County Antrim' prefers mythology to archaeology:

> The legend has it, Ossian lies
> beneath this landmark on the hill,
> asleep till Fionn and Oscar rise
> to summon his old bardic skill
> in hosting their last enterprise.

> This, stricter scholarship denies,
> declares this megalithic form
> millennia older than his time –
> if such lived ever, out of rime –
> was shaped beneath Sardinian skies...
>
> let either story stand for true,
> as heart or head shall rule. Enough
> that, our long meditation done,
> as we paced down the broken lane
> by the dark hillside's holly trees,
> a great white horse with lifted knees
> came stepping past us, and we knew
> his rider was no tinker's son.

'Stricter scholarship' on Stone Age Ireland has already revised itself, while Ossian's legend remains potent. To 'summon' Ossian is, in fact, to call up a quarter-millennium of intertwined academic controversy (as when one scholar attacks 'the myth of the unity of Celtic speech, ethnic extraction and culture')[3], cultural debate, political conflict and literary imagining that pivots on the publication of James Macpherson's *Poems of Ossian* in the early 1760s. Very loosely derived from Gaelic materials,[4] *Ossian* laments the Fianna in a potent generic blend of elegy and epic; the 'translations' being supposedly spoken by the bard who 'sits forlorn at the tomb of his friends'. Barren western landscapes and autumnal or wintry weather enhance the terminally melancholy mood that so impressed embryonic European Romanticism, and so reinforced what Clare O'Halloran terms 'the eighteenth-century vogue for the primitive, encapsulated in the belief that the best condition of man and human society was the earliest'. O'Halloran shows that eighteenth-century Irish antiquarians resisted Ossianism. They stressed the sophistication rather than primitivism of the Gaelic past, and sought to repatriate Oisin from Scotland (as did Lady Morgan in *The Wild Irish Girl* [1806]). Nevertheless, she concludes: 'In their complex attempts to repossess the Gaelic past, Irish writers and historians of all traditions could not escape the Scottish Ossian.'[5] Nor can they today when his legacy has assumed new guises and sparked off new controversies. In *Celticism* (1996), a timely symposium edited by Terence Brown, Joep Leerssen defines 'Celtic' as 'the history of what people wanted that term to mean'. He has also called Celticism 'impervious to paradigm-shifts'.[6]

Ossianic "Celts", yoked with equally suspect "Saxons", became key players in nineteenth-century cultural and political ideology. Thomas Davis's poem 'Celts and Saxons', which recruits support for the nationalist Young Ireland movement (1842-48), indicates how a nineteenth-century intellectual might invoke ethnology ('the science which treats of races and peoples') as routinely as academics today invoke its post-structuralist deposer. Davis lays out a flattering catalogue of the racial types that have battled and settled in Ireland: 'the proud Milesian...And the hard enduring Dane,/ And the iron Lords of Normandy/ With the Saxons in their train'. Mainly an appeal to Protestants ('Irish Saxons'), the poem draws on a developing ethnological theme: the theory of English origins called, with different inflections, Anglo-Saxonism, Teutonism or Teutomania. This theory explained English character and imperial success (the two being identified) in terms of supposed Nordic or Germanic qualities such as hardness and endurance. Davis's point is that such qualities should now advance the *Irish* nation. In 'The Celts' and 'The Woeful Winter' (a Famine poem) another Young Irelander, Thomas D'Arcy McGee, highlights the Celtic side of the opposition. McGee deplores present-day Irish weakness, mourns a 'mighty race,/ Taller than Roman spears' and salutes 'the primal poet' as their last vestige 'by miscalled lake and desecrated grange'. Only in Ossian's song do 'they live and love and bleed –/ It bears them on through space'. This suggests how Ossianism, itself entangled with the Jacobite defeat of 1745, can be re-activated by political need. McGee links the Fianna with the Famine when he regrets that 'the Celtic blood runs palely, that once was winy red', and that Celts have ceased to 'smite the Saxon as mallet striketh ball'.

Makings of 'Celticism'[7] can be found in Shakespeare's history plays,[8] i.e. in the first makings of the United Kingdom. Similarly, Anglo-Saxonism existed before its nineteenth-century apotheosis. It began in the sixteenth century, mainly under the aegis of the Protestant bishop John Bale who reacted against his past as a monk by denying Roman and French influence on England and preaching a purely Saxon church (Euro-scepticism begins here too). Later, Thomas Carlyle, Charles Kingsley and others would claim that the English were essentially a Teutonic race, blood-kin to the Germans, Dutch, Scandinavians and Americans. Kingsley's 'Ode to the North-East Wind' blends climate, Protestantism and machismo into racial assertion: ''Tis the hard grey weather/ Breeds hard English men...Come; and strong within us/ Stir the Viking's blood;/ Bracing brain and sinew;/ Blow, thou wind of God.' It was chiefly Tory periodicals, however, that promoted Teutomania.[9] In 1880 the ethnologist Grant Allen argued influentially that most British people were not Anglo-Saxons but Celts; and that this applied not only to their origins but also to the intermixture that Irish, Scots and Welsh immigration into England had produced.

Further, it was the 'Celtic' sections of the British Isles that had (whether by accident or design) dispatched most colonists to the New World.[10] The doctrines of Anglo-Saxonism had already lost intellectual credibility, while competition with Germany had calmed Teutomania. C.M. Doughty, who feared a German invasion, proposed a Celtic foundation-myth in his epic *The Dawn in Britain* (1906-7), a poem significantly admired by Edward Thomas and Hugh MacDiarmid.

To turn from legend and race theory to the 'stricter scholarship' of linguists and archaeologists. Hildegard L.C. Tristram argues that the nineteenth-century 'philological model', which itself created pan-Celtic consciousness, and which 'leaves out the social relevance of language peformance and the cultural aspect of...linguistic activities', retains an anachronistic influence in Celtic linguistic studies. Thus the notion that a language-community necessarily defines or connects people in other ways persists even among some scholars: 'very little sociolinguistic, psycholinguistic, cognitive or pragmatic research has been carried out in these languages'.[11] In *Celtic Britain and Ireland: The Myth of the Dark Ages* (1990), an overview of archaeological debates, Lloyd and Jennifer Laing conclude that 'Saxons' were well out-numbered by Romano-Britons; that 'a peaceful and nearly wholesale assimilation [between] Romano-British and Saxon cultures...by the seventh century took on the umbrella term of "Saxon" or "English"'; and that 'the origins of Dark Age Celtic art [lie] fairly substantially in the Romano-British repertoire'. This model, perhaps coloured by the 1990s, posits less invasion and massacre (warriors leaping imperially off ships) than coexistence, trade and cultural diversity. In any case, most archaeologists now stress the 'common cultural elements between Celt and Saxon' in the 'Irish Sea province'; and, as regards pre-history too, join with most anthropologists and linguists in contesting the idea that people, language and artefacts move together through time and space in a compact ethnic package.[12]

As for the pre-historic Celtic conquest of Britain: Simon James of the British Museum has recently 'outraged' Plaid Cymru and the Scottish National Party by stressing 'the "complete absence" of physical evidence of a composite Celtic people carrying out the necessary invasions', and by claiming that this tradition was invented at the time of Anglo-Scottish Union (1707).[13] Andrew P. Fitzpatrick judiciously summaries the debate about Iron Age Celts: 'The Celts of the European Iron Age may be obscured by modern studies; but they are not entirely a product of nationalistic myths, nor are they purely a creation of imperialistic ethnic definition in the nineteenth

century...criticisms of modern interpretation do not invalidate the
ancient sources themselves. Instead, they demand a willingness to
examine the regional variation and to explore the archaeology of
the Iron Age whilst recognising that it is a theoretical construct,
instead of merely the filling in of the details of a grand, united
scheme of "Celtic" Iron Age Europe.'[14] All this reminds us that
Celts as well as Saxons can appear in aggressive, invasive and heroic
guises. (The Horrible Histories series includes *The Cut-Throat Celts*
along with the *Vicious Vikings* and *Smashing Saxons*). Timothy
Champion finds that 'images of the Celts' in nineteenth-century
archaeology and ideology veer between representing them 'as war-
riors [and] as an artistic people'.[15] The alternation corresponds to
the Jacobite theme of the Celts' resurrection from their aesthetic
afterlife to become 'a mighty race' or nation once again. The pro-
gramme for the tenth Atlanta Celtic Festival (1996) portrays the
Celts as a coherent ethnic group and as a force to be reckoned
with – the old plot of their fall from world-imperium ('At one
time the Celts dominated the ancient world from Spain to Turkey')
to residuality, with a hint of political comeback by way of culture:
'Today's Celts thrive as cultural groups in France, Ireland, Britain,
Canada and the United States.'

But it is as a residual, and thereby poetic, formation that the
Celts have passed much of the last two centuries. Matthew Arnold
projected not only national and psychological, but also imaginative,
needs on to race. He supported "Saxon" hegemony as justified by
England's worldly skills; but helped the Celtic or mixed (Anglo-
Celtic) side of the ethnological argument with his much-criticised
lectures 'On the Study of Celtic Literature' (1865-6).[16] Arnold's
attraction to allegedly Celtic qualities (largely in *English* literature)
was determined by what he found wanting in contemporary England
and by what he wanted for his own poetry. According to Frederic
E. Faverty's useful study, *Matthew Arnold: The Ethnologist*: '[Arnold]
regarded Philistinism, Teutonism and utilitarianism as three aspects
of the same regrettable failing in the English'. He agreed with a
famous Irish judgment, 'For dulness, the creeping Saxons', and the
view that 'The Anglo-Saxon is England's sitting-part.' By reclaim-
ing its Celtic spirit, English culture would achieve an ideal balance:
i.e., it would be saved from becoming Germany. (For Faverty, the
'underlying confusion in Arnold's argument is that...he regards
racial qualities as constant and yet alterable.')[17] Arnold admired
certain attributes which he associated with Saxon genes: energy,
steadiness, honesty and morality. But he thought that in gaining
so much of the world, England had lost not only its soul but its

THE POETICS OF CELT AND SAXON

intelligence: flexibility, the capacity for self-criticism, the philo-
sophical faculty to place ideas in a wider context. France was the
'Celtic' country (French origin-myth had settled on the Gauls by
the later nineteenth century) where he found most critical intelli-
gence; Wales and Ireland where he found most soul.

To recapitulate Arnold's sins: under the influence of French
theory (Henri Martin's *Histoire de France* [1855] and Ernest Renan's
essay 'La Poésie des Races celtiques' [1859]), he characterises Celts
as spiritual, lively, sentimental, impressionable, volatile, passionate,
eloquent, quick, anarchic, feminine, ineffectual, defeated. 'Melancholy
and unprogressiveness' sum up the 'irresistible magnetism' they
possess for him. More than Renan's essay, however, Arnold's con-
stitutes a portrait of the artist, Romantic sensibility, poetry. This
is warranted by Ossianism. Since Ossian/Oisín 'the primal poet'
was sole survivor of the Fianna, Celtic qualities converge on the
poet; the poet becomes the ideal-typical Celt. As Thomas Gray's
influential ode 'The Bard' puts it:

> On a rock whose haughty brow
> Frowns o'er old Conway's foaming flood,
>   Robed in the sable garb of woe,
> With haggard eyes the poet stood...

Conversely, when Gray's bard plunges into the flood, the poet along
with the Celt becomes obsolete or residual. Patrick Sims-Williams,
who disputes the idea that a unique "natural magic" distinguishes
the poetry of the Celtic languages, suggests that there were 'at
least three strands' to the 'image of the Celtic bard, inspired by,
and expiring in, the rugged Celtic landscape': the observed impor-
tance of poetry and song to peripheral Irish, Welsh and Highland
communities; the historic flight of the Welsh bards to rocks with
haughty brows; the outdoor mysteries of 'the Druid in his oaken
grove'.[18] Yet, while envying the Romantic extremity attached to an
'intoxication of style' he thinks Celtic, Arnold diagnoses lack of
staying-power, measure and architectonic. Thus failure in battle,
business or politics is not wholly sublimated by success in art. Most
fundamentally, to quote the notorious phrase that Arnold took
from Martin, Celts are 'in revolt against the despotism of fact'.
But this, too, implies the condition of poetry in the later nineteenth
century: its haggard-eyed revolt against the despotism of factories
and realist fiction. Arnold projects not only Anglo-Celtic fusion or
Union, or the integration of his own literary personality, but also
artistic unity: the lyric poem pitched between passion and measure,
a power in the world again. (It could be a blueprint for the later
Yeats.)

Perhaps Ossianism was always keyed to culminate in the *fin-de-siècle* lyric. For Renan, notoriously, 'la race celtique s'est fatiguée à prendre ses songes pour des réalités'. During the hundred years from *Ossian* to Arnold, the Celts had become the barometer of Europe's wistful backward look from the beach-heads of modernity: 'les tons divins expirant ainsi à l'horizon devant la tumulte croissant de l'uniforme civilisation' (Renan).[19] Leerssen writes that the 'conflation between peripherality and timelessness [is] one of the dominant modes of nineteenth-century Celticism...The Celtic Fringe is a place of stasis, a place where time moves slowly or stands still...a place at the very edge of the real world...liminal, half-ghostly'. He cites the comic strip *Astérix* as proof of 'the extraordinary tenacity and persistence of such anachronistic imaginative schemata: the Celtic-Gaulish isolation and extra-historicity of Brittany (embracing megalith-builders, Gauls and Bretons) is a continuing... commonplace'.[20] Yet this is also the dream-time of nations which, to quote Benedict Anderson, always 'loom out of an immemorial past, and, still more important, glide into a limitless future'.[21]

In Ireland and Scotland, Celtic time figures the Jacobite nation in abeyance or waiting. Further, literary resistance to modernity, to scientific and technological progress, to Darwinism, was inevitably magnetised by the Celtic configuration. It was not just for Irish reasons that Yeats came on board. If, as Leerssen suggests, the Celts can be at once Self and Other in Irish, French and British Isles contexts – he coins the term 'auto-exotic' – it follows that, beyond antiquarianism or nationalism, they afford a repository, even a safe-deposit, for traditions, forms of cognition, forms of art, that the metropolis rejects or denies. Hence Celticism as, to quote Leerssen, 'a multi-genre, multinational phenomenon'.[22] In *The Celts: The Construction of a Myth* (1992) Malcolm Chapman argues that 'the continuity of the Celts [i.e. in narratives which link the Iron Age, *Ossian* and Irish traditional music] is not derived from anything intrinsic to these people, but...derives from a particular kind of culture-meeting – a meeting between a self-consciously civilising, powerful, centralising culture...and a much less powerful culture'. That such meetings occur and continue is indicated by the increasing attraction of pan-Europeanism to pan-Celticism. John Collis, another Celto-sceptic, comments: 'Not only have the "Celts" not gone away, they are in the ascendancy, and, like the Germani in the early twentieth century, are being invoked for political purposes. I find myself chairman of a committee of the Council of Europe promoting "Celtic Routes" for informed tourism. Worse, we find ourselves in a Europe which is undergoing major political change in which ethnicity is playing a major role.'[23] By analogy with Celticism, pan-Celticism may serve as an escape-route from inconvenient history into an alternative, aggression-free, un-imperial yet culturally superior Europe.

That Celticism still captivates the French *avant-garde* was shown by *L'Imaginaire Irlandais*, a literary festival held in France during Spring 1996. Parisian intellectuals raved about *celtique* spirituality, while Irish writers objected coarsely on the sidelines. Introducing contemporary Irish literature to the French public Gil Jouanard wrote in Renanesque style: 'Proposer la célébration de l'imaginaire irlandais, c'est énoncer un pléonasme: l'Irlande n'est qu'un morceau d'imaginaire abandonné au gré des flots.' Jouanard admits (without understanding) the role of the unconscious in all this when he represents his floating Ireland 'abandoned to the will of the waves', identical with the imaginary itself, as a 'pre-Cartesian' object of desire: 'cet imaginaire qui nous ramène...aux racines de notre in-conscient pré-cartésien'.[24] Heinrich Böll's *Irisches Tagebuch* (1957) has helped Germany to retain a 'romanticised and idealist image of [Ireland] as symbolising everything noble and good...Peace-loving and innocent...every man and woman is a poet' – as Gerhard Heim-ler wrote, when Ireland was the featured country at the Frankfurt Bookfair. When several European and American fashion designers were asked what qualities of style they associated with Ireland, they mentioned 'poetry and purity', 'folkloric Celtic charm', 'unspoilt... untouched naturalness', 'the powerful and irresistible allure of a nation with a soul of its own', 'the unique blend of the Catholic faith and Celtic tradition', 'the soul of Europe'.[25] It's easy, of course, to perceive Celticists rather than 'Celts' as mistaking dreams for realities. *John Bull's Other Island* satirises not only 'melancholy Celt' misreadings of Ireland but also complicity between the Celt/ Saxon stereotypes in preventing self-knowledge and mutual know-ledge. Louis MacNeice asks in *Autumn Journal*: 'Why do we like being Irish? Partly because/ It gives us a hold on the sentimental English/As members of a world that never was,/ Baptised with fairy water...' Celticism affects France's own image in a similar way: 'Foreigners tend to think of the French as mercurial, unpre-dictable, emotional and perverse. The French, more accurately, see themselves as methodical, rational and obedient to expected standards of taste and behaviour.'[26] Despite historical and cultural variables, certain items remain on the timeless Celtic menu: other-worldliness, liminality, spirituality, melancholy, excessive emotion, imagination, poetry. To deconstruct Celticism is always to de-poeticise. The 'creeping Saxon' belongs to prose.

As for Celticism's political impact and implications: there is, first, the obvious point that its construction was parochial in time and space. Just as individuals credit their achievements to character rather than context, so the ideological niches of Celt and Saxon derive from the industrial revolution and the European balance of power in the mid nineteenth century. In Ireland 'Saxons' were top dogs. France's decline relative to Germany and England was confirmed by its defeat in the Franco-Prussian war (1870-1). Thus today's 'Celtic Tiger' need not be an oxymoron; nor should Oriental Tigers revert to odalisques or geisha (I write as Yamaichi Securities goes bust) if their economies wobble. Arnold's political writings know that other forms of despotism account for Ireland's degraded state; he campaigned for Catholic civil rights and reform of the land system. It was another Arnold – poet-physician to the condition of England – who espoused Celticism. Yet, when he later opposed Home Rule, on the grounds that the Union *needed* its Celtic dimension, his racial theory fed his belief that the Irish were ill-equipped to govern themselves. There is an echo of Arnold's indispensable Celts, useless on their own, in Evelyn Waugh's wartime novel *Put Out More Flags* (1942) which regrets that 'the people who once lent fire to an imperial race, whose genius flashed through two stupendous centuries of culture and success...are now quietly receding into their own mists, turning their backs on the world of effort and action'.

Did race theory influence the approach of the UK political élite to the Irish Question? In *Anglo-Saxons and Celts* (1968) L.P. Curtis influentially argued that the 'Paddy' caricature and the 'Anglo-Saxonist image of the Irish Celt' affected the whole conduct of affairs. It designated the native Irish as not merely Other but inferior, and hence unsuited to 'Anglo-Saxon liberty'.[27] As we have seen, this was indeed a sort of loop-tape in Arnold's thinking. Yet Celt/Saxonism could feed English separatism, as well as Arnold's (not uncomplimentary) fusionism; and some historians, including Sheridan Gilley and R.F. Foster, play down the political force of such stereotypes. Gilley argues that the stereotypes derived from politics, not the other away round: 'The Irish were damned for disloyalty [to the Union] before they were damned as Celts.' There was also a 'complex relationship' between 'anti-Celtishness and anti-Catholicism'[28] (which explains the elisions between Celt and Catholic in the minds of Tom Paulin and one fashion designer). Anglo-Saxonism had been engendered by Protestantism; and, as Linda Colley shows in *Britons: Forging the Nation 1707-1837* (1994), war with France had built Protestantism into the emergent nineteenth-century ideology of "Britain". In this respect, as in others, Arnold's Celticism differs from Renan's. An anti-clerical with mystical inclinations, Renan praises the Catholic-Celtic race, as opposed to the belatedly converted 'race germanique', for being 'naturellement chrétienne'; whereas Arnold displays Anglican bias when he Celticises non-conformism along with Catholicism: 'The religion of Wales is more emotional and sentimental than English Puritanism; Romanism has indeed given way to Calvinism among the Welsh, – the one superstition has supplanted the other'. For English and Irish Protestants, Catholics were religiously not racially inferior, and this could be remedied by conversion. In Scotland, too, the reason why Celts and Scots were not cognate has a religious dimension – even despite the Gaelic-speaking presbyterians of the western islands. Writing on 'Anglo-Saxons into Celts: The Scottish Intellectuals 1760-1930', Christopher Harvie stresses the legacy of 'the Calvinist Covenanters who…saw themselves as bulwarks against the anarchy and Catholic credulousness represented by the Stuarts and the Highlands', and which produced in the 1830s 'a Scottish variant of full-blown Anglo-Saxonism' which was incompatible neither with nationalism nor with radicalism. Yet the long-standing influence of Yeatsian cultural nationalism (and hence poetry) helps the Celts to win out when Romantic Scotland is revived or constructed by Scottish literary intellectuals today. Harvie concludes: 'An increasingly potent national movement believes in the Celtic version, and has forgotten its Protestant and Teutonic forebears.'[29]

Within English (and Arnoldian) representations of Ireland we should perhaps allow for differences of sphere – political, religious, cultural, literary – even if their orbits overlap. Within the literary sphere itself there are several Irish 'characters', whose representation and reception have varied according to context. And, just as Celts are not always Irish, the Irish are not always Celts. Ape-like, lazy or violent Paddy is no magnetic melancholic. When Arnold cannot reconcile Renan's 'race…fière et timide…à l'extérieur, gauche et embarrassée' with 'the typical Irishman of Donnybrook fair' the clash of prejudices, popular and literary, disproves his thesis. To this day, tourists in Ireland bemusedly look for soul on the one hand, carnivalesque "craic" on the other. As for Irish self-perceptions, a group of 'Celtic' male strippers have described themselves as exporting to English women a doubly exotic thrill: 'a bit of the rough' and 'a pure Irish boy'.

In nineteenth-century texts the nuance of 'race' itself ranges loosely and dangerously between blood, nation and culture (as it does in Yeats's poetry). The Celtic languages were identified as

Indo-European in 1831; and this, together with the exclusion of the
semitic languages from the European family, promoted positive
images. Chris Morash sees the Celts as 'the social climbers of
nineteenth-century race theory', because they filled the mystic gap
left by the Jews. Some scholars venerated them as ancient, even
aboriginal, Aryans: 'guardians of a spirituality which stretched "from
the grey dawn of their pre-history onwards to our own era" '.[30]
Renan stresses the purity of Celtic blood: in Ireland 'la race est
restée pure de tout mélange avec l'étranger'. The sliding of 'purity'
between race and soul may be one reason why Irish nationalism
has a superiority as well as an inferiority complex. Although in
the 1890s most cultural nationalists preferred to talk of Gaels, not
Celts, Celticism as well as Catholicism influenced images of the Gael
as 'spiritual beyond the ways of men'.[31] But if Renan and Arnold
advanced the idea of Jewish difference from the Indo-European, it
was in Germany, the continental country most stirred by *Ossian*
and most prominent in Celtic scholarship, that Celtomania became
most darkly complicit with anti-semitism. Morash concludes: 'When-
ever we allow a poem, a novel or a film to put forward the idea
that the "Irish" and "Celtic" are synonymous terms, or that Irish
"Celts" somehow have a greater spiritual purity than other peoples
(as is currently the case with the marketing of a certain type of
ethereal music as "Celtic"), we are taking part in a discourse which
was not only racist in origin, but which has been instrumental in
the legitimisation of anti-semitism.'[32]

The Irish service of German propaganda radio during the Second
World War was run by the Celtic scholar Hans Hartmann, who, in
Robert Fisk's words, 'had an unhealthy fixation on the Teutonic
purity of Irish racial stock'. For Hartmann, the Celts were actually
more Teutonic than the Saxons, having 'remained more faithful to
the spirit and traditions of Europe than [had] the English'.[33]
There is irony here in that some Anglo-Irish thinkers, such as
Standish O'Grady, a disciple of Carlyle, had embraced "Saxon"
Aryanism as a means of asserting their traditional dominance in
the face of actual decline. (By a further irony, O'Grady's muscular
versions of Irish legend helped to empower the "Celt".)[34] Reiner
Luyken has discussed the links between other Nazi administrators
or propagandists and the cult of Celtic 'Volk'.[35] Breton and Spanish
Celticism in the 1930s made some compacts with fascism: one fac-
tor in Spanish 'over-valuation of the Celts' (which included Aryan
credentials) was 'to provide an historical legitimation of the Franco
regime's concept of fatherland through the representation of Spain
as a unified whole since time immemorial'.[36] The ideological role

of German 'celtologists' as regards Ireland is elaborated by David O'Donoghue in his study *Hitler's Irish Voices: The Story of German Radio's Wartime Irish Service* (1998). So a phrase like 'the soul of Europe' is less innocent than it might appear. One of the fascist-kitsch Sinn Féin murals in west Belfast includes Celtic tracery, a dolmen, Cathleen ní Houlihan wearing a green monk-like robe, and a dove that looks like an eagle.

New Age Celticism – not confined to music – is another meta-morphosis of Celtic 'Soul'. The Celtic sections of Irish bookshops serve up a heady ethno-eco-Christian-mystical brew to foreigners and natives alike. A current best-seller is John O'Donohue's *Anam Cara: Spiritual Wisdom from the Celtic World*, from which comes the following collage:

> The Celtic mind was neither discursive nor systematic. Yet in their lyrical speculation, the Celts brought the sublime unity of life and experience to expression. The Celtic mind was not burdened by dualism. It did not separate what belongs together... The Celtic mind adored the light. This is one of the reasons why Celtic spirituality is emerging as a new constellation in our times... Ireland is a land of many ruins. Ruins are sacred places full of presence... For the Celts, the world is always latently and actively spiritual... In the Celtic world there was no barrier between soul and body...The world of Celtic consciousness enjoyed this unified and lyrical sensuous spirituality... The pagan world and the Christian world have no row with each other in the Irish psyche... The Celtic tradition had a wonderful sense of the way eternal time is woven through our human time...the Irish landscape resisted linearity...the Celtic mind never liked the line but always loved the shape of the circle.[37]

Anam Cara is unconsciously influenced by *Ossian*, Renan, Arnold and obsolete archaeology, as well as consciously by early Christian Gaelic poetry (read along 'natural magic' lines). Donald E. Meek accounts for the genre to which it belongs as a reaction against materialistic, hierarchical and authoritarian structures, and notes: 'Celtic Christianity is...highly eclectic, bringing under one label a range of products, old and new. The focus is not on the Celtic texts themselves, but pre-eminently on the needs of the spiritual consumer...'[38] Twentieth-century "Celtic" poets, such as Seamus Heaney, are sometimes co-opted to supply the 'lyrical' goods specified above. In its Irish context, as regards both author and audience, *Anam Cara* reflects a need to redeem Catholic spirituality from the crumbling authority of the institutional Church (Celtic a-historicity has its uses), although O'Donohue's prelapsarian vision is conditioned by 'unifying' Catholic theological habits. He may also seek to recover a 'peace-loving and innocent' Celtic Ireland from the impression created by more recent events.

In his still fresh critique of ethnology, *The Saxon and the Celt: A Study in Sociology* (1897), J.M. Robertson deconstructs Celt/Saxonism and concludes: 'we ought...to look for the cause of differences of national culture and well-being in institutions, political and other...in anything, in short, rather than in primordial and perpetual qualities of race'.[39] Yet what begins as race theory can transfer to culture theory. And even if ethnic/cultural stereotypes follow rather than lead politics, they can be politically exploited. Ulster unionists, for instance, drew on the vocabulary of Anglo-Saxonism and Celticism to paint Home Rule as the absorption of 'progressive' Ireland by misty Ireland. As partition loomed, these concepts began to serve a two nations as opposed to a one nation idea. Dennis Kennedy cites a passage quoted by the *Belfast News-Letter* in 1919: 'Ireland is inhabited by two distinct nations, or at least nationalities...The larger is composed of Celts, whether by race or assimilation...the others of Saxon descent. The ethnic character of the two races is as violently opposed as is well-nigh conceivable. They are not less widely separated in their religion'. And in 1921 the paper approved a comment that endorsed the existence of 'two Irelands – the Protestant, Loyalist and Saxon-blooded and Saxon-minded Ireland, and the Roman Catholic, Nationalist and Celtic Ireland'.[40] Most Irish nationalist propaganda of the time holds just as little comfort for Davis's desired political fusion of so-called Celts and Saxons in Ireland, and for Arnold's desired cultural fusion of Celtic and Saxon 'genius' in England, the Union and poetry.

2

John Hewitt's poems 'Ireland' (1932) and 'Ulsterman' (1937) belong to this inherited scenario. In 'Ireland' the speaker identifies with 'We Irish' and with 'the Keltic wave that broke over Europe', but takes a Saxonist line on the defeatist forms of behaviour – and forms of 'poetry' – that Arnold deemed 'Celtic':

> We Irish pride ourselves as patriots
> and tell the beadroll of the valiant ones
> since Clontarf's sunset saw the Norsemen broken...
> The later men got nothing save defeat,
> hard transatlantic sidewalks or the scaffold...
>
> But we are fools, I say, are ignorant fools
> to waste the spirit's warmth in this cold air,
> to spend our wit and love and poetry
> on half a dozen peat and a black bog.

> We are not native here or anywhere.
> We were the Keltic wave that broke over Europe,
> and ran up this bleak beach among these stones...

Hewitt's desire that his fellow-Celts should again share in 'great tidal movements round the earth' points towards the isolationist Irish Free State. He tries to reconcile Celtic and 'Saxon-minded' Ireland by representing the Celt as mobile rather than beached on the fringe. Yet Hewitt himself became obsessed with what it meant to be 'native here'. 'Ulsterman', a poem of marked ethnological residues, raises the issue in an early and naive form:

> Far back the shouting Briton in foray,
> the sullen Roman with his tramping host,
> the fair beard plaited in the Saxon way,
> the horned prow torching terror to the coast:
>
> then the dark chaunting Kelt with cup and cross,
> the red Scot flying from a brother slain,
> the English trooper plowing whin and moss,
> the gaunt Scot praying in the thin grey rain.
>
> These stir and mingle, leaping in my blood,
> and what I am is only what they were...
>
> Kelt, Briton, Roman, Dane, and Scot,
> time and this island tied a crazy knot.

Ulster has induced a fraught version of Arnold's argument for hybridity.

Sixteen years later, in a chapter of autobiography called 'Planter's Gothic', Hewitt more optimistically proposed a model of 'the ideal Ulsterman': 'he must carry within himself elements of both Scots and English with a strong charge of the basic Irish'. Now he speaks culturally, if imprecisely, rather than in the ethnic idiom of 'mingling in my blood'; although in both cases the 'elements' appear discrete rather than smoothly blended. Elsewhere he alludes to 'an uneven and lumpy mixture'. Thus the Celt-Saxon dialectic influences Hewitt's characterisation of Ulster Protestants or 'Saxon-Scots' as he terms them.[41] In 'Saxon and Celt: The Stereotypes' Terence Brown quotes from James Barkley Woodburn's *The Ulster Scot: His History and Religion* (1914). The book is a contribution to the Home Rule debate which, for thirty years, had generated constructions of the Ulster Scot (and Scotch-Irish in the US) to combat the Celtic or Gaelic race-types that served Irish separatism. Woodburn represents his hero as 'stern, dogged, and strong of purpose; independent, self-contained. and self-reliant, able to stand on his own feet, and intensely proud of the fact...perhaps the main outstanding fact about him is his power to command'.[42] Brown's choice of quotation is not quite fair to Woodburn, who stresses culture (especially the presbyterian investment in education, as in founding Princeton University) and denies racial difference at the outset: 'There are not two races in Ireland: the whole population is a mixture of Celtic and Teutonic, and the Ulsterman has probably as much Celtic blood as the Southerner…The popular theory… that there are two distinct races in the island…is, like many of the opinions about Ireland, entirely erroneous.' Yet Woodburn strays into ethnological tropes when he connects a 'more virile stock' with a colder, Northern climate, suggests that the South has been 'enervated' by Catholicism and claims that the Ulster Scot possesses 'the passion, alertness and quickness of the Celt' in addition to his other merits. This implies that the 'Saxon-Scot' – apparently a paragon of all the virtues – has improved on the Saxon. Hewitt's cultural self-image as Saxon-Scot is less positive as well as less simplistic than Woodburn's, yet does not contradict it. For him, too, there is only a male of this dogged or rugged species. Hewitt's socialism made him critical of the unprogressive ('half a dozen peat and a black bog'); and his defining adjective for himself and for Ulster Protestants in general – 'stubborn' – accords with Woodburn's portrait: 'he is determined to the verge of stubbornness, and will accept no compromise'.[43] As compared with the Viking-Teuton wing of macho Anglo-Saxonism (see Ted Hughes), the Saxon-Scot wing appears less heroic and violent, less sexy, more like porridge than Valhalla.

Hewitt was not the first poet from Protestant Ulster to deal in stereotypes of self-reliant or stubborn Saxon and unreliable, elusive Celt. As Brown shows, Thomas Hamilton Drummond and Samuel Ferguson had preceded him. But Hewitt was first to translate characteristics ('an extroverted, stubborn inarticulate society') into aesthetics, because he recognised that Protestant self-articulation had become more imperative in the new context of Northern Ireland. He also saw that, despite the historical contribution of Ulster Protestants to Irish poetry, the art had somehow been ceded to the "Celts". Thus Hewitt's seminal essay 'The Bitter Gourd: Some Problems of the Ulster Writer' (1945) proposes for the Saxon-Scot a poetic character distinct from the Celtic and akin to the literary traditions of New England: 'The careful rejection of the rhetorical and flamboyant, the stubborn concreteness of imagery, the conscientious cleaving to the objects of sense which, not at all paradoxically, provides the best basis and launching-pad for the lonely ascents of practical mysticism, lie close to the heart of Ulster's best intellectual activity.' The oxymoron 'practical mysticism' affirms Hewitt's belief in the Saxon-Scots' 'strange amalgam of realism and roman-ticism'. Possibly a riposte to 'natural magic', the concept reclaims lost spiritual ground from the Celt by way of New England philosophers such as Emerson and William James (of Ulster Scots ancestry).[44]

But what about this 'dark chaunting Kelt' and 'rejection of the rhetorical and flamboyant' (whatever his self-image, Hewitt's verse can be both)? Culturally Methodist, intellectually atheist, Hewitt embraces the typical confusions of Celt/Saxonism when he merges Celt into Catholic ('cup and cross') as auto-exotic Other. Sometimes (see below) he echoes Arnold on Romanist superstition. Arnold describes the English as Germanic with 'hauntings of Celtism'; and chants and rituals, whether in chapel or sacred grove, fascinate Hewitt: a fascination that reconstitutes Yeats's 'Druid land…Druid tune' of the 1890s. For Hewitt, too: the Druidic cloaks the priestly; restores mysteries banished by the Reformation and Darwinism; figures Irish Protestant marginality; and secretes an ecumenical paganism. The Catholic-Celt haunts his psyche as a return of both the repressed and oppressed: the *frissons* of what has been called Protestant Gothic or Protestant magic.[45] In 'Once Alien Here' (1945) the Ulster Plantation violates "natural magic":

> The sullen Irish limping to the hills
> bore with them the enchantments and the spells
> that in the clans' free days hung gay and rich
> on every twig of every thorny hedge,
> and gave the rain-pocked stone a meaning past
> the blurred engraving of the fibrous frost.

The speaker's ethno-cultural scenario returns to its aesthetic origins (of which Hewitt appears unconscious) as dispossession becomes Celtic liminality, mystique, poetry. This triggers desire for poetry of a different cut:

> So I, because of all the buried men
> in Ulster clay, because of rock and glen
> and mist and cloud and quality of air
> as native in my thought as any here,
> who now would seek a native mode to tell
> our stubborn wisdom individual,
> yet lacking skill in either scale of song,
> the graver English, lyric Irish tongue,
> must let this rich earth so enhance the blood
> with steady pulse where now is plunging mood
> till thought and image may, identified,
> find easy voice to utter each aright.

The landscape/mindscape of 'Once Alien Here' combines Saxon-Scot and Celtic features: 'rich earth', 'rock and glen', 'mist and cloud'.

That it represents a regional adaptation of race-theory ('blood')
appears more explicitly in the tension between 'stubborn wisdom
individual' (Saxon-Scot), 'graver English' (Saxon minus Scot) and
'lyric Irish' (Celt). The latter phrase identifies the Celt with supe-
rior poetic power. Such encapsulations and Hewitt's sense that 'a
native mode' is to be found somewhere between Saxon and Celt
(the poem stops significantly short of Arnold's fusionism), owe more
to ethnology than to literary evidence. This is an ethno-critical
manifesto for "Ulster poetry". Yet, as in his dealings with Ossian,
Hewitt could also appropriate Celtic/natural magic. In 1953 he
symbolised the Hewitt family's origins in Kilmore, Co. Armagh as
'a spring well under a gentle thorn, a never ceasing source and jet
of folk magic and meaning'.[46]

'Enchantments', however, remain ambiguous. In 'The Colony'
(1953), an allegory which renders Northern Ireland as an outpost
of the declining Roman empire, Hewitt casts territorial unease into
Celticist metaphor: 'So our troubled thought/is from enchantments
of the old tree magic'. Such imagery becomes more negative as it
becomes more political. Celtic 'darkness', wilderness and forest,
the druidic grove, move across a spectrum from the mysterious to
the potentially, if excusably, malign. Poetic spells turn into lies or
superstition or black magic at some points where Celt and Catholic
merge in this Protestant imagination. In his uncollected discursive
poem 'A Country Walk in May' (1960) Hewitt calls himself and
his companions 'Irish of the planter's polity', once again caught
between Celt and Saxon. They are 'not black-browed, moody Gaels,
addicted much/ to the soft answer and the easy touch,/ the spume
of spangled words'. Yet – the walk takes place near Coventry, whose
art gallery Hewitt ran for fifteen years – they are still more emphatic-
ally not 'creeping Saxons':

> In Midland precinct or suburban lane,
> each moment makes our wide divergence plain
> from these goodhearted, cocksure, talkative,
> more-tolerant-than-any-race-alive,
> brave, cosy, but inhospitable folk,
> who gape at wit and roar at every joke,
> God's Englishmen.

The speaker clinches this hostile portrait with the comment: 'it's
their exceptions that have made them great'. So a 'Saxon-Scot'
may have severe reservations about his Saxon part or sitting-part.
Here Hewitt sings from the same hymn sheet as a Scottish Free
Church radical quoted by Christopher Harvie. In 1847 Hugh Miller
wrote of the English: 'I never yet encountered a better-pleased

people…Unthinking, unsuspicious, blue-eyed, fair-complexioned, honest Saxons.'[47] Louis MacNeice writes in similar but self-aware vein: 'Although brought up in the Unionist North, I found myself saturated in the belief that the English are an inferior race. Soft, heavy, gullible, and without any sense of humour…They were extraordinarily slow in the uptake.'[48] Common features of the negative "Saxon" stereotype, seen at its most complex in critical representations of the English by Anglo-Irish writers from Maria Edgeworth to Shaw to Elizabeth Bowen, are complacency, literal-mindedness, stupidity, lack of 'wit'.

It's too simple to see 'Country Walk' as confessing Hewitt's split identity or identification. Rather, even as the speaker subscribes to the binary stereotypes, he exposes their inadequacy as cultural analysis since they cannot fit him in. The underlying problem with the Ulster Protestant, as with the Lowland Scot, in the Celt/Saxon typology is that both their Saxon and Celtic credentials are suspect: neither as Saxon as Finchley nor as Celtic as Fingal's Cave. Matthew Arnold does not accept 'lowland Scotchy' verse as belonging to the Celtic strain; in which case the 'gloaming' of Samuel Ferguson's Ulster Scots ballad 'The Fairy Thorn' should not have influenced Yeats and the Celtic Twilight. Murray Pittock observes: 'The identification of Scotland as entirely Celtic was almost always one which sought to minimise differences between Highland and Lowland in the interests of patriotic unity…[Walter] Scott's mixed vision of Scots as Germanic and Celtic was by contrast a paradigm of his evolutionary Unionism'. Harvie nuances Scott's politics differently, calling him 'emotionally Jacobite and practically an integrationist Whig'.[49] Colin Graham's analysis of Ferguson's epic poem *Congal* (1872) discloses further twists in the Ulster/Scots effort to negotiate the powerful ethnic antithesis (with its concealed Anglican and Catholic hostility to presbyterianism). Here pan-Celticism serves a unionist effort to stress, more comprehensively than Arnold or Scott, 'the unity of the culture of the British Isles', thereby 'Celticising England' and bringing all Celts in from the fringe.[50] In a more recent twist a Northern Irish impresario, sensitive to cultural diversity, has broadened the remit of *Riverdance* by staging a dance-show that draws on Irish, Scots and Scotch-Irish (Appalachian) traditions. The show calls itself 'Rhythms of the Celts', however, and its publicity refers to '3,000 years' of distinctive Celtic expression.

Roy Hattersley has even recruited the Orange Order for Celticism, for 'the terrible beauty born of doom and gloom'. Hazily recalling Macpherson-Arnold's 'They went forth to the war, but they always fell' and misapplying Yeats's 'Easter 1916', Hattersley cites the

Protestant obsession with the Battle of the Somme and other 'memories of the past' as proof that the Portadown marchers of July 1995 are 'quintessentially Irish': part of a Thomas Moore ethos that is 'melancholy to the point of despair...heroic, tragic, poetic...do not expect the story to have a happy ending'.[51] It should alarm Orangemen that, in Hattersley's eyes, they have lost the Saxon world and gained an Ossianic soul. It is again relevant that Macpherson's original mythic narrative of doom and gloom has its context in Jacobite defeat: 'They are now forgot in their land; their tombs are not found on the heath'. If fairies can become tigers, then Celts and Saxon-Scots, Jacobites and Williamites, enchanters/chanters and planters, marginals and metropolitans, poets and bourgeois might change places. From this angle, Hewitt's attraction to Oisín seems at once prescient and prudential.

Yet one of his literary contemporaries, the novelist Sam Hanna Bell, managed to resist Ulster's residual race theory: 'it has been concluded that...the traditions of Ulster can be found only in Catholic homes because Catholics are more "poetic", less "materialistic" ...I consider [this] decidedly unfair to some very solid company directors I know'.[52] Forty years later Celticism and Jacobitism contribute to nationalist disdain for 'Protestant culture'.[53] Robert McLiam Wilson's novel *Eureka Street* (1996) shares Bell's distrust of trade-offs between race-type, stereotype, poetry and propaganda. Wilson satirises a poetry-reading largely attended by Belfast republicans: 'These people gathered close together, snug in their verse, their culture, they had one question. Why can't Protestants do this? they asked themselves. What's wrong with those funny people? Why aren't they spiritual like us?'[54]

3

The otherworldly poetics of Celticism have worldly dimensions, worldly effects. For some continentals today, Ossianism softens the edges of IRA violence (Wesley Hutchinson points out that Irish republicanism is the only political cause which has been supported both by *Libération* and Le Pen).[55] In 'forcing the periphery above the horizon of post-Culloden dispossession', to quote Pittock, Macpherson injected Jacobite politics into the bloodstream of European Romanticism. And in the 1890s, Pittock argues, 'Irish or Scottish nationalism, bound up with a Romantic vision of the Celtic past, was not only a politics suited to the Symbolist critique of modern culture, but also a direct attack on the constitutional integrity of the British state.'[56]

Pittock may overstate his case; but it accords with Hewitt's quest for poetic empowerment of the Saxon-Scot as unionist political hegemony looks shakier. One of Hewitt's best poems, 'A Local Poet', recalls his youthful inspiration in Celtic Twilight terms: 'He'd imagined a highway of heroes/ and stepped aside on the grass/ to let Cuchulain's chariot through...' And, indeed, 'Apparition', published in 1931, is a portrait of the artist in search of Cuchulain: 'I stood at twilight on a mound:/ The grass was wet beneath my feet:/ A dripping moon rose wet and round,/ And winds blew faint horns of retreat.//A shape of mist with shield and spear/ Stood in the bracken to his knees...' Fifty years later Hewitt would criticise the poetry associated with the Ulster Literary Theatre, an offshoot of the Dublin Revival: 'All this original verse was filled with fairies, tramps of both sexes, tinkers, turfcutters, mothers crooning cradle-songs in cabins in misty glens or by lonely shores...So from these voluble city dwellers there was not a word about where they lived and the people they lived among...'[57] Yet, as 'Ossian's Grave' indicates, he did not renounce 'shapes of mist' when he stepped off that twilit mound. His post-war project for Ulster literary regionalism sought a mystical sanction. 'Those Swans Remember' (1955), which Hewitt called 'a deliberate attempt to go beyond my usual flat plain manner of statement',[58] is neo-Yeatsian in 'link[ing] the dark Aegean to the Moyle' and in its symbolic galaxy of naturally magic animals such as the 'Salmon of All Knowledge' and the unicorn:

O white and gentle creature, come not near,
but through the shadows delicately pass
between the dark pool and the moonlit grass.

For Yeats, Oisín v. St Patrick figures the *fin de siècle* v. the Victorians; for Hewitt, 'Oisin blinking through his tears;/ Oisin pursued by Patrick's nagging words' figures his regionalist cultural agenda v. unionist philistinism.[59]

From the late 1930s to 1957 the Glens of Antrim, mainly populated by Catholic small farmers, served Hewitt as a microcosmic region within a region. This hilly northern coastal area, looking at Scotland across the Sea of Moyle, was his counterpart or counter to the West of Ireland in Revival ideology. Like the West for Revival Protestants, his 'chosen ground' staged Hewitt's closest encounter with Celtic-Catholic Otherness, causing him to rethink some inherited clichés. His Glens poems partly continue, partly revise, Revival and Celticist versions of landscape, culture and poetry. Hewitt's few West of Ireland poems register unease with a wholly wild environment and with the literary-political expectations it engenders. *His* turfcutter poem, 'Turf-carrier on Aranmore', dissociates the speaker from a turf-carrying boy, his donkey and 'the/ bare unprofitable mountainside', all 'native to this Druid air'. It also criticises the politics that permit such poverty. Less extreme, less 'Celtic', the Glens became a home from home: a psycho-cultural, auto-exotic landscape blending wild and tame prospects. A scholar of Ulster's topographical verse and art, Hewitt subscribes to this originally English mode, but stresses objective and subjective differences on the Saxon horizon, too. 'A Country Walk in May' rejects Warwickshire for 'The whin-bright ditch/ across the sloping moss of the long hill...the whinchat breaking from the cannavaun...and that sharp heathered cone'. In this Ulster alternative to English pastoral 'roughness edges all/ with timelessness and sadness, shewing man/ against all odds, a small precarious clan'. Here 'clan' identifies the exiled Hewitt, as well as mankind and perhaps Ulster Protestants, with Celtic losses.

At one end of Hewitt's register 'timelessness and sadness' try for the Ossianic sublime, but fall short. 'Garron Top' rather theoretically desires 'fundamental storm' on a height 'abstracted to the elements'. 'Freehold', a regionalist manifesto, hails 'historic Ulster, battlefield/of Gael and Planter' as a romantically remote Celtic fringe: 'last edge of Europe, cliff against the west/stemming the strong tides with its broken coast'. Yet Hewitt goes on to bind Celtic (and, subtextually, Saxon-Scot) settlement into the rebuilding of postwar society: his Celts scramble ashore 'to light their fires and build their wicker sheds'. 'Sunset over Glenaan' definitively stakes out Hewitt's 'chosen ground' as the area of hillside farms, its 'utmost limits' defined by the mountains' 'dark array'. This excludes the 'fat valleys' of 'the inland Planter folk' with their 'dulled prosperity'. (Renan contrasts 'la vulgarité normande...une population grasse et plantureuse' with the Bretons: 'une race timide' 'sentant profondément' who live where the wind is 'plein de vague et de tristesse'.) Fat Ulster Protestant valleys, like Midland precincts, contrast with each hilltop's 'cairn of dead/ and ancient memories of turbulence'. Pathetic fallacy, which survives knowledge of how some "Celts" became fringe, fuses terrain with racial character in ethnological fashion. The poem ends with the speaker claiming a stake in both Planter and Gael, and implicitly Celt and Saxon: 'I also share/ the nature of this legendary air'. As compared with the city, Glenaan gives 'nurture of the heart/ the rowan berries and the painted cart,/ the bell at noon, the scythesman in the corn,/ the cross of rushes, and the fairy thorn'. This catalogue reconciles Hewitt's opposites by transposing Celticism into the more domestic and folkloric idiom of Yeats's Sligo poems. Indeed, his most intimate experience of the Glens occurred 'before the rapid leap in technology changed the pace of rural life, when traditional usages and customs were still practised or vividly remembered'.[60]

Hewitt was aware of 'Moira O'Neill' as a precursor in Antrim pastoral. He called her *Songs of the Glens of Antrim* (1900) 'a unique event in our literary history', despite 'the limitations in the social background of the author' – i.e., her upper-class origins.[61] In 'Cuttin' Rushes' O'Neill makes an old woman speak thus: 'Rippin' round the bog pools high among the heather,/The hook it made me hand sore, I had to leave it go,/'Twas he that cut the rushes then for me to bind together./*Come, dear, come!* – an' back along the burn/ See the darlin' honeysuckle hangin' like a crown...' And here is Hewitt speaking (in 1948) as one of those 'Gathering Praties': 'a long four-acre field, half pale with stubble,/ half lengthwise ribbed with drills the digger broke/ in slow dark showers of mould.// We bent and picked/ and flung the tubers, if the proper size,/ into the slatted basket ...Then the half-buried praties daubed with mud/ were cold and wet to handle...' This is the Ulster agricultural poem well advanced on its road from O'Neill to Seamus Heaney. Hewitt does not let picturesque pastimes, such as ceilidhs or Halloween rites, drive out economics. 'Landscape' defers to the countryman's reading of its title as 'a map of kinship', 'a chart of use', 'a handbook of labour or idleness'. Without discarding the folkloric, Hewitt translates the forlorn or mistily utopian or saltily vital Celtic fringe of 1890-1910 into a more utilitarian, communitarian 'practical-mystical' locus.

Thus the Glens do not necessarily deliver what Samuel Beckett called 'the Ossianic goods'.[62] Nor do they always speak in 'the lyric Irish' tongue. 'Country Talk' begins: 'Partly from reading the books and hearing the plays,/ and partly because it has happened to us now and then,/ we expect the cadenced phrase and the singular image...but more often the wisest have no more style than a sod'. Stereotype yields to observation. And in 'Homestead' Oisín, as mediated by the Glens of Antrim, even re-orients Celt and Saxon:

> Oisin, I said, is my symbol, that shadowy man,
> warrior and bard returning again and again
> to find the Fenians forgotten and unforgotten,
> rising when bidden on the young men's lips
> to face defeat and go down and sleep in their cave.
> Oisin, who baffled Patrick, his older faith
> tougher than the parchment or the string of beads:
> Oisin after the Fenians...
>
> I have seen him since, can tell you where he whispers
> among the salleys and the blood-bright holly...

What the speaker calls his 'cloven nature' (material *versus* spiritual) harks back to Saxon and Celt, since it is figured by a legendary contention between Dan Lavery, the 'red-necked farmer' and Gillwirra MacCartan, 'the reed-voiced bard'. As elsewhere, Hewitt follows Yeats in using pagan myth to transcend Christian schisms. But he takes his own line on the quarrel between Oisín and St Patrick, poetry and religion. By relating Oisín's atheism to his own, he realigns Celt and Saxon, and recruits 'practical mysticism' to circumvent the sectarian. 'Homestead', which places poetry at the centre of an imagined community, mingles a mystical Saxon pre-cursor from New England with Celtic precursors from the poetry of "natural magic" that would later inspire *Anam Cara*: 'I shall often remember the Walden Pond,/and the grey beehive cells of the tonsured men...talking to God across the assenting grass'. Despite that rare nod to Christianity (if a Christianity close to Paganism), Hewitt's Ossianic poems generally celebrate Oisín 'who baffled Patrick'. At another level of this bafflement, 'May Altar' (1950) reflects on the confirmation of Catholic girls in the 'thorn-white Glens'. The poem accommodates both 'the chipped and battered statue of the Virgin' and the speaker's hankering for 'the pagan thorn', thus splitting Celticism from Catholicism while applying Ossianic balm to Ulster tensions.

Oisín does not have all the answers. And only intermittently does Hewitt find the poetic means either to resolve cultural inhibitions or to escape stereotypes of Self and Other. When an "Ulster" or "Northern Irish" poetry eventually transpired, its matrix proved much more complex than he had imagined, despite the ethnologi-cal continuities I indicate below. Yet the Glens of Antrim helped Hewitt to recast some tenacious ethno-critical themes. It is to his credit that he never adopts a Celtic persona – a strong temptation for Irish Protestant poets in the mid-century, as earlier. John Wilson Foster observes: 'it is a measure of the magnetism of Yeats and the Revival that certain Ulster writers changed their names and went, figuratively but usually literally too, to Dublin: Samuel Waddell remade himself as Rutherford Mayne...Anna Johnston as Ethna Carbery, George Russell as AE...'[63] Frank O'Connor and Patrick Kavanagh laughed at F.R. Higgins (a southern Protestant) for dressing himself up as a 'wild Celt' before he could write at all.[64] W.R. Rodgers, another poet from the Protestant North, sometimes played style-intoxicated Celt to Hewitt's sober Saxon-Scot: Hewitt's elegy for Rodgers calls him a 'wild hare'. Elsewhere in this book, I argue that Tom Paulin plays the wild Irish critic to a notionally Saxon audience (see pp.224-34). Yet for Hewitt too, despite his revisions of stereotype, an 'irresistible magnetism' linked the poetic with the Celtic, with 'the enchantments and the spells'. His original conditioning by the Celt/Saxon dialectic may have been as unfortunate (contrast MacNeice's lack of susceptibility) as it is revealing. Yet it moved him to overcome the negative Saxon-Scot image, whether internalised or externally imposed, as this affected poetry in Northern Ireland.

4

To sum up so far: Celticism and Anglo-Saxonism are interdependent; their dialectic derives from intellectual, literary, religious, cultural and political history in the British Isles and Europe; it has served both separatist and fusionist models of relations within and between "these islands"; even now, Celticist notions cling to poetry in ways that can be either positive or problematic; Northern Ireland brings its own 'crazy knot' to the saga. In the rest of this essay I will add to my earlier suggestions that Celticism has been less disadvantageous to Irish nationalism than is often maintained, and that hidden workings of ethno-criticism muddle poetic intercourse between Ireland and England – one effect being to make "Ireland" and "England" loom too large. Tom Paulin's account of the mutual attraction between domineering Protestant Anglo-Saxonism and 'relaxed Catholic Celticism' reproduces as much as notices complicity in stereotype. He accepts Celticism as an actually existing formation rather than 'the history of what people wanted [the term "Celtic"] to mean' (Leerssen). The exasperation of a Shaw or MacNeice is sharpened by knowledge that they will never be clasped to the sentimental English bosom with the same guilty fervour as the exotic Catholic-Celtic Other. If the Ulster Saxon-Scot is too Scottish, they are too Anglo.

Anglo-Irish writers, both nationalist and unionist, specialise in correcting English views of Ireland. Yeats's response to Arnold comes under this rubric, even if it did not appear so to the nationalist journalist D.P. Moran. Moran is the first of three nationalist commentators on Celticism whose attitudes may throw light on its wanderings between poetry and politics (the others are Declan Kiberd and Seamus Deane). In 1900 Moran, who advocated a Gaelic-speaking, economically self-sufficient 'Irish Ireland', attacked Yeats for propagating mysticism, mongrelism and the 'Celtic note':

A certain number of Irish literary men have 'made a market' – just as stock-jobbers do in another commodity – in a certain vague thing, which is indistinctly known as 'the Celtic note' in English literature, and they earn their fame and livelihood by supplying the demand which they have honourably and with much advertising created. We make no secret of the reason why we have dropped our language, have shut out our past, and cultivate Anglo-Saxon ways. We have done them all in the light of day, brutally, frankly – for our living. But an intelligent people are asked to believe that the manufacture of the before-mentioned 'Celtic note' is a grand symbol of an Irish national intellectual awakening. This, it appears to me, is one of the most glaring frauds that the cred- ulous Irish people have ever swallowed. I hope no one will think I am attacking the 'Celtic note' from an English literary point of view. I am looking at it merely from the point of view of the Irish nation, of which it is put forward as a luminous manifestation. Beyond being a means of fame and living to those who can supply the demand, what good is the 'Celtic note' in English literature to the Irish nation?[65]

While this has a sectarian subtext, there was good warrant for distinguishing the Gaelic from the Celtic, and for attributing a "Saxon" business sense both to Twilight literati and to Catholic Ireland. But Moran's core question – what good is the 'Celtic note' to the Irish nation? – typefies the utilitarianism of nationalism when it comes to literary representations. It follows that positive stereo- types (which, I am arguing, Celticism also fostered) will not always be contested with the same rigour. It also follows that Irish Protestant writers, whatever their cultural politics, cannot afford to let negative or simplistic representations go by default. Replying to a series of similar articles by Moran, Yeats stresses the need for 'the expression of Irish emotion and Irish thought' in both languages, and then insists: 'I have avoided "Celtic Note" and "Celtic Renaissance" partly because both are vague and one is grandiloquent, and partly because the journalist has laid his ugly hands upon them [and] I have argued that the characteristics which [Matthew Arnold] has called Celtic, mark all races insofar as they preserve the qualities of the early races of the world'. Then he subverts Moran by suggesting that those who would deny the Irishness of the 'delicate, obscure mysterious song of my friend "A.E."' are brainwashed by 'the cir- cumstance of a life which is dominated by England'. 'Entangled in the surfaces of things', they fail to appreciate writers 'who may be recognised in the future as most Irish'.[66] So Yeats retains the spirit, though not the letter, of Celticism as a passport to future accep- tance of himself and his movement as no less primordially Irish than the Gaelic League.

As Yeats says, he is interested in matters other than Ireland – poetry, for example. In 'The Celtic Element in Literature' whenever

Yeats remarks of Arnold 'I do not think he understood', 'I will put this differently' or 'I prefer to say', he pulls away from ethno-criticism to define a 'religious', mythic and symbolist aesthetic which he sees Arnold as having imperfectly intuited; just as he distances Arnold's ideas from Irish cultural debate: 'I do not think any of us who write about Ireland have built any argument upon them'. Yeats prefers 'ancient' and 'primitive' to 'Celtic': 'all the august sorrowful persons of literature...are indeed but the images of the primitive imagination mirrored in the little looking-glass of the modern and classic imagination'. He speaks less for revolt against fact than for literary revolution: the 'reaction against the rationalism of the eighteenth century has mingled with a reaction against the materialism of the nineteenth century'. When Yeats redeems Renan's dreamy Celt from negative stereotype – 'this "mistaking dreams" which are perhaps essences, for "realities", which are perhaps accidents' – the reversal heralds a symbolist poetry that rejects Arnold's 'measure'. Further, the Celts are not the only ancient show in town (the 'makers of the *Kalevala*' being nearest to 'the old way') and what might count aesthetically or spiritually is Celtic centrality, proximity to the metropolis, not liminality: 'Of all the fountains of the passions and beliefs of ancient times in Europe...the Celt alone has been for centuries close to the main river of European literature.'[67]

Discussing Yeats's Celticism (in *Inventing Ireland: The Literature of the Modern Nation*, 1996), Declan Kiberd seems more hypnotised by Celticism and by England/Arnold as inventor of Ireland, than Yeats ever was. In a chapter called 'The Last *Aisling – A Vision*' he fuses the *aisling*, the Gaelic dream-poem of Jacobite restoration, with Yeatsian cosmology. Asserting that 'A Vision, for all its arcane lore, was intended by [Yeats] to provide a spiritual foundation for the new nation state', he translates the gyres into the dialectic of Celt and Saxon: into 'the Anglo-Irish antithesis out of which Yeats and the Irish revival came'. It is Kiberd, not Yeats, who represents England and Ireland as a binary 'antithesis' to be 'transcended'; who declares the Primary (democratic, scientific, factual) gyre to be 'Anglo', and the Antithetical (hierarchical, aesthetic, visionary) gyre to be 'Celtic'; and who designates *A Vision* 'a Celtic constitution not solely for Ireland but for all the world, after the rough beast has come again'.[68] Despite 'all the world' this reading insists on the recognisably national character of the most 'arcane' Irish literature, and allows 'Celtic' lineaments to be a valid recognition-factor. Since Kiberd has previously been critical of Celticism as a 'colonial' strategy, and sceptical about Yeats's nationalist credentials,[69] it may be good news that he welcomes him back into the Irish fold. Yet he does so in terms that Yeats never really endorsed in the 1890s and abandoned soon afterwards. (Yeats's 'manly' aesthetic of the early 1900s is partly an effort to dissociate himself from a "Celtic" aesthetic of 'vague desires'.)[70] Kiberd now simplifies Yeats's early mindscape, projects it on to the complexities of his later career, and construes the poetic and philosophical effort to 'hold in a single thought reality and justice' as a Celtic manifesto. Having sheltered the Celts when down on their luck, poetry has become superfluous to political requirements.

Seamus Deane more consistently doubts that Celticism has done the nation service. His Clarendon lectures, published as *Strange Country: Modernity and Nationhood in Irish Writing since 1790* (1997) update his earlier contention that 'the romanticising of the Celt [became], in effect, the romanticising of the Irish Catholic', and that this racial/cultural patronage promoted political acquiescence in the Union. In *Strange Country* Deane says of the nineteenth-century Irish novel: 'The psychology of the Irish community – in its national form…is created as a form of energy, that is in need of appropriation, external control, so that it can become politically sober while remaining aesthetically vivacious.' More broadly, he focuses on the terms 'tradition' and 'modernity', arguing that European Celticism locked Irish nationalism into a posture which allowed the Union to figure as modernising: 'The Celt as a racial formation was now transposed from its nationalist, antiquarian origins of the eighteenth century into a pan-European *combinatoire* of evolutionary destiny, the preservation of difference, even of anachronism, as a refusal of those adaptations needed to survive into the world of international finance and the nation-state.'[71]

Yet Deane also suggests that the spectral, occult, regressive, libidinal 'lost world' of Celtic strangeness should not be altogether disowned by Irish nationalism. Nostalgia, some theorists now argue, can harbour future worlds. If so, the longest-running political advertisement in history – Macpherson's *Ossian* – is delivering at last. Deane's nostalgic package has a Jacobite shape. Modern national selfhood may even require 'the presence of archaic elements to articulate its difference from them'. Deane also sees 'occultism, theosophy, Gothic fiction, the twilight of the Celtic gods' as 'closely intertwined with Yeats's rediscovery of an Ireland that, to a large extent, spoke a different language, the Irish he could never master'. Further, Yeats's latterday Anglo-Irish canon (formerly condemned by Deane as ideologically unionist) now rebukes 'the Lockean-Whig interpretation of history' and threatens the British state's 'repression of the Irish nation and of the deep psychic energies it exemplifies'.[72] In thus equating the language of Protestant occultism with the Irish language as hidden Irelands, potential Irelands, Deane accepts Yeats's point to Moran and re-unites the literary and linguistic wings of the Irish Revival. Yet, like Kiberd, he validates a loosely and helpfully Celtic-nationalist Yeats at the expense of the later poetry – and poetry – the Protestant dissident, the shrewd political observer, the eclectic autodidact. Having earlier suspected Yeats's Celticism as a cloak for Saxonism, Deane now allows its utility to distort the Yeatsian dynamic in a different manner. His revised Yeats would always oppose 'nationality' to 'rationality',[73] always deplore the subjugation of the national psyche to the despotism of historical fact. Here nationalist neo-Celticism co-opts the Romantic, anti-Enlightenment element in postmodernist thought. Yeats's Fenians may yet 'rise, making clouds with their breath'.

Deane's critical shift intersects with the Celticist features, even the Celtic unconscious, of his autobiographical fiction *Reading in the Dark* (1996). This *Bildungsroman* concerns a child trying to read social codes and family secrets in Derry during the years that incubated the Northern Irish Troubles. The Northern Catholic sense of being at once cut off (from the Republic) and in waiting (for a United Ireland) consorts with the *aisling* figure of Celtic timelessness, suspension and ahistoricity. In representing a liminal, repressed, Jacobite existence, Deane draws on 'occultism...Gothic fiction, the twilight of the Celtic gods'. The text is full of deaths, hauntings, ghosts, desolation, wailing, winter, darkness. Some chapters, however, fringe Deane's dark Northern city with a more positively Celtic, mythically luminous countryside. 'Grianan', for instance, conjures the Ossianic in the manner of John Hewitt at Ossian's Grave. The child sits in a wishing-chair amid a stone circle:

> I imagined I could hear the breathing of the sleeping Fianna waiting for the trumpet call that would bring them to life again to fight the last battle which, as the prophecies of St Colmcille told us, would take place somewhere between Derry and Strabane, after which the one remaining English ship would sail out of Lough Foyle and away from Ireland for ever. If you concentrated even further, you would scent the herbal perfumes of the Druid spells...[74]

While the recruitment of the Fianna for Brits Out is placed as childish fancy, the first-person voice (as elsewhere in this text) reserves little narrative, historical or ironic distance. It is the voice of poetic sensibility in which childhood and adult imagination converge. Despite some sharp socio-political impressions, the book often depends on Celtic-poetic recognition factors. Michael Foley's very

different fiction, *The Road to Notown*, published in the same year
and portraying Catholic Derry of roughly the same period, met with
nothing like the same success. Foley's landscape is sociological, his
tone satirical, his structure more thoroughly novelistic. Blake Mor-
rison was one 'sentimental English' reviewer of *Reading in the Dark*
who got carried away: 'Magic and folklore swirl around...[the child's]
aunt tells him stories of possession and metamorphoses and sleep-
ing warriors; he learns how if you meet somebody with one green
eye and one brown you should cross yourself, "for that was a human
child that had been taken over by the fairies".'[75] In *The Road to
Notown* Derry youngsters watch *Z-Cars*. It is an irony (which Yeats
might enjoy) that Deane's mildly Celticist fiction should reach a
wider audience than his anti-Celticist criticism. But the phenomenon,
like Kiberd's and Deane's revaluation of the 'Celtic' Yeats, proves
George Boyce's thesis that Yeats has been a long-term political asset
to Irish nationalism, especially in its current conflict with the Saxon-
Scot, because he exported to England the 'Ireland of romance, song
...twilight'.[76]

5

One residue of Celticism is that Irish woodnotes are thought to be
wilder and more native than their English counterparts. Neil
Rhodes's essay 'Bridegrooms to the Goddess: Hughes, Heaney
and the Elizabethans' challenges this assumption. Rhodes explores 'a
thematic continuity between the work of [Ted] Hughes and [Seamus]
Heaney in the way they represent certain cultural antagonisms or
antitheses' and use 'the same kinds of oppositional formulae...to
represent the Anglo-Irish relationship'. His focus is Hughes's
influence, especially the ideas that culminated in *Shakespeare and the
Goddess of Complete Being* (1992), on Heaney's collections *Wintering
Out* (1971) and *North* (1975). These ideas interpret the nexus between
nationality and religion with reference to 'gender-based stereotypes'.
Hence Ireland as Catholic, instinctive, female; England as Protestant,
rational, male. I believe that Rhodes is right to see these mythic
histories as symbiotic (he supplies convincing intertextual detail),
and to add Hughes to the 'palimpsest' whereby in Heaney's *North*
'the divisions of modern Ireland are written over successively by the
lore of Iron Age Denmark, the Vikings and Shakespeare's England'.[77]
However, intermediary between Shakespeare and Hughes, the more
immediate source for all 'antagonisms or antitheses', may be the
'oppositional formula' of Celt and Saxon.

This returns us to Tom Paulin calling Hughes 'a domineering Anglo-Saxon Protestant drawn to a relaxed Catholic Celticism'. Paulin wonders, too, whether Hughes's myth 'isn't also a means of expressing historical guilt'. Yet Paulin fails to probe the Irish poetic Other who has abetted Hughes's 'construction of a myth in which the Germanic/puritan/masculine is eternally at war with the Celtic/Catholic/feminine'.[78] And guilt in Hughes, such as his view that Shakespeare desires to salvage 'the goddess of Catholicism... of Medieval and Pre-Christian England' from 'the young Puritan Jehovah', is a slippery psycho-cultural matter [79] – as, indeed, is victimhood in Heaney. Heaney's 1972 poem 'A Peacock's Feather', on the birth of an 'English niece', introduces Celts and Saxons into a binary blood-and-soil scenario that sets the English or Anglo-Irish big house against 'scraggy farm and moss'. He writes: 'May tilth and loam,/ Darkened with Celts' and Saxons' blood/ Breastfeed your love of house and wood'. (Outside the vocabulary pressed by the poets, one line of comparative enquiry might ask why Heaney should cultivate a Jungian *anima* whereas a Freudian *id* prowls and growls in Hughes's poetry.) In 1974, Heaney controversially politicised Hughes's Goddess and Jehovah as Cathleen Ní Houlihan violated by a 'new male cult', with a godhead in London, 'whose founding fathers were Cromwell, William of Orange and Edward Carson'.[80] But if Heaney partly recognised, partly imitated the 'antagonisms or antitheses' at work in Hughes's early poetry, this may have something to do with common ancestry in Robert Graves's *The White Goddess* (1946) of which there was a new edition in 1961. (Graves expressly rehabilitates the word 'tilth' in his poem of that name.) *The White Goddess* is a powerful carrier of gendered Celticist tropes into poetics which emphasise that the 'function of poetry is religious invocation of the Muse'. This tradition, in its English guise, Graves traces to Celtic rather than Anglo-Saxon origins. In passages that must have strongly influenced Hughes, Graves aligns classical, patrilinear, Apollonian poetry with England's (Protestant) desertion of the Mother-Goddess: 'The Civil Wars in England were won by the fighting qualities of the Virgin-hating Puritan Independents'.[81]

Heaney's 1976 lecture 'Englands of the Mind', a brilliant if perverse response to the language and rhythms of Hughes, Geoffrey Hill and Philip Larkin, thinks about English poetry in ethno-critical terms that ultimately invoke Celtic origins. He associates distinctive cultural qualities with the Anglo-Saxon, French and Latin strata of the English language: an Irish reading of poetic Englishness which gives priority to its oldest elements. For example, Heaney identifies an English desire 'to receive from the stations of Anglo-Saxon confirmations of ancestry', and sees that desire fulfilled, when he calls Hughes 'rightful heir to [the] alliterative tradition'. He also detects and approves an underlying Celtic 'beat': 'the poems beat the bounds of a hidden England, in streams and trees, on moors and in byres'; '[in "Pibroch"] fetching energy and ancestry from what is beyond the Pale and beneath the surface, we have the elements of the Scottish piper's *ceol mor*'. Here Anglo-Saxon has become the new Gaelic, while 'stations' reminds us that it was a language of pre-Reformation as well as pagan England.[82] Heaney's slender quatrain in *North* appears to aim at a smoothed-out Anglo-Saxon metre: 'love-den, blood-holt,/ dream-bower'. This poem 'Bone Dreams', the poetic equivalent to 'Englands of the Mind', explicitly harks back to 'the scop's// twang, the iron/ flash of consonants/ cleaving the line'.

Over twenty years later, Heaney's 'On a New Work in the English Tongue' glossed Hughes's elegies for Sylvia Plath (*Birthday Letters*, 1998) with the passage from *Beowulf* in which King Hrethel mourns his son Herebeard:

> Alone with his longing, he lies down on his bed
> And sings a dirge, suddenly without joy
> In his steadings and wide fields.
> Such were the woes
> And pains of loss that the lord of the Geats endured
> After Herebeard's death. The king was helpless
> To set to right the wrong that had been committed.

As a poem about poetry, 'On a New Work' performs various and curious translations of language, genre and gender. Its masculine idioms highlight the friendship of male poets rather than the death of a female one. But more significant for my purposes is the way in which *Beowulf* becomes the ground of authentic poetry, authentic emotion, the English Tongue. The poem begins by attacking contemporary literary shallowness ('Post-this, post-that, post-the-other') and the Heaney-voice re-affirms 'language that can still knock language sideways' by casting Hughes as an Anglo-Saxon lord/bard.[83]

The phrase 'hidden England' re-orients a famous coinage of Daniel Corkery who called his influential study of the Gaelic tradition *The Hidden Ireland* (for Corkery's influence on Heaney, see pp.97-99). Heaney represents Hill and Larkin as successively less in touch with this mysterious locus. He thus encourages in Hughes ideas of cultural recovery similar to those associated with a particular form of Irish nationalism. While "England", as in Edward

Thomas too, is always 'lost' beneath accretions, Thomas's sense of history tempers his myth-making. At one level, 'Englands of the Mind' knows perfectly well that it is dealing in literary constructs: '[Hill's] celebration of Mercia has a double-focus; one a child's-eye view close to the common earth, the hoard of history, and the other the historian's and scholar's eye, inquisitive of meaning, bringing time past to bear on time present and vice versa.' At another level, Heaney's romanticism reads other romanticisms literally (and then is read literally itself). Thus he implies that Hughes has reversed a long declension from the Anglo-Saxon origins of English poetry as foreign (French and Latin) elements infiltrated – Corkery thought the Norman conquest a disaster for English literature. Again, Heaney may over-politicise the language of *Mercian Hymns*: 'The native undergrowth, both vegetative and verbal, that barbaric scrollwork of fern and ivy, is set against the tympanum and chancel-arch, against the weighty elegance of imperial Latin.' As for Larkin, the 'native undergrowth' has vanished since he offers only 'the bright senses of words worn clean in literate conversation…a stripped standard English voice'.

It is by no means clear that Larkin's dealings with the psyche or with "England" are less 'native', more cerebral or 'literate' than Hughes's. Heaney reads all three poets in extremely interesting ways that elude English critics. But he also restores to England, *via* Northern Ireland, nineteenth-century ethno-critical concepts. In particular, his response to Hughes as Saxon/Protestant Other disregards the historical contingencies (post-war, post-religious, post-industrial) that engender and inform Hughes's myth. This reproduces the Jacobite a-historicity that conditions Heaney's own thinking about Northern Ireland. And, in a piquant reversal, he boosts Anglo-Saxonism by offering it the support of a now more vigorous Celticism. While eliding other dimensions of twentieth-century history in these islands, Heaney is as alert as Hewitt (for complementary reasons) to those aspects of postwar England that bespeak imperial decline and the dismantling of Protestant Britishness: 'The poets of the mother culture, I feel, are now possessed of that defensive love of their territory which was once shared only by those poets whom we might call colonial – Yeats, MacDiarmid, Carlos Williams.' Heaney's account of Geoffrey Hill's co-ordinates, like Hughes's version of Shakespeare, makes the most of Celtic-Catholic leanings: 'He is not the suppliant chanting to the megalith, but rather the mason dressing it. Hill also beats the bounds of an England, his own native West Midlands, beheld as a medieval England facing into the Celtic mysteries of Wales and out towards the military and ecclesiastical splendours of Europe.'[84]

Ossian began a process that led to race-theory, culture-theory, ethno-criticism. Heaney and Hughes return Celt/Saxonism to its origins in poetry, especially as a cluster of ideas about language: as ethno-linguistics perhaps. While these ideas have some etymological basis, they more crucially involve ethnic myth. In 'Englands of the Mind' Heaney quotes 'The Warriors of the North' and 'Thistles' to exemplify Hughes's northern Anglo-Saxon poetic foundations – phonetically a matter of consonants ('the Norsemen, the Normans, the Roundheads in the world of his vocables') and gutturals, psychically 'founded on a rock': 'The rock persists, survives, sustains, endures and informs his imagination, just as it is the bedrock of the language upon which Hughes founds his version of survival and endurance'.[85] Here one senses Heaney's complementary or counter myth of Irish vegetation, vocables and bog. Hughes can be more ambivalent about the bedrock than Heaney about the bog. In 'The Warriors of the North' the Vikings rape women and plunder 'the elaborate, patient gold of the Gaels' before 'the gruelling relapse and prolongueur of their blood//Into the iron arteries of Calvin'. Hughes's revised Anglo-Saxonism, retaining macho pagan heroics while rejecting latterday Protestantism, is guiltier about the Gaels than Kingsley's 'hard grey weather [breeding] hard English men' and stirring the 'Viking's blood'. Nonetheless, it is equally capable of sliding from an 'England of the mind' into functional stereotype and into unexamined reciprocity with Irelands of the mind. As a young man, Hughes knew 'The Wanderings of Oisin' by heart.

Hughes told Ekbert Faas that *Gaudete* (1977) aimed 'to find a balance "between German/Scandinavian, and ancient Britain/Celtic, betweeen Puritanical suppressive and Catholic woman worshipping"'.[86] *Remains of Elmet* (1979) also follows Matthew Arnold in seeking to redeem Anglo-Saxonism by way of Celticism. The sequence is most powerful as a set of images that question the effects of the wool-trade, the Great War, industry and de-industrialisation on landscape and community. Less persuasively, Hughes sets institutional England, epitomised by the Calvinist 'religious stonework' of 'Mount Zion', against a lost, natural, hidden Celtic world: 'The Calder valley [was] the last Celtic kingdom to fall to the Angles'. 'Remains' – 'their tombs are not found on the heath' – signals an underground liminality. It is unusual, since Doughty's *Dawn in Britain*, to find Celticism transposed to an English poetic landscape (although T.H. White's Arthurian influence may be relevant). In fact, Hughes's moors are more elementally bleak than anything in Heaney or Hewitt. Their aboriginal inhabitant, 'The Ancient Briton ...Under His Rock', is hailed in the language of primal Celtic purity:

'that waft from the cave,/ The dawn dew-chilling of emergence,/ The hunting grounds untouched all around us'. Hughes does not only wish to exorcise the imperial Protestant guilt of unancient 'Britain'; he also reproduces the sources of Celticism in Jacobitism and in Romantic resistance to modernity. Thus 'Crown Point Pensioners' suggest something older than mills, chapels and their demolishers: 'Attuned to each other, like the strings of a harp,/ They are making mesmerising music,/Each one bowed at his dried bony profile, as at a harp./Singers of a lost kingdom.' It seems significant that few English critics take Hughes's myth seriously in cultural or political terms (Rhodes notes the ridicule with which *Shakespeare and the Goddess of Complete Being* was greeted);[87] whereas Heaney's myth, as poetry and literary criticism, is often received more or less literally.

North (1975) is Heaney's most obvious extension of Celt/Saxonism, since its mythic field encompasses the Vikings and a Celtic goddess. But *Wintering Out* (1971), the collection in which his poetry first coped with the new demands of Irish history, contains a more subtly "Celtic" group of poems: 'Bog Oak', 'Anahorish', 'The Last Mummer', 'Gifts of Rain', 'Broagh', 'A New Song'. Like *Reading in the Dark*, although more urgently, *Wintering Out* conjures liminal, ghostly, hidden figures to signify historical repressions and stirrings: the 'geniuses' who encroach upon Edmund Spenser, the mummer's 'dark tracks', 'soft voices of the dead'. Their terrain is the dark, the river bank, 'moss and rushes'. Here, as in John Hewitt's differently angled poems, Celtic elusiveness haunts a northern – now inland – landscape which exhibits more tangible communal and agricultural contours than the misty West; while (see the quatrains quoted below) there is also textual hybridisation between the Celtic note and the Hidden Ireland. In its literary-critical dimension, *Wintering Out* revisits the questions about "Ulster poetry" that Hewitt was first to raise. Discussing (in 1972) Hewitt's *Collected Poems 1932-67*, Heaney suggests: 'Perhaps this two-way pull, back into the grave and eloquent mainstream of English and out into the shifting, elaborate, receding currents of the Irish experience, lies behind Hewitt's poetic voice, a voice that inclines to plainness but yields to the drift and suggestion of a rhythm, that begins to declare but evolves towards introspection...' [88] In finding Hewitt's Celt/Saxonism unproblematic and in accepting his opposition, in 'Once Alien Here', between 'graver English, lyric Irish', Heaney may identify his own poetics as more exclusively those of Celtic recession, reticence, introspection and drift, together with a hint of circles and whorled artifacts ('elaborate' is Hughes's adjective

for Gaelic art). Thus, when Heaney renders Anglo-Irish relations
as 'Our guttural muse' being 'bulled...by the alliterative tradition',
he has the Saxon-Scot Hewitt in mind as well as the Anglo-Saxon
Hughes. This poem, 'Traditions', allies 'correct Shakespearean'
with the linguistic effects of the Scottish plantation in south Derry:
'the furled/ consonants of lowlanders/ shuttling obstinately/ between
bawn and mossland'. 'Furl', in Heaney's usage here, seems to be the
Scots verb cognate with 'whirl', which also suggests the trundling
noise made by a cart.

'A New Song' again contrasts residual Irish with dominant Eng-
lish, and uses phonetic allegory to project changes in the literary-
political map:

> And Derrygarve, I thought, was just,
> Vanished music, twilit water,
> A smooth libation of the past
> Poured by this chance vestal daughter.
>
> But now our river tongues must rise
> From licking deep in native haunts
> To flood, with vowelling embrace,
> Demesnes staked out in consonants.

Matthew Arnold would approve this embrace between Celt and
Saxon, Planter and Gael, except that the Celtic element seems to
be taking over. Just as Hewitt revises Celticism in hope of poetic
empowerment, so Heaney revises it in the direction of political
empowerment: the 'enchantments and the spells' fight back as
'twilit water' proleptically, passive-aggressively becomes 'flood'. I
need not labour the point that there is no basis for allying Gaelic
with the 'vestigial', the recessive or vocalic; English (in which
Heaney writes) or consonants with macho aggression. Perhaps,
indeed, ethno-linguistics require Anglo-Saxon to be the 'bedrock'
since stricter allegorical logic might construe French and Latin
influence as rendering English less Teutonic. In 'Gifts of Rain'
Heaney represents his own sound as 'reed music, an old chanter//
breathing its mists/ through vowels and history'. 'Reed music', like
the 'windy boortrees' of 'Broagh', nods to Yeats's *Wind Among the
Reeds* from a related Celtic landscape of literary and political aspi-
ration. A century later, ripple-effects continue in Chapter XXXIX
of Derek Walcott's *Omeros* (1990). During a trip to Glendalough
in Co. Wicklow, with its relics of the Celtic Church, the narrator
hears 'a brook speak[ ] the old language of Ireland', tells how 'alder
and aspen aged in one alphabet' and regrets 'a nation/split by a
glottal scream'.

The risk of ready-made, much-processed myths is that they can prevent poets from noticing either things or words. Thus Tom Paulin's poetry, which attaches a negative rather than positive Saxon-Scot stereotype to Ulster Scots dialect, often falls for the idea that language and racial/cultural character are intimately connected. And mythic collusion between Hughes and Heaney may, at times, have inhibited more challenging dialogues – aesthetic and cultural – either between themselves or with their poetic compatriots. To remain fresh, myths need to cross-fertilise with new material (as they generally do in *Wintering Out*), and look outside the closed circuits of literature. In the 1990s, however, Hughes increasingly subjected poetry itself to ethnology. His essay 'Myths, Metres, Rhythms' (1993) takes ethno-critical essentialism to extremes:

> ...in some ways, the older Celtic traditions survived more intact and resilient than either [the new Chaucerian or the Old English tradition]. For one thing the actual nations survived, separate but attached, concentrated in isolation, like powerfully active glands, secreting the genetic remnants of a poetic caste selectively bred through many centuries. The different languages also survived, with the relics of their unique poetic traditions still sacred. When we speak of Chaucer as the 'fountain undefiled' of English poetry's delicacy, or of *Beowulf* as the buried reservoir of English poetry's strength, we are probably glossing over the fact that these two have spent so much of their time, to change the metaphor, like male and female spiders, trying to avoid or paralyse each other... But we are certainly overlooking the fact that without the enveloping, nurturing Celtic matrix, English poetry would be unrecognisably different and vastly deprived.

'Tis the voice of the Bard, the White Goddess, and the pure, timeless, holy, a-historical, feminine Celt. Not only Hughes's metaphor, but also his attraction to a 'poetic caste' is racial. And gender stereotype runs further rampant as he declares the Celtic matrix bride as well as womb: 'For various reasons, the Celtic presence is usually to be found supporting the Old English, and as time passes becomes less and less separable from it [so much, once again, for Latinate, Frenchified poets]...the relationship...can be viewed as a marriage in which the old or unorthodox tradition is the bride and the new, metrically strict orthodox tradition the groom.' The sexual analogy does not bear much inspection, but perhaps this *aisling* consummates the warm literary relations between Hughes and Heaney in a poetry of complete Anglo-Celtic being. In fact, Hughes contradicts himself in a Gravesian footnote which mentions the 'notoriously arduous poetic colleges of the old Celtic world'. Like Arnold, however, Hughes has nothing to say about actually existing Celtic languages let alone countries.

But the appeal of *relaxed* Celticism (and 'unorthodoxy') resides in Catholicism as much as in metre or the maternal body. Now operating in mythic overdrive, Hughes goes on to speak of Surrey's 'hard Reformation face' and to represent Hopkins's Catholicism as, like the time he spent in Wales and Ireland, 'a lonely, forlorn, backtracking effort to locate the divorced, unheard-of or thought to be defunct woman of the well-spring'.[89] Hughes's Afterword to *The School Bag* (1997), the second anthology he edited with Heaney, genuflects to the Catholic icon at the expense of the Protestant word. He recommends a bizarre method of memorising poetry by means of 'visualised images', and the Reformation's exclusive guilt for 'rote learning' would surprise historians of Catholic education in general and of the Christian Brothers in particular:

> In England in the seventeenth century, the Puritan/Protestant ascendancy of the Civil War made a serious bid to eradicate imagery from all aspects of life...The same spirit also banished from the schools the old-established techniques that used imagery and officially replaced them with 'learning by rote'. The discarded methods, dimly associated with paganism and Catholicism, were soon forgotten.[90]

To quote Hughes's poem 'Lovesong', he and Heaney may have ended up wearing each other's ethnological face. Hence Paulin's confusion about 'relaxed' Celticism: an ex-oxymoron that has moved as far from *Ossian* and haggard eyes as has Celtic Tiger – although the 'emotional and sentimental' legacy of Hughes's nonconformist background was shrewdly anticipated by Arnold. Henry Hart sees Heaney's Ireland as becoming more 'masculine'; Neil Rhodes contrasts his 'sober, classical' version of Ovid in *New Metamorphoses* (1994) with Hughes's aim 'to tap the savagery' beneath Ovid's civil surface.[91] Their anthologies, too, can be read as shifting symbiotic exercises: *The Rattle Bag* inclining more to a "Celtic" walk on the wild side; *The School Bag* reverting to a "Saxon" sense of educational and social responsibility. Is Hughes's eccentric Afterword a liminal riposte to the smack of firm government in the Foreword? There Heaney speaks authoritatively for both as wanting to make their second collaboration 'less of a carnival, more like a checklist'.[92] In its very title Heaney's *Redress of Poetry* assumes the neo-Arnoldian *gravitas*, the sweetness and light, that characterise these lectures from Arnold's Oxford chair, just as 'school bag' recalls school-inspector Arnold. Meanwhile, Hughes published the eccentric *Goddess of Complete Being*. On one level, Heaney and Hughes seem to settle between themselves (a process culminating in Heaney's *Beowulf*) the 'struggle for control of the language of authority between Jacobite and Hanoverian writers'[93] which underlay the nineteenth-century ethnic antics of Celt and Saxon. But, as Rhodes suggests, it may equally be time to abandon such oppositions as a way of 'writing about cultural politics' – and, indeed, writing poetry and criticism.[94] In bringing Celt/Saxonism back to the poetic point where it came in, Heaney and Hughes may have finally exhausted its literary credit. Yet 'impervious to paradigm-shifts', says Joep Leerssen. And Niamh is still calling

> Away, come away:
> Empty your heart of its mortal dream.
> The winds awaken, the leaves whirl round...[95]

Pastoral Theologies

1

This essay follows from the last two since ecology and ethnology are among the influences on what, lacking a better label, I will call "Irish pastoral poetry". Other systems of ideas, including religious systems, also condition how it is written and how it is read. Yet critics who discuss Irish poetry of Nature, country, landscape, rural community, place (not all the same thing) do not always declare their premises, test them against cultural particularities, or look for local variations on the ancient European genre. I see "pastoral" as a capacious generic umbrella – covering anti-pastoral, too – rather than as synonymous with 'escapism'. Tensions between Nature and culture, Nature and agriculture, Nature and society, Nature and art, 'bee-loud glade' and invasive history, have long defined the pastoral tradition. Further, as Jonathan Bate urges: 'Pastoral has not done well in recent neo-Marxist criticism, but if there is to be an ecological criticism the "language that is ever green" must be reclaimed.' In *The Environmental Imagination* (1995) Lawrence Buell writes similarly of American pastoral: 'Partly because [pastoral ideology] has been treated with much astringency of late, I shall stress its constructive potential rather than its role as a blocking agent or inducer of false consciousness.' [1] If Irish pastoral has, on the whole, been less severely judged, this need not mean that its 'constructive potential' has been realised. Perhaps a perceived tautology – what is Ireland if not greenly pastoral? – has been spared analysis. To focus on varieties of pastoral within the multi-generic field of the lyric poem may highlight Ireland's distinctive "green" idioms. Like other genres practised by Irish authors, pastoral poetry can be rendered either too indigenous (as when exclusively derived from Gaelic sources) [2] or too foreign (as when absorbed into critical vocabularies developed elsewhere).

In his review of John Barrell's and John Bull's *Penguin Book of English Pastoral Verse* (1978) Seamus Heaney is significantly alert to these issues. First, he asks if 'the story ends as quickly' as the editors (who call pastoral always 'false' and now 'lifeless') claim. Second, although he mentions twentieth-century English and Scottish poets who might have made the cut (Edward Thomas, Hugh MacDiarmid), it is Irish poetry that Heaney chiefly cites as showing more than 'occasional twitches' of the old tradition. Third, he rescues one kind of poem from disparagement as 'pastoral': 'I have occasionally talked of the countryside where we live in Wicklow [Glanmore] as being pastoral rather than rural, trying to impose notions of a beautified landscape on the word, in order to keep "rural" for the unselfconscious face of raggle-taggle farmland.'[3] This claim I find more questionable than Heaney's other challenges to Barrell and Bull. It implies that even the actualities of Wicklow are aesthetic ('beautified'), while even the aesthetics of Heaney's childhood environment are actual ('unselfconscious'). Certainly Heaney has translated a hitherto unremarked place into (beautiful?) verbal images. Yet the ratio of wildness or naturalness to cultivation, whether agricultural or artistic, depends on closer reading of landscapes and texts. Heaney's review belongs to the period of his 'Glanmore Sonnets', which worry about moving to a more self-conscious literary relationship with a new landscape. Yet 'Raggle-taggle farmland' ('Away with the raggle-taggle gypsies, O') indicates that, just as humanity has always intervened in landscape, literature is hard to avoid. This applies even to that pastoral touchstone, John Clare.[4]

So let us start again with varieties of pastoral and culture, and with a generic field constituted by intertextual dialectics rather than by absolute differences. The cultural agents include agriculture, the history of natural history, English Romanticism and – a neglected factor – religion. This essay owes much to a ground-breaking compilation: *Nature in Ireland: A Scientific and Cultural History* (1997), edited by John Wilson Foster and Helen C.G. Chesney. Foster speculates as to whether 'attitudes to animals and plants differ[ed] between the English and Scots Protestants and the native, Catholic Irish (qua Christians)'. He also asks: 'Did the popularity of the Bible among the more fundamentalist northern Protestants inhibit a scientific approach when their southern, broader-church Protestant co-religionists were starting modern science in Ireland?'[5] In a chapter on Belfast's reception of Darwinism, David N. Livingstone finds that the Catholic Church blamed Protestantism in the person of John Tyndall (an Orangeman from Co. Carlow) for science being made the vehicle for materialism; while some Presbyterians managed to attack both evolution and Catholic resistance to the idea. They argued that it was Catholics who were 'secularising the physical sciences' by separating science from faith.[6] But the Irish Catholic Church's hostility to Darwinism, and to scientific modernisation in general, was more powerful. Although the presbyterian belief in education came under stress, presbyterian anti-Darwinism did not effect 'the cultural exclusion of science'.[7] The Irish Church's rearguard action was more prolonged than in other Catholic countries; and the Irish language (which ousted Nature Study from primary schools) also helped to marginalise science until the 1960s. Thus such issues still touch late twentieth-century poetry. In *Nature in Ireland* Dorinda Outram suggests that the 'construction of the Irish "nation" as a monolithic alliance between nationalism and Catholicism left little space for the moral systems that had accompanied science and the Enlightenment.' But since Catholics who wanted to "do" science were variously obstructed by the Church (some making scientific careers outside Ireland), perhaps sectarian dynamics, as in the Darwin row, were equally at work.[8] Outram criticises Foucault's account of 'natural history' for, among other inattentions to particularity, 'completely excluding the theological dimension so strong in the English, and hence Anglo-Irish tradition'. This omission illustrates, she says, 'the insensitivity of universalistic accounts to the differences between "cultural domains" '.[9] Her objections also hold for 'universalistic accounts' of pastoral poetry.

2

Religion is one context for Patrick Kavanagh's 'On Reading a Book on Common Wild Flowers' (1954), a poem interested in its own pastoral bearings:

> O the prickly sow thistle that grew in the hollow of the Near Field
> I used it as a high jump coming home in the evening –
> A hurdle race over the puce blossoms of the sow thistles.
> Am I late?
> Am I tired?
> Is my heart sealed
> From the ravening passion that will eat it out
> Till there is not one pure moment left?
>
> O the greater fleabane that grew at the back of the potato-pit.
> I often trampled through it looking for rabbit burrows!
> The burnet saxifrage was there in profusion
> And the autumn gentian –
> I knew them all by eyesight long before I knew their names.
> We were in love before we were introduced.
>
> Let me not moralise or have remorse, for these names
> Purify a corner of my mind;
> I jump over them and rub them with my hands,
> And a free moment appears brand new and spacious
> Where I may live beyond the reach of desire.[10]

Like Heaney in the passage quoted above, Kavanagh contrasts unselfconscious and conscious responses to natural phenomena.

The exaggerated formality of his title and apostrophes – 'O the prickly sow thistle' – parodies verse that, like botanical taxonomy, seems remote from hands-on rural experience. Similarly, 'profusion' echoes and mocks the polysyllabic 'burnet saxifrage'. The author of that great anti-pastoral poem *The Great Hunger* also plays off vulgar flower-names (fleabane) against loftier (autumn gentian). The speaker's familiarity with these flowers is underlined by his having treated them almost with contempt, simply as the furniture of his world: 'I used it as a high jump', 'I...trampled through it'. Yet the state of being 'in love before we were introduced' is not just a state of innocence. At one level it asserts the primacy or authenticity of "country poet" (the poet whose work draws on affiliations to a specific countryside and community) over "Nature poet" (the poet who must depend on 'introductions'). The world that Kavanagh stakes out, the world in which he situates the flowers, is a farm world. The 'hollow of the Near Field', and 'the potato-pit' are taken for granted as reference-points for wild Nature. But, partly by betraying its botanical know-how, the poem also dismantles this opposition. The names are what remain to be relished as physically as their referents: 'I jump over them and rub them with my hands'. (As with Edward Thomas – whom Kavanagh read – things and words, belong to the same planet.) Here country poet and Nature poet cross-fertilise.

Jumping and rubbing facilitate the Wordsworthian leap from primal vision ('eyesight') to transcendence ('a free moment'). The poem's starting-point is Kavanagh's distance, in time and space, from his Monaghan farm (he has now lived for fifteen years in Dublin). Like Wordsworth, the speaker prolongs or procures vision through 'recollection'. To know by eyesight is local intimacy, instinctual response and ultimately the Romantic Eden which Kavanagh calls 'that childhood country' and Heaney the 'illiterate'; to know the names represents adult cognition after the Fall. However, a tentative synthesis between these epistemologies 'purifies' fallen 'passion' and 'desire' in a visionary zone 'brand new and spacious'. 'Transubstantiation' may be a better word than 'transcendence' for the effect whereby the flowers are declared to be present in their names as the experience in the poem. The speaker also gives himself absolution for loss of primal contact ('Let me not moralise or have remorse'). Kavanagh's Catholicism recognises that Wordsworth's structures retain a dimension of faith, but he gives it new vesture and a firmer presence. At odds with the authoritarian Irish Church established in the 1850s, his poetry invokes a residual, localised form of Irish Catholicism in which everyday things are 'woven with religion in the texture of country life'.[11]

To sum up: 'On Reading a Book on Common Wild Flowers' is
marked by the Irish small farm in the mid twentieth century; by
Catholicism; by tensions between country poetry and Nature poetry
– also between hands-on experience and science; by the deepest
Wordsworthian emotional and artistic structure (in *Patrick Kavanagh:
Born-Again Romantic* Antoinette Quinn emphasises Kavanagh's
assimilation of the Immortality Ode).[12] Another context is Dublin.
The rural cosmos distilled into the poem, into 'a corner of my
mind', obliquely resists the city – source of the 'ravening passion'
that lies in the future inhabited by the speaker. "Urban" and "pas-
toral" poetry are too often seen as antithetical, or the latter as a
wilful refusal of the former, rather than (like country and Nature
poetry) as dialectical. Doctor Johnson remarked that pastoral 'has
nothing peculiar but its confinement to rural imagery'.[13] Even if a
poet prefers one or other locale – although many move imaginatively
between city and country – language, culture and cognition elide
or elude the binary confines. Apart from the abundant evidence of
pastoral complexity and streetwise simplicity; to quote Louis
MacNeice, the '*chosen* voice and mood' of any lyric poem are 'set
defiantly in opposition to what they must still co-exist with'.[14] 'On
Reading a Book on Common Wild Flowers' defies over-botanical
Nature poetry and city poetry on different flanks.

Nor do country and city always occupy the same ideological
spaces. Raymond Williams himself stresses the uniqueness of the
English case in which early industrialisation and rapid urbanisation
had reciprocal effects on pastoral writing. Some critics, however,
apply Williams in a rather confused way to Ireland, as when the
Literary Revival is held solely responsible for rustic stereotypes.
Since the Revival was conditioned by Romantic-aesthetic recoil
from the industrial revolution, the west of Ireland becoming a
Lake District with a difference (see below), it is unsurprising that
'pavements grey' should be taboo. Yet there was complex inter-
play, with generic consequences for Irish pastoral, between a liter-
ary ideology (mainly associated with Protestants) and a sociology
(mainly associated with Catholics). Until Dublin began to expand
after 1960, "the country" also enjoyed a status that reflected the
historical importance of the land question and the economic
importance of agriculture to the Republic. The former's resolution
in the early 1900s consolidated a nation neither of folkloric peas-
ants nor urban workers but of independent farmers closely allied
to the Catholic Church (Kavanagh's *Great Hunger* protests against
the restrictive social codes promoted by this alliance). James H.
Murphy sums up the consensus on post-Famine Catholic Ireland:

There is agreement that, increasingly throughout the nineteenth century and decisively after the foundation of the Irish Free State, Irish society came to be dominated by a lower middle-class establishment of farmers and shopkeepers...it was Ireland's 'nation-forming class'.[15]

Kevin Whelan's article 'Town and Village in Ireland: A socio-cultural perspective' probes the deeper reasons for 'the late completion of our urban network'. Whelan's historical explanation includes the 'centrifugal effect of the townland...as opposed to the centripetal functions of tightly controlled manorial systems elsewhere in Europe'; and, later, the 'dominant Irish farm family system... geared to maintain social networks which transcended or ignored village life [and which constituted] an intensely localised cellular system based on extended families'. Incipient village/town systems were successively blighted by the Reformation; by tensions between the estate (improving landlords) and the State; by the dismantling of British/Protestant urban institutions – although these were gradually replaced by Catholic equivalents. Whelan argues that all this established a 'porosity of the Irish urban system to rural influences', which meant that 'in the period from 1850-1960' 'country triumphed over town'.[16] The Republic still lags behind comparable European countries as regards urban infra-structure.

Insular rural Catholicism helped to produce the introversion of the Free State. In rural Northern Ireland, Catholic disaffection created a still more sequestered community. Nor have Ulster Protestant farmers, a substantial class, exactly been in the vanguard of social and political change. Thus Irish circumstances, throughout most of this century, did not parallel the destruction of rural communities in England, although labourers had to leave the land in Ireland, too. Hence, up to a point, the power of morally conservative values in both nationalist and unionist politics; and, in the Republic, the correlation between resistance to such values and the growth of Dublin. Eamonn Hughes argues that, ideologically, 'The rural is the site of homogeneous Ireland; the urban is resisted precisely because it is potentially the site of heterogeneous Ireland.'[17] Kavanagh's poetry, in taking the strain of his journey from small farm and self-contained Catholic community to the city, from claustrophobia to agoraphobia, see-saws across several historical faultlines. Its trajectory repeats that of Wordsworth's 'Michael'.

In January 1998, reviewing the Republic's 25 years in the EU, Fintan O'Toole wrote: 'The availability of huge subsidies for farming and food products reshaped rural society and all but destroyed the remnants of the small-farming class that had been at the heart of the old nationalist idea of self-sufficiency.'[18] The number of family farms fell from 278,500 in 1960 to just under 160,000 in 1992. Ironically, agriculture fed the economic transformation which has ended the Church's national hegemony and tilted the balance of cultural power towards the city. Of course, the 'reshaping' of rural society is part of the picture too. Nor do all liberals live in the city or conservatives in the country. In 'The Myth of Modernisation', Luke Gibbons makes this point; and also claims that a metropolitan élite, rather than Irish rural society, historically destabilised by famine and emigration, has promoted conservatism: 'The bogey of traditionalism and rural values can no longer be used…as a scape-goat for a regressive politics that emanates from the metropolitan centre.'[19] But Gibbons's claim itself stems from the continuing struggle between homogeneous and heterogeneous Ireland. It is a way of rescuing nationalism and Catholicism from charges of regression; it ignores the original 'nation-forming class' whose obedience to the Church *resulted from* insecurity; it disregards con-temporary voting patterns – more liberal east of the Shannon – and the clientalist political networks which derive from the 'localised cellular system' and which prevent the metropolis from going it alone. Also, many citizens retain umbilical links with a country home-place.

Rural Ireland, in the ideological guises (small-farming, nationalist, western-mythological) feared by the arch-Dubliner and prophet of heterogeneous Ireland – James Joyce – is not dead yet. *A Portrait of the Artist as a Young Man* presents a dialectical opposition between Dublin and an Irish countryside which haunts the subjectivity of Stephen Dedalus as dark, secretive, communal ('the thoughts and desires of the race to which he belonged flitting like bats, across the dark country lanes'). To Stephen "the country" is seductive in its mystery but alarming in its atavism; "the city" is the locus of self-hood, art and 'life', however painfully so, or the summons to these where Dublin-as-seaport faces Europe. Stephen records in his diary:

> John Alphonsus Mulrennan has just returned from the west of Ireland. European and Asiatic papers please copy. He told us he met an old man there in a mountain cabin. Old man had red eyes and short pipe. Old man spoke Irish. Mulrennan spoke Irish. Then old man and Mulrennan spoke English. Mulrennan spoke to him about universe and stars. Old man sat, listened, smoked, spat. Then said:
> – Ah, there must be terrible queer creatures at the latter end of the world. –
> I fear him. I fear his redrimmed horny eyes. It is with him I must struggle all through this night till day come, till he or I lie dead, grip-ping him by the sinewy throat till…Till what? Till he yield to me? No. I mean him no harm.

Here Stephen's emergent literary idiom clashes with both rural languages of the Revival: Gaelic and the Hiberno-English of J.M. Synge and Lady Gregory. Yet, viewed from more heavily urbanised societies, Ireland *is* "the country" or "the West". By the same token, *Ulysses* has often been installed as the verbal metropolis of "international" modernism, as if (Dublin)-Trieste-Zurich-Paris were not a European axis with many metropolitan variables. These influence what, as well as how, the text sees. Joyce's self-irony produces Haines, the English enthusiast for the Revival who barely notices his urban surroundings as he rushes off to buy Douglas Hyde's *Love Songs of Connaught*.

The point is that specifically Irish modes of "country and city" condition literary works. Nor is it a simple matter of pastoral idioms masking city-based power, since power may also base itself in/on the country. Seamus Heaney's 'Station Island' (1984) enacts an artistic rite of passage which on one level moves away from rural, as well as Northern Irish, origins; at another, reaffirms his variety of pastoral. By invoking Joyce/Dedalus, the last canto implicitly links Heaney's current mobility between Dublin and America (in the image of 'elver-gleams in the dark of the whole sea') with an artistic selfhood that has flown by communal nets. Nonetheless, Heaney makes 'Joyce' walk an unlikely country road, speak in a Heaney voice ('That subject people stuff is a cod's game') and look 'wintered hard and sharp as a blackthorn bush'. 'Changes', from the same collection, pits the cultural strengths of Heaney's childhood 'omphalos' – the pump around which the farm now orbits in imagination, whose 'citadel' once sheltered a nesting bird – against the urban universe that his child, like the reader, is liable to inhabit:

> ...I said, 'Remember this.
> It will be good for you to retrace this path
>
> when you have grown away and stand at last
> at the very centre of the empty city.

3

Daniel Corkery, dedicated to the 'living pieties' of Catholic rural Munster, helped to fashion the cultural ideology of the Irish Free State.[20] In *The Hidden Ireland* (1924), his tribute to the Munster Gaelic world and its poetry, Corkery says: 'The Gaels never made of their own the cities and towns'; and contrasts the 'alien-minded city' (Cork) with the countryside that sustained the suppressed yet

vital culture of the Gael: 'a closeness to the land, to the very pulse
of it, that those Planter houses could not even dream of '.[21] The
trope of an organically vigorous life, persisting against the odds
outside the planters' artificial and doomed walls, recurs in nation-
alist writing as a sturdier version of Celticism. Joyce resists this
anti-urban trope, whose revision Gibbons resists in turn: a new
generation of Dublin and Belfast novelists has been tough on rural
pieties.[22] Yet the Ireland of townlands and small towns, however
regionally diverse, however subject to socio-economic change,
however viewed authorially, remains a rich literary locus (as in the
fiction of John McGahern, Patrick McCabe and Dermot Healy).
Heaney, as we have seen, owes some of his rhetorical confidence
to the positive resources of Catholic-rural Ireland, denied its
nation-forming apotheosis in the North, but even there drawing
strength from its wider, deeper power. Heaney read Corkery as a
schoolboy. He gave a lecture called 'Homage to Daniel Corkery'
when he was writing his early poems.[23] One of his northern men-
tors was the Corkeryite fiction-writer, Michael McLaverty.
    The Irish contexts of Heaney's pastoral are not only significant in
themselves. They filter what he takes from other sources. Corkery's
Hidden Ireland gave him, he wrote in 1983, his 'sense of a relation-
ship to a hidden Ulster', 'a concept of identity' and a means of
'relating my literary education [to] the heritage of the home ground'.[24]
The opening paragraph of Heaney's Nobel lecture 'Crediting
Poetry' also suggests how he translated into his own terms, the
terms of sequestered rural Ulster Catholicism, the notion of a hid-
den, archetypal, poetically enriching domain:

> In the nineteen-forties, when I was the eldest child of an ever-growing
> family in rural County Derry, we crowded together in the three rooms
> of a traditional thatched farmstead and lived a kind of den-life which
> was more or less emotionally and intellectually proofed against the out-
> side world. It was an intimate, physical, creaturely existence in which
> the night sounds of a horse in the stable beyond one bedroom wall
> mingled with the sounds of adult conversation from the kitchen beyond
> the other. We took in everything that was going on, of course – rain in
> the trees, mice on the ceiling, a steam train rumbling along the railway
> line one field back from the house – but we took it in as if we were in
> the doze of hibernation. Ahistorical, pre-sexual, in suspension between
> the archaic and the modern, we were as susceptible and impressionable
> as the drinking water that stood in a bucket in our scullery: every time
> a passing train made the earth shake, the surface of that water used to
> ripple delicately, concentrically, and in utter silence.[25]

Whatever else may be going on here, Heaney presents the foundations
of his pastoral as combining the pre-reflective with a pre-modern

latency. His autobiographies often efface his urban experience, including 15 years in Belfast. Yet society underpins the 'den-life' depicted above. From Whelan's 'socio-cultural perspective', as contrasted with that of mythic autobiography, the passage evokes the 'intensely localised cellular system, based on extended families' which has characterised Irish rural culture.

To put it another way: the ease with which Heaney's cultural hinterland lends itself to Corkery's cultural myth is one sign that his poetry did not originate as an encounter between unmediated Irish landscape and Wordsworth. Corkery's *Hidden Ireland* is itself touched by English Romanticism. Nonetheless, when he and Wordsworth mingle in Heaney's aesthetic, he brings his own strong flavour. Although a view of Heaney as Wordsworth Redivivus seems more or less axiomatic among English critics, Nicholas Roe and Seán Lysaght make cases for the limits of his Wordsworthianism. And they do so in religious terms, both theological and cultural. Roe's essay 'Wordsworth at the Flaxdam' compares the role of the Wordsworthian 'spot of time' in 'Death of a Naturalist' and in a passage (about trapping woodcocks) from *The Prelude*:

> To make a very rough distinction, Wordworth's imagination inhabits the child's feelings, whereas…Heaney dwells fruitfully on contingent nature. Wordsworth recreates the child's nervous onward hurry… Rather than explore a comparable inner territory… Heaney's poem conveys the texture of landscape itself…The imaginative life of Wordsworth's spot of time is internal, in 'Death of a Naturalist' it is disengaged and external to the child.
>
> …these recollected moments in *The Prelude* internalise the redemptive structure of Milton's Christian epic as a prerogative of the poet's imagination. Wordsworth is in effect his own Satan but he is also his own redeemer, for each spot of time enacts a fall that contains the promise of future restoration. It is therefore possible to see *The Prelude* as in some degree dependent upon the inner light and private intercession of Protestant theology, and closely related to the spiritual journal and autobiography of puritan tradition. 'Death of a Naturalist' suggests that Heaney is drawn to the Wordsworthian spot of time, but unable to admit its redemptive adequacy.[26]

Nonetheless, just as 'Station Island' may be *Catholic* 'spiritual journal and autobiography', 'contingent nature' and 'the texture of landscape itself' are hardly value-free. Heaney's language of sensation imprints certain kinds of physical texture with psychological appeal. What 'Squarings' would later call 'Ground of being' emphasises weight, luxuriance, states between the solid and fluid, between fecundity and decay ('green and heavy-headed/Flax had rotted there'). Also, Heaney ultimately sets bounds to the poem's immersion in the outer world and to the poet's status as 'naturalist'. The intimation of (masculine) sexuality coincides with a withdrawal from "Nature" when the sensations it offers cease to be pleasurable and controllable, when collecting frogspawn exposes the child to 'a coarse croaking that I had not heard/Before'. There are similar withdrawals in other early poems with a similarly ambiguous issue. 'Death of a Naturalist' discredits 'Miss Walls's' bowdlerised Nature study about 'daddy frog' and 'mammy frog', but without refiguring biology in/as wild Nature. It does not, for instance, follow another of its models, Ted Hughes's 'The Bull Moses', into an adolescent epiphany that internalises the dark powers of animal and id. Heaney's 'The Outlaw', about Kelly's 'unlicensed bull', humanises and domesticates the bull's sexuality as 'the unfussy ease of a good tradesman', wholly in control – as Kelly of him, the poet of the poem. In 'Death of a Naturalist' how to conceive "Nature" in adult terms is left open at the moment of fallen knowledge: 'And I knew/ That if I dipped my hand the spawn would clutch it'.

Nature's vengeance on the boy-naturalist endorses a recoil from scientific curiosity that preserves Nature's primal mystique as a poetic resource. 'Churning Day', at a remove from wild Nature, constitutes a spot of time in which speaker and child appear more at home. The moment is communal rather than individual, transubstantiative rather than redemptive, instinctive rather than interrogative; and it involves a domestic female animal and a domestic female ambience. What comes from the 'hot brewery of cud and gland and udder' lends itself to processing or control in terms which fuse butter-making and poem-making until 'in the house we moved with gravid ease'. In this pregnant enclosure ('den-life' as in 'Crediting Poetry'), this maternal poetic matrix, no disturbing gap opens up between sensation and thought as humanity works on Nature: 'Our brains turned crystals full of clean deal churns'. Later I will suggest that farmwork goes deep as an analogy for writing poetry. By defining his imaginative co-ordinates (which include the Marian tradition) in part implicitly against those of Wordsworth and Hughes, Heaney begins to stake out a path whereby his "Nature" diverges from modes in which English pastoral poetry inclines either to Protestant religious structures or to (related) 'naturalist' enquiry. His 'Digging' is not quite Thomas's.

He continues, however, Wordsworth's critique of those who 'murder to dissect' and violate the spirit in the woods. Perhaps because post-Darwinian Catholicism had so firmly separated faith from science, Heaney seems at ease with what Wordsworth owes to Romantic *Naturforschung* (Nature study) 'based on the identity of nature and spirit' and opposed to positivistic science.[27] In two essays, 'Heaney vs Praeger' and 'Contrasting Natures: The Issue of Names', Seán Lysaght analyses Heaney's relation to Nature as natural history. Lysaght's first essay questions a passage in Heaney's lecture 'The Sense of Place' (1977). After concluding that Kavanagh and John Montague share 'a feeling for their place that steadies them and gives them a point of view', Heaney criticises the celebrated Irish naturalist Robert Lloyd Praeger for lack of similar steadiness in his odyssey *The Way That I Went* (1937):

> [Praeger's] point of view is visual, geological, not like Kavanagh's, emotional and definitive. His eye is regulated by laws of aesthetics, by the disciplines of physical geography, and not, to borrow a phrase from Wordworth, by the primary laws of our nature, the laws of feeling.[28]

This parallels the beautified *versus* the raggle-taggle. Lysaght comments that Praeger's book does include Romantic 'feeling' for the countryside (it has epigraphs from Shelley and James Thomson), and suggests that Heaney's real quarrel with Praeger is that his own 'variety of local allegiance...bases itself on an idea of cultural and demographic antecedence which seeks to deny [Praeger's variety] full access to the atavistic mysteries of the land'. Yet Heaney's sense of mystery – and application of Wordsworth's 'primary laws' – may be Catholic before it is nationalist. In any case, a poetry of rural community/ place again acquires credentials that "Nature poetry" ('aesthetics') lacks; while science is disqualified from laying down 'primary laws'. It is a matter of culture as well as theology, or culture follows theology. As Lysaght says, 'For historical reasons, the growth of field natural science in Ireland, with centres in Belfast and Dublin, was almost exclusively a Protestant achievement.'[29] Praeger (1865-1953), the most influential figure in the history of Irish natural history, begetter of the pioneering Clare Island Survey, began his work in Belfast and moved to Dublin.[30] The argument does not only pivot on insiders *v.* outsiders, farmers *v.* ramblers, authenticity *v.* distance. Irish religious history further explains why Heaney does not much identify with Wordsworth the 'naturalist', walker, evangelist for 'Presences of Nature...Visions of the hills/ And Souls of lonely places'. Few of his poems occupy that point of the pastoral spectrum where Nature becomes a detachable Idea or Mission or occasion for reading a 'Book on Common Wild Flowers'.

The Way That I Went, a journey through Irish landscapes, can hardly show intimate 'feeling' for every corner, and certain kinds of taxonomy have never been locally generated. Heaney's critique of Praeger reproduces the nationalist synecdoche whereby one Irish

'place' fits all. In his second article, however, Lysaght finds greater
variety in Heaney's practice than in his theory, arguing that he
'has courted two different attitudes to naming and identification.
The first...is tribal and territorial, implying that the place and its
name have a peculiar flavour that can only be savoured and safe-
guarded by the natives; this carries with it the implication that
names are ultimately untranslatable. The second view is more uni-
versal, taking its cue from geology and natural history, and tran-
scending the confines of sectarian or cultural disputes.'[31] Lysaght
quotes, as an example of the latter, 'The Peninsula', in which Heaney
'rediscovers the attractions of the seashore and its wildlife':

Now recall

The glazed foreshore and silhouetted log,
That rock where breakers shredded into rags,
The leggy birds stilted on their own legs,
Islands riding themselves out into the fog

And drive back home, still with nothing to say
Except that now you will uncode all landscapes
By this: things founded clean on their own shapes,
Water and ground in their extremity.

Yet Heaney's special focus and appeal as a pastoral poet remain
to be defined. Nor would I agree that 'geology and natural history'
often come centre-stage. In 'The Peninsula' to 'uncode' landscape
(probably the Ards Peninsula in Co. Down) is to encode a reflexive
language for selfhood and poetry: the repeated 'their own', 'riding
themselves'. In this finely etched 'prospect of the mind', Heaney
reconciles himself with Praeger more through aesthetics ('silhouetted',
'shapes') than through science. The poem belongs to a landscape
series, including 'Whinlands', 'Shoreline' and 'Bogland', that char-
acteristically conjures a whole physical ambience rather than puts
isolated features under a (naturalist's) microscope. In 'Fosterling'
(which links Flemish genre painting with home ground and Ulster
Scots speech) Heaney reflects on his art of landscape: 'I can't
remember never having known/ The immanent hydraulics of a
land/ Of *glar* and *glit* and floods at *dailigone*./My silting hope. My
lowlands of the mind.' 'Immanent hydraulics' aptly defines his
seductive word-environments, at once palpable and yielding, phys-
ical and metaphysical. Individual flora and fauna are named or
highlighted less frequently than one might suppose, being stitched
into the rich overall texture, although here and there they flash out
vividly: the 'kingfisher's blue bolt at dusk', the 'rowan like a lip-
sticked girl'. But if Heaney has moved from Kavanagh's "country"
poetry towards "landscape", or aestheticises wild Nature, he still

resists Nature poetry. 'Serenades' ironically plays the literary reso-
nances of nightingale and sedge-warbler against the familiar 'ack-ack/
Of the tramp corncrake/Lost in a no-man's land/Between combines
and chemicals'.

Neil Corcoran refers to Heaney's 'reciprocal relationship with
Nature'.[32] Terence Gifford, in *Green Voices*, 'sees no reason to
avoid describing this relationship as one that assumes a unity with
nature...the assumption that human life is organically unified with
the natural world'. All this may, or may appear to, be the case; but
Gifford, despite heading one chapter 'The Social Construction of
Nature', does not investigate the cultural basis for such 'assump-
tions' (including Heaney's 'confident assumption of connectedness
with the feminine forces of the natural world'). Perhaps he con-
siders them more "natural" in an Irish poet. He also asks: 'How
does the green language of Heaney, coming out of a culture under
stress differ from that of Hughes...confronting an environment
under stress?'[33] Again, Gifford does not specify Heaney's 'culture' –
equated with Northern Irish politics – or give reasons for judging
either the Irish environment ('combines and chemicals'?) or English
culture stress-free. If 'unity with nature' is indeed an effect in/of
Heaney's poetry, what 'connections' are being made?

> Hide in the hollow trunk
> of the willow tree,
> its listening familiar
> until, as usual, they
> cuckoo your name
> across the fields.
> You can hear them
> draw the poles of stiles
> as they approach
> calling you out:
> small mouth and ear
> in a woody cleft,
> lobe and larynx
> of the mossy places.
>
> ('Oracle')

Here the child-poet, at once voice and ear, performs the 'act of
complaisance with natural impulses' that Heaney favours in his
discussions of pastoral poetry during the 1970s. Wordsworth, whom
Heaney may render too complaisant, 'is drawn into himself even as
he speaks himself out, and it is this mesmerised attention to the
echoes and invitations within that constitutes his poetic confidence'.[34]
Being inside a tree is a mask to which Heaney's poetry returns,
and which accompanies its returns to 'itself': 'I fall back to my

tree-house and would crouch/Where small buds shoot and flourish in the hush' ('Glanmore Sonnets', V). If Wordsworth is the poet as pantheist, Heaney is the poet as animist, spirit-voice of trees or 'mossy places', creator of nests in which to dwell.

No pastoral poem can avoid anthropocentrism – not even when Derek Mahon/Nerval advises: 'your brusque hegemony/ Means fuck-all to the somnolent sun-flower/ Or the extinct volcano'. Yet, as I argue in ' "The Business of the Earth" ', the power-dynamics between humanity and the natural world vary from poem to poem and poet to poet. The speaker of a Heaney poem often disguises his anthropocentrism, even from himself, by virtue of being "centric" in other ways: strategically placed at the centre of the world the poem summons and arranges. Heaney's favourite geometry of centre and circle is reiterated in 'Crediting Poetry': 'concentric ripples'; 'poetry [makes] possible a fluid and restorative relationship between the mind's centre and its circumference'.[35] (Contrast the disconnected 'centre of the empty city' in 'Changes'.) Heaney also patrols, like a farmer, the boundary between domestic and wild. Since animism is a form of psychic projection, the animist does not necessarily quarrel with the farmer whose intimacy with wild Nature issues in control: 'Mapping the furrow exactly' ('Follower'). Historically speaking, 'Animistic beliefs do not necessarily promote reverence for nature.'[36] In contrast, Ted Hughes's brand of animism strongly identifies with wild Nature or with Nature as wild. Whereas Heaney implicitly aligns poetry with the invention of agriculture, favouring the vegetable rather than the animal or mineral, Hughes identifies with poetry's more primitive communal origins. He wears animal masks, hunter-gathers poems, exposes his imagination to bare rock, and desires cosmic powers to overwhelm human cognition. Hughes represents man as Nature; Heaney represents Nature as man (Kelly's bull). It is the difference between 'ghost-crabs' and 'the spirit of the corn'. Hughes's own farm-poems (in *Moortown*, 1987) depict animal husbandry as an elemental struggle.

Discussing *Field Work*, Gifford refers to Heaney's notion of 'art as finding expression for the earth itself'.[37] In the first Glanmore sonnet Heaney's speaker is more tentative and more humanistic than this implies: 'Now the good life could be to cross a field/ And art a paradigm of earth new from the lathe/Of ploughs'. Here *Field Work* defines itself as *Georgics*: again, Heaney's 'earth' is not Thomas's. The speaker does not seek to express 'the earth'; he proposes working with 'earth' as a metaphor for poetic expression: 'Old plough-socks gorge the subsoil of each sense'. The sequence is divided between – and about – images that hark back to the family farm, and images that represent their author or his aesthetic as less authentically *in situ*. Sonnet III begins: 'This evening the cuckoo and the corncrake/(So much, too much) consorted at twilight'. The sestet still more explicitly acknowledges the poem's Wordsworthian scenario of 'retreat' into wilderness and solitude:

> I had said earlier, 'I won't relapse
> From this strange loneliness I've brought us to.
> Dorothy and William – ' She interrupts:
> You're not going to compare us two...?
> Outside a rustling and twig-combing breeze
> Refreshes and relents. Is cadences.

The last two lines introduce yet another consciously Romantic trope and further disclose the extent to which these sonnets debate pastoral itself. Yet, despite some effects of psychic disturbance, they still do not altogether internalise the spot of time: here the 'strange loneliness' that characterises post-Wordsworthian English pastoral is also culturally 'strange'. Rather, as above, Heaney resolves tension in the 'complaisance with natural impulses' which generates poetry. But 'natural impulses' operate under controlled conditions. What is 'outside' depends on and fulfils interior needs.

The 'self' of Heaney's poetry, then, moves between instinct (animism) and control (agriculture), but its own boundaries appear quite firmly drawn. It rarely dissolves into the unconscious ('subsoil') or cosmic flux or earthly ecosystem – as happens in Hughes and Thomas. Instead, the cosmos moves centripetally towards the human figure. What Heaney most values in Wordsworth is 'a prolonged moment of equilibrium during which we feel ourselves to be conductors of the palpable energies of earth and sky'.[38] In 'Gifts of Rain' a farmer conducts energies so that 'sky and ground//are running naturally along his arms/that grope the cropping land'. The self-doubt of 'Exposure' is set against a less amenable natural backdrop, although (like 'Refreshes and relents') it tends to harmonise with the human 'voice': 'Rain comes down through the alders,/Its low conducive voices/Mutter about let-downs and erosions'. And here again is the figure of the masking, camouflaging tree: 'Taking protective covering/ From bole and bark'. The egotistical sublime comes wrapped in negative capability. (A comparison with Thomas's 'Aspens' might be instructive.)

Yet there are further dialectics at work. It is in Heaney's poems of 'exposure', poems in which the speaker has left imaginative home base, sometimes for the coast, that the natural world most powerfully intrudes its Otherness, or challenges and re-orients human solipsism. 'The Peninsula' is one example. So is this cosmic image from 'Exposure', at once scientific and aesthetic: 'A comet that was lost/ Should be visible at sunset,/ Those million tons of light/ Like a glimmer of haws and rose-hips'. Thus 'Exposure' and the 'Glanmore Sonnets' might also be read as *Eclogues*, or as an argument between georgic and eclogue, 'silage' and 'bay tree', ploughman-poet and the Arcadian artificer who asks 'What is my apology for poetry?' A more recent example is 'Postscript' (to *The Spirit Level*, 1996) which evokes 'ocean…wild/ With foam and glitter' and a lake 'lit / By the earthed lightning of a flock of swans'. This kinetic conjunction, where sea and inland water coincide, is said to 'catch the heart off guard and blow it open' – open also to Yeats's symbolic western language. 'Off guard', however, may be telling.

If Heaney is a Green or environmental poet, it is usually not in the sense that he subordinates human consciousness or human rights to ecosystems, but in the sense that the fabric of his poems heals modern splits between/within self and world. He 'assumes' what Wordsworth aspires to reassert. Hence his imaginative ease among sense-impressions and our ease among his poems. He invites us into the tree house to become at home in landscape. His poems therapeutically 'assuage' or 'appease' or 'restore' (to use his own verbs for poetry's healing touch) because, even when their content darkens, they eschew alienation such as Thomas's 'I cannot bite the day to the core' or Larkin's 'None of this cares for us'. Heaney is not a 'post-pastoral' poet (Gifford) who has digested Wordsworth and Thomas and moved on. Rather, some aspects of his sensibility hark back to a pre-Reformation, pre-Cartesian order. His animism is rooted in Catholicism as well as in Romantic Nature and, as with Kavanagh, the former protects the latter from the crisis of faith it undergoes in Thomas. What Heaney calls 'some vestigial sense of place as it was experienced in the older dispensation' enables a 'feeling, assenting, equable marriage between the geographical country and the country of the mind'. This is also landscape apprehended or manifested through religious signs: 'a diminished structure of lore and superstition and half-pagan, half-Christian thought and practice'.[39] Heaney does not reproduce the overt Catholicism in Kavanagh's wish to 'know God the Father in a tree'; but confidence in the identity between spirit and matter blesses his own 'marriages' between geography and mind. Protestantism, because more deeply implicated in the rise of capital, science and technology (although this is now disputed), may have more relent-lessly pursued the logic of Christian anthropocentrism – hence also begetting the ecological reaction against it. Yet Irish Catholicism, which kept in touch with a pre-Enlightenment 'natural world redolent with human analogy and symbolic meaning'[40] – partly because unofficial Catholicism preserved 'the older dispensation', partly because official Catholicism resisted science – has *ipso facto* never doubted human centrality. When the proponents of an emergent Celto-Catholic ecology 'claim a moral perspective for environmental awareness, grounding it in our responsibility to appreciate the natural world as God's first revelation',[41] they continue the theological tradition of 'immanence' whereby Nature encodes messages from the creator to mankind. Heaney's most recent collections, *Seeing Things* (1991) and *The Spirit Level* (1996), explicitly read the poet's surroundings for immanence, for signs of 'where the spirit lives'.

Of course Heaney's pastoral theology intersects with English 'Romantic ecology'. Its images remind us of Nature's presence and thus function as a bridge 'from anthropocentric to more specifically ecocentric concerns'.[42] And why should he and Kavanagh so readily internalise Wordsworth's equivalence between primal vision and imagination when they disregard other elements in his poetry? Did their own personal and cultural histories reproduce events in nineteenth-century England, making them receptive to the compensatory psychic structures that Wordsworth put into lyrical currency? Certainly, as the physical, social and cognitive world of 'that childhood country' recedes in time and space, its poetic surrogate transubstantiates it more emphatically. In this sense, Heaney does for old Catholic-rural Ireland what Yeats did for Anglo-Ireland. The spot of timelessness in 'Markings' parallels the end of 'On Reading a Book on Common Wild Flowers', but without the ambiguity of Kavanagh's 'may live':

> All these things entered you
> As if they were both the door and what came through it.
> They marked the spot, marked time and held it open.
> A mower parted the bronze sea of corn.
> A windlass hauled the centre out of water ...

Compared with Kavanagh, Heaney begins at a farther point from the way of life for which 'Digging' is really an elegy, just as he begins at a farther point from Catholic orthodoxy. Whereas Kavanagh initially identified poet and ploughman, it is Heaney's father who has ploughed, dug or sold cattle. Thus Heaney half-becomes his own "primitive" in a form of Romantic retrospect at once psychological and cultural. This makes him all the more protective of the amniotic security that lay about him in his Mossbawn infancy: 'To this day, green, wet corners, flooded wastes, soft rushy bottoms, any place with the invitation of watery ground and tundra vegetation ...possess an immediate and deeply peaceful attraction'. Heaney's 'life of sensations' can figure as a security blanket. When he defines poetry as 'fortifying our inclination to credit promptings of our intuitive being' or appealing to 'the first recesses of ourselves, in the shyest, pre-social part of our nature',[43] he implies the origins of the lyric poem in primary narcissism: in desire to restore the seamless instinctive union between infant and world, between subject and object; in mourning for loss of the maternal body. Assisted by Catholic epistemology, Heaney's imagination both guards and affirms those instinctive recesses, 'the hiding places'. That such 'den-life' simultaneously evokes a lost or receding domain enhances the power of his pastoral. For some readers, Hidden Ireland reproduces vanished England, making the countryside a real presence once again.

One difference from Wordsworth, whether psychological or theological or both, is that Heaney's poetry rarely announces: 'The things that I have seen I now can see no more'. The very title of Seeing Things seems to contradict Wordsworth by claiming that the capacity to 'see into the life of things' need not weaken with age. Some poems possibly over-insist on their access to primal vision, and on the speaker's selfhood as thereby 'fortified', 'entered', 'confirmed', 'corroborated' or 'ratified'. Nor, again, is this quite the understanding of selfhood associated with Wordsworth's poetry or with the development of "Protestant" individualism in its various cultural and conceptual guises. Selfhood in Heaney seems to require validation from communal or external forces that are then maximised in the poet/persona as a clan in its chieftain. A trope of identity-as-circularity, identity-as-poetry, the circumference returning to the centre, recurs in Seeing Things and The Spirit Level: 'both the door and what came through it', 'whatever is given//Can always be re-imagined', a salmon picking up 'unheard concentric soundwaves', 'whatever was in store/ Witnessed itself already taking place', 'Strange how things in the offing, once they're sensed,/ Convert to things foreknown', 'What happens next//Is undiminished for having happened once', 'My last things will be first things slipping from me'. Even time-burdened Thomas Hardy acquires 'a ripple that would travel eighty years/Outward from there, to be the same ripple/ Inside him at its last circumference'. These closed circuits can turn Heaney's later pastoral into a hyper-Arcadian realm that excludes personal, as much as public or natural, history. In Outcasts from Eden: Ideas of Landscape in British Poetry since 1945 Edward Picot sees Heaney's recent work as shaking off the Edenic backward look: 'Heaney's feeling that the internal world of ideas must be given precedence over the external world of things and places takes us at last beyond the confines of the Eden myth.' I would argue that this is to misread the (albeit shifting) ratio beween control and Nature that has characterised Heaney's pastoral from the outset. Unlike Hughes's, his Eden is never 'an undisturbed primitive state': it pivots theologically on the poet as Adam.[44] Auden writes of Eden-Arcadia: 'Change can occur, but as an instantaneous transformation, not through a process of becoming...Temporal novelty is without anxiety, temporal repetition without boredom.'[45] Heaney tends to concede change on one plane then cancel it on another. His 'You' is not *ipso facto* less self-centred or integral than his 'I', while the repeated 'things' and what/whatever construction verges on the vague rather than the mysterious. He also repeats a global 'all' which, in the conclusion of 'Poet's Chair', serves a transubstantiative collapse of distinctions between child and man, 'seeing' and writing, event and memory, Nature and artefact, man and poem. The embryonic poet is again situated centrally, between agriculture and wild:

> My father's ploughing one, two, three, four sides
> Of the lea ground where I sit all-seeing
> At centre field, my back to the thorn tree
> They never cut. The horses are all hoof
> And burnished flank, I am all foreknowledge.
> Of the poem as a ploughshare that turns time
> Up and over. Of the chair in leaf
> The fairy thorn is entering for the future.
> Of being here for good in every sense.

This remembers Kavanagh's sonnet 'October' which begins by uniting past and present on a transcendental plane: 'O leafy yellowness you create for me/A world that was and now is poised above time'. Yet despite affirming 'the prayering that the earth offers', 'October' includes 'regret for youth passing' and ends in subtly cadenced doubt as to whether the seasons of Nature, agriculture and human life synchronise. Here 'pastoral enclosure' does not subsume historical time into 'poem', while 'heavily' carries a lot of weight into future Octobers haunting the present tense of the final couplet:

> It is October over all my life and the light is staring
> As it caught me once in the plantation by the fox coverts.
> A man is ploughing ground for winter wheat
> And my nineteen years weigh heavily on my feet.

4

The northern pastoral poetry of Kavanagh, Heaney and John Hewitt is aware, sometimes jealously so, of a more extensive Irish tradition: western pastoral. Ironically, a western landscape (by Paul Henry) graces the cover of Kavanagh's Penguin *Selected Poems*: evidence that, from London, all Irish literary countryside looks the same. This is not to deny regional hybridisations or to imply that northern poets do not write western poems: poets from the urban Protestant North have particularly, though not exclusively, developed the tradition that Yeats did most to establish. However, poetic western pastoral itself belongs to a larger cultural complex. As Tim Robinson says of the Aran Islands: 'After the antiquarians came the linguists, ethnographers and folklorists, and then the writers, poets, film-makers and journalists.'[46] In Gaelic and English, in prose and drama, in the visual arts and cinema, in tourism and postcards, in politics and ideology, in pilgrimages, fashion, oyster festivals, poetry festivals and summer schools, the West continues to generate mean-ings. Meanwhile, Irish poetry itself is still sifting Yeats's original aromatic blend of *Ossian,* mysticism, aestheticism and Co. Sligo, still unmaking and remaking the Yeatsian West. The pastoral structures he pioneered can be obscured by ambivalence about Yeats's continuing presence in Irish poetry and by reductive judgments like Declan Kiberd's view of his resort to Sligo as a 'refusal of history', which derives from Protestant guilt and which has led poets of other denom-inations astray. Kiberd castigates 'the number of poems set on the Aran Islands, or in west Kerry, or on the coast of Donegal – all written by artists who act like self-conscious tourists in their own country'.[47]

As I indicate below, there is also western anti-pastoral and anti-western pastoral: Joyce inaugurated a tradition of scepticism about the literary 'journey westwards'. Kiberd, however, echoes Heaney on Praeger. He implies that Irish Catholics should/can never imagi-natively travel in Ireland since they already belong to the single trans-ferable national place: the universal parish or geographic collective. Hence the contrary image of Irish Protestant writers as literary playboys of the western world. Kiberd reads contemporary poetry according to a historical prejudice. The charge of tourism, like the charge of aesthetic or scientific detachment, imputes a suspect out-sider (at best), colonial (at worst) status. It invokes landlordly pros-pects and English travel-narratives, even though by 1900 the West had become the focus for a wide range of Irish literary, linguistic and political aspirations. It signified, if with different inflections, not the single transferable place but the model place: Platonic

Ireland.[48] Nonetheless, there was incipient tension between the western Gaeltacht – given a prelapsarian status by linguistic nationalism, and to which notions of representativeness thus attached – and literary liberties. The more the West slipped from model to microcosm, the more the old man with redrimmed eyes spoke English, smoked and spat, the more it became critique. The clash between Synge and the nationalists who resented *The Playboy of the Western World* was a clash of expectations that turned on the difference between an ideal-typical locus and an experimental artistic site. This play about how a community deals with an outsider tests its audience, as do poets from "Protestant" backgrounds who adopt a western locale. Such poets sometimes try to pre-empt deracination by laying the speaker's status on the line: Louis MacNeice in 'Western Landscape' (1945) calls himself a 'visitor...disfranchised in the constituencies of quartz and bog-oak'. Critics may over-interpret such deprecations, which are dialectical or interrogative as much as defensive, as when Terence Brown suggests that the imagined western places of Yeats, MacNeice, Richard Murphy and Michael Longley 'all can be read as insecure assertions of an Irish identity established through association with place that a man or woman of Catholic nationalist stock feels no need to make'.[49] The literary point may be that "the West" is not where you live. It is eclogue rather than georgic.

Nor is 'Irish identity' the be-all and end-all as regards the intersections between culture, genre and form that constitute western pastoral. There are many reasons why it should incline more to eclogue than to georgic, although the difference is not absolute: 'Innisfree' launched both kinds of Irish pastoral in their modern guises. Patchily settled, tragically evacuated by Famine, inhospitable to cultivation, vulnerable to social breakdown, romantically open to sublime and beautiful constructions, the West has inspired indigenous georgics,[50] but has more often been a site for projection and speculation. Its time-setting is future-eternal rather than past-perpetual, its psychological setting desire rather than memory. Innisfree's cabin (modelled on *Walden*) will have to be built before apiculture can commence. Or, as Yeats symbolically pleads in 'Meditations in Time of Civil War': 'honey-bees,/Come build in the empty house of the stare'. Virgil's *Eclogues* ('one of Yeats's reference books')[51] with their conscious artifice and social critique, set between country and city, civil strife and future golden age, death and love, lucky Tityrus and unlucky Meliboeus, seem an apt ancestor for western pastoral. Overall, its horizon is utopian rather than (like Kavanagh's and Heaney's) Edenic, according to Auden's distinction between the gyres of pastoral:

> Our dream pictures of the Happy Place where suffering and evil are
> unknown are of two kinds, the Edens and the New Jerusalems. Though
> it is possible for the same individual to imagine both, it is unlikely that
> his interest in both will be equal and I suspect that between the Arcadian
> whose favourite daydream is of Eden, and the Utopian whose favourite
> dream is of New Jerusalem there is a characterological gulf...Eden is a
> past world in which the tensions of the present world have not yet arisen;
> New Jerusalem is a future world in which they have at last been resolved.[52]

In 'The Fisherman' Yeats dresses his utopian poetics, his ideal
Irishman and ideal audience – 'A man who does not exist,/ A man
who is but a dream' – in exotic 'Connemara clothes'. In fact, the
poem dramatises a decision to write pastoral, while the context of
that decision – alienation from a dystopian environment rendered
as urban ('the catch-cries of the town') – indicates that territorial
politics may condition Irish eclogue as much as georgic.

Twenty years earlier, Yeats's 'Song of the Happy Shepherd' had
moved from nostalgia for Eden – 'The woods of Arcady are dead'
– to the utopian imperative 'dream thou!' This poem indicates the
intellectual origins of Yeatsian eclogue in resistance to materialism
and Darwinism. Like the Catholic Church, the Shepherd rejects
the 'Grey truth' and 'star-bane' of scientific progress. Born in the
same year as Praeger, Yeats had abandoned his youthful entomology
for 'almost an infallible Church...of poetic tradition', then of occult-
ism, magic, legend and philosophy. This was his riposte to being
'deprived by Huxley and Tyndall, whom I detested, of the simple-
minded religion of my childhood'.[53] Yet some scientific habits stuck
(John Wilson Foster observes that Yeats 'classified Irish fairies and
fairy tales in an almost Linnaean system').[54] In 1886 he precociously
fused Darwinism with *anima mundi* as a way of attacking George
Eliot's emphasis on 'conscious man': 'she knows nothing of the dim
unconscious nature [of man] the world of instinct which (if there
is any truth in Darwin) is the accumulated wisdom of all living
things from the monera to man while the other is at the very most
the wisdom gathred during four score years and ten'. Yeats would
later consider natural selection inartistic because it exalted 'accidental
variations'.[55] Yet, as in that early alliance with Darwin against Victorian
moralism and tunnel vision, his antagonism to science weakens
whenever science serves the cosmological claims of poetry. The poet-
scientist Miroslav Holub approvingly quotes Yeats's pronouncement
of 1896: 'The more a poet rids his verses of heterogeneous knowledge
and irrelevant analysis, and purifies his mind with elaborate art,
the more does the little ritual of his verse resemble the great ritual
of Nature, and become mysterious and inscrutable.'[56]

That seems designed to put Wordsworth in his place. Yeats also identified Wordsworth – or what Michael Baron terms 'Victorian Wordsworthianism' – with a myopic focus on 'conscious man', with philosophical and ethical 'utilitarianism'.[57] Thus when Yeats defines his own aesthetic against Wordsworth's, he not only distinguishes Irish literature from English; he lays the foundations for modern western pastoral. Evidently Yeats's post-Darwinian crisis of faith made Wordsworthian "Nature" appear less secure, as a compensatory spiritual resort, than 'elaborate art' boosted by the occult. Nonetheless, their differences belong to the sphere where Romantic aesthetics meet the 'inner light and private intercession of Protestant theology...spiritual journey and autobiography' (to quote Nicholas Roe). Recent comparative discussion has taken Yeats's rhetorical hostility to Wordsworth ('that typical Englishman')[58] less literally. It has found philosophical overlaps, points of aesthetic agreement, intertextual echoes, recourse to Wordsworthian models. For example, Baron argues that Yeats's investment in orality and search for a 'language that expresses communal and local affections and pieties' acknowledge Wordsworth; whose texts, in turn, are more divided about such issues than Yeats's view that he lacked 'the dramatic sense' allows.[59] In 'Yeats and the Ghost of Wordsworth' Maneck H. Daruwala compares Yeats's 'To a Young Beauty' and Wordsworth's 'To a Young Lady Who Had Been Reproached For Taking Long Walks in the Country'. His article reveals Yeats's relation to Wordsworth as an antinomy rather than an antithesis: 'Wordsworth's "Young Lady" is a child of Nature, Yeats's – he hopes – a child of Art.' Yet, as Darwula reminds us: 'Much early Romantic poetry is concerned not with nature but with the human mind in nature; later Romantic poets such as Yeats stress the anti-mimetic and inward movement. Wordsworth's emphasis on art is submerged, while Yeats stresses human nature in an aesthetic world.'[60]

By the same token, Yeats's emphasis on Nature may be 'submerged'. In his parallel between the little ritual of art and the great ritual of Nature, aestheticism keeps the door open for science. This perspective questions binary judgments such as Patrick Sheeran's:

> Throughout his work Yeats evinces a striking lack of interest in nature or landscape per se. Hills, mountains, plains and rivers are important to him not so much for their intrinsic or even aesthetic value but insofar as they can be made to symbolise a world elsewhere or because they are connected with a particular incident. Yeats is above all fascinated by two things: landscape as symbol and landscape as shaped by man.[61]

Frank Kinahan argues that critics have too easily agreed (at times with Yeats himself) that Yeats was not 'an observer'; whereas the 'natural world provided the poetry of his youth with as many images as his folklore and occult sources combined'. Kinahan quotes Oliver St John Gogarty's praise of the 'accurate and fitting...scenes Yeats introduced into ["The Stolen Child"]' and Gogarty's comment that 'When he was a youth, he took it all in'.[62] Writing on William Allingham (in 1888) Yeats bears this out: 'Perhaps...to fully understand these poems one needs to have been born and bred in one of those western Irish towns; to remember how it was the centre of your world, how the mountains and the river and the roads became a possession of your life forever'.[63] Here georgic and eclogue overlap: Yeats's remembered Eden drives his quest for Utopia. And while he draws the line at wildflowers as an English poetic fetish,[63] taking in birds, trees, water and weather is another matter. All appear in that autumnal pastoral 'The Wild Swans at Coole':

> The trees are in their autumn beauty,
> The woodland paths are dry,
> Under the October twilight the water
> Mirrors a still sky;
> Upon the brimming water among the stones
> Are nine-and-fifty swans.
>
> The nineteenth autumn has come upon me
> Since I first made my count;
> I saw, before I had well finished,
> All suddenly mount
> And scatter wheeling in great broken rings
> Upon their clamorous wings.
>
> I have looked upon those brilliant creatures,
> And now my heart is sore.
> All's changed since I, hearing at twilight,
> The first time on this shore,
> The bell-beat of their wings above my head,
> Trod with a lighter tread...

The speaker is an observer: lake-watcher and bird-counter, seeing and looking, alert to the lakeside in a rainy season (limestone geology makes the Coole lake prone to flooding). The precisely indicative syntax of the first stanza keeps the first person singular in abeyance. And when he does come on stage, it is as the arena for a characteristic conflict in Romantic Nature (compare Edward Thomas's 'October') between reading the scene as human psychology and as alien: 'Unwearied still, lover by lover,/ They paddle in the cold/Companionable streams or climb the air'. Yeats transfers human concepts: 'lover by lover'. But the poem also knows that swans mate for life, and the ironical oxymoron 'cold/ Companionable' implies a co-operation within natural systems that human consciousness fails to comprehend let alone match. The scene is, of course, subject to the aesthetic gaze as well as to naturalist observation: 'The trees are in their autumn beauty' unites both kinds of perception, as does the visual equilibrium between water and sky, aurally reflected by the assonantal chiasmus 'Mirrors...brimming'. The poem's poised opening is itself mirrored at the beginning of the last stanza: 'But now they drift on the still water,/ Mysterious, beautiful'. Yet the addition of mystery to beauty underlines Nature's Otherness and the point that the aesthetic gaze has been disturbed – historically, as well as during the poem itself (nor is twilight what it was). The swans's interruption of the speaker's observing, gazing, counting and stylising – 'scatter wheeling in great broken rings' – is itself choreographed and orchestrated. Yet 'before I had well finished', like the unrhymed lines, dramatises the refusal of Nature to stay 'still'. It neither submits to science nor 'imitates art'. The poem ends with questions that envisage further losses of control:

> Among what rushes will they build,
> By what lake's edge or pool
> Delight men's eyes when I awake some day
> To find they have flown away?

As in other swan-poems, the swans seem a meta-symbol for Yeats's inspiration: stillness and motion, elusive vision and finished art. Ear and eye render their pan-aesthetic appeal: 'clamorous wings', 'the bell-beat of their wings'. Besides looking, Yeats listens to Nature, whose sounds may be symbolically in tune with favoured rhythms, one ritual validating another ('bell-beat', wind among the reeds, the curlews' 'sweet crystalline cry' that ends 'Paudeen') or initiate some 'clamorous' counterpoint. In 'Coole and Ballylee, 1931', a work of greater heart-soreness, the swan-symbol refers to the poem itself in less plangent terms as 'sudden thunder' and arrogant purity. Yet the actual bird has not vanished. The lines 'That stormy white/ But seems a concentration of the sky' marks the point where the rituals of art and Nature touch. So does Yeats's salute to 'those brilliant creatures', bird and icon, an evolutionary marvel. 'Brilliant' links a luminous, numinous whiteness with the idea that the swans' creaturely existence has a complexity independent of, but equal to, the mind's creativity. Yeats's does not always mediate so finely or humbly between Nature and art as he does in 'The Wild Swans at Coole'. Yet the poem suggests how his sensitivity to natural phenomena sets limits to their co-option as art-objects, sets difficult standards for 'beauty'.

If, in Sheeran's phrase, Yeats is 'fascinated by...landscape as symbol and landscape as shaped by man', symbol depends at some level on observation; landscape shaped by man is won from the wild. At once cultivated and wild (now a Nature reserve), Coole Park provided the makings of "Coole": a rich pastoral locus in which to explore the dynamics of house, garden and wilderness. 'The Wild Swans at Coole' gives its suggestive name to the collection (1917) that stakes out the ground of Yeats's later eclogue, particularly in his two elegies for Robert Gregory: 'In Memory of Major Robert Gregory' and the deliberate eclogue 'Shepherd and Goatherd'. This is also the collection in which Yeats's tower/house at Gort begins a symbolic career, complementary to "Coole", in which the variables of its natural environment impinge on the aesthetic, social and metaphysical endeavour it figures. At the beginning of 'The Phases of the Moon' an unexplained sound may signify that 'A rat or water-hen/ Splashed, or an otter slid into the stream'; at the end, a bat that 'circled round [the toiling poet] with its squeaky cry' implies coincidence between the gyres of mind and moon. But even when local birds or animals are most explicitly symbolic, the persuasiveness of the symbol depends on observation: 'What tumbling cloud did you cleave,/ Yellow-eyed hawk of the mind' ('The Hawk'); 'the mountain grass/ Cannot but keep the form/ Where the mountain hare has lain' ('Memory'). Robert Gregory triggers Yeats's portrait of the ideal landscape artist (although he has a complementary expertise in 'all the lovely intricacies of a house'):

VII

For all things the delighted eye now sees
Were loved by him: the old storm-broken trees
That cast their shadows upon road and bridge;
The tower set on the stream's edge;
The ford where drinking cattle make a stir
Nightly, and startled by that sound
The water-hen must change her ground...

IX

We dreamed that a great painter had been born
To cold Clare rock and Galway rock and thorn,
To that stern colour and that delicate line
That are our secret discipline
Wherein the gazing heart doubles her might...

In stanza VII, as in 'The Wild Swans at Coole', the aesthete-naturalist observes with eye and ear. Natural and man-made features of the tower's landscape, like domestic and wild animals, mingle rather uneasily in his consciousness ('the stream's edge', 'shadows', 'startled'). Stanza IX reverses the delighted eye's trajectory in a progressively inward movement from 'cold Clare rock' to aesthetics to the emotional power generated by artistic 'discipline'. The seeming paradox of 'the gazing heart' telescopes this process, while 'doubles her might' puts down inartistic mere sincerities. The female pronoun adds to the suggestion that observation is integral to poetic 'might'. 'Human nature in an aesthetic world' (Daruwala) does not erase but transposes its natural ground.

Given the stress on 'heart' in 'The Wild Swans at Coole' and elsewhere, Yeats might have apologised for his youthful remarks on the 'Saxon' (in part, revenge for the melancholy Celt stereotype): 'He is full of self-brooding. Like his own Wordsworth, most English of poets, he finds his image in every lake and puddle. He has to burthen the skylark with his cares before he can celebrate it. He is always a lens coloured by self.'[65] In 'The Symbolism of Poetry', Yeats firmly detaches symbolism from subjectivism: 'the beryl stone was enchanted by our fathers that it might unfold the pictures in its heart, and not to mirror our own excited faces'.[66] When John Eglinton (in 1898) thought that the Irish literary movement could do with some Wordsworthian 'high seriousness' as opposed to a diet of symbols and legends, Yeats replied that poetry was the 'revelation of a hidden life', 'the only means of conversing with eternity left to man on earth'.[67] Thus Yeatsian pastoral – in theory – objectively voices a symbolic locus. It does not subjectively describe and moralise according to the utilitarian agenda 'Let Nature be your teacher'. This may boil down to a difference between high church and low. If, as Wilde says in 'The Decay of Lying', Wordsworth 'found in stones the sermons he had already hidden there', Yeats may have found in beryl stones the 'hidden life' he had already hidden there. Yet deeper differences are at stake when aestheticism stresses the poet's hierophantic role in ordering mysteries. That, for Yeats, Nature is the material form of *anima mundi* (a concept viewed as heretical by the Catholic Church) makes his early pastoral mystical rather than pantheistic or animistic. And, in structural terms, the more poetry moves from description to symbol, and from meditation to drama, the greater its ambition to speak for a less personal 'self' on the earthly stage (*the* delighted eye', '*the* gazing heart'). Overall, Yeats's template defines western pastoral as an objectifying genre with large metaphysical potential. This includes the in-built generic self-consciousness induced by Ireland on the one hand, aestheticism on the other. Western pastoral will also become a forum for aesthetics.

In Yeats's early western poems, symbolism situates the self in cosmic Nature (Joyce's joke about 'universe and stars'). 'Who Goes with Fergus?', for instance, projects sexual and spiritual desire on

to 'the shadows of the wood,/...the white breast of the dim sea/
And all dishevelled wandering stars'. His later eclogues emphasise
the house, flaunting their own formal architecture or 'secret disci-
pline' as, under pressure of history, Yeatsian pastoral becomes less
mystical and more cultural. The last stanza of 'In Memory of Major
Robert Gregory' ('seeing how bitter is that wind/ That shakes the
shutter') prepares for the secular prayer of 'A Prayer for My
Daughter'. This poem, although future-oriented towards an Irish
New Jerusalem, begins in 'great gloom' since the 'tensions of the
present' (Auden) have not been resolved and because they implicate
the next generation: 'Once more the storm is howling, and half-
hid/ Under this cradle-hood and coverlid/My child sleeps on.' Here
western pastoral acquires more distinct political contours: taking
shape as 'excited reverie' in an unstable space between shelter (also
the poem itself) and storm, in an unstable interregnum between
turmoil and Utopia. (This is one way in which Heaney's 'Exposure'
inclines to eclogue.)

Yet Nature does not only symbolise contemporary violence or
propaganda: it relieves socio-political stress. Critics have noted
Yeats's surprising resort to Wordsworth and Coleridge as he lays
down ideal qualities for his daughter and the future:[68]

> May she become a flourishing hidden tree
> That all her thoughts might like the linnet be,
> And have no business but dispensing round
> Their magnanimities of sound,
> Nor but in merriment begin a chase,
> Nor but in merriment a quarrel.
> O may she live like some green laurel
> Rooted in one dear perpetual place.

Auden says: 'to become an inhabitant of new Jerusalem it is abso-
lutely required that one be happy and good'. This Lucy-like figure
redeems woman from corrupted mythic artifact ('that great Queen,
that rose out of the spray'), substituting a symbolic presence which
is animistically closer to Nature – Daphne, rather than Aphrodite or
Cathleen Ní Houlihan. Yeats condenses Nature into his favourite
symbols, tree and bird, while 'one dear perpetual place' simultan-
eously pulls back the troubled nation to a natural-utopian western
microcosm. On the aesthetic front, the nation's sources in denatured
intellect – the poet's 'dried up' mind, the 'opinionated mind' of
Irish politics – yield to a bird's 'magnanimities of sound'. The phrase
links Yeats's art, daughter and ideal Ireland. (In 'On a Political
Prisoner' Constance Markiewicz undergoes a similar redemptive
metamorphosis into a 'rock-bred, sea-borne bird'.) This part-spiritual,

part-organic model – a great-souled natural voice – inspires the architecture resumed later in the poem: 'And may her bridegroom bring her to a house/ Where all's accustomed, ceremonious...Ceremony's a name for the rich horn/And custom for the spreading laurel tree'. Thus Yeats translates desirable systems, social and artistic, into natural processes – fluid, fertile, abundant – which are seen as underlying them. All this can, of course, be read as a naturalisation of woman or power. More positively, it enacts artistic and cultural therapy that takes a wounded psyche, a wounded Ireland, back to basics (compare 'Stream and Sun at Glendalough' in which Nature and art restoratively fuse at a bad moment: 'Through intricate motions ran/Stream and gliding sun'.) In its constructive aspect 'A Prayer for My Daughter' seems a version of Virgil's 'messianic' Golden Age *Eclogue* IV.

Much of this, especially the classical-pastoral Horn of Plenty, still humanises Nature. Wild Nature is given more autonomy in 'Meditations in Time of Civil War' in proportion as that sequence probes the durability, even validity, of the civilisation which 'architect and artist...rear in stone'. The poet-protagonist assumes the traditionally pastoral role of exile from the world of action, forced to rethink in rural seclusion. When Nature invades humanity's 'loosening' architecture the effect seems paradoxically constructive and instructive. In 'The Stare's Nest by My Window' the 'mother birds bring grubs and flies', while the human element has only mutual destruction to show: 'Last night they trundled down the road/ That dead young soldier in his blood'. Here another unexpected echo (Wilfred Owen's 'Dulce et Decorum Est') suggests how western landscape is taking the strain of postwar Europe. In each stanza, admission of human failure is followed by a refrain which appeals to the creative spirit of/as Nature: 'My wall is loosening; honey-bees,/ Come build...' Earlier, 'My House' has reintroduced the tower in its natural and man-made setting:

> An ancient bridge, and a more ancient tower,
> A farmhouse that is sheltered by its wall,
> An acre of stony ground,
> Where the symbolic rose can break in flower,
> Old ragged elms, old thorns innumerable,
> The sound of the rain or sound
> Of every wind that blows;
> The stilted water-hen
> Crossing stream again
> Scared by the splashing of a dozen cows...

The 'Old ragged elms, old thorns innumerable', unsusceptible to control, to pruning or counting, remind humanity of its own (ragged) place in Nature. These undeclared symbols are ironically juxtaposed with the 'symbolic rose' which needs no soil, but whose creative 'flowering' might 'break' its artifice: art becoming Nature to utopian effect. In 'The Road at My Door', visited by combatants from each side, the poet partly chafes at his impotent retirement, partly takes quietist bearings from observation (again) of female nurture in Nature: 'I count those feathered balls of soot/ The moor-hen guides upon the stream,/ To silence the envy in my thought'. (Moorhens also appear in 'Easter 1916'.) The Yeatsian eclogue is not an artificial refuge from war or Nature, but an arena where its own investment in artifice is challenged by both.

The birds in 'Meditations' are humbler than the symbolic swan that vanished in 'Nineteen Hundred and Nineteen' and will reappear in 'The Tower'. Like his humbler animals, they figure the poet's vulnerable flesh rather than invulnerable work. Art in Yeats's poetry turns to Nature when dismayed by mortality as well as humbled by history. 'At Algeciras – A Meditation upon Death' begins with (almost) neutral natural-historical data:

> The heron-billed pale cattle-birds
> That feed on some foul parasite
> Of the Moroccan flocks and herds
> Cross the narrow Straits to light...

until rhythmic crescendo imparts the usual symbolic aura to birds in the trees: 'In the rich midnight of the garden trees/ Till the dawn break upon those mingled seas'. The temporal depth of the trees, the spatial sweep of the seas, exemplify how Yeats's natural images attract or express a cosmic frame. The poem continues to question 'the Great Questioner' by spelling out the two approaches it has so far taken to Nature: science and symbolism:

> Often at evening when a boy
> Would I carry to a friend –
> Hoping more substantial joy
> Did an older mind commend –
> Not such as are in Newton's metaphor
> But actual shells of Rosses' level shore.

That the scientist should appear more 'metaphorical', the poet more empirical, is a neat irony which underwrites Yeats's claims for his own cosmology.

Another conscious irony in 'Algeciras' is that the rhyme 'boy'/'joy' echoes the Immortality Ode. So does the last section of 'Meditations in Time of Civil War', which begins with a phantasmagoria of natural and artificial images, all of which have appeared in the sequence or elsewhere in Yeats:

I climb to the tower-top and lean upon broken stone,
A mist that is like blown snow is sweeping over all,
Valley, river and elms, under the light of a moon
That seems unlike itself, that seems unchangeable,
A glittering sword out of the east. A puff of wind
And those white glimmering fragments of the mist sweep by.
Frenzies bewilder, reveries perturb the mind;
Monstrous familiar images swim to the mind's eye.

Social and poetic architecture are threatened by defamiliarising forces that upset relations between the eye, the mind, 'the mind's eye', 'reverie' and landscape under a moon that may be Nature or art, like the 'fragments...of mist'. Yet the kaleidoscope will form new patterns. Yeats concludes: 'The abstract joy,/The half-read wisdom of daemonic images,/Suffice the ageing man as once the growing boy'. Like 'At Algeciras', this resists Wordsworth by playing ironically on joy/boy. 'More substantial joy' and 'abstract joy' qualify the absolute natural joy of Wordsworth's 'vision splendid'. Once again, natural history and 'daemonic images' belong to the same cognitive cosmos. Yeats consistently rejects Wordsworth's notion of the child and proto-poet as 'Nature's Priest' rather than apprentice to a system of symbolism, but even his celebrations of his own creativity somehow affirm the created world. 'Ageing' and 'growing' stress Nature as process, work in progress, while 'abstract' again links science and art. The aesthete does not suffer the diminishing returns of youth, subjectivity and Eden. At the same time, he knows that human victories over Nature are make-believe. 'The Man and the Echo' admits to losing the struggle as the speaker recognises himself in animal Nature: 'A stricken rabbit is crying out,/And its cry distracts my thought'.

5

At the end of 'Meditations in Civil War' the Celtic Twilight returns to imbue political and conceptual chaos with otherworldly strangeness. Yeats bequeathed this glimmering instability to his successors in western pastoral. He also bequeathed landscapes in which settlement and wildness interpenetrate, in which Utopia is desired and doubted, in which flora and fauna go in and 'out of nature' and in which, to quote Louis MacNeice's 'Western Landscape', we find 'affirmation and abnegation together'. I will glance at this large legacy under four headings: art, (social) architecture, mysticism, ecology.

MacNeice shares with Yeats underlying pastoral structures as well as western affiliations.[69] For instance, his resort to eclogue in the 1930s parallels the motivation behind Yeats's 'Shepherd and Goatherd'. Both poets exploit the frank artifice of classical eclogue – as dialogue and competition between herdsmen poets – to explore conflicts about art, Nature and social duty.[70] Yeats's personae deprecate their elegies for Gregory, whose own achievement does not console his mother's grief: 'There's nothing of him left but half a score/ Of sorrowful, austere, sweet, lofty pipe tunes.' Here again death – identified as death 'in the great war beyond the sea' – chastens artifice, as it does more explicitly in MacNeice's 'Eclogue by a Five-barred Gate' (modelled on Virgil, *Eclogue* III). Personified as the judge of two shepherds' songs, 'Death' criticises them for failing to 'quote/The prices of significant living and decent dying'. None of MacNeice's eclogues, named as such, has a western Irish setting, although he called 'Valediction', his landscaped farewell to Ireland, an eclogue, and 'Eclogue from Iceland' may be a displacement exercise. However, his eclogues theorise his western poems. For example, 'Eclogue for Christmas', modelled on Virgil, *Eclogue* I, moves between country and city in order to criticise escapist modes of both which are 'Rotting the nerve of life and literature'. MacNeice makes the city, submerged in Yeats, an explicit context for the mid-century pastoral of 'a bastard/Out of the West by urban civilisation'. He also takes Yeats's dialectic of retreat *versus* engagement into new circumstances.

History enters MacNeice's pastoral as modernity, 1930s Europe, post-Treaty Ireland. 'The Hebrides' (1937) focuses on cultural survival in a subsistence community which only just keeps 'the folk-fancier or the friendly tourist' at bay. Here the poet as sociologist succeeds to the poet as 'folk-fancier'. At the same time, MacNeice's Hebridean 'brave oasis in the indifferent moors' also symbolises all pastoral enterprises since herding and agriculture began and localises the civilised values currently at risk: 'And while the stories circulate like smoke,/ The sense of life spreads out from the one-eyed house/ In wider circles through the lake of night/ In which articulate man has dropped a stone'. Two years later, in 'The Closing Album', MacNeice introduced the Second World War into western pastoral less subtextually than Yeats had introduced the First. This sequence of Irish snapshots can be read both as an elegy for Yeats and as reinscribing western pastoral with contemporary history and politics.[71] Just as in 'The Hebrides' ominous signs threaten the Ossianic refrain 'On those islands', so history slides incongruously under a timeless West: 'a hundred swans/ Dreaming on the harbour:/ The war came down on us here' ('Galway'). Following up this implication that Ireland has reverted to Tír na

nÓg in opting out of Europe, MacNeice's 'Neutrality' indicts de
Valera's wartime policy as irresponsible pastoral. He caricatures
Yeatsian language and symbolism ('A Knocknarea with for navel a
cairn of stones...the shadow and sheen of a moleskin mountain')
and exposes them to western seas where the mackerel now feed
'on the flesh of your kin'.

Conditioned by relief from war, 'Western Landscape' resumes
but also dissects the aesthetics of 'shadow and sheen':

> In doggerel and stout let me honour this country
> Though the air is so soft that it smudges the words...
>
> O grail of emerald passing light
> And hanging smell of sweetest hay
> And grain of sea and loom of wind
> Weavingly laughingly leavingly weepingly –
> Webs that will last and will not.

The poem follows its title in blurring boundaries between place
and representation, visual and verbal art, practice and theory. The
over-the-top assonantal refrain initially makes the text itself an
entrapping 'web' that recycles Yeats's 'woven world-forgotten isle'.
Woman, much entangled in the weave of the West, inhabits these
adverbs as 'A deaf-dumb Siren that can sing/ With fingertips her
falsities' (the mythic frame of some western pastorals is Homeric
rather than Celtic). Nor is the Siren the only body in a landscape
that includes 'the broken bog with its veins of amber water'; in
which 'the distant headland' is 'a sphinx's fist, that barely grips the
sea'; in which 'the mitred mountain weep[s] shale'. Here Nature
partly allows, partly disproves anthropocentric pattern-making:
'Webs that will last and will not'. When the speaker asks: 'what/
Is the hold upon, the affinity with/ Ourselves of such a light and
line?' the West represents what is perpetually unsatisfied in aesthetic
desire itself. More than Yeats, MacNeice internalises climatic in-
stabilities whereby 'our minds become, like the earth, a sieve,// A
halfway house between sky and sea' ('Donegal Triptych'). 'Western
Landscape' is based on Achill Island: an environment that lends
itself to Heraclitean metaphysics and aesthetics. 'The Strand', which
also belongs to MacNeice's Achill group, defines his aesthetics of
the West and the West of his aesthetics in a way that exposes the
human 'brave oasis' to 'webs that will last and will not'. The first
three words ('White Tintoretto clouds') promise that Nature imi-
tates Art. But the next phrase twists the sight-lines: 'beneath my
naked feet'. Family and cultural history are implicated in the aes-
thetic questions raised by 'The Strand'. The poet's father, even in
Anglican clergyman garb, has always been at home in the West

('A square black figure whom the horizon understood'), whereas the son knows that his own wish for such reciprocity is hopelessly paradoxical: 'This mirror of wet sand imputes a lasting mood/ To island truancies'. The last lines exchange Tintoretto clarity and square figure-in-the-landscape for a flux of light and water in which 'shaping' power shifts to Nature, and the poem's self-image becomes not a static but a moving mirror:

> And the mirror caught his shape which catches mine
> But then as now the floor-mop of the foam
> Blotted the bright reflections – and no sign
>
> Remains of face or feet when visitors have gone home.

Recent western poetry renews this dialectic between art and instability, which includes a destabilised self. Michael Longley's 'Landscape' cuts 'imagination' down to the diffuse materials on which it works ('Here my imagination/ Tangles through a turf-stack/ Like skeins of sheep's wool'), and subjects 'thought' and the poem itself to the natural world's centrifugal dynamics:

> A place of dispersals
> Where the wind fractures
> Flight-feathers, insect wings
> And rips thought to tatters
> Like a fuchsia petal.

Finally, beside water, 'A mouth drawn to a mouth/ Digests the glass between/Me and my reflection'. As in MacNeice, bodily fragments, corresponding to perceptual disorientation, litter the western environment. The aesthetics of 'The Strand' reach a further point of dissolution in Longley's 'Watercolour' (*The Ghost Orchid*, 1995) in which a painter, whom the sitter addresses, elides his image into the landscape: 'My pullover a continuation of the lazybeds/ You study through the window'. The painter's materials are themselves 'natural' – water and a brush of 'goose-quill and sable' – so the picture/poem always in process, always in the present tense, shares in the instabilities it tries to capture: 'One drop too many and the whole thing disintegrates./In this humidity your water-colour will never dry.' Yet there are counterweights to this art of disintegration. Each of Derek Mahon's short Aran Islands poems, 'Recalling Aran' and 'Epitaph for Robert Flaherty', contains the word 'perfect'. The western island is many things: Tír na nÓg, national microcosm, twilight zone, battleground of tradition and modernity, resort of truancy, and (see below) Zen shrine or Nature reserve. Mahon goes back to first principles by making it an artefact, itself a poem. His 'dream of limestone in sea-light' and 'islands of dark ore' reconceive Yeatsian origins by identifying Aran with a quintessential aestheticism, with definitive form. The resultant symbol, however, 'measures' life together with art ('final', 'simple', 'pure'):

> Reflection in that final sky
> Shames vision into simple sight –
> Into pure sense, experience.
> Four thousand miles away tonight...
> I clutch the memory still, and I
> Have measured everything with it since.

'Reflection', an ambiguous word that appears in three of the poems quoted above, has been peculiarly co-opted by the aesthetics of western pastoral.

'Loosening masonry', in its more literal aspect, can also turn western landscape into a 'place of dispersals'. Poetry dwells on derelict pre-Famine buildings, gapped drystone-walls, townlands diminished by emigration, abandoned island cottages, the remains of 'ancestral houses'. In such ruins western landscape, as an elegy for human obsolescence, for 'articulate man', becomes historical. Meanwhile, as social critique, it reproaches the failure of Irish colonial and utopian architecture alike. Some poems by Richard Murphy, particularly in *Sailing to an Island* (1963) and *The Price of Stone* (1985), make up for cultural and natural instabilities by their stress on houses and building, their desire to propitiate 'time's auctioneers' and atone for its exploitations. The sonnets of *The Price of Stone,* themselves consciously built, give voice to western buildings in various states of repair, with sins to exorcise and losses to grieve. 'Lead Mine Chimney' speaks of industrial decay: 'Pointlessly standing up'; 'Connemara Quay' confesses its failure to do 'all those things/Goodwill intended when I was designed/ To end the poor land's hunger'; 'Kylemore Castle 'Built for a cotton king 'had to be faced in stone/ Dressed by wage-skeletons'; 'Family Seat' has survived its past: 'They've all been buried in their name-proud vaults./ Paraplegics live here now, and love my faults'; 'Rectory begins: 'My porous rock foundations can't keep down/ Rising damp from arcane rheumatic springs'. This figures an antithetical anarchism that undermines Murphy's stonework and approves Nature's subversion of human structures and institutions. Empty western landscape can sometimes appear liberating rather than elegiac.

How 'peopled' is western pastoral? Poets may be silenced between the Scylla of emptying the landscape and the Charybdis of populating it in a politically incorrect manner. Murphy, who lived for years in a house he built in Cleggan, Co. Galway, still did not go native according to Patrick Crotty in *Modern Irish Poetry: An Anthology* (1995): 'Murphy is perhaps the last Anglo-Irish poet, fascinated by native modes of existence which appear more instinctive than his own...Murphy's concern with building, boat restoration and sailing – and indeed with poem construction – might be said to embody a diminished, solitary version of the colonist's "civilising" imperative'.[72] The dynamics of Otherness depend on country and city as well as coloniser and colonised; they may also have a psychological basis. Yeats, although criticised for patronising the locals, does not really co-opt 'the peasant' in Wordsworth's style. Just as Heaney splits his self-image between primitive and sophisticate, so Yeats peoples his pastoral with nomadic archetypes who dramatise his own passions, whether spiritual or sexual. The anarchic impulse that flickers in Murphy goes back to Synge and his influence on Yeats's wilder West: its psychic resistance to religious, moral and political systems, its tramps and crazies, its brutalities, its outlands of road and mountain.

Nevertheless, an implicitly Protestant poetic entry into western Catholic communities tends to walk on tiptoe. When MacNeice calls himself 'disfranchised' he uses severance from the landscape to imply other exclusions, political and religious. Similarly, Michael Longley's verse-epistle 'To Derek Mahon' represents the two poets, when visiting the Aran Islands (Inisheer) at Easter, as 'strangers in that parish', although also as hypothetically becoming 'islanders ourselves' through symbolic ecumenical ritual where eclogue meets georgic: 'we bent/ Our knees and cut the watery sod/ From the lazy-bed where slept a God/We couldn't count among our friends'. Here western landscape is inscribed with Irish religious apartheid. In his anti-pastoral 'Mayo Monologues', however, Longley assumes the imagined voices of local people to criticise the psycho-cultural deformities of a dystopian West. 'Self-heal', for example, is spoken by a girl recalling a maltreated boy who approached her sexually: 'I might have been the cow/Whose tail he would later dock with shears,/And he the ram tangled in barbed wire/That he stoned to death when they set him free.' Besides being where you don't live, the West (as in Synge) also provides ways of looking at how we all live. MacNeice's sequence 'A Hand of Snapshots', whose context is the emigration of the 1950s, schematises all frequenters of western landscape as The Left-Behind, The Back-Again, The Once-in-Passing and The Gone-Tomorrow. His photographic metaphor again insists on shifts of focus and angle which are ultimately aesthetic. By laying out dialectical perspectives from which the landscape might be conceived or imagined – permanent residence, expatriation, holiday visits – MacNeice recognises the potential of western pastoral to explore the metaphysical as well as cultural problematics of 'home': 'what now is merely mine, and soon will be no one's home' ('The Left-Behind'), 'Born here, I should have proved a different self' ('The Once-in-Passing').

Patrick Sheeran has attacked readings of Yeats's landscapes as colonial, inauthentic and reactionary. Trying to set his 'ancestral houses in a more humane context', he proposes that they exemplify Heideggerian 'dwelling': i.e. visions of 'peace in a protected place', the right to which has been won by cultivation as well as building. Sheeran's desire to transform Yeats the Settler into Yeats the Dweller fits Yeats's own graph of unease in 'In Memory of Major Robert Gregory'.[73] But if the Tower as symbolic dwelling oscillates between fortification and home, if 'almost settled' still covers all the edifices of western pastoral, 'dwelling' should not be construed too literally. Residual utopian microcosms, like their Revival precursors, are chiefly constituted by values, by inner geography. The tower builds in 'All those that manhood tried, or childhood loved/ Or boyish intellect approved'. And, as Gregory's death indicates, all human settlement is 'a brave oasis'. Often too homely for Yeats, 'home' is a more prominent word but equally moveable feast in Michael Longley's poetry. In 'The West', for example, Belfast and a familiar Mayo cottage mutually complicate each other's existence and meaning: 'I listen for news through the atmospherics,/A crackle of sea-wrack, spinning driftwood,/ Waves like distant traffic, news from home'. Yet the West retains its utopian horizon in symbolising the ideal earthly home that might be anywhere: 'finding my way for ever along/ The path to this cottage, its windows,/ Walls, sun and moon dials, home from home'. Paul Durcan, whose poetry visits the West from an implied Dublin rather than an implied Belfast, also writes a western poetry of 'home' in which, to quote Peter McDonald, 'origins and destinations have become relative, and, perhaps, of secondary importance'.[74] 'Going home to Mayo, Winter 1949' returns to (rural-Edenic) origins in that it remembers a childhood visit to 'my father's mother's house'. The memory marks a split: 'But home was not home and the moon could be no more outflanked/ Than the daylight nightmare of Dublin City'. Here the child-poet, for whom the towns on the way to Turlough are 'magic passwords into eternity', may be captured at a moment when the West engenders a new utopian cycle within which more poets from Catholic backgrounds will be driven to eclogue. 'Home' in Durcan's 'The Dublin-Paris-Berlin-Moscow Line', however, upsets the opposition of country and city, east-coast and west-coast

Ireland: 'From the shores of the Aran Islands/ To the foothills the
far side of the Caucasus/ These are the terraced streets/ That smell
of home to us.'

Poets from all backgrounds have found it easier to fabricate
spiritual homes than dear perpetual places out of western materials.
Halfway through 'Western Landscape' the question, 'How do we
find continuance/ Of our too human skeins of wish/ In this inhuman
effluence?' points in the mystical direction which persistently clings
to the aesthetics of western pastoral. The speaker-seeker identifies
with St Brendan and a long tradition of quests to 'undo/ Time in
quintessential West'. His theological excursus culminates in a quint-
essential definition of western pastoral itself: 'The west of Ireland/
Is brute and ghost at once'. This marks a post-Enlightenment post-
Darwinian gap between Spirit and Nature, together with the desire
to close it – to replace poetic consubstantiation with transubstanti-
ation, perhaps. However, the poem's overall tendency, as in 'O
grail of emerald passing light', reflects MacNeice's belief that the
poet must remain Lancelot the grail's seeker rather than Galahad
its finder: [75] 'Flitting evolving dissolving but never quitting...'

'Quintessential West', grail of Celtic cultists as well as poets, also
provokes anti-western pastoral. In 'The Mayo Tao', which begins
'I have abandoned the dream kitchens for a low fire/ and a pre-
scriptive/ literature of the spirit', Derek Mahon parodies the quest
for 'immanence' by measuring the western timelessness sought by
the urban poet against a meagre outcome:

> I have been working for years
>   on a four line poem
>   about the life of a leaf.
> I think it may come out right this winter.

Yet the poem treads a fine line between self-irony and self-epiphany:
'the mountain paces me/in a snow-lit silence'. Paul Durcan's
'Loosestrife in Ballyferriter' more robustly satirises a whole tradi-
tion of spiritual tourism:

> I stood in the delivery ward outside the Gallarus Oratory,
> Overtaken by coachload after coachload of tourists
> From Celtic, from Medieval, from Modern times,
> Expiring, only to be given birth to, in that small black door-space.

Like Mahon, Durcan is really attacking shallowly motivated west-
ern pilgrimages. 'Loosestrife in Ballyferriter' has a Gaelic refrain
which translates as 'The White Strand, the White Strand,/ Where is
my father, where is my mother?' Referring to the Blasket Islands, the
speaker asks: 'Was it the Irish who burned us out of our island

homes?' By invoking an ideal West as measure of the Republic's failings, Durcan sets the utopias of the 1890s against dystopian outcomes. 'Loosestrife' epitomises how his mockery or subversion of traditional tropes clears the ground for vision. First, he tears up the old western space-time maps by introducing trans-historical coach-tours or European and eastern vistas: the Caucasus, the title-poem of his first collection 'O Westport in the Light of Asia Minor', the 'French Ireland' that the rebellion of 1798 failed to produce by 'the scimitar shores of Killala Bay' ('Backside to the Wind'). Secondly, Durcan is unique in fusing the West as prelapsarian Eden ('*White Strand*') with the West as New Jerusalem ('French Ireland'). There may be Catholic theological residues in his easy equations of brute with ghost. In 'O Westport' the West becomes the locus for the Creation itself: 'And standing on the mountains of their dread [they] saw/The islands come up through the mists'. Thus poetry finds it hard to eliminate ghost from the West whose dystopian mode has reached its nadir in drama – not to mention the sitcom *Father Ted*. In Martin McDonagh's play *The Lonesome West* (1997) (the title is taken from Synge) the parish priest complains, just before committing suicide: 'Jeez. I thought Leenane was a nice place when first I turned up here, but no. Turns out it's the murder capital of fecking Europe.' [76] Unlike Durcan's West, McDonagh's appears almost wholly 'brute': material, materialist, desacralised and deromanticised. Eden (*The Lonesome West* concerns fratricidal brothers) and New Jerusalem are absences rather than potentialities. And if this is western anti-pastoral, McDonagh's *The Cripple of Inishmaan* is anti-western pastoral directed at Robert Flaherty's film *Man of Aran*. The play contrasts with Derek Mahon's attraction to Flaherty's Aran as the shrine of aesthetic desire: 'islands of dark ore'.

Mahon and Durcan, then, draw on western spiritual reserves – the one as a dimension of the aesthetic, the other as a dimension of the national. The late Seán Dunne makes the reserves themselves a site for unironical Tao or Zen. The Basho-like 'four-line poems' that constitute his sequence 'The Healing Island', in *Time and the Island* (1996), are also influenced by the religious ideas of Thomas Merton. Dunne's east-west fusion theology irradiates phenomena so intensely that the poetry appears to put human arrogance aside and draw readers deep into therapeutic mysteries:

> Flowers teem on ditch and wall.
> Packed as mussels, firm petals part.
> Frail stems teach the most:
> Thin as tissue, they outlast gales.

Des O'Rawe writes: '*Time and the Island* argues its case through poems which are, like Thomas Merton's motto for the truly spiritual life, "free *for* the world rather than free *from* it".' [77] Yet this echoes MacNeice on western missions: 'enter[ing] solitude once more to find communion/With other solitary beings, with the whole race of men' ('Donegal Triptych'). And here, in fact, western pastoral co-habits with the Marxist theory of Christopher Caudwell (see p.151). A significant shift in *Time and the Island*, however, is that its spiritual synthesis has absorbed ecology. The history outlined earlier explains why ecology should be a relatively new source or form of Irish pastoral theology, especially for poets from Catholic backgrounds, and why it should matter that Seán Lysaght calls his second collection *The Clare Island Survey* (1991). In fact, the contrasting titles of Lysaght's and Dunne's collections indicate that the ecological eclogue also veers between ghost and brute, its islands between shrine and Nature reserve. Yet Yeats prefigured the point where counting swans marks environmental anxiety. And, thanks to him, Beauty and Nature continue a significant dialogue in western pastoral. Ecology does not transform or replace, but extends and redefines, the pre-existing interplay between aesthetics, metaphysics and politics.

In his preface to a reissue (1997) of Praeger's *The Way That I Went* Michael Viney writes diplomatically:

> Fifty years ago in Ireland, being 'interested in nature' was largely the preserve of a minuscule group on the margin of mainstream society, and in the schools nature study was still all but crowded out by other priorities. Today's popular support for the goals of Birdwatch Ireland and the Irish Wildlife Trust along with... other groups with a stake in the conservation of nature, speak for a cultural enrichment which, for subtle historical reasons came late to this island. But the impulse for it was well-nurtured, if not actually planted in the national psyche by the book called *The Way That I Went*. [78]

Viney, author of the influential *Irish Times* column 'Another Life', can also take credit for steering 'the national psyche' (a phrase normally reserved for Famine commemoration) towards Nature and environmental awareness. In the Preface to *A Year's Turning* (1996), which concentrates twenty years into a quintessential western calendar, Viney judges that 'Thallabawn has taught us a relationship with nature, open equally to science and poetry, that is the moving spirit of this book.' [79] An Englishman, Viney has absorbed the literary, cultural and scientific traditions that conditioned Edward Thomas's poetry, and which continue to generate ecological theory and practice as well as literature. The same crossing of Irish western

pastoral with originally English modes and their 'Anglo-Irish' out-
reach can be detected in the prose of Tim Robinson, the poetry of
Michael Longley. There are some clear differences between this
pastoral hybrid and the Heaney-Wordsworth georgic. For instance,
it doubly problematises its own construction: wariness about in-
truding on other people's landscapes meshes with wariness about
human intrusion on Nature. Just as Thomas asks whether poetry
constitutes and models a holistic way of apprehending landscape,[80]
so in *Stones of Aran: Pilgrimage* (1986) Robinson agonises over the
'problem' of 'taking a single step as adequate to the ground it clears
as is the dolphin's arc to its wave':

> The dolphin's world…is endlessly more continuous and therefore pro-
> ductive of unity than ours, our craggy, boggy, overgrown and over-
> built terrain, on which every step carries us across geologies, biologies,
> myths, histories, politics etcetera, and trips us with the trailing *Rosa
> spinosissima* of personal associations.[81]

Robinson's pursuit of a 'wholeness beyond happiness', figured by
an impossibly holistic step, implicates the physics and metaphysics
of 'earth-dwelling' in the larger ecological sense. His intricate
journey round the perimeter of Arainn Mór parallels what 'walking'
means to Thomas: a fluid syntax of relations in time and space.
The step of the sentence quoted above also resembles MacNeice's
ever-frustrated voyage towards becoming 'part of a not to be parted
whole', except that to substitute a dolphin for St Brendan changes
(up to a point) the theological bearings. After *Pilgrimage* came *Stones
of Aran: Labyrinth* (1995), the two subtitles interpenetrating as
grail-quest and interior quest. In Longley's poetry the questing
traditions of western pastoral encounter images of birds, flowers
and animals which hover between endangered fact and tentatively
therapeutic symbol. In the 'Mayo Monologue' called by the flower-
name 'Self-heal', prospects of symbols 'breaking in flower' remain
doubtful. The title ironises the girl's failed attempt to teach 'the
names of flowers' to the disturbed boy. Again, as a political rather
than psychological resort, 'Bog Cotton' is 'useless…though it might
well bring to mind/ The plumpness of pillows, the staunching of
wounds'. As compared with MacNeice as well as Yeats, the ratio
between the aesthetic and the natural-historical has shifted in a
way that affects symbolic dispositions. MacNeice poses, even as he
precisely visualises, 'the heron in trance and in half-mourning'. His
images fall into sculpted ('sphinx's fist') or painterly ('emerald…light')
attitudes, however fragile. Not impressionist panoramas but environ-
mental microcosms, Longley's poems dwell on natural detail in a
way that adds an ecological horizon to western pastoral's unstable

aesthetics and problematic earthly home. This is also a politics of form, hovering between art and Nature, questioning human constructions as well as presence. 'Spring Tide', in which seawater destabilises habitats, ends with an apology for poetry:

> By a dry-stone wall in the dune slack
> The greenish sepals, the hidden blush
> And a lip's red veins and yellow spots –
> Marsh helleborine waiting for me
> To come and go with the spring tide.

Here the language of natural history outranks the language of art, thus reversing the Yeatsian order. Despite seeming likeness to the human body, a suggestion of female come-hither, the alien veins and 'yellow spots' begin to translate the literal fact of the orchid passively 'waiting' into an active rejection of anthropocentric, anthropomorphic poetics: 'waiting for me' raises false expectations in speaker and reader. Nor can common or uncommon wildflowers be taken for granted as in the Kavanagh universe.

None of the writers quoted above allows ecology to subsume (though it may include) all other artistic steps across the 'craggy, boggy, overgrown and overbuilt' terrain of western pastoral itself: Irish history would prevent this in any case. An old joke underlines the extent to which western landscape has attracted competition as well as interaction between epistemologies. In *The Book of the Burren* Cilian Roden tells how, in 1910, two unionist naturalists agreed to construe 'the blue Gentian, white Mountain Avens and red Bloody Cranesbills on a Burren hillside' as a miraculous apparition of the union jack in 'the western extremity of the United Kingdom'.[82] Foster/Chesney's *Nature in Ireland* interweaves natural history with economic, social and political history. Patrick Sleeman reports that 'during the brutal Cromwellian campaign, wolves were said to have increased, due to the general state of disorganisation'. Eoin Neeson shows how, after the Tudor conquest, 'the relationship between timber and economic dominance...played a profound part in subsequent historical development'.[83] Tim Robinson initially stands back from history to set Aran in geological time ('the geographies over which we are so suicidally passionate are, on this scale of events, fleeting expressions of the earth's face');[84] and poets, too, exploit western rocks to deflect political passions. Yet this is not escapism but strategy, to which other ecological perspectives also contribute. Just as winds of the Anglo-Irish war and Civil War shake Yeats's western shutters, just as the world wars have left undernoted traces, so the Northern Irish conflict has sometimes entered western pastoral to renew the dialectic between Utopia and dystopia that goes back to Virgil's first *Eclogue*: 'en quo discordia civis/ produxit miseros' – 'To such a pass has civil dissension brought us'.

Michael Longley's 'The Ice-cream Man' splits its screen between Belfast, where 'They murdered the ice-cream man on the Lisburn Road/ And you bought carnations to lay outside his shop', and a botanical visit to the Burren. He transmutes the latter into a wreath and litany of flower-names: 'I named for you all the wild flowers of the Burren/ I had seen in one day: thyme, valerian, loosestrife,/ Meadowsweet, tway blade, crowfoot, ling, angelica...' Here Irish pastoral touches base with its religious hinterland; as it does for similar tragic purposes in Seamus Heaney's 'The Strand at Lough Beg': 'I...gather up cold handfuls of the dew/ To wash you, cousin. I dab you clean with moss/ Fine as the drizzle out of a low cloud./ ...I plait/ Green scapulars to wear over your shroud.' Both elegies turn to the natural world for help with mourning and protest; both involve conundrums about Spirit and Nature. Yet a closer look might reveal metaphysical or theological differences – within the generic field of Irish pastoral poetry, within the common poetic ritual of grief.

'Something Wrong Somewhere?'
Louis MacNeice as Critic

1

I'll begin with a dozen quotations – some of MacNeice's *obiter dicta* on the limits and failings of literary criticism, especially in its response to poetry:

> The literary critic fails through being literary.[1]

> Marxists do not as a rule make helpful literary critics (exception: Christopher Caudwell).[2]

> All that a critic can do is lay stepping stones over the river.[3]

> The critic's view of art is essentially static; the artistic process is essentially dynamic.[4]

> Literary criticism's great vice is that it will take any individual poet as a pure specimen of any one tendency or attitude.[5]

> Criticism based on the assumption that a poem is a mere translation of facts outside itself is vicious criticism.[6]

> the man who reads a poem and likes it, is doing something far too subtle for criticism.[7]

> Critics often tend to write as if a condition were the same thing as a cause.[8]

> the big critic, who writes whole books, is often plugging some perverse general theory of poetry which leaves no room for seven poets out of ten. The little critic, who writes book reviews, seems compelled, partly by lack of space, partly by laziness, to prefer the snap generalisation, the ready-made label, to any decent down-to-earth analysis.[9]

> In a world where most of the sceptics are cold pike and most of the enthusiasts melting jellyfish, [Randall] Jarrell stands out as someone well equipped with not only a heart but with several grains of salt.[10]

> According to my reviewers, taken collectively (and I am confining myself to more or less favourable reviews), I am a writer they can place quite simply: I am a surprisingly feminine, essentially masculine poet, whose gift is primarily lyrical and basically satirical, swayed by and immune to politics, with and without a religious sense, and I am technically slap-dash and technically meticulous, with a predilection for flat and halting and lilting Swinburnian rhythms, and I have a personal and impersonal approach, with a remarkably wide and consistently narrow range, and I have developed a good deal and I have not developed at all.[11]

> Quotations are too often used either to save thought or to show off.[12]

My penultimate quotation might cause a cold-pike sceptic to sneer that MacNeice's gripes stem from the critical reception of his own poetry. But he does cite 'more or less favourable reviews', and goes on to say (this is 1949): 'Most living poets have been similarly treated by reviewers. Can something be wrong somewhere?'

Discussion of MacNeice's criticism has mainly asked how it serves, and serves to explicate, his poetry. For instance, one line of commentary ties it to his central role in assimilating and challenging Yeats's aesthetic.[13] This essay is less concerned with the themes that plot MacNeice's artistic direction or with the critical strategies that help him to negotiate anxieties of influence (although both will crop up) than with his broader practice as critic in a less specialised era. Practice generates theory – his usual, but not invariable, order of priorities – when he thinks about poetry or when the conceptual inadequacies of poetry criticism provoke him. A subtext here may be the encounter between a classicist/ philosopher and failures to take responsibility for literary-critical language. At the beginning of *The Poetry of W.B. Yeats* (1941) MacNeice underlines the provisionality of his terms:

> The literary critic's judgements are never more than approximately true. To make his points he has often to over-stress them. Sometimes, especially when I am taking – or refusing to take – Yeats at his word (his own statements about poetry are usually unqualified), I may seem to be forgetting that a poem – or a poet – is a complex unity, that is, complex but a unity (or a unity but complex). I may seem to make a facile use of such concepts as 'emotion', 'personality', 'system', 'belief', using them with an unwarrantable rigidity. For this I apologise in advance.[14]

> Most literary critics must find themselves repeatedly on or over the verge of self-contradiction. This is because criticism implies the application of standards of a certain rigidity; if the critic relaxes his standards too far, he is lost in flux. But if he does not relax them, he is certain to be unjust to the particular subjects of his criticism, to be guilty – if only on a small scale – of the sin of Procrustes.[15]

Although MacNeice writes about other literary topics (fiction, drama, translation, academic books, most kinds of Irish writing), poetry is usually on the critical mind that Richard Ellmann terms 'always discontented with its own formulations'.[16] In 'Pleasure in Reading: Woods to Get Lost In' (1961) MacNeice says: 'Of the works that I "turn to time and time again" the great majority are in verse. It is like having a taste for distilled liquors, natural in someone who is in the distillery business.'[17] All creative artists are, deep down, self-serving critics, although some disguise it better than others. Yet the ratio between subjectivity, or the selfish gene, and objectivity varies from poet-critic to poet-critic. They may open a narrower or wider window on perennial questions. We do not trust them equally as guides to the best malt. Nor do MacNeice's irony and frank polemic seduce us into reading his criticism naively, as melting-jellyfish scholars read the self-representations of contemporary poets. The current dichotomy, or perhaps collusion, between hard theory and soft criticism is not only a new guise for pike and jellyfish. It is a fulfilment of trends against which MacNeice warns.

I want to develop this proposition with reference to four related points: what the 'critical faculty' means to MacNeice; some literary-critical positions shared by MacNeice and Auden in the later 1930s; MacNeice's take on the intertwined issues of poetic tradition and literary generation; and a recurrent motif in his writings about poetry – a motif which is dialectical, as he said all criticism should be: that is, the tension between his sense of form and his openness to anarchism, to writing that breaks all the rules, including his own. Hence his delight in the eclecticism of Apuleius: 'It is hard to find a writer who combines such dissimilar qualities – elegance and earthiness, euphuism and realism, sophistication and love of folklore, Rabelaisian humour and lyrical daintiness, Platonism and belief in witchcraft, mysticism and salty irony.' Yet, he continues: '[Apuleius] was predominantly an artist; the *Golden Ass* is not just a mixture but a blend.'[18] Like other critical formulations by MacNeice, this bears on postmodernism, form and meaning.

2

MacNeice's criticism is conditioned by a variety of material, literary and intellectual contexts. His most substantial essays on poetry, 'Poetry Today' and 'Subject in Modern Poetry', and the two full-length critical books, *Modern Poetry* (1938) and *The Poetry of W.B. Yeats*, are products of the decade when he was making his name and his early aesthetic, and during which he was briefly tempted to become a full-time writer. His Clark lectures, assembled in the posthumous *Varieties of Parable*, were delivered after he had left the BBC staff to go freelance. His more occasional reviews and articles of the 1940s and 1950s are the critical memoranda of a man other-wise occupied – as poet, broadcaster, writer for radio, translator, adept of the George salon. The important essay 'Experiences with Images' (1949) is an exception, although that, too, seems to be 'required writing' in Philip Larkin's sense. But if the opening sen-tences respond to a commission, they also illustrate four character-istics of MacNeice's critical interventions: their analytical thrust,

their dialectical structure, their self-consciousness about the kinds of
authority they claim, their air of being proved on his creative pulses:

> How do I use images? In trying to answer this question (and I shall
> merely scratch the surface) I find it hard to be honest. There are two
> such strong but opposite temptations – to oversimplify, make it all
> sound neat-and-easy (here comes the Master Craftsman counting his
> brass tacks) and to make it all sound alarmingly but glamorously mys-
> terious (here comes Inspiration falling off her tripod).[19]

MacNeice wrote for periodicals whose very names now 'accen-
tuate a thirst', to quote his 'Elegy for Liberal Poets'. Alan Heuser's
bibliography lists *New Verse, Horizon, The Listener*. The *London
Magazine* and *New Statesman and Nation* (the latter less recognisably)
persist. Here he could count on a Left-liberal readership for whom
literature, culture and politics interpenetrated. This was still more
or less the case when he died in 1963. In a recent essay on F.R.
Leavis, 'The Critic as Journalist', Stefan Collini asks:

> where does cultural criticism happen? Where do those debates take place
> in which a society's conception of itself is fought out and fought over, in
> which standards of argument, of intellectual and aesthetic excellence,
> even of general human flourishing, are articulated and brought to bear on
> the transient issues of the day?...there must be a strong presumption
> that different answers would obtain for different times and places. At
> present, for example, much of this criticism may be carried on in media
> other than print journalism, and there is also some reason to think that
> literature may be less looked to as a source of value or legitimation
> than when 'literary scholarship' first established itself. None the less,
> the starting-point for this essay is the suggestion that for the middle
> decades of the twentieth century in Britain one particularly plausible
> short answer to this general question would be 'literary journalism'.[20]

During these decades the vocabularies of 'big critic' and 'little
critic' were not as distinct as they have since become. Noting the
tendency, MacNeice laments – in the tone of one glad to be an
academic *manqué* – that Yeats, Shaw and Joyce 'should now be at
the mercy of the evergrowing tribes of humourless scholars'.[21] He
was not routinely hostile to academic criticism. In 1952 he began a
review of Rosamond Tuve's *A Reading of George Herbert* by regret-
ting a dumbing down of poetry: 'Between the two World Wars,
when poets still thought it was proper to learn and to think...'[22]
Like other poets of his generation he was intellectually stimulated
by I.A. Richards, if partly to disagreement. He wrote in 1940: 'Not
that I accept Richards's complete severance of poetry from beliefs;
a poem flows from human life with which beliefs are inevitably
entangled'.[23] Auden-MacNeice's 'Last Will and Testament' has fun
with Richards's scientific model of literary criticism:

Item, to I.A. Richards who like a mouse
Nibbles linguistics with the cerebral tooth
We leave a quiet evening in a boarding-house

Where he may study the facts of birth and death
In their inexplicable oddity
And put a shilling in the slot for brains and breath.

The poets also bequeath 'Our humour, all we think is funny,/ To
Dr Leavis and almost every psycho-analyst'. Nonetheless, academic
criticism has a presence and a role in the cultural world they are
sending up. MacNeice's own critical principles coincide with Rich-
ards's stress on understanding, objectification and demystification
as opposed to 'preconceptions', 'stock responses' and deference to
'authority'. In 'Poetry, the Public, and the Critic' (1949) MacNeice
accepts that Richards definitively 'exposed the pitfalls that trapped
his Cambridge undergraduates when they passed judgments on
poetry', and continues: 'Those pits are as wide as ever – "stock
responses", the obsession with "message", etc – and even profes-
sional critics fall easily, not to say happily, into them.' [24] Tuve's
book influenced his 'parable' poems and his ideas about parable, as
did Graham Hough's *Preface to 'The Faerie Queene'* (1962). And
he knew that poets could be as daft as academics. Writing (for the
New Statesman) about an amusingly controversial election for the
Oxford Chair of Poetry in 1961, he says: 'That either Graves or
Leavis is likely to commit absurd generalisations and injustices in
his lectures does not really matter. What undergraduates need is
provocation.' Yet the same article restates MacNeice's deep resis-
tance to Oxford mentalities: 'I marvelled once again at what Oxford
does to her captors or infiltrators. Whether they come from the
Redbrick enclaves or from Cambridge, they seem to pick up over-
night the soft-spoken malice, the ostentatiously throw-away display
of inside information, the heavy-lidded thin-lipped irony, the
addiction to verbal arabesques, the exquisite verdigris of cynicism,
that have traditionally characterised this city of sneering spires.' [25]
    Certainly this is remote from MacNeice's own critical manner.
The overlaps between Heuser's *Selected Literary Criticism of Louis
MacNeice* and *Selected Prose* (not only the reviews in both volumes)
suggest that, for MacNeice, literary criticism is never a detachable
category. His radio scripts involved literary themes and adaptations;
he put contemporary poetry on the air. Similarly, the literary-critical
stratum of his poetry does not just flag up reflexiveness or inter-
textuality for the benefit of academe. MacNeice's eclogues enter the
debate about literature and society in the 1930s.[26] *Autumn Journal*
more obliquely mingles literary and social criticism as it re-reads a

variety of texts in the light of Munich. These include the classical canon, the Bible, Yeats's 'Meditations in Time of Civil War', *The Waste Land*, Auden's 'Spain', his own earlier poetry. A different example of literary criticism holistically entering poetry, and conceiving poetry holistically, is the tender *Dunciad* 'Elegy for Minor Poets'. Here poetry figures less as 'Inspiration' or the work of a 'Master Craftsman' than as a function and analogue of life itself:

> Who were too happy or sad, too soon or late...
>
> Who were lost in many ways, through comfort, lack of knowledge,
> Or between women's breasts, who thought too little, too much,
> Who were the world's best talkers, in tone and rhythm
> Superb, yet as writers lacked a sense of touch,
> So either gave up or just went on and on –
> Let us salute them now their chance is gone...

When MacNeice defines one enemy of promise as living 'in the wrong time or the wrong place' he obliquely expresses gratitude (this is the mid 1940s) to his own historical situation which has underlined the unpredictable chemistry between talent and contingency.

'Elegy for Minor Poets' is linked with 'Western Landscape' and 'Woods' in its use of pastoral tropes to reflect on poetry. MacNeice allegorises the creative process as a journey through implicitly English and Irish landscapes: 'Who often found their way to pleasant meadows/ Or maybe once to a peak...Some who go dancing through dark bogs are lost'. In 'Woods' this mixed terrain is given more psycho-cultural than aesthetic contours: 'Each wood is the mystery and the recurring shock/ Of its dark coolness is a foreign voice'. The poem represents its author's sensibility as imprinted by the interplay between physical environment, childhood and adolescent emotion, reading ('the picture-book', Malory, Keats, *A Midsummer Night's Dream*, Herrick). 'Western Landscape', as we have seen (p.123), manifests and debates the metaphysical extreme of MacNeice's aesthetic spectrum. What all three poems share as acts of criticism (which is not all they are) is a sense of poetry as entangled with community, history, culture and autobiography, though not reducible to any of these. MacNeice's autobiographical prose, as well as poetry, crosses into literary criticism; for example, the satirical passage (in *The Strings are False*) on Stephen Spender's *Trial of a Judge* and its reception by communists. This includes a portrait of a woman who attacks the play's liberal tendency: 'She spoke precisely and quietly, never muffing a phrase (you could see her signing death-warrants).'[27] Conversely, *Modern Poetry*, subtitled 'A Personal Essay', incorporates 'literary autobiography, i.e. the history of my own reactions to and demands from poetry, in reading and writing it, over a number of years starting from early childhood'.[28]

This self-interrogating 'case-book' method (redeployed in 'Experiences with Images') also reflects the empiricist bent of the mind 'discontented with its own formulations'. MacNeice, philosophically trained, took neither the premises nor the structures of poetry for granted. In one dimension his poems ceaselessly probe relations between metaphysics and aesthetics, perception and form, flux and pattern.[29] Thus he was not against theory, but against its propensity to arrogance, to absence of discontent: 'And oh how much I liked the Concrete Universal,/ I never thought that I should/ Be telling them vice-versa/ That they can't see the trees for the wood' (*Autumn Journal* XIII). In 'Poetry Today' (1935) he binds aesthetic theory to practical trial and error: 'To banish theory is as much of a half-truth and a whole lie as to make theory omnipotent. The functions of theory are propaedeutic, prophylactic, and corrective; just as in learning to play tennis. When it comes to the point, the work is done with the hands.'[30] By the same token, the critic should not be 'more interested in producing a watertight system than in the objects which are his data'.[31] In *Modern Poetry* MacNeice maintains that a 'poem is not an abstracted circle, but rather a solid ball'.[32] So if we, as critics, are to get our hands on that ball, we will have to 'descend from metaphysics into history'.[33] More historicist than postmodernist in intellectual temper, MacNeice argues that the 'new similarities' produced by poetic conjunctions can only be appreciated with reference to the old similarities current 'at a particular time'.[34] He regards Marxist criticism as mostly too metaphysical for this task.

In part owing to his intellectual tussles with Anthony Blunt, MacNeice usually represents aestheticism and Marxist literary theory (mid-century style) as inversions of each other. This is so when he calls for 'a responsible criticism' in 'Poetry, the Public, and the Critic' (1949):

> most critics pass by on the other side. But then most critics, unlike creative artists, are snobs and will only preach to the converted. This is true not only of the aesthetic critic who prefers to leave the 'average reader' on the other side of a gulf, but also of the Marxist critic who says that nothing can be done about the gulf until there has been a revolution.[35]

In the same essay MacNeice insists that critics need to be *more* responsible than poets. Whereas anarchist poets may be allowable, 'there is not much place for the anarchist critic'. He approves E.M. Forster's view of criticism's job as 'education through precision'.[36] Elsewhere MacNeice calls verse itself 'a precision instrument'.[37] So criticism should aim at being precise about precisions. Similarly, it should be critical about a criticism: i.e., literature's 'criticism of life'. MacNeice has no difficulty with Matthew Arnold's definition, given sharper point by the 1930s. In *Modern Poetry* he declares it 'part of a poet's legitimate business to say what he thinks are the best or the next best goods for man'.[38] Accordingly, it is part of a critic's legitimate business to evaluate such value-judgements. This demand, however, is not met when critics neglect their duty of precision towards the artistic matrix; when they assume that there is 'a stock set of answers...to a stock set of questions'; and when they acquire the 'superficial habit of fastening on something in a poem which can be easily labelled and then making [their] own label the differentia of the poem'.[39] In the introductory chapter to *The Poetry of W.B. Yeats* MacNeice contrasts Yeats and Rupert Brooke, as he considers relations between a poem, 'the life of the poet', and 'the life outside [the poet]'.

> Brooke's paeans to war *are*, on analysis, self-contradictory; they are a sentimental falsification that, unlike the lover's, has no profound natural sanction. The fact that many of his contemporaries agreed with Brooke does not vindicate his poems. It merely widens the basis of the lie...If we now turn to Yeats, we will find that he also at times – and also from sentimental motives – misrepresented the world in which he was living. But it seems to me that there is an important difference between his approach and Brooke's. Brooke, under the mask of realism, flatly asserts that something which is bad is good; what is more, he trumpets his mistaken belief in the manner of one who wishes to convert others. Yeats, who repudiated realism and does not use the tone of a crusader, may present certain facts coloured or distorted by his own partisan feelings but he allows the reader to see that this presentation is founded on an 'as if'.[40]

Here MacNeice practices and proposes a fine critical balance in which aesthetics inform history and ethics, and *vice versa*. This is "value-judgment" in a comprehensive sense.

The Poetry of W.B. Yeats already corrects the 1930s half-truth that 'a poem must be *about* something'.[41] By 1960 MacNeice had expelled the last traces of reportage or journalism from his creative and critical systems. His Clark lectures conclude with a salute to 'good parable writers' for being concerned with 'the kind of truth that cannot be, or can hardly be, expressed in other ways'.[42] Yet if his stress has decisively shifted to parabolic 'inner conflict' or 'inner light', he 'still holds that a poet should look at, feel about and think about the world around him'.[43] He does not anticipate, in both senses of the verb, the latter-day concordat between Marxism and postmodernism. Despite his admiration for Beckett, he finds Golding's 'world of moralities and story-lines' a relief after the

metaphysical extreme of *The Unnamable* (which he compares to
Hindu esotericism and Christian 'accounts of the Negative Way').[44]
At this yogi end of the spectrum there can be no criticism of life.
The political 1930s, it seems, indelibly stamped MacNeice's critical
attitudes and attitude to criticism. The well-known Preface to
Modern Poetry declares the term itself integral to poetry. Here
MacNeice sharpens up Arnold, as well as Horace's *utile* and *dulce*,
as he envisages the critical spirit moving vigilantly between the
aesthetic, ethical and socio-political spheres:

> The poet...is both critic and entertainer (and his criticism will cut no
> ice unless he entertains,...Propaganda, the extreme development of
> 'critical' poetry, is also the defeat of criticism...The writer today should
> not be so much the mouthpiece of a community...as its conscience, its
> critical faculty, its generous instinct.

The asyndeton makes the last-named qualities permeate one another,
with 'critical faculty' intermediary between conscience and gener-
osity. Conversely, when *Autumn Journal* foresees that the propaganda
war against Hitler will mean becoming, like the enemy, 'uncritical,
vindictive', the latter state derives from the former. 'Criticism' is
the last word of *Modern Poetry*: 'When the crisis comes, poetry may
for the time be degraded or even silenced, but it will reappear, as
one of the chief embodiments of human dignity, when people once
more have time for play and criticism.'[45]

'Responsible criticism', then, interprets and parallels the respon-
sibilities of poetry itself; and its course, whereby aesthetics never
quite loses touch with ethics, appears contrary to the Negative
Way. During the war MacNeice thought that Auden had sold out
in saying: 'Others must be regarded aesthetically and only oneself
ethically.' This is because 'Ethics presupposes not only judgement
upon others but calculated interference with them'.[46] It is relevant to
note why MacNeice warms to certain critics, literary and otherwise.
He likes precision, argument, conviction, resistance to (con)tem-
porary fashions, refusal to fudge. Thus he praises T.S. Eliot's 'pre-
cisely tentative essays' (despite their 'catchwords') for promoting a
'general movement towards clarity and rigour'; Honor Tracy for
'saying a great many things which few Irishmen would have the
guts and few Englishmen the wits to put down in black and white';
Tuve for putting Herbert in context and for bridging the 'pseudo-
historical gulf' which had made it impossible to read Spenser;
Randall Jarrell, in *Poetry and the Age*, for 'stick[ing] his neck out'
and 'tell[ing] you exactly which poems by anyone he thinks are
his best, he will quote from these abundantly, and he will tell you
exactly why he admires what he quotes'.[47]

3

Years earlier, this had been MacNeice's own method with Auden and other contemporaries. It exemplifies the MacNeice-Auden relationship (though not necessarily its balance of literary power) that MacNeice's response to Auden is on the record, whereas relatively little runs the other way. Auden's *Selected Poems* of MacNeice is a significant – and, of course, post-dated – exception. His selection shows taste (in recognising that the late 1940s to the late 1950s was a dull stretch for MacNeice), but not always insight (in largely overlooking the Irish dimension). According to Craig Raine,[48] the Faber files disclose that MacNeice outsold Auden in the 1930s. However, it was not the common reader who canonised Auden, but a literary-Left grouping whose agenda was itself informed by English national priorities. Auden left England partly because he feared he would be co-opted by the Establishment which eventually absorbed most of his contemporaries, though its Anglo-American cousin may have sometimes caught him. Of course, Auden's groupies misread Auden, just as they could not read some dimensions of MacNeice, and critical reception during the decade generally missed the significant reciprocities and differences between the poets. Again, although Auden writes with splendid precision about poetry – witness the essay on D.H. Lawrence – his characteristic critical mode became aphorism rather than analysis (MacNeice calls *The Enchafèd Flood* 'a book of typically staccato criticism').[49] He also diversified into a greater range of cultural commentary after moving to the US. Even during the 1930s, MacNeice's essays and reviews, as contrasted with the prose in *The English Auden*, more often work with the hands and work on poetry. While Auden also generalised brilliantly about education and psycho-analysis, MacNeice was defining 'the new poetry', and defining it in more concrete terms than those emanating from the politically inflected Auden-worship, or self-worship, of other young poet-critics.

There is tension between MacNeice's sense of where Day Lewis and Spender fail and his need to affirm a poetic dynamic not exclusively of Auden's making. Obviously one reason why he wrote about poetry was to protect his own work against the 'ready-made labels' and 'stock set of questions' that reviewers brought from their reading of Auden and of the times. Hence, in part, the auto-biographical strategy of *Modern Poetry*, which allows him to cite and quote himself for illustrative purposes. In the earlier essay 'Poetry Today' MacNeice calls Spender 'a naif who uses communism as a frame for his personal thrills' and remarks that Day Lewis...has

committed lamentable ineptitudes while pleading for the cause',
although he praises the innovative qualities in their less pretentious
work.[50] He notes the pressures of the Zeitgeist – not least, literary
hype – on all the poets, including Auden:

> Auden's great asset is curiosity...He reads the newspapers and samples
> ordnance maps. He has gusto, not literary gusto like Ezra Pound, but
> the gusto which comes from an unaffected (almost ingenuous) interest
> in people, politics, careers, science, psychology, landscape and mere
> sensations. He has a sense of humour. To say he is an Aeschylus as
> some people have done, is merely stupid and might encourage him to be
> pompous. His job is to go on observing things from his very unusual
> angle and recording them...in his very individual manner.[51]

In *Modern Poetry* this repositioning of Auden and the poetic
movement in MacNeicean terms becomes more explicit. Whereas
Day Lewis, in *A Hope for Poetry* (1934), had seen the post-war poet
as 'appealing above all for the creation of a society in which the
real and living contact between man and man may again become
possible',[52] MacNeice does not stray into socio-political speculation.
He concentrates on changes in diction, rhythm, imagery, and rela-
tions with readers. These changes, initiated earlier in the century,
have taken a new direction – rather than revolutionary turn – in
the 1930s. He calls Auden and Spender 'participants' (as contrasted
with Eliot, Pound and Empson) because they are 'more interested
in the world of concrete people'. Discussing 'obscurity' and the
effect of audience on structure, he says:

> On the whole, modern poetry is becoming more lucid, and that because
> its subject is less esoteric. The suggestions of the Symbolists may still
> be occasionally used, but for an end outside themselves. On the other
> hand, rhetoric (which the Symbolists banned) will be used, as by Auden,
> but similarly not for its own sake – not as it was used by so many Latin
> poets. True rhetoric presupposes a certain scale of values, certain con-
> ceptions of good and evil. Such a scale of values, however uncertain
> and fluctuating, is implicit in the poetry of Auden and Spender.[53]

Although *Modern Poetry,* according to MacNeice's later view, still
over-stresses 'the half-truth that a poem must be *about* something',
meaning is conceived as a function of 'true rhetoric' as opposed to
detachable subject-matter. Thus he says of diction: 'modern poets
often use terms borrowed from various spheres of technical writing
– psychological, scientific, or sociological. Such language is valid
provided the poet is himself in a position to use it naturally and
provided the ideal normal reader can be expected to understand it.'[54]
Ultimately, a sense of the times (which remains imperative) depends
on the sense of timing encoded in artistic calculation: 'it is desirable
that poets like these should write honestly, their poetry keeping

pace with their lives and with their beliefs as affecting their lives, neither lagging behind in an obsolete romanticism nor running ahead to an assurance too good to be true'.[55] So the shifting site of poetry can be found somewhere between Eden and Utopia.

Modern Poetry ratifies the aesthetic convergence of MacNeice and Auden as they 'rode and joked and smoked' in Iceland. (This interlude recalls Robert Frost and Edward Thomas in August 1914.) *Letters from Iceland* is a central 'critical' text of the 1930s because it pivots on relations between poetry, literary criticism and history. If MacNeice likes to interweave criticism *in* poetry with criticism *of* poetry, or presses on generic boundaries, the results are both distinctive and part of a wider collaborative project – not just with Auden. Thirties texts do not spare literature when they criticise systems and institutions: Gordon Comstock's brooding on the hierarchy of bookshop shelves in *Keep the Aspidistra Flying* ('Dead stars above, damp squibs below'); the mutually ironic inter-play of English history and English literary idioms in Virginia Woolf's *Between the Acts*. Leaving aside Marxist dismissals of "bourgeois" form, what differentiates thirties critique from current theory is that it usually seeks not to disprove but to improve or prove literature. MacNeice writes at the beginning of *The Poetry of W.B. Yeats*:

> War does not prove that ["escapist" or "realist" poetry] is better or worse than the other; it attempts to disprove both. But poetry must not be disproved. If war is the test of reality, then all poetry is unreal; but in that case unreality is a virtue. If, on the other hand, war is a great enemy of reality, although an incontestable fact, then reality is something which is not exactly commensurable with facts.[56]

Letters from Iceland does not disprove poetry even if it dismantles textual hierarchy in the spirit of Auden's 'Letter to Lord Byron': 'The pious fable and the dirty story/ Share in the total literary glory'. 'Iceland' figures as a verbal free-for-all with contributions from the sagas, proverbial lore, travellers' tales, geological and sociological reports, a parish register, guidebooks, Nazi doctrine ('*Für uns Island ist das Land*'), awful recipes, the poets' own multi-generic writings. As Tom Paulin has shown,[57] in disclaiming literary authority they deepen their critique of fascism: Auden's 'ogre, dragon, what you will', MacNeice's 'shouting wall of flesh'. Yet, of course, positions are thereby taken. 'The dirty story' as ironical collage is a strike against ominous 'unreality'. Collage democratises rather than rela-tivises a text whose epistolary mode, dialogic impulse and formal choices declare poetry an art of communication. Thus popular or non-literary culture appears neither for its own sake nor to depose,

in blanket terms, "the category of literature". Sometimes it marks a
vital solidarity, sometimes a morbid symptom: 'We hope one honest
conviction may at last be found/ For Alexander Korda and the
Balcon Boys/ And the Stavisky Scandal in picture and sound//
We leave to Alfred Hitchcock with sincerest praise/ Of *Sabotage*'
('Last Will and Testament'). Critical discrimination cannot relax
in any cultural sphere. Nor is it enough 'To give his ogreship the
raspberry/ Only when his gigantic back is turned'. 'Subversion', that
much abused term, means something. For example, Auden's witty
history of poetry gets serious, or discloses its seriousness, when he
queries the tendency of *fin-de-siècle* and modernist aesthetics:

> So started what I'll call the Poet's Party:
>   (Most of the guests were painters, never mind) –
> The first few hours the atmosphere was hearty,
>   With fireworks, fun, and games and every kind:
>   All were enjoying it, no one was blind;
> Brilliant the speeches improvised, the dances,
> And brilliant, too, the technical advances...
>
> Today, alas, that happy crowded floor
>   Looks very different: many are in tears:
> Some have retired to bed and locked the door;
>   And some swing madly from the chandeliers;
>   Some have passed out entirely in the rears;
> Some have been sick in corners; the sobering few
> Are trying hard to think of something new.

This agrees with various judgements by MacNeice on the 1890s
and after. His attack on 'Pure Form' in 'Eclogue for Christmas' is
elaborated in his critical prose: 'The nineties poets did to some
extent criticise life, but their own lives were both limited and
artificial, and the small portion of them, which on a strict aesthetic
censorship they admitted into their poetry, was still more so';
'Samarcand and the [Georgian] linnets were consolations for the
armchair. So, though superficially very different, were the poems of
the Imagists. Imagism was a branch from the stump of Pure Form
– a salutary movement in that it insisted on clarity and precision
...but itself escapist and bad in that the imagists had nothing to
say. One must be clear and precise *about something.*'[58]

A new collection of essays, *Rewriting the Thirties: Modernism and
After* seeks to 'challenge the persistent aftermyth of the thirties as
a homogeneous anti-modernist decade'. If the myth is too simple,
although its phrasing here seems questionable, so is 'rewriting' the
thirties (in an oddly Whig spirit) as 'a troubled but symptomatic
transitional phase between modernist and postmodernist writing,
art and politics'.[59] As regards poetry: its practitioners, of course,

are not tethered to single decades. Lively aesthetic dialectics con-
tinued between Yeats (whom I do not reckon a "modernist"), Eliot,
Pound and younger poets whose horizons were European in new
ways. The dialectic, however, was neither homogeneous nor resolved.
While the huge influence of *The Waste Land* cannot be denied,
neither can the reaction against the poem's aesthetic (not just the
vulgar Marxist reaction) nor the 'rewriting' of Eliot's scenario in
explicitly political or religious directions. Current attempts to make
the British 1930s, especially Auden, more "modernist" may involve
special pleading, as when Stan Smith terms *The Orators* a post-
modernist assault on the 'universalising pretensions of modernism'
that 'cocks a snook at the metropolitan high priests of culture'.[60]
We can discuss *The Orators* – as we can the ironically metropoli-
tan, tactically localist, ethically universalist *Letters from Iceland* –
without requiring the vocabulary of postmodernism; before which
it was possible to cock snooks or give raspberries or prolong
undergraduate anarchism, and for readers to get the point. Some
approving definitions of postmodernism as deconstructive play
among the rubble, or with the rubble, might consider how *Letters
from Iceland* employs and tests 'the airy manner'. Dissolving the
British 1930s into a mid-century 'transitional' phase (and so eliding
'the English Auden' into 'the American Auden') erases the decade's
distinctiveness as a time when few writers could evade a heightened
consciousness of history, any more than can subsequent readings.
    That applies to Eliot[61] or Woolf as much as to Orwell, Auden and
MacNeice. And if those writers who survived would change tack
again, the Auden who influenced the New York School, for instance,
still carried some 1930s baggage (Byron was important to Frank
O'Hara, too). Insofar as it concerns poetry, the argument about
whether "postmodernism" is modernism by the same means, or a
successor that has lightened up, can be referred to the dialectical
(generic and formal) diversity of the 1930s, not only in Britain. As
the clash between Woolf and MacNeice (see below) indicates, gen-
erational vantage-points make a difference. 'Transitional', like
'troubled', is a euphemism. Both adjectives cancel history and liter-
ary history to embrace the prestige of modernism/postmodernism
in aptly atemporal style: a manoeuvre that could return us on a
looptape to the 1890s. Strangely, even leftwing critics succumb.
David Bromwich, however, has compared 'the Marxist-postmodern
encounter' to the German Communists' attack on social democracy
'in order to stage a purer confrontation with the Nazis: a strategy
that at its first trial did not work out well'.[62] And, writing from the
Left, Alex Callinicos in the opening sentence of *Against Postmodernism*

echoes Auden on 'the Poet's Party': 'This book is an attempt to
challenge the strange mixture of cultural and political pessimism
and light-minded playfulness with which – in a more than usually
farcical reprise of the apocalyptic mood at the end of the last cen-
tury – much of the contemporary Western intelligentsia apparently
intends to greet our own *fin de siècle*.'[63] Callinicos notes the current
exhaustion of avant-garde radicalism in its political mode, and this
is exactly where the 1930s came in, where forms took different
turns: 'the sobering few/ Are trying hard to think of something
new'. Whatever political radicalism may reside in art need not
depend on modernist rupture any more than on social realism –
the collapse of the Soviet Union has accelerated the ideolological
flight from the latter to the former. And, given what happened to
poetry in that quarter, the opportunistic pact between Marxism
and literary postmodernism is bad news for MacNeice's 'critical
faculty'. For the 1930s poets (with their eye on the "war poets",
too) relations between the politics of form and forms of politics
were cast into a fresh kaleidoscope. At one moment modernist rel-
ativism may be critique; at another, it may be convention.

MacNeice's 'Epilogue' to their shared book fixes and dramatises
the historical moment of aesthetic consensus between himself and
Auden: 'Still I drink your health before/ The gun-butt raps upon
the door.' Their consensus turns on the difficult imperatives of
audience and community; on the necessary fusion of entertain-
ment with criticism (Auden's 'parable art'); and on how to read –
and continue – the history of poetry in the twentieth century.
Letters from Iceland is a channel between MacNeice's mid-thirties
essays and eclogues on the one hand, *Modern Poetry* and *Autumn
Journal* on the other. 'Letter to Lord Byron', which epitomises
the book's liaisons between literary and social criticism, certainly
influenced MacNeice, although in *Modern Poetry* he blends his
own idiom with Auden's when he calls the poem 'a mass of con-
temporary criticism, autobiography and gossip' in an 'elastic form,
able to carry…discursive comments…on a world of flux and con-
tradiction'.[64] 'Letter to Lord Byron' prompted the different elasticity
of *Autumn Journal*, as did the tonal togetherness of 'Last Will and
Testament'. This 1930s 'ending' combines saturnalia, foreboding,
apologia and benediction in a cultural critique that implicates the
poet-testators. After Iceland, MacNeice reviewed Auden's *Look
Stranger!* and *Oxford Book of Light Verse* (dedicated to E.R. Dodds).
His review of the former praises Auden for his capacity to develop,
for exhibiting 'that criticism of life which is the function of a major
poet', for his 'eye which keeps the balance between emotion and

intelligence', for his entertainment-value, and for having 'something to write about'.[65] He welcomes the *Oxford Book* as representing poetry's 'many-sidedness', calls Auden 'one of the few living poets whose poetry can walk in the street without falling flat on its face', and concludes: 'As a comment on poetry or the nature of poetry or the function or anything-else-you-like of poetry, this book is worth a hundred laboured volumes of literary criticism.'[66]

But it was not a matter of MacNeice's criticism propagating Auden's values. Discussion of Auden's late-thirties re-alignment overlooks the close exchange between the poets at this period: an exchange which, up to a point, meant that they changed places. Their convergence helped MacNeice to be more political (critical) in his poetry, helped Auden (after his Spanish apotheosis) to be less so. They began to blend entertainment and criticism in new ratios. Meanwhile, there were MacNeicean resonances in Auden's self-extrications from his false position as leader of the literary Left. To quote some of his apostasies: 'Poets are rarely and only incidentally priests or philosophers or party agitators. They are people with a particular interest and skill in handling words in a particular kind of way...Apart from that, they are fairly ordinary men and women'; 'We can justly accuse the poets of the nineties of ivory towerism, not because they said they were non-political, but because the portion of life which they saw as poets was such a tiny fragment.'[67] MacNeice's politics had long been informed by the irony of Auden's aphorism: 'That movement will fail: the intellectuals are supporting it.'[68] But unlike Auden, as their disagreement over Yeats shows,[69] MacNeice did not think that the collapse of 'clever hopes' or utopian theories meant that all had failed: that poetry could have no effect on or in history. In 'The Poet in England Today: A Reassessment' (1940) he writes: 'If the artist declines to live in a merely political pigeonhole, it does not follow that he has to live in a vacuum. Man is a political animal, not a political cog.'[70]

Not having subscribed to most premises of Marxist literary criticism, MacNeice never leapt to the opposite extreme. But, as my preliminary quotations show, there was an 'exception' to the rule of his hostility – an exception that outlasted the 1930s. He admired Christopher Caudwell who 'makes heavy reading, but at least he is trying to get beneath the surface'.[71] MacNeice quotes Caudwell in 'The Tower that Once', his reply to Virginia Woolf's famous polemic 'The Leaning Tower' (*Folios of New Writing*, Autumn, 1940). Here he is countering Woolf's assumption that 'all these writers of the Thirties were the slaves of Marx, or rather of Party Line Marxism':

Marx was certainly a most powerful influence. But why? it was not because of his unworkable economics, it was not because of the pedantic jigsaw of his history, it was because he said: *'Our job is to change it'*... some at least of these poets – in particular Auden and Spender – always recognised the truth of Thomas Mann's dictum: 'Karl Marx must read Friedrich Hölderlin.' Even an orthodox Communist Party critic, Christopher Caudwell, in his book *Illusion and Reality*, insisted (rightly) that poetry can never be reduced to political advertising, that its method is myth and that it must represent not any set of ideas which can be formulated by politicians or by scientists or by mere Reason and/or mere Will – it must represent something much deeper and wider which he calls the 'Communal Ego'. (*Folios of New Writing*, Spring 1941) [72]

Caudwell defines the Communal Ego as follows: 'the instinctive ego of art is the common man into which we retire to establish contact with our fellows'; 'that paradox of art – man withdrawing from his fellows into the world of art, only to enter more closely into communion with humanity'. Caudwell sees poetry as originating in and reproducing – though more and more faintly – 'the rhythmic introversion of the tribal dance [in which] each performer retired into his heart, into the fountain of his instincts'.[73] *Illusion and Reality* was published in 1937. It is unclear whether MacNeice had read it by the time *Modern Poetry* went to press; but his opening chapter, 'A Change of Attitude', includes what seem endorsements rather than parallels. First, he agrees with the diagnosis of 'Marxist critics' (and hence with the historical analysis in *Illusion and Reality*) that the 'divorce between the poet and other men or between the poet and himself as a man' corresponds to 'the rigid differentiation both of classes and functions in a capitalist society'. Second, Caudwell says 'Language is a social product', 'the poet can only live with words socially'; MacNeice (attacking Parnassianism, Symbolism and Imagism) says: 'the trouble with words is that every word is a community product'. Third, Caudwell stresses 'Not an abstract man in abstract nature, but men as they really live and behave, who must live concretely before they come to speculate abstractly, and whose abstract speculations therefore will bear the marks of their concrete living'. MacNeice ends the chapter by reaffirming poetry as emerging from the encounter between 'concrete living... a system of individuals determined by their circumstances, a concrete, therefore, of sensuous fact and what we may call "universals"' and 'a concrete poet...the whole man reacting with both intelligence and emotion'.[74]

All this amounts to more than surface agreement or coincidence. Perhaps Caudwell's Communal Ego and 'concrete living' (a *leitmotif* in *Illusion and Reality*) helped MacNeice to understand poetry's

relation to society as a matter of origins, structures and mechanisms
rather than of content or authorial ideology. Such ideas ignited
MacNeice's communalist sense of Ireland and of the classical Greek
poets for whom life 'meant life within a community'[75] – both soci-
eties are paradigmatic in *Autumn Journal*. He implicitly connects
the Communal Ego with Yeats's 'unity of being' and with his own
holistic vision of fifth-century Athenians who 'plotted out their life
with truism and humour/Between the jealous heaven and the callous
sea' (*Autumn Journal* IX). In 'Donegal Triptych' he insinuates
Caudwell's definition of the poet into western pastoral (see p.130).
Also, unlike Caudwell, he did not think that poetry would come
into its own in a communist society. For Caudwell, the 'movement
forward from bourgeois culture to communism [which] is also a
movement back to the social solidarity of primitive communism'
will allow poetry to be more artistically 'individual'. Nonetheless,
Caudwell's analysis of poetry as tapping into social collectivities ('all
the complex history of emotions and experience shared in common
by a thousand generations') cuts across simplistic dismissals of the
lyric as bourgeois. It also refined the 1930s literary cross-cutting
between Marx and Freud. In a chapter on 'poetry's dream-work',
Caudwell calls poetry 'an inverted dream' which 'flows from reality
down to the instincts' whereas dream 'flows from the instincts to
the boundary of reality'.[76] This consorts with MacNeice's interest
in dreams and with his later emphasis on 'dream logic' as a struc-
ture and strategy of parable. In *Varieties of Parable* he again invokes
Caudwell to boost an aesthetic which readjusts, but also reaffirms,
relations between the psyche and society:

> I have suggested that any parable writer, in whatever form, is concerned
> with the projecting of a special world. How far such a special world
> must also be a private world is open to argument…often, both in novels
> and in plays, and most frequently in poetry, the author is dealing not
> with man the political or social animal…but with man the solitary animal.
> In these latter cases the special world tends to become a private world.
> But even if this is so, it need not mean that we cannot share it with its
> creator. Given the same historical and geographical background many
> people's privacies tend to overlap. This has not only been proved by the
> psychologists, whether Freudian or Jungian, but has been maintained
> even by a Marxist critic, Christopher Caudwell, in the objectivist, over-
> topical 1930s.[77]

4

Poetic movements may have greater stamina than political move-
ments. Hence, in part, MacNeice's interest in literary tradition,
literary generation and their relation to history. By supporting and
interpreting (in a more selfless way than his peers) a dynamic in
which he also shared, MacNeice faced into the crux that he iden-
tifies at the beginning of 'Subject in Modern Poetry' (1936):'The
literary critic includes the literary historian, but it is notoriously
difficult to write the history of one's own times'.[78] Perhaps the
effort to do so, culminating in *The Poetry of W.B. Yeats*, kept
MacNeice in touch with history in general. He was helped by his
belief in the very existence of a movement, in an imaginative col-
lectivity. Like Caudwell, MacNeice subscribes to a socialism of
the creative process that contrasts not only with the 'Auden as
leader' model, but also with (positive and negative) post-Romantic
versions of the poet as solitary, solo performer, non-communal
Ego. Equally, the Communal Ego questions the easy equation of
(post)modernist polyvocality with anti-authoritarian politics.

I have suggested that MacNeice's attraction to Caudwell's Marxist
analysis may have been conditioned by Irish factors. Certainly, the
intersection between an Irish sense of genealogy and a socialist
sense of collectivity gave him an insight into how tradition works
– an insight *that* it works. This, in turn, benefited his successors.
Poets are coy about their links to contemporaries: X will say of Y
and Z: 'I had a drink with Y after meeting Sam Beckett in Paris,
and Z gave my first book a rave review, but I wouldn't call us a
movement.' Such disavowals, often credited by allegedly streetwise
critics, disregard the commonality exerted by more impersonal
pressures: by mechanisms of tradition, by the mutual awareness
that shapes difference, and by the obligation, as MacNeice puts it,
to 'do our duty by the present moment'.[79] The 1930s collaborations
brought into the open what is more usually latent. With reference
to the New York School, Geoff Ward has argued that critics neglect
the dynamics of 'coterie' (MacNeice's term is 'clique'). Besides
offering a 'humanist refuge against temporality'[80] and permutations
of stimulus, coterie engenders sibling rivalry, sibling differentiation,
family romance. Most importantly, however, it stakes out the aes-
thetic field of 'the present moment'.

MacNeice does his critical duty by coterie and by the present
moment when he speaks as survivor amid the ruins of the thirties
Left intelligentsia. 'The Tower that Once' is one of three replies to
Woolf's attack. The others ('The Falling Tower' and 'Below the

Tower') are by Edward Upward and B.L. Coombes. John Lehmann, editor of *New Writing*, adds a 'Postscript': part-obituary, part-apologia for Woolf. He stresses 'the astonishing vitality of her interest in what was being attempted by the living artists, poets, novelists around her'.[81] Upward and Coombes criticise her article from a primarily political viewpoint. Upward finds 'some truth in Virginia Woolf's accusation that [the 30s writers] were half-hearted and their work was filled with confusion and compromise', but on the different grounds that they were not socialist enough:

> At times they seemed afraid to hate and afraid to love...A socialist writer would be likely to choose as his 'hero' a character of historic proportions, but the writers of the thirties tended to choose as their heroes either very ordinary people or else frustrated intellectuals or even criminals. They could not really admire their heroes. And in their search for someone or something to admire they fell into philo-sophical abstractions and psychological obscurities.[82]

Coombes, a miner-writer, fastens on Woolf's tacit dismissal of the working class's future as well as past literary contribution (she says: 'Take away all that the working class has given to English litera-ture and that literature would scarcely suffer'). He argues that the working-class writer and 'the Leaning Tower writer' need one another, since the former lacks education and the latter lacks 'the closeness of men who live and work together; who eat the same food at the same time, and who speak the same language'.[83] Only MacNeice makes a strictly literary-historical and literary-critical case, claiming (as he does elsewhere) an authority that resides in 'my generation':

> [Mrs Woolf] should not attack my generation for being conditioned by its conditions. Do not let us be misled by her metaphor of the Tower. The point of this metaphor was that a certain group of young writers found themselves on a leaning tower; this presupposes that the rest of the world remained on the level. But it just didn't. The whole world in our time went more and more on the slant so that no mere abstract geometry or lyrical uplift could cure it.[84]

This insists on the nexus between history and literary tradition. MacNeice notes that neither Woolfian modernism nor Georgianism could have been simply reheated in the 1930s. In *Between the Acts*, on which she was then working, Woolf herself bears out MacNeice's point, as well as Lehmann's sense of her creative curiosity, by fac-ing the world on a slant and by modifying her method to 'write historically', as Peter Widdowson puts it.[85] She may thus be in denial (although true to her distrust of over-polemical literary feminism) when she argues that the 'Leaning Tower' generation cannot write unconsciously owing to its hyper-consciousness of class and history. Hence the writers' 'Discomfort; pity for themselves; anger against society' and their tendency to create scapegoats for their own indissoluble membership of the bourgeoisie: 'They cannot throw away their education; they cannot throw away their upbringing.'[86]

MacNeice had a personal spur to refute Woolf's argument in that she uses *Autumn Journal* ('feeble as poetry but interesting as autobiography') to exemplify 30s scapegoat-hunting and autobiographical fixation. It may be her feelings of exclusion from male intellectual privilege that speak, since she largely quotes from the poem's critique of Oxford (which resembles her own critique of Cambridge) but misses MacNeice's self-ironic tone. If Woolf is right about autobiography, though wrong to see it as proof of literary incapacity, she is on shakier ground in celebrating the nineteenth century as a stable era during which writers could ignore war, believe that 'Life was not going to change' and allow the unconscious to do its work. MacNeice easily finds contrary evidence; but his two shrewdest points have to do with generational perspective. Woolf asks her juniors how they can imagine the classless society which they have not experienced. This not only damns superficial utopianism; it denies literature's power to write into the future, to participate, however obliquely, in historical change. MacNeice says: 'Mrs Woolf deplores our "curious bastard language", but I notice that in the next stage of society and poetry she looks forward to a "pooling" of vocabularies and dialects.' The second point is again the inevitability of being 'conditioned by our conditions', not only passively: 'We were right to throw mud at Mrs Woolf's old horses and we were right to advocate social reconstruction and we were even right – in our more lyrical work – to give personal expression to our feelings of anxiety, horror and despair (for even despair can be fertile).'[87]

This dialectic appears to involve several paradoxes. Woolf has temporarily forgotten her own radical past in which technical innovation contributed to the kind of 'destruction' she now deplores. And she takes a conservative line – on genre and language – with writers whose aesthetic would be reckoned less "modernist" than hers. Thus, rather than a neat 'transition' in which postmodernism struggles to be born, we find MacNeice opposing her with concrete living and concrete poets: 'It is carrying the Nelson eye too far to pretend that Auden and Spender did not bring new life into English poetry.'[88] Yet if Woolf defends "tradition" here, Mac-

Neice elsewhere defends it against experimental excesses that derive from her generation rather than his. MacNeice always denied that 'my generation' had thrown out tradition:

> All the experimenting poets turned their backs on mummified or theo-rised tradition, but the more intelligent realised that living tradition is essential to all art; is one of the poles. A poem, to be recognisable, must be traditional; but to be worth recognising, it must be something new.[89]

In *Modern Poetry* he puts this more succinctly: 'All experiment is made on a basis of tradition; all tradition is the crystallisation of experiment.'[90] A later essay, 'The Traditional Aspect of Modern English Poetry', written for an Italian audience in 1946, plays the European card against those traditionalists and anti-traditionalists for whom the term means the poetic traditions of the nineteenth century. MacNeice concludes: 'Most of the younger generation have returned to more regular forms, while trying to be their masters, not their slaves...believers in meaning (though not necessarily in a wholly rational meaning) they try, in the European tradition, to convey it by all the means at their command – and most of these means, on analysis, are traditional.'[91]

In 'The Tower that Once' MacNeice calls the 'mutual misun-derstanding of the literary generations' 'one of the evils of our time', adding: 'my own generation has often been unjust to its immediate predecessors'.[92] He was to experience such injustice himself. Reviewing two anthologies (in 1957) he says: 'This game of pigeonholing literary generations has gone too far...Posterity may find our generations closer to each other than we care to think'. His complaint is not just personal pique or loyalty to old comrades, but an objection to the myopia and amnesia of the 'small critic', the unhistorical anthologist: 'Mr Fraser classifies the 30s poets, mentioning particularly Auden and myself, as "Augustans", who were succeeded by "romantics".'[93] MacNeice's readings of the poetic 'present moment' always imply long vistas and hence high standards, whether provided by the classics (a rarer point of refer-ence in poetry criticism today), by his touchstones in English lit-erature, or by the foundational roles of Yeats and Eliot in the twentieth century. His alternative title for *Varieties of Parable* was *From Spenser to Beckett*. Similarly, he likes Randall Jarrell's habit of mentioning his contemporaries 'in the same breath as Dante, Shakespeare et al'.[94] Had MacNeice lived to edit the *Oxford Book of Twentieth-Century English Verse*, for which he was contracted, something exciting might have happened.

5

For instance, as compared with Larkin, MacNeice would probably
have made more sense of aesthetic dialectics since 1900. (Anthony
Thwaite recalls that he planned 'to begin with Hardy and Housman,
and then the bulk of the book would give solid prominence to
Yeats, Eliot, Lawrence, Muir, Graves, Owen, and Auden'.)[95] His
criticism in the 1930s, from 'Poetry Today' onwards, often engaged
with the repercussions of the *symboliste* and *vers libre* revolution
which 'released poets from the suffocation of the Victorian salon'.[96]
"Modernism", of course, was not yet a separate or segregating lit-
erary-critical category. MacNeice's analyses of Eliot's technique
stress its points of contact with traditional forms: 'in Eliot, who at
first sight seems formless and prosy, we strike patches almost too
deliberately lifted from his private classics'. He continues, in a
passage that still typically looks at 'living tradition' from the angle
of poets with choices as opposed to determinists plugging 'some
perverse general theory of poetry':

> Eliot's verse was only free in that he allowed himself to ring the changes
> quickly; one moment conversation; the next moment Senecan senten-
> tiousness (for the latter the traditional blank verse line is always crop-
> ping up again; but thanks to quick change juxtapositions it had tem-
> porarily regained its freshness). But other poets were bound to want a
> more stable medium. There were two ways of obtaining this: to loosen
> the verse more (as in *Cathay*, 'The Journey of the Magi', etc., Walt
> Whitman and Blake's Prophetic Books) or to tighten it up to the tension
> of blank verse and heroic couplets by devices which would make it
> appear new. Abstractly, these are alternatives; actually the New Poets
> have compromised between them.[97]

MacNeice's simplest explanation of 'changes in technique' is that
poets get bored, modes get played out, fashions look dated, the
band-waggoners drop off: 'In poetry, of course, we keep in with
the old fashions while we practise the new ones; and the old ones
owe their freshness to the freshness of the new ones.' Thus free
verse, a liberating reaction against the Victorians rather than
against 'all the past', may itself become constricting. Nor was 'the
traditional line used in blank verse and in the rhyming couplet'
always 'the same line'.[98] MacNeice's chapter on 'Rhythm and Rhyme'
in *Modern Poetry* begins by setting out the effects unique to free
verse and by defending the 'poise' that differentiates even the
'baldest' type from prose. He goes on to say, however: 'But in
general I myself prefer the more regular kinds of verse because I
think that if you are going to poise your phrases at all they will
usually need more poise than can be given them by the mere

arranging of them in lines. Few poets have the *élan* of Whitman or Lawrence and most free verse, consequently, is thin and not memorable.'[99]

MacNeice prefers 'the more regular kinds of verse' because they provide more scope, open up more 'rhythmical variations' (he gives examples). Here his belief in 'variousness' meets his belief in proportion – which is not a contradiction. As we have seen, MacNeice dislikes one-dimensional readings of poetry, mono-rail literary trajectories. Thus in 'Subject in Modern Poetry' he rejects the poles of 'psychic automatism' and 'pure propaganda', of 'visceral parrot-talk' and 'bill-plastering'.[100] Yet this is hardly conciliatory language. In desiring genuine complexity to crystallise out of 'the interflux of extremist principles',[101] MacNeice does not seek a safe middle way. When he calls most of the great poets 'compromisers', he means that criticism should 'try to work out for each poet a kind of Hegelian dialectic of opposites'.[102] In *Autumn Journal* IX he disparages the Hellenistic poets for 'turning out dapper little elegiac verses/…carefully shunning an over-statement/ But working the dying fall'. A few poets, however, manage to keep all the balls in the air all the time. He suggests that Herbert and Yeats are better models (not the same as better poets) than Donne and Hopkins because they 'are more *classical*' in the proportions of their verse. As contrasted with Donne's, 'Herbert's conceits very rarely stick out offendingly but are usually organic parts of a whole; nearly all his poems are in balance. His first virtue is *construction*; equal second are the sureness of his music and the purity of his diction which, of course, are part and parcel of his construction.'[103] MacNeice brilliantly cuts through to the kernel of Yeats's self and anti-self by renaming them Jekyll and Hyde: 'the poet as he thinks he is or consciously wishes to be' *versus* 'his suppressed and subordinate self (or the self which, as a poet, he would wish to suppress or subordinate)'. He adds: 'Hyde complements and corrects Jekyll, sometimes indeed by sabotage'.[104] And when MacNeice attacks the disproportionate Pound of the *Cantos*, it is because Pound's extremism (tied in with rhythmical 'monotony', see below) returns poetry to a 90s corner: 'For very many years he has been repeating, rather hysterically, that he is an expert and a specialist, but he has specialised his poems into museum pieces'.[105] That is, Pound no longer listens to 'Hyde'. In 'Elegy for Minor Poets' it is disproportion that wrecks the talents of those who 'were too happy or sad, too soon or late', 'thought too little, too much', 'were too carefree or careful'.

Over-specialised poets and critics resist or fear the 'many-sidedness' of Auden or Apuleius, the fact that Yeats is 'a federation'.

Celebrating Yeats's transgressive 'little mechanical songs' in the persona of Crazy Jane, MacNeice deplores 'the puritanical book-reviewer who demands that any one poet should be all the time a specialist, confined to his own sphere (the reviewer allots the sphere), and all the time self-consistent. If a poet has been labelled serious, he must never be frivolous. If the poet has been labelled "love-poet", he is taken to be declining if he shows the Latin quality of "salt".' MacNeice urges the poet not to 'bother with this Procrustes who has to live by his bed'.[106] While relevant to Yeats and his masks, not to mention good advice for reading poetry in general, the polemic expresses MacNeice's weariness with being crassly labelled by critics according to Audenesque or Wordsworthian premises. His interchangeably negative terms for bad critics are 'puritanical' and 'procrustean' – terms that evoke ways in which proportion or variety might be resisted on either side of the Irish Sea.

MacNeice subtly characterises the trap of repetition for both poet and critic when he asks 'whether any one mood or idea can valuably be expressed more than once with exactly the same emphasis'.[107] So proportion means continual dialectic – the gyres – rather than succumbing to aesthetic specialisation or a single critical perspective and hence to stasis. It means altering the angle, choosing a different canvas, and not, like Pound, 'using the same cadences again and again for glamour, and the same contrasts again and again for brutality (or reality)'.[108] Discussing 'rhyme' in *Modern Poetry*, MacNeice proposes how 'one may compromise between...two schools of thought'; i.e., the case that rhyme is musical and 'makes for memorability', and the case 'that, being obviously artificial, it suggests insincerity and that it lulls the reader into a pleasant coma'. MacNeice outlines the 'compromise' as follows: 'One can use rhyme in a poem, but not continuously or not in the expected places...One can use internal rhymes, off-rhymes, bad rhymes; one can rhyme a stressed against an unstressed syllable'.[109] His own poetry sometimes falls into procrustean traps. That it escapes is connected with his internalisation of proportion. He says of Pound: 'Quantity must always affect quality. A metre of green, as Gauguin said, is more green than a centimetre, but a bucket of Benedictine is hardly Benedictine.'[110]

The invitation to give the Clark lectures stimulated MacNeice to theorise. *Varieties of Parable* obviously illuminates *Solstices* (1961) and *The Burning Perch* (1963). Less obviously, and despite his attention to prose and drama, these lectures re-open the question of "modern poetry". MacNeice's attitude to free verse was always out of line with "modernist" poetics as retrospectively constructed by the old-style American literary academy. The mid-Atlantic postmodernist academy, also favours free verse (not 'the *élan* of Whitman or Lawrence') now read, rather than written, with an eye to discontinuity, fragmentation, indeterminacy etc. Since modernist structural relativism shifted from consciousness to language, the highest poetic virtue, for some critics, is to 'break the syntagmatic chain' – however monotonous the effect, however disproportionate its currency. Many-sided poets, including MacNeice, tend to reserve chain-breaking or "aporia" for purposeful variation, for specific deadlocks or contradictions. Thus MacNeice maintains that Beckett's silences 'are there to throw the words into relief '.[111] Despite his own fertility in image and symbol, MacNeice argues that symbolism (and its progeny) has been over-valued and its relation to other elements of poetic structure, such as syntax, ill-defined. Again, it depends on proportion. The ascendancy of symbol (as Yeats discovered) may produce atrophy elsewhere. MacNeice's first lecture begins by explaining why he has opted for 'parable':

> 'Symbolism' for instance has been vastly overused and to some critics a symbol means something very plastic while to others it means something quite rigid. As for the adjective 'symbolical', it is a notorious get-out or let-out word, used by authors when they want to get away with a murder they're not quite sure they have committed. At the same time the word is too wide in its reference: in language at least it is not possible not to use symbols, since all language, on ultimate analysis, is by its nature symbolical.[112]

Later in the lecture he disagrees with some of Martin Esslin's views on Beckett and Pinter (which include comparing the Theatre of the Absurd to 'a Symbolist or Imagist poem'). MacNeice notes Esslin's assumption 'that when people lose belief in God they also have to give up discursive thought and logic'; criticises him because he 'perceives and appears to approve of a "devaluation of language" '; and remarks that 'he goes too far in postulating the peculiarity of the modern world'. To Esslin's complaint that Sartre and Camus use an 'old [dramatic] convention', he counters: 'Mr Eliot's theory...that in a dislocated world poetry must be dislocated too, has been disputed now for several decades.' He approves Graham Hough's critique of the 'growing belief that all the work of literature is done by images, not by syntax or dianoia [the mental faculty used in discursive reasoning]'. and finds Eliot guilty of 'indulging' his images.[113] 'Broken images' and broken syntax – although juxtaposition can be a form of syntax – do not exhaust all the creative or critical possibilities even as regards rupture. And Eliot's breaks throw his missing links, as well as words, into relief. Brian Vickers's attack on Paul de Man's diminished

sense of classical rhetoric, which leads him to sever categories of
language from processes of thought, is relevant:

> In the hands of de Man rhetoric no longer means oratory, civic eloquence,
> moving the feelings, or constructing the whole of an artistic discourse; it
> refers to a few well-known tropes, not even figures. The modern frag-
> mentation of rhetoric is carried further, reducing it from persuasion or
> 'actual action upon others' to the workings of a self-contained 'intra-
> linguistic figure or trope'. It has been made introverted, solipsistic.[114]

Being interested in cognition, parable makes more room for
syntax and thereby 'true rhetoric' (MacNeice) than does symbol-
ism. Yet MacNeice's mastery of the Greek, Latin and English
syntactical repertoire need not mean that he conceives syntax or
rhetoric in positivistic terms any more than, in *Autumn Journal*,
he conceives the Ancient Greeks as 'Models of logic and lucidity,
dignity, sanity'. In a fine essay on MacNeice's classicism Peter
McDonald points out that the three classical scholars whom he
really admired are noted for their 'distance from a conventionally
rationalist, humanist idea of classicism'.[115] The best-known work
of his friend and mentor E.R. Dodds is *The Greeks and the
Irrational*. Perhaps MacNeice (and Beckett) can be seen as devel-
oping the inverted gyre of Yeatsian rhetoric, and hence as produc-
ing ambiguity more in the manner of *The Turn of the Screw* than
of *The Waste Land*. Poetry, of course, always makes a difference to
syntax, to tropes and figures. Matei Calinescu, in the very act of
defining postmodernism, knows that poetry has anticipated him:
'A certain degree of undecidability of meaning…has always been a
feature of poetry.'[116] For MacNeice, this is also a key feature of
parable, except that 'undecidability' is an existential as well as
philosophical problem. At the end of his poem 'The Taxis' the
cabby tells the passenger who has always thought himself 'alone
tra-la': 'I can't tra-la well take/ So many people, not to speak of
the dog'. This poem destabilises the boundaries of the self by darkly
exploiting, rather than by glibly abandoning, syntax, symbol, story,
dialogue, refrain, stanza. 'Parable' does not cover every kind of
poetry (MacNeice makes careful distinctions). But, as a way of
defining poetry, it may cover more than symbolism.

McDonald notes that MacNeice was in some ways a belated
practitioner and theorist of parable.[117] Auden had reinvented para-
ble in the 1930s and moved on. In *Varieties of Parable* MacNeice
calls Auden an *'anima naturaliter parabolica'* and notes: 'From the
first he has been very ready to use a sampling system, a kind of
synecdoche, the part standing for the whole: hence in his early
poems the continual use of pioneers, mountaineers, engineers, scouts,

spies, and so on as types of the advance guard of contemporary
humanity – or sometimes just types of humanity.' Yet he adds: 'If
at times [Auden] is a parabolist, he is not a consistent or sustained
one'. MacNeice finds 'something atomic' in Auden's method as in
Eliot's (that is, images may have a private, arbitrary, free-standing
significance), and contends that in *The Age of Anxiety* 'this poet,
like the more obviously descriptive type of poet, is getting his
effects by enumeration rather than by fusion'.[118] In MacNeice's
most complex parable-poems 'fusion' (not the same as "unity")
engages all the elements of form. And if these play their part pro-
portionally, they may do so communally. MacNeice's theory in the
early 1960s, as close to his practice as it was in the 1930s, takes
the Communal Ego into every aspect of poetic structure. And
parable, pan-generically, gives poetry an enhanced communal pres-
ence: 'the parabolist, whether he uses prose or verse, is following
a poetic rather than a documentary procedure'.[119]

6

MacNeice's later perspectives on "modern poetry" enter the fore-
ground of another poem with a literary-critical dimension. 'All
Over Again' is the last poem in *Solstices*:

> As if I had known you for years drink to me only if
> Those frontiers have never changed on the mad map of the years
> And all our tears were earned and this were the first cliff
> From which we embraced the sea and these were the first words
> We spread to lure the birds that nested in our day
> As if it were always morning their dawnsong theirs and ours
> And waking no one else me and you only now
> Under the brow of a blue and imperturbable hill
> Where still time stands and plays his bland and hemlock pipe
> And the ripe moment tugs yet declines to fall and all
> The years we had not met forget themselves in this
> One kiss ingathered world and outward rippling bell
> To the rim of the cup of the sky and leave it only there
> Near into far blue into blue all over again
> Notwithstanding unique all over all again
> Of which to speak requires new fires of the tongue some trick
> Of the light in the dark of the muted voice of the turning wild
> World yet calm in her storm gay in her ancient rocks
> To preserve today one kiss in this skybound timeless cup
> Nor now shall I ask for anything more of future or past
> This being last and first sound sight on eyes and ears
> And each long then and there suspended on this cliff
> Shining and slicing edge that reflects the sun as if
> This one Between were All and we in love for years.

Earlier I quoted MacNeice's remark that Yeats 'may present certain facts coloured or distorted by his own partisan feelings but he allows the reader to see that this presentation is founded on an "as if"'. This alludes to the well-known idea that poetry in general is so founded. 'All Over Again', syntactically and tactically founded on 'as if', is a love poem about love poetry and about poetry. The title conflates this perennial lyric genre with the perennial emotion from which it derives: 'Notwithstanding unique all over all again'. 'As if' is an impossible condition from the outset. The impossibility of having 'known you for years', or writing the first and last love poem, merges into the impossibility of abolishing history ('the mad map of the years'), the impossibility of poetry ever delivering a golden world ('as if it were always morning'). Yet these impossibilities cannot disprove 'as if'. Nor is fictionality admitted for its own sake, but for the sake of human pain and hope. The poem's scenario, Jon Stallworthy tells us, evokes the Cape in South Africa.[120] Yet there is nothing arbitrary or 'atomic' about an Eden laid out as sea, sky, sun, dawn chorus, hill, the 'ripe moment tugging' (which implies the tree of knowledge), 'ancient rocks' and 'cliff'. The latter's final appearance as a two-dimensional 'Shining and slicing edge' is again partly self-referential. It recapitulates the poem's parabolic landscape as a vertiginous dynamic which yet 'shines' with 'all' it tries to hold in suspension.

That this modern love poem comments on its own project (always a feature of the genre, but rarely to such a pitch) appears in the relations between syntax, 'rhythm and rhyme' and literary allusion. These advertise their presence and hence the intricate devices required to construct 'One kiss ingathered world and outward rippling bell'. The elisions of the punctuationless sentence are not always smooth, but snag on ambiguity and disjunction as when 'drink to me only' seems to introduce a further conditional clause 'only if', or the inversion 'still time stands' might imply stasis or the reverse, or when 'hemlock' succeeds to 'bland'. The poem's breathlessness and catchings of breath are one measure of 'as if'. So is a rhetorical palette which includes oxymoron, parison (the 'as if' structure), elaborate ploche (the repetitions of kiss, sky, cup, year, blue), polysyndeton which multiplies connectives (the series of 'of' constructions), asyndeton which eliminates them ('sound sight'), adynaton or the inadequacy of the speaker ('Of which to speak requires new fires of the tongue'). More broadly, the syntax enacts movements of ingathering and outward rippling as it amasses or disperses the highly condensed verbal ingredients that belong to the 'ripe moment'. Thus 'some trick/ Of the light in the dark of the muted voice of the turning wild/ World' is expansive in its polysyndeton yet compressed in blending language, perception and cosmos. There is also compression, and a comment on poetic compression, in 'Near into far blue into blue'; and in the Cummings-like use of 'then and there', and 'Between' to stand for the time/ space relations that the poem hypothetically remakes 'in this skybound timeless cup'. The syntagmatic chain is stretched, twisted and buckled to dramatise the half-problematic, half-exhilarating relations between future and past, cause and effect, experience and speech, identity and flux, love and time, poetry and posterity.

Another 'Between' is the sonnet framed by the first five and last five lines with their rhymes of 'if', 'cliff' and 'years'. Repetition is the common ground where rhetoric meets poetic form in rhythm and rhyme. 'All Over Again' encompasses great variation as regards the latter (all the kinds of rhyme MacNeice lists in *Modern Poetry*). This may be the poem where MacNeice both vindicates and most fully realises his addiction to internal rhyme. It is 'as if ' it provided cups of sound in which to delay movement through time: 'And the ripe moment tugs yet declines to fall and all/ The years we had not met forget themselves in this/One kiss...' The effect resembles pouring champagne into a pyramid of glasses. The most inclusive concept for all 'repetition-devices' is 'refrain'. In *The Poetry of W.B. Yeats* MacNeice enlarges his defence of rhyme into a defence of refrain and attacks rigid notions of its 'rigidity'.[121] Refrain cannot be about sameness without also being about difference. The multiple and metamorphic refrains of 'All Over Again' (perhaps another sense of its title) suggest that once you repeat sounds you are irretrievably making cognitive patterns from language/ experience; yet at the point of repetition the pattern has already changed: 'and these were the first words/ We spread to lure the birds that nested in our day...' This, reflexively rhymed on 'words'/ 'birds', evokes Caudwell's 'complex history of the emotions and experience shared in common by a thousand generations'. It also indicates that MacNeice's later poetry can encompass relativity of consciousness ("modernism") and relativity of language ("postmodernism") while remaking "traditional" form. Indeed, 'All Over Again' may dramatise precisely this encounter. That Adam's naming enterprise runs into difficulties, contradictions, aporia, is hardly news for poetry defined as a compound of 'as if ' and 'all over again', the latter phrase being ambiguously poised between recurrence and endings.

MacNeice weaves more quotation than usual into his web of repetition and variation: Ben Jonson, his own poems ('Snow', 'Meeting Point', 'Eclogue by a Five-barred Gate', 'To Posterity'), Walter

Pater's description of the Mona Lisa which Yeats set out (at the beginning of the *Oxford Book of Modern Verse*) as a poem beginning 'She is older than the rocks...', Yeats's own play on 'ancient' and 'gay' in 'Lapis Lazuli', Eliot's 'still point of the turning world', perhaps Housman's 'blue remembered hills'. These allusions, which go with the flow, again stress 'all over again': the persistence of motifs and devices that link the lover and artist, the objects of love and of art, and all to their earthly habitat. As ever, MacNeice takes a long view of the poetic enterprise, of tradition, even as he rearranges its landscape according to new pressure from "proportion" and from his renewed sense, in the early 1960s, of how modern institutions threaten communication while making it more urgent. Time's 'bland and hemlock pipe' is a social as well as mortal enemy with which MacNeice's parabolic structures critically engage. Writing on *Solstices* for the *Poetry Book Society Bulletin*, he reaffirms some of his thirties principles, including poetry's critical duty: 'I have also, perhaps...found it easier than I did to write poems of acceptance (even of joy) though this does not – perish the thought – preclude the throwing of mud or of knives when these seem called for'. And, once again, with his own reviewers clearly in mind, he attacks procrustean literary criticism:

> Poets are always being required – by the critics and by themselves – to 'develop'. Most critics, however, to perceive such development, need something deeper than a well and wider than a church-door. In certain poets of our time the changes are conspicuous enough; in others, such as Robert Graves, a careless reader might complain that the menu is never altered.[122]

MacNeice returns to the question 'Can something be wrong somewhere?' which he had raised in 'Poetry, the Public, and the Critic' written for the *New Statesman* twelve years earlier. Its context was a commissioned series of articles on the arts and their audience (Raymond Mortimer dealt with the visual arts, Desmond Shawe-Taylor with music). In this essay I have often quoted from what appears a crucial *précis*. It is here that MacNeice pinpoints the complementary deficiences of big and little critic, the mirror-image snobbery of aesthetic critic and Marxist critic, the undesirability of the 'anarchist critic', the crying need for 'responsible critics', the revealing contradictions in the reception of his own work. He also cites both Richards and Caudwell, whose reciprocity in his thinking opens channels between New Criticism and Marxism. The article begins: 'The critic is by his nature a go-between. In some periods he can fulfil his nature merely by calling from a window, while in others, as in our own, he has great gulfs to cross.'

In debating whether 'the gulf between [a community's] poets and its readers' is now 'unbridgeable', MacNeice stresses, as in the 1930s, what the reader shares with the poet: 'Ordinary conversation is nearer to lyrical poetry than cold prose'; 'when [the reader] himself is poeticising, i.e. talking…he will…use all sorts of hidden allusions, double meanings, irony, hyperboles, and fancy variations from baby-talk to "meaningless" swear-words; he will also play many tricks with rhythm.' However, the reader may not recognise poetry as a heightened version of everyday talk which must compensate for the speaker's physical absence. The critic, therefore, has an 'educational' role in connecting the reader with the poet who 'is somewhere around in the community'. MacNeice's ideal sense of that role combines Caudwell with Richards. The poet, he says, uses words as 'a means of communication', 'for an end which is at once social and personal' (he quotes 'the instinctive ego of art'). This requires analytical 'hard work' from the critic on such matters as perspective, 'prose meaning', prosody. After 'the critic has thus discussed what kind of poem he is dealing with, and whether it is good of its kind, he can then, if he likes, go on to a third and more difficult question: what is the value of this kind of poem?' Meanwhile, in default of responsible criticism, 'neither salon shibboleths nor Inner Voice gush will help'.[123]

Fifty years on, in more atomised circumstances, shibboleths and gush are still around. So is a swollen academic sector, whose greater control over the reception of poetry was abetted by MacNeice's bête noire, Ezra Pound: buckets of literary-critical Benedictine. Gail McDonald concludes Learning to be Modern: Pound, Eliot, and the American University by stressing Pound's compatibility with the 'Puritan inheritance [perhaps MacNeice sniffed this out]…the nineteenth-century American college, the core curriculum, and Irving Babbitt'.[124] MacNeice, in contrast, inhabited a less rarefied literary environment, and desired better-proportioned relations between 'Poetry, the Public and the Critic'. His own criticism moves from aesthetic manifesto to socio-cultural critique to review to academic article without violent changes of stylistic and tonal gear. Perhaps, among other factors, his refusal to pander to academic audiences, both as critic and poet, has kept him off some syllabuses – and thus distorted their maps of the century. I have argued elsewhere that MacNeice's creative and critical endeavour to juggle the legacies of Yeats and Eliot is crucial to the evolution of poetic "modernism" on this side of the Atlantic, and that many consequences of his endeavour are to be seen in contemporary Northern Irish poetry.[125] This is a historical reason why MacNeice's criticism

- how grateful we are to Alan Heuser's editing – must not be neglected.

There is also a philosophical reason: MacNeice's appeal to 'honesty' as an objective for poet and critic alike. On the whole, he seems remarkably alert to his own subjective motives; his analytical and dialectical inclinations standing him in good stead. But 'honesty', given MacNeicean dreamwork, does not signify some kind of "Honest Ulsterman" bluntness. Certainly, one of honesty's opposites is 'lies', but in no merely factual sense. In *Autumn Journal* IV the protagonist tells his 'honest' lover, only half-ironically, that 'even your lies were able to assert/Integrity of purpose'. He also praises her 'special strength/Who never flatter for points nor fake responses'. Honesty, then, seems close to 'integrity': another favourite term, denoting not a static condition but a complex radar that warns against betrayal of creative instincts, critical principles and their delicate mutuality. The opposite of this, in turn, seems to be 'trimmer' (a category less current in these flabbier times). MacNeice calls Yeats's *Collected Poems* (1950) 'the record of an artist who remained single-minded in a world of trimmers and who, for all his posing, had integrity'.[126] For the critic, 'honesty' means not faking it, trying not to become an intellectual fashion-victim nor to compromise when a judgment might prove unpopular or imprudent. In the holistic critical climate of *Autumn Journal* dishonest literary criticism belongs to the same ethos as 'the trimmers at Delphi and the dummies at Sparta' who symbolise the betrayal at Munich.

In Praise of 'In Praise of Limestone'

I am one of those who think that Auden's inspiration gradually ran out or ran shallow. The second half of the massive *Collected Poems* mostly leaves me cold. But in 1948 Auden wrote a defence of shallowness which reconnected his poetry – though too briefly – with its underground streams. Unlike all those later poems of 'slick and easy generalisation' (to quote 'Letter to Lord Byron') in slick and esoteric metres, 'In Praise of Limestone' makes real demands on technique. For a start, its form has mimetic point: the capaciously long lines; the free elegiac couplets trellised with a leisurely and elaborate syntax; the anapaestic rhythms; the liquid assonances; the sudden alliterative clusters. 'In Praise of Limestone' brings the Auden landscape sensually and rhythmically alive again:

> If it form the one landscape that we, the inconstant ones,
>> Are consistently homesick for, this is chiefly because
> It dissolves in water. Mark these rounded slopes
>> With their surface fragrance of thyme and beneath
> A secret system of caves and conduits; hear the springs
>> That spurt out everywhere with a chuckle,
> Each filling a private pool for its fish and carving
>> Its own little ravine whose cliffs entertain
> The butterfly and the lizard; examine this region
>> Of short distances and definite places...

Midway between symbol and discursiveness, the poem occupies the site of parable. But this is an unusual parable, a meta-parable, in that its discourse interprets and justifies its symbolism. At one level, 'In Praise of Limestone' speaks from behind its own scenes, from the interval between inspiration and embodiment. It takes shape as a meditation upon why it takes the shape it does: 'If it form...' The self-referential opening and closing lines body forth poetry (images, sounds, texture, text, subtext) as a geology which is also a physiology. 'In Praise of Limestone' comes full circle: the speaker begins by suggesting how to read it and ends by suggesting how it came to be written:

> Dear, I know nothing of
> Either, but when I try to imagine a faultless love
>> Or the life to come, what I hear is the murmur
> Of underground streams, what I see is a limestone landscape.

Yet the writing and the reading 'dissolve' into one another. From

'If it form...Mark...hear' to 'what I hear...what I see', from genesis
to revelation and back again, from the physicality of Nature to the
physicality of poetry, 'In Praise of Limestone' invokes its own
becoming in the imaginations of author and reader.

By analogy with fractal geometry (particularly dramatic in lime-
stone), which includes the idea that geological irregularity remains
constant over different scales, the conclusion epitomises the poem.
But so do other passages which reproduce its overall contour of
'short distances and definite places'. Thus the sequence beginning
'hear the springs/ That spurt out everywhere', which then conveys
the miniaturisation of grand masses in limestone ('Each...carving/
Its own little *ravine* whose *cliffs* entertain...'), itself miniaturises the
poem's larger orchestration of spurts and carvings and implies that
individual poems are fractal phenomena. The syntax typically rep-
licates itself, often in triplicate, as with the imperatives Mark/hear/
examine. In the second phase of the poem we are told to 'Watch,
then, the band of rivals as they climb up and down / Their steep
stone gennels *in twos and threes*, at times/*Arm in arm*, but never,
thank God, *in step*' [my italics]. 'Never' sparks off another triad:

> accustomed to a stone that responds,
> They have never had to veil their faces in awe
> Of a crater whose blazing fury could not be fixed;
> Adjusted to the local needs of valleys
> Where everything can be touched or reached by walking,
> Their eyes have never looked into infinite space
> Through the lattice-work of a nomad's comb; born lucky,
> Their legs have never encountered the fungi
> And insects of the jungle, the monstrous forms and lives
> With which we have nothing, we like to hope, in common.

The way in which semi-colons prolong a sentence, or sentences
begin at unpredictable points of the line, produces an impression that
the poem's structure has ramified (is ramifying) by metamorphic
fractal fertility rather than according to an architectural grand plan.
From the outset, even the phrases that introduce what look like
discrete stanzas have the air of retracing previous steps before mov-
ing on: 'If it form'; 'Watch, then'; 'That is why, I suppose'; 'They
were right, my dear, all those voices were right/And are right...'.

So whatever else 'In Praise of Limestone' may be, it is a Helicon
poem like Robert Frost's 'Directive' – another meta-parabolic land-
scape. 'Directive', published in *Steeple Bush* the year before Auden
wrote 'In Praise of Limestone' (a few verbal parallels suggest that he
may have taken note), encodes many layers of Frost's life and work.[1]
Like Auden, Frost begins with homesickness, with nostalgia for an
imagined topography at once spatial and temporal, art and life:

Back out of all this now too much for us,
Back in a time made simple by the loss
Of detail, burned, dissolved, and broken off
Like graveyard marble sculpture in the weather,
There is a house that is no more a house...

The journey takes in mountain country, woods, apple trees and
much Frostian self-quotation en route to a 'lofty and original'
spring: 'Here are your waters and your watering place./ Drink and
be whole again beyond confusion'. This ending, too, condenses
the poem, just as the poem condenses Frost's poetry and its 'stays
against confusion'. Like 'Directive', 'In Praise of Limestone' fea-
tures 'springs' and 'waters' that evoke the unconscious sources,
resources and effects of poetry, although Auden's undercurrents
seem more Freudian than Jungian – ever-'spurting' streams rather
than 'original' fount. This points to other differences between the
Frost and Auden landscapes. For instance, when Frost links geol-
ogy and physiology ('Great monolithic knees the former town/
Long since gave up pretence of keeping covered'), he does so in a
manner which separates, rather than fuses, country and city as
imaginative space. Limestone's fractal metamorphoses comprehend
society as well as Nature and art. Again, Frost's 'dissolved, and
broken off/ Like graveyard marble sculpture in the weather' implies
an investment in wholeness which differs from Auden's more positive
sense of creative tension between the human artifact and the natural
or historical forces that tend to 'dissolve' it.

Another difference is that, while both poems are constructed as
guided tours, Auden supplies an apparently more didactic guide.
'Directive' delays the imperative mood ('If you'll let a guide direct
you/ Who only has at heart your getting lost...'), but Auden intro-
duces it almost at once. Yet this is a muted, self-aware register of
Auden's didactic voice, liable to modulate into the confessional
voice of 'we, the inconstant ones'. Michael Wood has discussed
the complex play of pronouns and perspectives in 'In Praise of
Limestone' as offering the reader a spectrum of roles between
'inclusion and instruction'. For instance, 'we' can provisionally
choose to align ourselves with or against the 'inconstant ones', and
our alignment may (inconstantly) alter as we read on. At least up
to the point where the speaker's voice becomes 'unmistakably per-
sonal' (and ultimately the artist's voice), we must consider where
to locate ourselves with reference to the objective and subjective
points of the poem's compass.[2]

In the first phase, the didactic voice unexpectedly changes gear
as the landscape metamorphoses from an object of 'examination'

to the maternal body. The exclamation draws us in (although women readers may draw back):

> What could be more like Mother or a fitter background
>   For her son, the flirtatious male who lounges
> Against a rock in the sunlight, never doubting
>   That for all his faults he is loved...?

Edward Upward reads 'In Praise of Limestone' as 'very much a personal family poem about [Auden's] brothers and his Mother, and, not least, about himself '.[3] Certainly (like 'Directive' again), the poem seems to be both a summa of the poet's *paysage moralisé* and a 'secret system' encoding personal history.[4] It is clear that this involves a closeted homosexual narrative (for which 'secret system' might itself be code) and that, in its aspect as 'mad camp' or Auden's erotic Muse, limestone also takes on the contours of the male body 'entertaining' its lovers and itself. Although the maternal rock is said to be a 'background' for 'her son, the flirtatious male', the effect is again one of mutation rather than distinction. And limestone's androgynous gendering leads back, or feeds back, into its aspect as art: 'whose works are but/ Extensions of his power to charm'. This is Auden's familiar notion that art begins in childhood attention-seeking, in a desire to 'entertain our friends', in strategies of 'pleasing or teasing' – as does sex. The poem's punningly combined portraits of poet and homosexual (each placates Fate with 'a clever line/ Or a good lay') encompass narcissism, promiscuity and mature self-reproach. There may be another triad here whereby family history and sexual history are layered with literary history. Thus the 'brothers' as blood-brothers or the gay brotherhood, merge into *literary* 'rivals...engaged/On the shady side of a square at midday in/ Voluble discourse': a passage that evokes many faded photographs. In portraying, it seems, his contemporaries as not 'in step' but as competitive and disputatious, Auden begins to reflect on constructions of the English 1930s, on differences between the decade as seen or recollected from within and from outside. As he does so, he reiterates and interprets his abdication from literary leadership.

Despite its non-judgmental ethos (the 'rivals...know each other too well to think/There are any important secrets'), 'In Praise of Limestone' is not altogether permissive as a work of literary criticism, especially since Auden includes himself in the critique:

> So, when one of them goes to the bad, the way his mind works
>   Remains comprehensible: to become a pimp
> Or deal in fake jewellery or ruin a fine tenor voice
>   For effects that bring down the house, could happen to all
> But the best and the worst of us...

These ways of 'going to the bad' signify the crowd-pleasing temp-
tations to which some artists have always yielded, but may also hit
specific targets. In contrast, Auden writes one contemporary, Louis
MacNeice, approvingly into the poem. A paraphrase of MacNeice's
wartime 'Prayer Before Birth' implies that the shared principles of
Letters from Iceland survive:

> Not to be left behind, not, please! to resemble
> The beasts who repeat themselves, or a thing like water
>   Or stone whose conduct can be predicted, these
> Are our Common Prayer, whose greatest comfort is music
>   Which can be made anywhere...

Compare the ending of 'Prayer Before Birth':

> I am not yet born; O hear me,
> Let not the man who is beast or who thinks he is God
>   come near me.
>
> I am not yet born; O fill me
> With strength against those who would freeze my
>   humanity, would dragoon me into a lethal automaton,
>   would make me a cog in a machine, a thing with
>   one face, a thing, and against all those
>   who would dissipate my entirety, would
>   blow me like thistledown hither and
>   thither or hither and thither
>   like water held in the
>   hands would spill me.
>
> Let them not make me a stone and let them not spill me.
> Otherwise kill me.

Auden's quotation from MacNeice reaffirms their solidarity with
regard to poetry ('music/Which can be made anywhere') and their
common wariness of determinist ideologies. And as he assimilates
MacNeice's imagery of stone and water – which criticises both the
over-determined and the over-fluid consciousness – into the creative
indeterminacy of 'limestone', he implies that indeterminacy does
not preclude ethical vigilance.

'In Praise of Limestone', then, incorporates a collective as well
as an individual apologia. Earlier in this phase of the poem, lime-
stone has been interrogatively recast as a historical landscape, the
(literary) 1930s regarded from the 1940s:

>   A backward
> And dilapidated province, connected
> To the big busy world by a tunnel, with a certain
>   Seedy appeal, is that all it is now? Not quite:
> It has a worldly duty which in spite of itself
>   It does not neglect, but calls into question
> All the Great Powers assume; it disturbs our rights.

The rhetorical question is spoken in a voice that represents the 1930s as passé or déclassé and which repeats the old charge, from Stephen Spender and other writers (though not MacNeice), that Auden's departure for the US in 1939 was a cop-out or sell-out.[5] One literary history encoded by the poem concerns the argument about poetry and 'worldly duty' which began in the 1930s, and is not over yet. Auden has already replied to his critics by tilting 'In Praise of Limestone' towards his 1940s positions, as in the initial images of the 'private pool' and 'its own little ravine'. In his early poetry, such recesses (valleys) were associated with escapism, until redeemed as the locus of poetry in 'In Memory of W.B. Yeats': 'It survives/ In the valley of its saying'. Now, 'the local needs of valleys' seem his favoured aesthetic habitat. 'Paysage Moralisé', a sestina from 1933, indicates how Auden's parabolic map has changed, not only in its 'dissolving' of clearcut allegorical topography but in the value attached to particular locales:

So many, doubtful, perished in the mountains,
Climbing up crags to get a view of islands,
So many, fearful, took with them their sorrow
Which stayed them when they reached unhappy cities,
So many, careless, dived and drowned in water,
So many, wretched, would not leave their valleys.

Is it the sorrow; shall it melt? Ah, water
Would gush, flush, green these mountains and these valleys,
And we rebuild our cities, not dream of islands.

Before asking whether the Auden landscape is to be judged passé or escapist, 'In Praise of Limestone' has characterised other aesthetics in terms of the extreme adventures, the 'skyline operations' ('Missing') assigned to 'mountains' in the 1930s:

                              That is why, I suppose,
    The best and worst never stayed here long but sought
Immoderate soils where the beauty was not so external,
    The light less public and the meaning of life
Something more than a mad camp. 'Come!' cried the granite wastes,
    'How evasive is your humour, how accidental
Your kindest kiss, how permanent is death.' (Saints-to-be
    Slipped away sighing.) 'Come!' purred the clays and gravels,
'On our plains there is room for armies to drill; rivers
    Wait to be tamed and slaves to construct you a tomb
In the grand manner; soft as the earth is mankind and both
    Need to be altered.' (Intendant Caesars rose and
Left, slamming the door.) But the really reckless were fetched
    By an older, colder voice, the oceanic whisper:
'I am the solitude that asks and promises nothing;
    That is how I shall set you free. There is no love;
There are only the various envies, all of them sad.'

Auden's well-known formulation (in the early 1930s) of the writer's responsibility – to 'Make action urgent and its nature clear' – is repudiated by the tone in which he not only denies his own literary leadership but also questions literature *as* leadership in all the guises figured by 'immoderate soils'. 'In Praise of Limestone' has deeply absorbed the dialectic of 'The Prolific and the Devourer', a crucial transitional work in its brilliant distinctions between the creative and political minds and in its self-analytical sense of how the latter may corrupt the former: 'The Dictator who says "My People": the Writer who says "My Public"'; 'To be forced to be political is to be forced to lead a dual life...only too often the false public life absorbs and destroys the genuine private life'; 'One of the best reasons I have for knowing that Fascism is bogus is that it is too much like the kinds of Utopias artists plan over café tables very late at night'. 'Immoderate soils' voice the 1930s literary call to be Commissar or Yogi (Caesar or saint). The 'clays and gravels' express the especially insidious temptation to become the former, to make things happen: 'The voice of the Tempter: "Unless you take part in the class struggle, you cannot become a major writer".' [6] The 'oceanic whisper' may invert the call to sainthood as a call to the grand refusal: to nihilism or death or the condition of the nomad looking into 'infinite space' somewhere beyond history and beyond poetry. Although the 'best' as well as 'worst' may hear all these calls, Auden implicitly places them as Tempter's voices, appeals to the egotistical sublime. He also rebukes his own former susceptibility in that he parodies the topographical imperatives of 'Spain' and other poems. The contrast between limestone and 'a crater whose blazing fury could not be fixed' may also deprecate café-table political posturing and acknowledge the limitations of an (English?) poetics remote from 'monstrous forms and lives'.

Yet this is a postwar poem, and during the war 'monstrous forms' and 'blazing fury' had come uncomfortably close to home. In 'Letter to Lord Byron' Auden had already ironised the connection between extreme landscape and extreme views: 'Besides, I'm very fond of mountains, too;/ I like to travel through them in a car...' In fact, 'In Praise of Limestone' answers the question 'is that all it is now?' with 'Not quite'. Earlier we have been told: 'this land is not the sweet home that it looks,/ Nor its peace the historical calm of a site/ Where something was settled once and for all'. This, presumably, can be read in personal, political and aesthetic terms, as well as situating the poem's own terrain somewhere between home and history, the domestic and 'worldly' spheres. Like 'Not quite', the lines contest the notion that all (30s) passion has been spent or

understood, the notion that Auden's poetry has really opted out
('home, sweet home'), dated, settled for middle-aged middle gear.
There is life yet in the old dog beneath the skin.

How, then, does 'In Praise of Limestone' reinterpret the 30s
commitment to 'worldly duty'? The opening lines set out a paradox
('we, the inconstant ones...consistently homesick for') on which
subsequent dialectic depends. This dialectic attaches values to
adjectives in the Yeatsian manner. One set of adjectives, again as
applicable to sexual as to literary behaviour, belongs to limestone:
inconstant, short, definite, flirtatious, ingenious, local, external,
evasive, accidental. Some of these adjectives acquire an unusually
positive resonance, just as the opposing adjectives take on totalitarian
overtones: important, moral, infinite, grand, big, busy, great, remote.
As Prolific and Devourer, poetry and ideology, meet again, lime-
stone's strategic self-deprecation both undermines the opposition
and assumes its own moral aspect: 'it disturbs our rights...[makes]
uneasy...rebukes...reproaches'. At first this corrective role is con-
fined to subversion and carnivalesque: 'these gamins,/ Pursuing the
scientist down the tiled colonnade/ With such lively offers'. Yet the
poem goes on to make more absolute claims for limestone as not
only a permissive, non-judgmental society or homosexual Utopia,
like that desired at the end of 'Through the Looking-Glass' ('Free
to our favours, all our titles gone'), but the ante-chamber to 'a
faultless love/ Or the life to come'. Lucy McDiarmid comments in
Auden's Apologies for Poetry that ' "In Praise of Limestone" turns
almost literally into a rite as it invokes the Apostles' Creed'.[7]

This key-change into idealism raises the question of whether
Auden, if not a 'saint-to-be' (although all the poem's voices may
represent tendencies of his – and everyone's – psyche), now sub-
ordinates poetry to religion. McDiarmid argues that, at this period,
'Every poem becomes an apology, undermining its own significance
and alluding to the value it cannot contain'. That explains the dead-
ness of later Auden; confession being possibly good for the soul
but usually bad for art. However, it is doubtful that 'In Praise of
Limestone' can be classified as 'a poem of *Sehnsucht*, of longing for
what is not itself ', or that 'poetry is not-limestone and limestone is
not-text'.[8] This Helicon poem which comes full-circle, this fractal
model of the creative gyre, seems to satisfy its own 'homesick' urges
(in part for the English Auden and English pastoral), to please and
praise itself. Surely Auden internalises limestone in a way that
contrasts with the split consciousness and unconscious subjectivity
of the 'anti-mythological' poet who calls 'The sun the sun, his
mind Puzzle'. Accordingly, from another angle, he externalises

limestone: so there is nothing outside the limestone text, so that it functions as subject and object. The point about limestone is its friability and mutability. It draws attention to Nature as artist, underlines the proximity of rock to architecture, of statue to flesh, of wilderness to garden, and thereby nudges the imagination of *homo faber*, of 'Eros, builder of cities':

> From weathered outcrop
> To hill-top temple, from appearing waters to
> Conspicuous fountains, from a wild to a formal vineyard,
> Are ingenious but short steps...

Limestone, as our minds play over it, as it represents the play of our minds, questions fixed boundaries between life or Nature and civilisation or art: 'These modifications of matter into/ Innocent athletes and gesticulating fountains'. Yet, despite such democratic access, such easy intercourse, categories are not dissolved or deconstructed in order to abolish them. 'In Praise of Limestone' can equally be read as celebrating a timeless creative and formalising principle: the human urge to modify matter. The shifts from 'weathered outcrop/ To hill-top temple', from 'waters' to 'fountains', condense the species' historical 'ingenuity' into Auden's own processes of image-making and 'verbal playing', his conspicuous versatility as displayed by the fountains and temples of the poem itself. (Here he contradicts the Marxist perspective of 'Spain' in which 'the diffusion/ Of the counting-frame and the cromlech' is marked off as 'all the past'.) All this, of course, counters criticism of his alleged 'inconstancy' as artist; whether critics target his departure from England, ideological shape-changes or textual revisions. In my view, Auden replies to his critics more completely than in the related apologia ' "The Truest Poetry is the Most Feigning" ' or in the Foreword to his 1966 *Collected Shorter Poems*. 'The Truest Poetry', whose tongue-in-cheekiness Philip Larkin missed in his review of *Homage to Clio*,[9] provocatively reaffirmed art for art's sake in the prosaic, philistine 1950s:

> Be subtle, various, ornamental, clever,
> And do not listen to those critics ever
> Whose crude provincial gullets crave in books
> Plain cooking made still plainer by plain cooks...

> What but tall tales, the luck of verbal playing,
> Can trick our lying nature into saying
> That love, or truth in any serious sense,
> Like orthodoxy, is a reticence?

(Larkin, who quotes this, may have taken it not only literally but personally.) ' "The Truest Poetry" ' strategically overstates poetry's fictiveness and insincerity, its ideological and ethical irresponsibility ('Re-sex the pronouns, add a few details...'). The Foreword, in contrast, insists on poetry's duty to its author's 'feelings and beliefs'. Auden says: 'A dishonest poem is one which expresses, no matter how well, feelings or beliefs which its author never felt or entertained.' Thus whether he praises dishonesty or deplores it or possibly practises it (in rewriting and censoring history), he espouses the fallacy that language is detachable from meaning. While ' "The Truest Poetry" ' knows this, its subtexts sabotaging its surface argument, the Foreword suggests that Auden cannot read his earlier poems in their full complexity:

> Critics, I have observed, are apt to find revisions ideologically significant... I have never, consciously at any rate, attempted to revise my former thoughts or feelings, only the language in which they were first expressed when, on further consideration, it seemed to me inaccurate, lifeless, prolix or painful to the ear...On revisions as a matter of principle, I agree with Valéry: 'A poem is never finished; it is only abandoned.' [10]

Written earlier, 'In Praise of Limestone' is able to mediate between the positions of ' "The Truest Poetry" ' and the Foreword, partly because the 1940s Auden is still productively arguing with the 1930s Auden, truth with fiction, history with transcendence. Limestone figures neither as 'the life to come', nor yet as correlative for a humbly chameleon poetry 'never finished...only abandoned'. As Nature, the body, civilisation, art, this symbol possesses and asserts the fertile, self-renewing spaciousness of Yeats's 'images that yet/ Fresh images beget' in 'Byzantium' (another Helicon/workshop poem). And its parabolic logic leads the speaker to realise the interdependence of truths and fictions, absolutes and embodiment, imagination and faith, Earth and Arcadia (Utopia, Paradise): 'Dear, I *know* nothing of/Either, but when I try to *imagine* a faultless love/ Or the life to come...' What follows is poetry not theology. Thus 'In Praise of Limestone' may be a meta-parable in distinguishing not only the Auden landscape but also the *poetry* landscape from the mental worlds of saint and Caesar. Yet, like MacNeice's Lancelot, poetry-as-limestone pursues the ideal. In the previous essay I argued that MacNeice and Auden do not permit a neat reading of twentieth-century poetry in these islands as moving, despite a 'pink decade' blip, from modernism to postmodernism. Certainly 'In Praise of Limestone' subverts 'grand narratives', but perhaps more their grandeur ('a tomb/In the grand manner') than all possibility of narrative. The poem makes no bones about offering its own limestone narrative, telling its own stories. To suspect authority, in the homosexual-anarchist style shared by Auden and Isherwood, is not to rule out authorship. That style may have contributed to latterday postmodernism, but it has a politics. At the end, Auden is close to the Dante who was 'simply a poet asking himself how you would describe heaven'.[11] By setting 'knowledge' against 'imagination' as the antinomies between which poetry has its being, he resolves his recurrent muddle about perfection of the life/work in an embodiment, and a faith in embodiment, that parallels Yeats's closure in 1939: 'Man can embody truth, but he cannot know it.'[12]

Larkin, Decadence and the Lyric Poem

1

Historical distance is lengthening for all Larkin's readers. Bri-nylon, loaf-hair and Belfast herring-hawkers now seem as archaic as Edward Thomas's plough and charcoal-burners. Honeymooners take planes not trains. Yet, as Larkin's images become more historical, they also become less sociological. Meanwhile the publication of the *Selected Letters* and biography has reinforced the psychological tendency in Larkin criticism. That is the line I intend to follow in this essay, although my focus will be the interdependence of the psychological and the aesthetic. I will also speculate about Larkin and the lyric poem.

Nowadays terms like 'multivocal' or 'dialogic' are applied to Larkin's poetry.[1] But his medium is surely the mask-lyric – a medium he could not escape, despite his desire to write novels. And his masks are fewer and thinner than those of poets whose embrace of the outer world is less problematic. Larkin's psycho-drama turns on a first-person speaker, and is usually produced by what Yeats calls 'those traditional metres that have developed with the language'.[2] This does not mean that Larkin should never be read against the grain of his own structures or of his efforts to control his reception. Further, what he might be protecting, what might be at stake in his poetry, is the lyric's very survival. One of his gyres is the losing and finding of faith in form. And, for Larkin, form as pattern is inseparable from form as mystery. In 'Sad Steps', for example, 'The hardness and the brightness and the plain/ Far-reaching singleness of that wide stare' unites the lyric artifact with its inspiration. This self-referential symbol reinstates what 'Medallion of art!…Immensements!' has defensively mocked. Larkin may not always succeed in rhetorically outflanking his doubts and doubters. Jake Balokowsky, surely well into literary theory by now, lurks on the next page of the *Collected Poems*. Yet it goes too much against the grain, concedes too much to theoretical premises and critical vocabularies that Larkin resisted, if we turn him into a postmodernist. That seems a risky way to restore his canonical fortunes. I prefer to highlight some aspects of his own theory which are pre-modernist and invoke Decadence. Several critics, myself included, have already discussed Larkin as (to quote his youthful self-description) a '*fin de siècle* Romantic' (*Letters*, 10), however heavily disguised as a

mid-century suburbanite. But the biographical disclosures provide a
new context for this emphasis, and perhaps this emphasis provides
a new context for them.

One result of tracking Larkin back to the 1890s is to open the
borders of his "Englishness" in a British Isles and European rather
than Anglo-American direction. Cyril Connolly writes that the Irish
movement aimed to 'discover what [explosive] blend of Anglo-
Irish and French...would knock the pundits of London off their
chairs'.[3] Leaving aside the disputed lineage of Larkin's symbolism
(and there may be several kinds of symbolism, transcendental and
non-transcendental, in his work), his decadent inclinations are not
only a matter of Yeats, Celtic fever and a voice heard singing of
Kitty or Katy. They align him with poets who, at different stages
of the twentieth century, absorbed principles of aestheticism that
survived in their forms if not their surface content. Such poets are,
for example, Edward Thomas, Robert Graves and Derek Mahon
(Mahon's different 'blend of Anglo-Irish and French' is especially
apropos). Larkin's letters to J.B. Sutton, with their air of Stephen
Dedalus showing off to his mates, prove how right James Booth is
to call him an 'existential aesthete'.[4] Even the letters that worship
D.H. Lawrence face towards Lawrence's gem-like flame rather
than his social circumference: 'I have been thinking recently that
Lawrence's beliefs are pure (in the sense of utter, most sensitive
and refined) aestheticism...More & more I believe in a central
pavilion of mystery, whose various sides are emblazoned with dif-
ferent emblems' (*Letters*, 56-57). In 1946 Larkin came up with the
following Beardsley- or Yeats-like emblem: 'I see [life] mainly
composed of sex, death and art, perhaps art as an acrobat going
round the ring with his left foot on a black horse, death, and his
right on sex, a white one.' He goes on to say: 'Still, I distrust
theorising about life like this: the only worthwhile theories, or
statements of belief, are works of art.' Changing idiom again, he
adds: 'All else is just farting Annie Laurie through a keyhole'
(*Letters*, 125). We might find all these linguistic and tonal registers
in a Larkin poem. Here they significantly converge to make the
point that art comes first. Some months earlier he had told Norman
Iles, in the terms of Wilde's preface to *Dorian Gray*: 'your attitude
is predominantly ethical & mine aesthetical...you aim at increased
positiveness of character while I aim at increased negativeness, a
kind of infinite recession in the face of the world...You see, my
trouble is that I simply can't understand anybody doing anything
but write, paint, compose music' (*Letters*, 87-88). Later he told
Sutton that he needed a friend who 'consciously accepts mystery

at the bottom of things...the kind of artist who is perpetually kneeling in his heart – who gives no fuck for anything except this mystery, and for that gives every fuck there is' (*Letters*, 106). 'Infinite recession in the face of the world' certainly characterises the fiction that Larkin wrote during the decade of apprenticeship that laid down his themes. *Jill* (1946) and *A Girl in Winter* (1947) leave their protagonists in solipsistic states of suspended animation, between sleep and waking, dream and actuality, life and death, life and art. The last paragraphs of *A Girl in Winter* so closely parallel the ending of Joyce's 'The Dead' as to suggest not so much plagiarism as affinity with its cadences, its ambiguous swoon. One shared motif is marriage – reassessed or rejected. In 'The Dead' Gabriel Conroy's self-image has been shattered by his wife's story about her romantic dead lover, Michael Furey. In *A Girl in Winter* Katherine Lind has decided against marrying her unromantic lover, Robin. Gabriel's 'soul' approaches

> that region where dwell the vast hosts of the dead... His own identity was fading out into a grey impalpable world: the solid world itself which these dead had one time reared and lived in was dissolving and dwindling... It had begun to snow again. He watched sleepily the flakes, silver and dark, falling obliquely against the lamplight... His soul swooned slowly as he heard the snow falling faintly through the universe and faintly falling, like the descent of their last end, upon all the living and the dead.

Katherine focuses on

> the snow and her watch ticking. So many snowflakes, so many seconds. As time passed they seemed to mingle in their minds, heaping up into a vast shape that might be a burial mound, or the cliff of an iceberg whose summit is out of sight. Into its shadow dreams crowded, full of conceptions and stirrings of cold, as if icefloes were moving down a lightless channel of water. They were going in orderly slow procession, moving from darkness further into darkness...Yet their passage was not saddening. Unsatisfied dreams rose and fell about them, crying out against their implacability, but in the end glad that such order, such destiny, existed. (*Girl*, 248)

Larkin's entropic cold and dark is more absolute (and closer to the narrative voice) than Joyce's. He never could complete the third novel which was supposed to 'develop logically back to life again' from 'the frozen wastes' (*Letters*, 109). M.W. Rowe has argued that after *Jill*, 'Sexually and artistically [Larkin] had begun to sort himself out.'[5] Yet, perhaps not quite. Rather, the ceaseless mutual sorting out between sex and art was to find its proper genre. His attempt to write fiction had returned him almost full circle to the liminal reverie where lyric poems are conceived: a mix of passivity and heightened awareness. Larkin's spectral fictional surrogates finally leave the social world to inhabit his favourite symbols of tree, wind, snow, night, and to abstract from life 'the maddened surface of things' (*Jill*, 243), the 'orderly slow procession' towards oblivion (*Girl*, 248). Yet there is development in the androgynous proto-poetic personality so strangely adumbrated in these novels. Whereas John (a truly weak man) remains at the mercy of feverish dreams, the dreams which Katherine and Robin share (she being the dominant partner) yield to an idea of 'order'. Larkin's contemporaneous letters to Sutton feature solitary epiphanies that more deliberately transpose Nature into art: a scene that 'appeared to me like a picture'; a bird's 'beautiful, ingenious twists of sound' (*Letters*, 145-46).

Psychological factors (to be considered later) helped to avert Larkin's gaze from wartime England. But the war itself was revolving the kaleidoscope of forms. Larkin's sensitivity to winds of literary change after 1940 is suggested not only by the exhaustion of his Audenesque, but also by his admiration for Cyril Connolly. Andrew Motion reveals that, at the memorial service for Auden, Larkin blurted out to Connolly, 'Sir, you formed me!' Connolly's *The Condemned Playground: Essays 1927-1944* (1945) was 'my sacred book'.[6] Larkin wrote an introduction to the 1985 reprint in which he quotes Connolly's axiom that 'the true function of a writer is to produce a masterpiece', and says: 'What strikes the reader most forcibly is his commitment to literature, to the notion that being a writer is the practice of a morality as well as an art.'[7] Connolly explains his title as signifying 'Art itself...man's noblest attempt to preserve Imagination from Time, to make unbreakable toys of the mind, mudpies which endure', yet an attempt always shadowed by 'evanescence'.[8]

Larkin had already, it seems, internalised *Enemies of Promise* (1938) – a book whose influence on poetic careers is incalculable.[9] Connolly's warning about the 'clasping tares of domesticity' must have fallen on receptive ground. Connolly speculates that domestic happiness may 'replace that necessary unhappiness without which writers perish', and recommends the modern discipline of being alone in a hotel bedroom. Larkin certainly remembered Connolly's later phrase about judging a writer by 'the resonance of his despair' (*Letters*, 478). In *Enemies of Promise* Connolly also speculates that a lyric poet has a better chance than a prose writer of resisting both the poppies of escapism and the thistles of politics, since 'he is entrusted with the experience of the ages, he is not a political conscript, nor can he be accused of escapism if he confines himself to celebrating the changing seasons, memories of childhood, love or beauty'.[10] Here Connolly ignores the cries of 'universalism' that might be uttered by theorists then as now. But a passage in *The Condemned Playground* directly sets about Marxist commissars in a manner that could be Larkin's: 'They are obsessed by a profound hatred of art and are prepared to devote their lives to gratifying it. To do this they occupy a fortified position, either at a university, or in an advanced political party, or as a publisher, and then proceed to castigate the artist...'[11]

Perhaps Connolly's formative effect went deeper than to confirm Larkin's sense that a married artist was a contradiction in terms; or to advise that the serious writer should avoid a profession too close to his own vocation – preferably finding camouflage among the salaried middle class. The questions he was asking about art and the writer's life in England (*The Condemned Playground* is partly a 'condition of England' work) became sharper in the late 1930s. Connolly calls the war 'the enemy of creative activity', and holds that 'writers and painters are wise and right to ignore it... Since they are politically impotent, they can use this time to develop at deeper emotional levels, or to improve their weapons by technical experiment.' This is particularly urgent because 'they have so long been mobilised in various causes' that they are losing faith in the disinterested intellect.[12] The larger argument of *Enemies of Promise* and *The Condemned Playground* is an attack on long-term English philistinism and short-term left-wing puritanism. It is a plea for style. In reaction against the realist excesses of the 1930s Connolly insists, for instance, on the precision of poetic language: 'Poetry, to stand out,' he says, 'must be a double distillation of life that goes deeper than prose. It must be brandy as compared to wine...This distillation...can only be achieved by a writer who maintains his sensibility and integrity at a high pitch and concentrates on the quality of his production.' Connolly also declares that the vogue for vernacular is dying and that 'mastery of form' waits in the wings. While he concedes the legacy of colloquial writing to 'a balanced literary budget', he advises young authors not to borrow from the realist 'the flatness of style, the homogeneity of outlook, the fear of eccentricity, the reporter's horror of distinction, the distrust of beauty...'[13] When Larkin is praised for using everyday idiom, some critics seem to forget that his lyric reacted against, as well as absorbed, the 1930s; that 'balance' is what counts; that his most crudely colloquial moments are associated with the withdrawal of beauty. Connolly's first *Horizon* editorial stated: 'Our standards are aesthetic, and our politics are in abeyance.' Larkin ends his introduction to *The Condemned Playground* by saluting the 'sober idealism' of 'the passages from war-time issues of *Horizon*', and by bringing 'art' and 'morality' still closer together: 'In the narrow corner of the mid-war years, it was Connolly's commitment to the morality of art that surfaced again, a vision of something beyond the condemned playground...' [14]

Other poets in the early 1940s also reaffirmed the aesthetic in ways that varied according to age, context and temperament. Larkin's contemporary, Keith Douglas, made every word 'work for its keep'.[15] Larkin's senior, Louis MacNeice, turned away from 'reportage'. But none was so magnetised as Larkin by 'pure aestheticism', or fell for the most visionary strata of Yeats. Larkin's emerging literary personality, then, matches the profile of an aesthete. In an earlier essay, 'Poète Maudit Manqué', I argued that Larkin's psychological affinities with the immature Yeats are as significant as his technical debts to the mature Yeats, and that these affinities amount to more than what Andrew Motion calls, with respect to *The North Ship,* 'a sentimental version of Yeats's preoccupation with love, sexual tristesse and death'.[16] If Larkin himself seems to concur ('not because I liked his personality...'),[17] artistic personality is what counts. The section of Yeats's *Collected Poems* that most centrally influenced *The North Ship* was *The Wind Among the Reeds,* in which Yeats's yearning, prostrated, frustrated lyric persona of the 1890s reaches its apotheosis. *The Winding Stair,* written 30 years later, comes next in influence. In his Introduction to the reissue of *The North Ship* Larkin recalls his reading and writing habits (1943-1946):

> Every night after supper before opening my large dark green manuscript book I used to limber up by turning the pages of the 1933 plum-coloured Macmillan edition, which stopped at 'Words for Music Perhaps', and which meant in fact that I never absorbed the harsher last poems. This may be discernible in what I wrote.[18]

But, to judge from internal evidence, he also knew Yeats's *Last Poems and Plays* (1940).[19] Thus the broader point to be discerned is that Larkin, in keeping with his aesthetic relish for intensely coloured book-covers, bypasses the historical-political Yeats altogether. Even when he imitates a Yeats poem with this dimension, as when he bases 'Born Yesterday' on 'A Prayer for My Daughter', he redirects his borrowings into purely individual channels. Whereas Yeats's 'daughter' as 'a flourishing hidden tree' disseminates cultural values, the 'ordinariness' that Larkin's poem desires for Sally Amis resides in a personal 'Catching of happiness'. *The Wind Among the Reeds* and *The Winding Stair* are notable for the extremity of the former's despair, the latter's 'joy', love poetry being a prominent genre in both. Larkin describes the poem he added to the reissued *North*

Ship ('Waiting for breakfast, while she brushed her hair') as 'show-[ing] the Celtic fever abated and the patient sleeping soundly'.[20] But 'fever' captures not only his 'infatuation with Yeats's music', but also his indelible identification with the sublimated sexuality, the ambiguous desire for some 'burning' consummation, that shapes Yeats's *fin-de-siècle* exhaustion and apocalypse:

> If grief could burn out
> Like a sunken coal,
> The heart would rest quiet,
> The unrent soul
> Be still as a veil;
> But I have watched all night
>
> The fire grow silent,
> The grey ash soft:
> And I stir the stubborn flint
> The flames have left,
> And grief stirs, and the deft
> Heart lies impotent.
>
> (*North Ship* XVIII)

Here Larkin restores Crazy Jane's image for sexual awakening ('nothing can be sole or whole/That has not been rent') to the virgin state and Yeats's nineties scenario of the heart growing old. In contrast, 'All catches alight' begins *The North Ship* in the most positive and imperative mood of *The Winding Stair*: 'Every one thing,/ Shape, colour and voice,/ Cries out, "Rejoice!"' Yeats's 'joy' (with added emphasis from D.H. Lawrence), like his proposal to 'cast out remorse' in 'A Dialogue of Self and Soul', may have impressed Larkin as an antidote to 'impotence'. This produces some odd mood-swings in *The North Ship*, even if the oscillation anticipates subtler dialectic in later poems. 'Winter' ends:

> Then the whole heath whistles
> In the leaping wind,
> And shrivelled men stand
> Crowding like thistles
> To one fruitless place;
> Yet still the miracles
> Exhume in each face
> Strong silken seed,
> That to the static
> Gold winter sun throws back
> Endless and cloudless pride.

Early Larkin both follows and resembles the early Yeats in that a solitary persona, whose masculine identity may be problematic, exists at a distance from the possibility of mutually fulfilled desire.

Elaine Showalter characterises the decadent male aesthete as homo-
sexual in spirit if not always in practice. Decadent writers turn
women into icons and fetishes: 'They appear as objects of value only
when aestheticised as corpses or phallicised as *femmes fatales*.' [21] It
has been well established that Larkin's poetry presents female images
in such terms. Women figure, indeed, as images, as 'beauty', as art-
objects, photographically or pornographically posed, best enjoyed
at a spectatorial distance. However, this is less easy to attack from
a feminist angle when it becomes the problem that a poem explores,
as in 'Wild Oats', which recognises the force of 'Unlucky charms',
or 'Latest Face'. In 'Latest Face' the speaker is a divided Pygmalion
who desires to protract the male gaze ('Your great arrival at my
eyes'), who hesitates to expose the 'statue of your beauty' to 'real
untidy air'. Larkin's negative images of women also conform to
decadent attitudes. The last stanza of 'Latest Face' attaches 'mur-
derous' power to a woman desired and denied. His poems are hard
on women who require effort and money, lose virginal purity, lose
their looks ('mug-faced wives'), talk or nag (virtually synonyms):
'the drivel of some bitch/ Who's read nothing but *Which*'. Evidently
the main trouble with 'unspeakable wives' is that they speak; while
in 'Wild Oats', the split between 'bosomy English rose/ And her
friend in specs I could talk to' implicitly portrays the former as
rendering the speaker speech-less. Galatea, then, should never
come to life. She *is* art: art as the higher pornography – immobile,
silent, disempowered – art for a male audience in need of solace
and for which the male poet is the medium. The admirer of 'Latest
Face' says: 'I contain your current grace'. Larkin rounds off the
introduction to *All What Jazz* by imagining his readers as men
oppressed by 'cold-eyed lascivious daughters on the pill' and 'age-
ing and bitter wives' (their sons are merely accused of laziness,
jeans and cannabis); and for whom, 'deserted by everything that
once made life sweet', he prescribes Doctor Jazz (*RW*, 298). Even
the empathy with desexualised maternity in 'Afternoons' – 'Their
beauty has thickened./ Something is pushing them/ To the side of
their own lives' – is couched in the language of aesthetic detach-
ment. At one level it is Larkin's sensibility that pushes such images
to the side. Similarly, the 'you' of 'Maiden Name' is coldly told that
she has disqualified herself as Muse: 'you cannot be/ Semantically
the same as that young beauty'. Woman as beauty, beauty as woman
has split between her permanent 'shape' in imagination and her
'depreciating' contingency in life. By marrying she has doubly
'confused' her identity. Larkin's manuscript note 'you are not she'
echoes Dorian Gray's rejection of Sybil Vane.

But the question of "misogyny" becomes more complex when
we consider Larkin's own gender-identifications. What happens to
women in his poetry projects his own desires, fears, self-hatred. He
can imagine nothing worse than being pushed to the side of his
own life. And women are not only the ideal or its negation, Eros or
Thanatos, the 'figurehead with golden tits' and her 'black-/ Sailed'
opposite. Less iconic females personify the suffering caused by the
ideal's failure to deliver. The poet is an 'Ugly Sister', who com-
pensates in art for lack of beauty in life. The 'friend in specs' is his
female double. In 'Love Songs in Age' and 'Faith Healing' women
are victims/victims are women, if unaesthetically so: 'Moustached in
flowered frocks'. Yet the androgyny here may go deeper. At times
the male speaker represents himself in the conventional female role,
without agency, waiting for a romantic lover to 'bear [him] off
irrevocably' ('Places, Loved Ones'). More broadly, the Larkin-
speaker tends to be passive: a sleeping princess waiting for life to
start. The early poem 'I see a girl dragged by the wrists' expresses
the desire 'To be that girl'. She is less a Muse than a better self,
another sister-figure, whose desires are masochistically fulfilled in
subjugation. To take a different tack, Larkin does not discount women
as artists, but recognises himself in the poetry of Christina Rossetti,
for instance: 'Life, and the world, and mine own self, are changed/
For a dream's sake'; 'O hope deferred, hope still.' [22] There is also
his career as 'Brunette Coleman', female author of lesbian soft porn.
    Andrew Motion construes Larkin's interest in lesbianism as
transitional between a homosexual and a heterosexual orientation.[23]
But even if the latter were comfortably or fully achieved – *Jill* and
A Girl in Winter enact a transvestite rite of passage towards imagi-
native androgyny – 'Brunette' is bound up with his continuing
pornographic tastes after the Oxford years. M.W. Rowe makes
extremely persuasive claims for the deep-seated significance of
Larkin's 'lesbian' phase. Perhaps, if we were to diagnose Larkin as
a decadent, it might enhance his reputation. Critics would talk about
transgression instead of sexism. Yet, while Lisa Jardine, commenting
on the *Selected Letters*, sets limits to the transgressive ('a steady
stream of casual obscenity, throwaway derogatory remarks about
women, and arrogant disdain for those of different skin colour or
nationality'),[24] the case is not met either when critics play down
Larkin's schoolgirl fantasies: when they term them 'mild' or 'face-
tious ventriloquism'.[25] In fact, they appear disturbingly obsessive, and
the biography evokes a hinterland of disturbance that stretches into
the burnt diaries and includes trace elements of several *fin-de-siècle*
sins: *'Twas wine or women, or some curse'* – Lionel Johnson's homo-

sexuality and alcoholism, Ernest Dowson's predilection for very young women. This brings us back not only to the psychology of the aesthete, but also to why aestheticism attracts a certain kind of psychology, and how this influences Larkin's lyric.

2

I wrote on Larkin as *poète maudit* without knowing the half of it. At least people who expect poetry to be cosy or poets always to be Mr nice guy – or gal – have had a shock. They may now be more attuned to the precise resonance of Larkin's despair in 'fulfilment's desolate attic'. Here I want to propose a psychological model that might fit Larkin: a model that particularly applies to decadent writing, and one that accounts for some of its strengths as well as weaknesses. This is the psychology of narcissism, and I will be drawing on various accounts of it.[26] Narcissism has been described as both a personal and cultural phenomenon, and as operating across a spectrum from the pathological to the normal. It is characterised by difficulties in moving from the grandiose idealised self of infancy to realistic self-esteem, and also from solipsism to relationship. The role of the mother is seen as crucial in promoting a realistically grounded selfhood. The female images in 'Next, Please' correspond to narcissistic images of the good and bad mother. Their opposition marks an impasse between the bountiful, all-giving figure of infancy, and the mother who encourages the reluctant child to renounce immature 'habits of expectancy'. On the one hand, narcissism is regressive. The narcissistic self withdraws, not exactly out of selfishness or self-love, but in response to threats to its integrity – Larkin's 'infinite withdrawal in the face of the world'. His poems and letters reiterate the fear of being invaded, diluted, controlled or possessed by another. Spending the self is equated with spending money – you don't get it back. This is a third sense in which the woman of 'Maiden Name' has 'confused' her identity. This is the poignancy of the women in 'Afternoons'. On the other hand, narcissism can be progressive if its 'strivings for wholeness and perfection' are transformed into a 'quest for virtue and beauty'.[27] So Larkin's withdrawal also represents 'the complete & utter solitude so necessary for any worthwhile artistic creation' (*Letters*, 157). The monastic 'singleness of that wide stare' is the poet's integrity as well as the moon's. The letter to Norman Iles, which contains his phrase about withdrawal, also contains a narcissistic image for the kind of self-dramatisation in which his future lyrics will specialise, and which will ideally transform life into art: 'I conceive the creative process as depending on an intricate arrangement of little mirrors inside one, and by continual care and assiduity and practice these mirrors can be cleaned and polished, so that in the end artistic perception is a whole-time and not a part-time thing.' David Punter begins *The Romantic Unconscious: A Study in Narcissism and Patriarchy* (1989) by proposing that it 'is the function of the ego to construct: to construct for itself a series of defences, and simultaneously to construct in the world a specular image of itself, which turns out to be an image of the defences themselves, inscribed with the markings of evasion, which figure in the world as the mystery to be explored, the tiger face peering from the suspected unconscious'.[28]

I would suggest that borderline narcissism fits the conflicts that Larkin's poetry both manifests and explores. The art called into being by the progressive aspect of narcissism is inseparable from the pathology of its regressive aspect which becomes its theme – in part consciously, in part unconsciously. Among other features of narcissism which correspond to Larkin's demeanour in life or art are 'the endless circling of desire upon itself', 'a remarkably rigid self-structure, which is most resistant to change' and narcissistic rage. The latter is directed against people and circumstances that 'fail to support...fantasies of omnipotence and total control'.[29] Narcissistic rage is the rage of Titch Thomas against the girl on the poster. It is the abuse and envy in some of Larkin's letters. And, inevitably, death above all threatens narcissistic 'self-structure': 'a special way of being afraid/No trick dispels' ('Aubade'). Logically, 'Basic conflicts associated with ageing, chronic illness, physical and mental limitations...are specially intense [for the narcissist], for such experiences make it more and more difficult for the grandiose self to deny the frail, limited and transitory character of human existence'.[30] The speaker of 'The Old Fools' experiences narcissistic rage when he contemplates the idea that 'the bits that were you/Start speeding away from each other for ever/With no one to see'. And the poem starkly contrasts the point where primary narcissism begins – 'the million-petalled flower/Of being here' – with its ultimate mockery: 'hideous inverted childhood'.

A final relevant feature of the narcissistic personality is that it evades Oedipal conflict (and hence coming to terms with the adult world). This would be too visceral and bruising for the rigid self to contemplate. Béla Grunberger concludes that 'It is not a question of taking the father's place but of acting as if the father had never existed.' Yet such behaviour marks a site of damage. Guinn

Batten, discussing narcissism and 'Shelley's Absent Fathers', suggests that 'neither dispassionate reason nor the will to resist the death drive can ever, finally, govern the self so long as the self (the ego) is constructed narcissistically and melancholically through its identification with the moral Law of an absent Father. For his love not only may be missing – indeed, it may metamorphose into desire and/or even hatred.'[31] Larkin does not, in fact, assume the patriarchal position. The father is strikingly absent from his poetry. The speaker of 'Dockery and Son' treats the idea of fatherhood like news of a bizarre custom from another planet. When Larkin's father was dying, Larkin suffered from a sense of being 'irrevocably marked out as a failure, a coward'. He told Sutton: 'I feel that I have to make a big mental jump – to stop being a child and become an adult' (*Letters*, 145). His elegy for his father, 'An April Sunday brings the snow' curiously consigns the father to the domestic sphere, as a jam-maker, and the final line lacks either memorial or dynastic assurances: 'sweet/And meaningless, and not to come again'. The mother looms much larger. 'Reference Back' can be read as a portrait of the artist unable to resolve his relationship with his mother and so exorcise the regressive aspect of his narcissism. 'Home' in this poem is made up of 'unsatisfactory' spatial and generational relations. This adjective is attached to the hall, a room, 'your unsatisfactory age...my unsatisfactory prime'. Mother and son are in separate spaces yet the axis of their connection remains fixed. The only sphere in which unsatisfactoriness briefly mends is the sphere of art: 'The flock of notes those antique negroes blew' creates 'a sudden bridge', just as the poem itself does. Larkin displaces his own birth on to music made 'The year after I was born' and displaces procreation – becoming a father himself might have been a more tangible bridge – on to creation, art ('flock of notes'). But at the end the underlying impasse (where the absent father may be buried) is stated rather than resolved: stated as an opposition between childhood paradise lost, 'what we have as it once was', and adult powerlessness to regain it: 'just as though/By acting differently we could have kept it so'. The speaker is narcissistic in that he cannot conceive a form of adult agency that might mediate between the 'Blindingly undiminished' and 'satisfactory' selfhood. Even if 'blinding', as in 'I Remember, I Remember', nuances primal worlds as deceptive, it mourns the loss of their integrity. Here the self is determined, rigid, not fluid. It refers back.

Larkin's poems, of course, know more than their speakers. They may also know more than their author. His protestations about transparency contradict his sense of mystery. In any case, the prominence of the first person singular/single seems tied in with narcissistic anxiety about the self, its bearings and boundaries. His focus is individuation not individualism. The difference between the poet and those 'Neurotics' in whom 'stalemate…grinds away' is that he can represent neurosis. His unhappiness can 'write black' and write back. He can analyse, ironise, sublimate, pursue 'the quest for beauty'. Singleness thus becomes a virtue, a vocation. Probably we have seen the last of a brand of Larkin criticism that regards him as a shy, witty bachelor or 'nine-to-five man who had seen poetry', in Seamus Heaney's somewhat patronising formula, rather than an artist whose art is entangled with personality disorder. Yet artistic singleness is not (and cannot be) a wholly resolved choice. Thus, for Larkin, 'the toad *work*' represents both stalemate ('Its hunkers are heavy as hard luck') and discipline. As the latter, it prevents him from joining those who 'turn over their failures/ By some bed of lobelias'. Nine-to-fiveness and poetry are not distinct, the one mundane, the other transcendental: they mutually stake out a site of conflict. More positively, 'Poetry of Departures' proposes to test poetry by staying put. 'Reasons for Attendance', also situated on this dialectical faultline, asks 'Why be out here?/ But then, why be in there?' There can be a negative answer to both questions. Down one unhappy masculine vista lurks 'Mr Bleaney'; down the other, where work conspires with marriage, lurks 'Arnold'. Ultimately the two fuse as terminally dreaded role-models. Mr Bleaney represents a pointless solitariness unredeemed by creative fruits: 'But if he stood and watched the frigid wind/ Tousling the clouds…' Here the wind, whose motion so often (in Romantic style) symbolises creative power for Larkin, implies the double absence of sexual/social and artistic potency. I have argued elsewhere that the syntactical labyrinth of the last two quatrains conceals a suicidal black hole.[32]

There may be parallels here with Woody Allen. Larkin and Allen share eccentric looks, defensive wit, incapacity to cohabit, obsession with death (Allen's 'I just don't want to be there when it happens'), agoraphobia, phobia about daily minutiae, an interest in youngish women, self-fascinated self-analysis. The seeming clarity of Larkin's structures does not make him a rationalist. Poets like Ted Hughes, who theorise and mythologise the unconscious, possibly tell us less about it than do '*naturally* fouled-up guys'. Larkin's psycho-drama taps into inescapably shared experience – the ordeal of adolescence – that it does not necessarily declare on the surface. For Larkin in 1947 his 'creations' were 'conscious peaks of cones that have their roots in the unknown…One bores a tiny hole – then (with luck) a fountain hits one in the eye. Bash!' (*Letters*, 141). On the one hand, he is wary of grubbing up the mysterious roots of poetry – hence his attacks on 'those chaps who go round American universities explaining how they write poems' (*RW*, 71); on the other, he often splits his voice (as does Woody Allen) between analyst and patient. His letters to Sutton compulsively dissect his 'soul-history'. In this they resemble Edward Thomas's letters to Gordon Bottomley, which similarly represent their author as 'tangled up in the web of... self-consciousness' (*Letters*, 159), and which similarly underlie poems written later on. Influenced by John Layard, Larkin read books about psychology and analysed his dreams. In 'If, My Darling' – whose readers should not really have been surprised by the *Selected Letters* – the artist-analyst shows us round his unconscious ('a string of infected circles'), although his aggression towards the woman addressed may disclose unanalysed layers. Larkin is always interested in other poets whose art arises from psychic crisis. For example, his probing of Emily Dickinson's 'disturbed, if not arrested development' hardly does her poetry justice, but its terminology evokes features of his own interior landscape. He finds 'somewhere within [her forms]...a deep fracture, that chills the harmless properties into a wide and arctic plain where they are wedged together eternally to represent a life gone irrevocably wrong' (*RW*, 193). There are echoes of this, and perhaps of Dickinson's poems, in his own 'Love Again'. Here the speaker lacks an 'element// That spreads through other lives' and his lack has 'Something to do with violence/ A long way back, and wrong rewards,/ And arrogant eternity'. Like Dickinson, Larkin could not stop writing letters to the world.

At the end of the Dickinson article Larkin calls poetry 'an affair of sanity, of seeing things as they are' (*RW*, 197). But this is partly a tribute to himself for not going mad, for managing his neurosis, for 'making [poems] of it' (*RW*, 68). Twenty-five years earlier, in poems and letters of the late 1940s, he had tried to locate the fracture in his own psyche. His diagnosis appears at its simplest in such formulations as 'the split in me...comes between what I admire and what I am' and 'I never like what I've got' (*Letters*, 149, 165). He refers to 'blockage', to 'mutually neutralising' qualities (*Letters*, 144, 152). Several poems also focus on split and blockage (more subtly represented in his mature work): 'Deep Analysis', 'Neurotics', 'I am washed upon a rock', 'Sinking like sediment through the day'. Two longer self-analytical poems that correspond to the narcissistic model are 'Many famous feet have trod' and 'On Being Twenty-six'. 'Many famous feet have trod' establishes a

Manichean separation between 'lineage of sorrow' and 'lineage of joy' which prefigures the doubled ships of 'Next, Please' and the polarity of 'Reference Back'. Central to 'lineage of sorrow' is what Larkin terms 'the instinct-to-turn-back', and which turns out to be narcissistic regression: 'Instinct that so worships my own face/ It would halt time herewith/ And put my wishes in its place:/ And for this reason has great fear of death.' 'On Being Twenty-six' ends:

> I kiss, I clutch,
>
> Like a daft mother, putrid
> Infancy,
> That can and will forbid
> All grist to me
> Except devaluing dichotomies:
> Nothing, and paradise.

If other poems, including most of those discussed above, move beyond the narcissistic dichotomies, it is not because they resolve them, but because they conceive them in more symbolic, dramatic and hence more exploratory terms. Thus 'Wild Oats' provides a richer scenario for self-accusation like that just quoted ('too selfish, withdrawn,/ And easily bored to love'). Some poems go further in their 'striving towards wholeness and perfection'. By imagining fulfilment as female, subject to another's agency like the 'girl dragged by the wrists', 'Wedding Wind' circumvents the stasis of Larkin's male personae and brings 'lineage of joy' to Yeatsian and Lawrentian life. Here 'wind' and 'joy' combine in a dangerous energy at once creative and procreative, the inversion of 'Mr Bleaney': 'Can it be borne, this bodying forth by wind/ Of joy my actions turn on, like a thread/ Carrying beads?' 'Born Yesterday' also projects the poet empathetically into a woman as fulfilment, woman as the future. This poem hopes that blockage, into which the speaker claims special insight (something 'That, unworkable itself,/ Stops all the rest from working'), might be redeemed in another life. 'At Grass', another poem that mentions 'joy', has been plausibly discussed by Simon Petch and Andrew Swarbrick, not as Blake Morrison's post-imperial *tristesse*, but as an embracing of 'anonymity', of post-identity.[33] To put it another way, the symbol enables Larkin to turn regression into progression. To get beyond society is not to drop out but to shed inessentials. The horses' years of co-option contrast with their merging back into undifferentiated Nature. This condition has a prelapsarian aura: paradise regained. The rhythm that introduces 'the groom, and the groom's boy' evokes benign nurturing with no strings attached, like putting a child to bed: 'Only the groom, and the groom's boy,/With bridles in the evening come.' Yet somehow the emotion is ideal rather than infantile. 'Unmolesting meadows', as a version of Eden, does incorporate Larkin's sense of its opposite: 'violence/A long way back', abuse, sex and society harrassing the self. Yet here the cadenced assonance from which 'evening' emerges, together with the placing of 'come', seems to accept the course of life rather than grimly wait for death. 'Meadows' is no mere poeticism despite the echoes it summons. In Larkin's poetry 'fields/Too thin and thistled to be called meadows' imply many kinds of loss.

3

The word 'Eden', with retrospective irony, occurs in Larkin's poem of 'Arrival' in Belfast. His passage to Belfast had already produced the interestingly titled 'Single to Belfast' ('I travel/ To unknown from lost') and a more positive poem of departures, of the self in motion and metamorphosis – 'Absences'. Yet the antithetical speaker of 'Arrival' sees himself as the serpent entering Eden and infecting a city, his ego fixed in a 'style of dying only'. 'Arrival' is one of Larkin's poems that 'shudder at the side' (*Letters*, 157) of life, society and relationships – all of which were now impending more urgently. It thus may or may not be a paradox that he has been thought to express the 'seasons of an English soul'.[34] I want, in the final stages of this essay, to take my argument into the "English" Larkin, into his quarrel with others, and make this the basis for a last look at the Larkin lyric.

One factor in the shock caused by Larkin's letters was a feeling that he had been taken to the bosom of England under false pretences – a serpent indeed. A deeper factor may have been unease as to what that said about English bosoms. If the condition of Larkin speaks to the condition of England, what kind of national or cultural neurosis are we talking about? Mr Bleaney's room looks darker than it did. But it may be significant that the poetry's ambivalence about socialisation had not previously shocked the bourgeoisie. Larkin's minimalist and masochistic sense of society as 'customs and establishments', as rules rather than roots, may have struck further chords. Yet narcissistic withdrawal is haunted by its alter ego: the ghost of a full social presence. This is strangely figured by symbolic glimpses of meadows, a farm or fertile countryside with abundant waters, crops, flowers, sheep and cattle. It evokes, perhaps, the redeemed England of Blake's or Lawrence's millenarianism: the farm where the poet might unironically be 'really myself', yet also violate the narcissistic boundaries by engaging with a generous multiplicity, not 'dilution' but 'increase' or 'punctual spread of seed'. The last stanza of 'Here' tries to resolve the dichotomy whereby Larkin values separateness, 'removed lives//[that] Loneliness clarifies', yet cannot wholly reject collectivity if in an ethereal form: 'Luminously-peopled air ascends'. This lure of utopian coherence, healing splits within the self and between self and society, must also have attracted readers.

Of course, the problem with all symbolic Englands (and indeed Irelands) is where to put the people. Here an aesthete must face the paradox that he has withdrawn into art to express life: a paradox summed up in Yeats's poem 'The Dolls' and in Larkin's remark to Sutton that 'Every now and then I am impelled to try to declare a faith in complete severance from life: and I can never quite do it' (*Letters*, 93). Like the dolls, who object to 'A noisy and filthy thing', Larkin's poetry shudders at the fleshly family, at children. It is generally kinder to animals: '*Mam, we're playing funerals now*' ('Take One Home for the Kiddies'). When gardening, he tried 'to cover up [worms] again so that the birds shan't see them' (*Letters*, 524). Children, however, affront the narcissist's prior claim on selfishness. They are 'kiddies' or 'nippers': an alien species who have pushed his own childhood aside. Larkin's flower imagery involves a narrative whereby the 'Tightly-folded bud' of the self comes to its own fruition: poetry as self-seeding male virgin-birth. A phrase cut from 'Mr Bleaney' is 'Too stingy barren'.[35] So if marriage and children are structural to condition-of-England literature, Larkin shares the inhibitions of E.M. Forster in *Howards End*. He was interested in Lawrence's childlessness, and wondered about its basis (*Letters*, 166). Yet I agree with those critics who see 'The Whitsun Weddings' as succeeding because the spectator is drawn into the scene, because solitude empathises with society and joins it in symbol, in visionary procreation. The poem's climactic 'arrow-shower' implicitly spreads the poet's seed, too: his phantom children, his luminous people. So here the artist becomes necessary to society, the poem becomes symbolically equivalent to society. No one else thinks of 'how their lives would all contain this hour'. The dark side of 'The Whitsun Weddings' has, perhaps, more to do with gender than with class: that is, with Larkin's anxieties about virginity. For the women in the poem, marriage is tribal initiation as violation: 'a religious wounding'. But here again the perspective is complicated by the speaker partly approving, partly aligning himself with the wounded women, partly criticising them for succumbing. As with *Howards End*, it seems a matter of lying back and thinking of England.

In other poems Larkin finds it harder to create a persuasive English microcosm – if that is his objective. Insofar as he really cares about 'customs and establishments' for their own sake, these become more abstract, out of touch, out of date. The failure of 'The Dance' is a case in point. The author cannot detach himself from a protagonist frozen in the narcissistic posture of adolescent jealousy. Similarly, the codes that he resists lack wider resonance as well as longer currency. There are two main moods in which Larkin sought to construct a social bridge between alienation and forms of national identity. The first is sentimentality, the second nostalgia. I would distinguish between them and suggest that nostalgia has more going for it as an emotional and literary structure, because truer to aesthetic narcissism. Style and sentimentality don't mix.

For me, the masks of sentimentality in Larkin go by the names of John Betjeman and Barbara Pym. The one stands for what he might have been as a more socially alert poet, the other for what he might have been as a novelist. Here, I think, Larkin deceived himself. His advocacy of these writers may compensate for his own distance from what he saw as 'ordinary' experience. This is why he sounds like John Major travestying Orwell when he praises Pym for expressing 'the underlying loneliness of life...the virtue of enduring this, the unpretentious adherence to the Church of England, the absence of self-pity, the scrupulousness of one's relations with others, the small blameless comforts' (*RW*, 243-4). Comforts like alcohol and pornography, no doubt. Or not like them. Similarly, he praises Betjeman's 'defiant advocacy of the little, the obscure, the disregarded', and uses him to berate a confused contemporary hit-list: 'all the modernisers and centralisers and rationalisers who are bent on making things easy for the motorist, or safe for the kiddies' (*RW*, 206-8). Perhaps Larkin's implied solution is that the motorists should run over the kiddies – on the lines of 'Why don't birds eat *weeds*?' (*Letters*, 524)

Larkin's regard for Pym and Betjeman is also linked with his increased stress on the priority of 'feeling'. But 'feeling', like its objects, operates as an exclusive and somehow diminished category. In all this, too, there is a kind of heresy against the aesthetic which panders to the philistinism Connolly had deplored. Up to a point, Larkin's *Oxford Book of Twentieth-Century English Verse* spreads that heresy. In fact his philistine mask often constitutes the protective clothing of the aesthete in England (compare Evelyn Waugh), just as his humdrum mask camouflages oddity and romanticism. But in the context I am discussing these masks eat into the face. Larkin is a better poet of self-pity than of pity. And his perception of the 'ordinary' as gleaned from Pym and Betjeman patronises people from an aesthetic perspective. This is not the gospel of life he once inhaled from Lawrence, nor his transformation of 'dull' in 'Born Yesterday'. Nor, conversely, is it the existential horror of being Mr Bleaney. It is pretending that 'what you settled for' – or what you think other people have settled for – 'Mashed you, in fact'. Further, it does not take in, let alone like, much that has happened in England since 1950. Even when the poet champions 'Crowds, colourless and careworn' against the trendy liberal academic who voices 'Naturally the Foundation will Bear Your Expenses', his implied rebuke to the speaker does not encode a counter-idiom that goes beyond simple populism. Larkin subscribes to the spirit of John Carey's later polemic *The Intellectuals and the Masses*, but his imaginative flesh is weak. Crowds are Other unless redeemed as 'Luminously-peopled air'.

Betjeman, of course, may also be reckoned a kind of aesthete – the border between sentimentality and nostalgia is blurred – but a coarser one than Larkin. If nostalgia is the narcissist's version of history, it marks loss and absence. The sentimentalist's version of history is conservation and heritage. Nor is Larkin's nostalgia necessarily for empire, as Tom Paulin – who misreads 'Afternoons' in this light – would have it.[36] It may, however, imply vacuums left at home by empire, which become more apparent as the superstructure implodes. Indeed, his 'England' may scent the further implosion of 'Britain'. 'Home', a word that hovers between the psychological and cultural, is always problematic in Larkin's poetry. On the most basic level, just as 'condition of England' texts require babies, they also require houses. Yet his letters suggest deep neurosis about the whole business of acquiring one himself. He wrote along 'Dockery and Son' lines to Norman Iles in 1972:

> I'm glad you feel satisfied with your life – no reason why you shouldn't. When I look back on mine I think it has changed very little... For the last 16 years I've lived in the same small flat, washing in the sink, & not having central heating or double glazing or fitted carpets or the other things everyone has, and of course I haven't any biblical things such as wife, children, house, land, cattle, sheep etc. To me I seem very much an outsider, yet I suppose 99% of people wd say I'm very establishment & conventional. Funny, isn't it? (*Letters*, 460)

Larkin's literal difficulty with home-making lies behind one of the best definitions of nostalgia (the ache for home), when the contents of 'Friday Night in the Royal Station Hotel' culminate in 'The headed paper, made for writing home/ (If home existed) letters of exile'. Home is sometimes a private or interior sanctuary: 'And not a fieldglass sees them home', 'Your beauty had no home till then'. It is more often an 'unsatisfactory' familial locus. In 'Home is so Sad' home is space, furniture and artifacts evacuated of meaning. Pictures, unplayed music and 'That vase' constitute a kind of failed poem for which the poem's nostalgia voyeuristically compensates:

> You can see how it was:
> Look at the pictures and the cutlery.
> The music in the piano stool. That vase.

Mr Bleaney 'Telling himself that this was home' is sadder still. Home as England, England as home, take colour from the word's psychological as well as cultural accretions in Larkin's poetry. England and home positively coincide when conditions are right for some kind of emotional or spiritual assent to the national being. Such conditions, fulfilled in 'The Whitsun Weddings', are rare. In 'The Importance of Elsewhere' what is *not* home betrays inner estrangement from what should be: 'Lonely in Ireland, since it was not home,/ Strangeness made sense'. In 'Homage to a Government', as in 'Home is Sad', the spirit has deserted the outer fabric: 'We want the money for ourselves at home…Our children will not know it's a different country'. On a more reflective level, 'Church Going' and 'An Arundel Tomb' do not seek to conserve churches and tombs. They raise questions about gaps between spirit and fabric; about the meaning of "home" as tradition, institution, artefact; about the fit between 'shape' and 'purpose', between 'attitude' and 'identity'.

David Gervais observes that, unmediated by history, the English past 'lies alongside the present' in Larkin's poetry 'without being part of it, not as its life-blood but as a back-drop or stage-set'.[37] Yet 'Church Going' and 'An Arundel Tomb' admit flux in general if not in particular: 'A shape less recognisable each week,/ A purpose more obscure'; the 'endless altered people…Washing at their identity'. Moreover, the aesthetic stylisation of history is centrally *about* distance, about yowling across the gap from present to past, about inviting the reader to 'look' at MCMXIV or the 'earl and countess [lying] in stone', just as we look at 'That vase' or 'that girl'. This demonstrative strategy has blind spots, since it nostalgically 'leaves us free to cry', but it also points to empty spots. Ted Hughes's First World War photograph-poem 'Six Young Men' contrasts with 'MCMXIV' in urging the reader to identify with their lives and deaths, perhaps over-insistently: 'That man's not more alive whom you confront/And shake by the hand, see hale, hear speak loud'. 'MCMXIV' emphasises 'archaic' distance in a way that makes the past more immediate when the freeze-frame relaxes: 'the men/

Leaving the gardens tidy,/ The thousands of marriages/ Lasting a little while longer'. Larkin's poem of contemporary marriage, 'The Whitsun Weddings', may avoid history in a different way. Despite taking shape as movement through time and space, as a culturally dynamic narrative, the pagan/ Christian symbolism situates the present mythically rather than historically. In the very foundations of his art Larkin had rejected the pressing 1930s sense of history. And narcissism personalises history, even when Larkin's speaker knows he is doing so: 'I thought that it would last my time' ('Going, Going'), 'Which was rather late for me' ('Annus Mirabilis'). England going tends to coincide with Larkin ageing. In Larkin's letters – and, to an extent, in his poems – historical change impinges as images to be liked or (more often) disliked. Yet, his very preoccupation with form makes him sensitive to where shapes have become unrecognisable, where 'England' might not be working, where community needs to be imagined afresh.

The absences of 'Friday Night in the Royal Station Hotel' signal the obverse of community:

> Light spreads darkly downwards from the high
> Clusters of lights over empty chairs
> That face each other, coloured differently.
> Through open doors, the dining-room declares
> A larger loneliness of knives and glass
> And silence laid like carpet. A porter reads
> An unsold evening paper. Hours pass,
> And all the salesmen have gone back to Leeds,
> Leaving full ashtrays in the Conference Room.
>
> In shoeless corridors, the lights burn. How
> Isolated, like a fort, it is –
> The headed paper, made for writing home
> (If home existed) letters of exile: *Now*
> *Night comes on. Waves fold behind villages.*

I disagree with Andrew Swarbrick's view that this haunting, formally lop-sided, sonnet 'thrills to residual presences' and 'broods on empty chairs and passing hours simply because they are there'. Here Swarbrick follows Barbara Everett's concept of a *positively* 'philistine aesthetic' in Larkin. This, she says, relishes 'factuality' and 'workaday transience' in images that, however intense, refuse to be 'symbolist'. Everett also sees 'Friday Night' and 'Show Saturday' as similar in their dealings with 'poetic objects'.[38] Before arguing that 'Show Saturday' is sentimental, I want to claim 'Friday Night' – which Everett and Swarbrick read sentimentally – for nostalgia and for symbolism (perhaps for a more Anglo-Irish than English aesthetic). The poem repeats key-words from 'Here', but to mark absence rather than hypothetical presence. This 'empty', 'lonely', 'silent', 'Isolated' 'fort' (an imperial echo?) is surely another sad home keeping up a pointless vigil. Its only resident (except for the porter, who seems part of the furniture) is a ghostly observer who has absorbed Cyril Connolly on unhappiness in hotel bedrooms. Here it will always be a dark Friday night of the soul. The poem does not anticipate the salesmen's cheery return on Monday morning. This 'station hotel', then, figures all our makeshift residences. Larkin's derelict objects throw a bleak 'light' on those for whose comfort they were shaped, and whose own obsolescence they encode. In this mood he approaches Beckettian defamiliarisation and Derek Mahon's 'terminal' zone where 'A sunken barge rots/ In the mud beach/ As if finally to discredit// A residual poetry of/ Leavetaking and homecoming'. (Mahon also approaches Larkin, since this poem, 'Going Home', is set in Hull.) 'Friday Night' is a letter of exile. It ends with another that gives its symbolism a further distillation. The closing italics take psychic England – hotel, station, Leeds, villages are both interior and exterior – deeper into the shadows, into dissolution: *'Now/ Night comes on. Waves fold behind villages.'* This reverses the direction of 'Here' towards a life-affirming coast-line where 'Hidden weeds flower, neglected waters quicken'. Larkin's fondness for the ambiguous 'fold' – which may herald unfolding or enfolding – condenses one of his gyres. As a sheep-fold (in 'First Sight'), the 'Tightly-folded bud' of Sally Amis or the erotic promise compressed into 'fold of untaught flower' in 'Spring', it signifies birth and the prospect of 'Earth's immeasurable surprise', 'the million-petalled flower/ Of being here'. In 'The Winter Palace' the word confirms the initial melancholy intuition with which the lambs in 'First Sight' contemplated 'a wretched width of cold'. 'The Winter Palace' ends: 'Then there will be nothing I know./ My mind will fold into itself, like fields, like snow'. The waves that *'fold behind villages'* at the end of 'Friday Night' complete the entropy of 'Light spreads darkly downwards' as they carry the poem's consciousness into permanent exile, beyond land and habitation.

Literature plays both a thematic and a structural role in Larkin's nostalgia. As with photographs and tombs, so with 'voice[s]…heard singing'. Larkin's attacks on 'litty' poetry obfuscate the extent to which his own poems invoke others. But he invokes literature not just as texts, but as life. Such is, after all, the religion of art. One reason for the success of 'MCMXIV', 'How Distant' and 'The Explosion' may be that they are framed by literary ancestors (the war poets, Lawrence) who enable him to imagine communal experience. Distance ('The Explosion' seems retrospective, too) symbolically

charges the experience so that 'the chance sight// Of a girl doing
her laundry in the steerage/ Ramifies endlessly', and it is not only
in death that the explosion's victims are 'larger'. If I call 'Show
Saturday' and 'To the Sea' sentimental rather than nostalgic it
because their contemporary scenarios involve more duty than beauty
('Let it always be there', 'helping the old, too, as they ought');
whereas the melancholy of 'Friday Night' has a decadent glamour.
In condition-of-England spirit, Larkin tries to imagine continuities:
'regenerate union' in his awkward phrase. There'll always be an
England'? or a UK? But, 'Unchilded and unwifed', and according
to the narcissistic pattern, he has more difficulties with the future
than with the past. Yet the past may harbour forgotten futures.
This is the positive function of nostalgia. Meanwhile sentimentality
rules out such potentiality by pretending that something is really
'there'. Larkin's poetry becomes sentimental when 'in there' forgets
'out here'. Decadent writing is characterised by millenarianism as
well as by aestheticism. It set in motion the possibilities on which
Yeats and Lawrence capitalised. These possibilities survive, however
faintly, in Larkin: in the nuance of 'morning', in a thrush 'Astonish-
ing the brickwork' ('Coming'). 'How Distant' and 'The Explosion'
exhilarate because they involve romantic departure and romantic death,
rather than humdrum duty. And they end with images of creation
and resurrection that renew *fin-de-siècle* or millenarian possibility:
'feet/ Inventing where they tread', 'shows the eggs unbroken'.

I will end by criticising 'Show Saturday' from a different angle,
and contrasting it with 'Cut Grass'. This will be my final claim that
the quintessential Larkin lyric expresses life at its intense moments,
that it is brandy not wine, symbol and music not statement or story,
that it remembers Yeats and Lawrence rather than attends to
Kingsley Amis shouting *'How d'you mean?'* (*Letters*, 223) Both
poems belong to the variable later years of Larkin's writing when the
synchronicity required for inspiration proved elusive. According to
his diagram of 1951, his thoughts, feelings, imaginings, wishes and
verbal sense had to meet at a crossroads (*Letters*, 173). At this period,
perhaps only three of them would turn up. There are more fre-
quent splits between symbol and statement, poetry and *vers de
société*. But Larkin not writing is more interesting than most other
poets producing a collection every three years. Not writing, or a
poem not working, proves the mystery and its psychological roots.

This is why Larkin the aesthete won't let Larkin the sentimen-
talist (or Everett's 'philistine') fake 'Show Saturday'. The rhythm
obstinately refuses to animate the elements of the poem, the glue
of assonance coming unstuck despite some wishful alliteration:

'Bead-stalls, balloon-men, a Bank'. As the speaker says: 'each scene is linked by spaces/ Not given to anything much'. Because the images seem a catalogue of separate items, randomly assembled, the microcosm remains atomised. James Booth and Barbara Everett would disagree with this judgment on different counts. Booth has argued that the failures of rhythmic and social coherence in 'Show Saturday' are true to the realities of modern fragmentation, and that to ask for more ('more' as in Seamus Heaney's imagined communities) would falsify English life.[39] For Everett, the images that the poem itself places on show portray the artist humbling himself before 'ordinariness': 'The artist as such has no standing, but sets his goods among the "lambing-sticks, rugs,// Needlework, knitted caps, baskets, all worthy, all well done".' [40] Such mock humility hardly becomes an aesthete – and the cost is clumsily knitted phrases as well as atomised images: 'There's more than just animals', 'manes/ Repeatedly smoothed', 'scrubbed spaced/ Extrusions of earth'. The worthy lines quoted by Everett sound ugly – 'the beat of tired prose', says David Gervais.[41] That Larkin is writing sentimentally is betrayed by implicit aesthetic hatred of the bourgeois, wifed and childed, middle England he is attempting to make poetic: 'wool-defined women,/ Children all saddle-swank'. (As for society, others will do that for us.) It is also betrayed by occasional images and cadences that belong to nostalgic Larkin rather than to would-be Betjeman. Perhaps his real poem lurks somewhere in this collage: 'Folk sit about on bales/ Like great straw dice…long immobile strainings that end in unbalance…A recession of skills…the ended husk/Of summer that brought them here for Show Saturday …Not noticing how time's rolling smithy-smoke/ Shadows much greater gestures…' Time rolling, the seasons, recession, balance, skills, images that hold the stylised gaze: all these most profoundly draw Larkin – as 'Cut Grass' illustrates:

Cut grass lies frail:
Brief is the breath
Mown stalks exhale.
Long, long the death

It dies in the white hours
Of young-leafed June
With chestnut flowers,
With hedges snowlike strewn,

White lilac bowed,
Lost lanes of Queen Anne's lace,
And that high-builded cloud
Moving at summer's pace.

The movement here, languorous with assonance, seems in tune with seasonal rhythms and bio-rhythms: 'Long, long the death// It dies...'; 'And that high-builded cloud/Moving at summer's pace'. In fact, the poem is about rhythms, about the 'breath' that produces it. Andrew Swarbrick feels that there is something missing if 'Cut Grass' 'works by an accumulation of images, all intensifying a lyrical moment but incapable of adding to it'. Even if Larkin (not necessarily reliable) thought the poem too purely 'music', the work-ethic that informs Swarbrick's comment would have him sweating to produce more 'Show Saturdays'.[42] 'Cut Grass' is not a lyrical moment but a momentous lyric. It evokes a whole tradition of encounters between (to quote Cyril Connolly) Imagination and Time. Echoes of other lyrics can be picked up in the almost exaggerated full rhymes, in the concentration on white flowers, in the proximity of snow to June, in the stresses enriched by inversion, in the tug of cadence (and decadence) against quatrain. The flower name 'Queen Anne's Lace' adds a touch of aesthetic décor or camp to a supremely nostalgic gesture that lingers over mortal losses. Larkin is especially qualified to imply that lyric poetry originates in the cry of primary narcissism against ultimate doom. His symbolism blends the natural world, the human body, human artefacts into a seamless sigh of lament and desire. And once again he stylises Nature as (visual) art. 'That high-builded cloud' sounds like Yeats consolidating Edward Thomas's 'high cloudlets' in 'Adlestrop'. If 'Cut Grass' is indeed a poem about poetry, it also symbolises how the imperfections of Philip Larkin's life have been subsumed into perfection of the work and protection of the lyric.

The Millennial Muse

While anthologies survive, the idea of poetic tradition survives. They house intricate conversations between poets and between poems, between the living and the dead, between the present and the future. In more polemical converse with one another, some anthologies dramatise the contest over aesthetic terms and values; all, as time goes by, betray the hidden forces that also shape canons. A. Alvarez puts the matter more bitterly, when he calls 'the English scene...savage with gang-warfare which, at a distance, can be dignified as disagreements between schools of verse'. But even "neutrality" implies selection and direction. Edward Lucie-Smith, who set out to compile 'an extremely broadly based, non-partisan anthology', *British Poetry since 1945* (1970, 1985), confesses in his 'Introduction to the Revised Edition': 'There is no avoiding the fact that making an anthology is a form of criticism.' Colin Falck's and Ian Hamilton's attempt to soften their choosily slim *Poetry since 1900* (1975) as having been 'compiled over a longish period with no particular theory in mind', founders on: 'there must surely be people...who would welcome a collection of modern poems which do not insult their intelligence or their common sense'. Andrew Crozier denies that his introduction to *A Various Art* (1987), coedited with Tim Longville, involves any 'polemic apology or manifesto'; but to call 'the poetry generally on offer' elsewhere 'either provincial or parasitically metropolitan' seems opinionated enough. John Muckle prefaces *The New British Poetry* (1988), edited by Gillian Allnutt, Fred d'Aguiar, Ken Edwards and Eric Mottram, with a statement whose own agenda contradicts its bid for the high ground: 'The majority of recent anthologies have tended to assert the claims of one particular group, a particular idea about poetry...this approach has led to the more adventurous and hard-hitting kinds of contemporary poetry being marginalised, whilst a narrowly defined orthodoxy gets on with running the show'. So there is no escaping canons – neither at a hard-hitting oral performance nor in a theory that calls ' "Objective and "representative"...man-made words or illusory concepts' (Allnutt). And, like it or not, it is the most aesthetically partisan anthologies – *Des Imagistes* (1914), Michael Roberts's *Faber Book of Modern Verse* (1936), Robert Conquest's *New Lines* (1956), Alvarez's *The New Poetry* (1962, 1966) – that influence the practice of poetry.

Harold Monro writes: 'to each decade its poet: Centuries think in different terms'. As the millennium blows the stars about the sky, as 'twentieth-century' ceases (not before time) to be synonymous with 'modern', I want to revisit some anthologies that, with modern self-consciousness, whether in retrospect or prospect, short-term or long, have sought to signpost the century. My focus will be less 'who's in, who's out?' than the anthologists' changing and conflicting rationales. All published in metropolitan England, the anthologies include those already mentioned; Monro's *Twentieth Century Poetry* (1929); Roberts's *New Signatures* (1932); W.B. Yeats's *Oxford Book of Modern Verse* (1936); C. Day Lewis's and L.A.G. Strong's *A New Anthology of Modern Verse 1920-1940* (1941); Kenneth Allott's *Penguin Book of Contemporary Verse* (1950, 1962); G.S. Fraser's *Poetry Now* (1956); Conquest's *New Lines 2* (1963); David Wright's *The Mid Century: English Poetry 1940-60* (1965); Philip Larkin's *Oxford Book of Twentieth-Century English Verse* (1973); D.J. Enright's *Oxford Book of Contemporary Verse 1945-1980* (1980); Michael Schmidt's *Eleven British Poets* (1980); Blake Morrison's and Andrew Motion's *Penguin Book of Contemporary British Poetry* (1982); Michael Hulse's, David Kennedy's and David Morley's *The New Poetry* (1993). Bent on getting the last word, four more anthologies made the millennial deadline: Sean O'Brien's *The Firebox: Poetry in Britain and Ireland after 1945* (1998); Simon Armitage's and Robert Crawford's *Penguin Book of Poetry from Britain and Ireland since 1945* (1998); Peter Forbes's *Scanning the Century: The Penguin Book of the Twentieth Century in Poetry* (1999); and Michael Schmidt's *Harvill Book of Twentieth-Century Poetry in English* (1999).

By generic definition, anthologies locate themselves in time – even those organised thematically, alphabetically or by poem rather than author. Beyond dates and literary period, some highlight the age, some the art. There are also variations within these variations. To take the generic temporal location first, and leaving aside thematic anthologies (love, birds, beasts, politics etc), anthologists attach poetry to history by pronouncing their enterprise epochal, contemporary, or new. Any two of these categories may merge. The epochal anthology claims to speak for an age: Yeats plotting the gyres 'from three years before the death of Tennyson to the present moment'; Larkin ambiguously nominating the century as his co-editor ('poets judged either by the age or by myself to be worthy of inclusion...poems judged by me to carry with them something of the century in which they were written'); Schmidt beginning and ending in globally millennial style: 'Modernism in its various forms is the defining movement of the twentieth century'; 'An

anthology that takes Modernist bearings is an anthology that believes
it is possible to find coherence within so large a body of work, from
so many corners of the world.' "Contemporary" anthologies are
usually mid-period reckonings by mid-life anthologists, anxious for
their own generational values, whose watchword is "representative".
Like epochal anthologies (and the recently extended *Golden Treasury*),
they tend to collapse in a lottery of names when the "new" impends.
Enright holds his nerve, but Allott (1950) admits to being 'less
and less selective as [he] approached the present', because 'the
sorting-out process of time has operated' less on the 1940s. The
recent 'since/after 1945' anthologies, although covering a longer
time-span, have contemporary rather than epochal aims: 'to reveal
the strength and diversity of its chosen period' (O'Brien), 'to rep-
resent in the strongest way the pluralism of modern poetry from
these islands' (Armitage/Crawford). Both anthologies (see below)
ultimately succumb to numbers. Although the flavour of antholog-
ical epochs is somehow suggested by the oldest and youngest poets
included – Walter Pater to George Barker (Yeats), Wilfrid Scawen
Blunt to Brian Patten (Larkin) – the youngest are hostages to for-
tune. In fact, Larkin avoided decisions about the last stretch by
franchising it to Anthony Thwaite's 'superior knowledge of pre-
sent-day literature'. How poet-anthologists engage with juniors as
well as seniors reflects their own creative psychology. Larkin's
reluctance to write a will, to appoint/anoint heirs, seems another
refusal of the patriarchal position.

"New" anthologies cover the shortest period, being future-oriented
and edited by young men in a hurry (Morrison and Motion are
"new" despite 'contemporary' in their title). Alvarez's Preface to
the 1966 *New Poetry*, recalled his original manifesto as 'an attempt
to read the entrails and prophesy the direction poetry might soon
take'. "Contemporary" anthologies (or until PR culture demanded
upbeat words like 'strength') often have plangent or defensive
introductions: 'A certain dissatisfaction with contemporary British
achievement, not only in poetry but in every branch of literature,
is undoubtedly widely felt' (Fraser); 'English poetry of the last
twenty years is considerably more varied and alive than is generally
realised or admitted' (Wright); 'In terms of spectator sport…poetry
…has sunk in the hierarchy to around the level of marbles or yo-yo'
(Enright). In contrast, the "new" anthologist's tone is confident, brisk,
peremptory: 'The poet is, in some ways, a leader'; 'The most glar-
ing fault awaiting correction when the new period opened was the
omission of the necessary intellectual component from poetry'; 'What
poetry needs, in brief, is a new seriousness'; 'Typically, they show

greater imaginative freedom and linguistic daring than the previous poetic generation'; 'Every age gets the literature it deserves.'
Writing on English and Irish anthologies, Carol Rumens comments:
'Perhaps the desire to elect leaders and order everyone else to fall into step behind is a quirk peculiar to English male anthologists'.[1]
(Fraser in 1950 laments the absence of a 'new dominating poetic personality'.) Latter-day 'pluralism' possibly over-compensates for this *vice Anglais* of addiction to hierarchies rather than galaxies.
Monro's anthology and *New Signatures*, separated by three years, contrast as the prematurely epochal and the impatiently new. Monro mingles "Georgians" and Imagists – not always poles apart – while surmising that 'the strong influence of Mr T.S. Eliot is [most] indicative of future tendencies...up to 1940'. Yet *New Signatures* was already ratifying 'a clear reaction against esoteric poetry' and a return to 'the possibilities of counterpointed rhythm'. The deep epochal swell carries cross-currents that are hard to read if one is caught up in them.

Yet for poet, critic or common reader to trust 'the sorting-out process of time' (an increasingly unstable concept) is to lose time.
Superficial first impressions turn into lazy received opinion, then into academic dogma that roots like couch-grass. And when, for instance, a poet like Keith Douglas falls between anthologies (he is not in Allott), the art becomes damagingly ignorant of itself.
Douglas himself understood how the true shock of the new challenges readers and writers: 'Poetry is like a man, whom thinking you know all his movements and appearance you will presently come upon in such a posture that for a moment you can hardly believe it a position of the limbs you know.'[2] *The Faber Book of Modern Verse* may owe its long influence to a unique fusion of the epochal and the new.

Anthologies also attach their contents to history by social, political or cultural hooks. Poetry would die if it never permitted, and if it too easily permitted, such attachment. In fact, the language of poetry's "relevance" changes – perhaps more than its conditions and contexts do in themselves. The most comprehensive way to situate poetry in the century is, of course, by invoking "modernity" whether negatively like Yeats ('Eliot...describing this life that has lost heart'), or positively like Michael Roberts in *New Signatures*:
'new knowledge and new circumstances have compelled us to think and feel in ways not expressible in the old language at all'.
In Roberts's *Faber Book* modernity, conjoined with the politics of the 1930s, has become 'crisis of a general kind [that] arouses a personal conflict in many poets'. Indicating that the terms of the

conflict may be 'intellectual', 'theological' or 'political and aesthet-
ic', Roberts goes on to say: 'Sometimes, as in Donne, several of
these terminologies are superimposed, serving as metaphors for
each other'. This is a more metaphysical account of negotiations
between poetry and modernity than Alvarez's related insistence on
modernity-as-crisis when, nearly thirty years later, he surveys 'the
last half-century'. Alvarez highlights 'the forces of disintegration
which destroy the old standards of civilisation', and continues: 'Their
public faces are those of two world wars, of the concentration
camps, of genocide, and the threat of nuclear war'. Nonetheless,
Roberts and Alvarez are alike in urging a twentieth-century con-
textual imperative, while being less concerned with poets' "com-
mitment" than with their interiorisation of the modern world – for
Roberts mainly through consciousness, for Alvarez through the
unconscious ('new depth poetry' influenced by D.H. Lawrence).

Such juggling of exterior and interior states contrasts with the
more polarised views of Peter Forbes and Michael Schmidt at this
fin de siècle. Forbes's epochal anthology speaks for 'the twentieth
century in poetry'; Schmidt's for poetry in the twentieth century.
Scanning the Century is literally and metaphorically all over the
place as it tries to make poetry (not only in English) tell the cen-
tury's story: 'primarily the story of world events and the new
moods thrown up by technical and social change'. But there are
too many stories, too many moods, both in poetry and the century,
for this or any other volume to capture. Hence Forbes's hectic
mixing of the bad and good news: 'For when the twentieth century
was not engaged in orgies of mass destruction, the dominant mood
was one of vivacity, a classless, unstuffy *joie de vivre*...' So that's
all right then. He groups poems according to categories at once
incongruous and not quite distinct: the world wars, the Holocaust,
Vietnam, 'Low Dishonest Decade: The Thirties', 'Prelude to a War:
Fascism v. Communism 1933-1939', 'From Neutral Tone to Angry:
The Fifties', 'Behind the Curtain: Communism 1945-1989', 'Younger
than that Now: The Sixties', 'Lost Tribes: The Middle East 1948-',
'Aftermath: The Seventies', 'A Stumbling Block: Ireland', 'Mother
Nature on the Run: The Environment', 'Trains and Boats and
Planes: Travel', 'Time Was Away: Love & Sex', 'All the Lonely
People: The Individual', and, just in case he's missed anything:
'The Way We Live: Existence'. It's not even that sport gets as
much space as the Holocaust, but that Forbes's categories lurch
between historical event, literary period, media-packaged decade
and cultural practice arbitrarily patched into the time-scheme
(sexual intercourse virtually begins in 1963, religion does not

begin at all). Further, despite the presence of foreign poets from
Cavafy to Durs Grünbein (*b.* Dresden, 1962), an English (not
British Isles) late twentieth-century perspective prevails. This can
seem trivial *vis à vis* the weightier material, as in the long section
'Workout in Reality Gym: The Eighties & Nineties', largely Eng-
lish in authorship, and given a shallowly Marxist gloss: 'The
emblematic activity of the period seems to be the workout – a
physical regime for lives no longer compelled to be physical,
symptom of a late stage of capitalism in which artificiality has
overtaken necessity.'

Forbes's notional model for bringing his chosen poetic images
'into some sort of relationship, as a newspaper does' seems to be
Louis MacNeice's *Autumn Journal.* He could do worse. But *Autumn
Journal*, for all its variousness, observes proportion as a formal and
ethical principle. Even if the poem's structure depends on fragile
conjunctions, MacNeice does more than juxtapose the elements of
an unstable world:

> The cylinders are racing in the presses,
>   The mines are laid,
> The ribbon plumbs the fallen fathoms of Wall Street,
>   And you and I are afraid.

Autumn Journal is not itself a newspaper but a multi-dimensional
verbal symbol, a syntax working centrifugally and centripetally.
Thus the lines quoted above could easily be filed under several of
Forbes's categories: 'All the Lonely People', 'Low Dishonest
Decade', 'Prelude to a War', 'The Media', 'Science and Technology'.
And there are some misfiles, even by his narrow criteria. For
instance, MacNeice's 'The Cyclist' has little to do with 'Mother
Nature' being "about" youth, mortality, sensory pleasure, gather ye
rosebuds ('these five minutes/Are all today and summer'). Nor is
Philip Larkin's 'Essential Beauty' really a concerned comment on
the advertising industry. The 'documentary realism of this book',
is not only 'at odds with [the] postmodern approach to history and
reality', as Forbes states, but with the poetic approach to them.
Perhaps the ultimate misreading is when a biographical appendix
calls Patrick Kavanagh's *The Great Hunger* (whose title symbolises
repressed lives in mid twentieth-century Ireland) 'the epic poem
of Ireland's most terrible human tragedy, the starvation of millions
by the potato famine'.

On the one hand, Forbes knows that poems move around. His
"historical" choices are often written after the event. Thus under
'World War I' he prints Larkin's 'MCMXIV' and Paul Muldoon's
'Truce' (while omitting Rosenberg and Sorley). On the other hand,

he barely realises that good poems have many occasions. 'Truce' is more immediately a political parable for Northern Ireland. But neither can it be neatly filed under 'Ireland: A Stumbling Block'. If Forbes referred 'Truce' to both histories – inconsistently, he dates categories but not poems – he would provide a richer contextual sense of how the century has entered and shaped poetry. In crossing two histories, Muldoon evokes others. Forbes does not include Derek Mahon's 'A Disused Shed in Co. Wexford'. Is it because this poem puzzles him by speaking so widely and deeply to modern history? Or because he has ruled out mycology as a category? *Scanning the Century* may have always been a grandly impossible project. But it needed, at least, finer feeling for how history works back and forth inside and outside poems. In what conceivable versions of history (London dinner-party? hippie nostalgia?) is Ireland 'a stumbling block', the 70s an 'aftermath'?

It is precisely the insular notion that history can be put on hold which has often denied so-called "war poets" their full aesthetic presence – and this despite the impetus that poets of the Great War gave to the 1930s. Introducing *Eleven British Poets* Michael Schmidt avoided this fallacy when he praised Keith Douglas's 'powerful originality', while following Roberts and Alvarez on poetry and history: 'Recent history has illuminated the destructive potential of human nature assisted by technology and ideology… Societies have altered, and language too speaks differently'. Twenty years on, *Twentieth-Century Poetry* suggests that Schmidt has changed tack (even though he cites Roberts's *Faber Book* as his model): 'It sometimes seems that the second half of this century has been lavishly preoccupied – when it claims to be preoccupied with poetry at all – with other things, with poetry's context, its usefulness, its witness and moral probity construed in the light of the age's shifting preferences and concerns.' In a hostile review of *Scanning the Century* he deplores 'the primacy of subject-matter over form, the precedence of "witness" over the claims of poetic art'.[3]

Schmidt now advocates a poetry of 'communion' as opposed to a poetry which 'is immediately political and deeply wedded to what it takes to be its community of concern'. Yet this opposition is not borne out by the contents of an anthology more prudently "mainstream" than is its editorial polemic. There are indeed excellent grounds for resisting most of the socio-political vocabularies inflicted on 'poetry since 1945'; but where these vocabularies err is not in introducing the theme of relevance at all, but in being alert only to the most obvious kinds (such as Tony Harrison's verbal class-warfare). Day Lewis, atoning for past sins, sensibly says in the introduction to *A New Anthology of Modern Verse*: 'I don't think you can make either the next war or the machine a Muse or a mainspring of poetry'. Perhaps the same goes for 'since/after 1945', though it depends on how anthologists nuance the arbitrariness of all period-defining dates. Unlike Armitage/Crawford, O'Brien excludes post-1945 poems by Graves, MacNeice and Auden because 'To have included work by poets who became established in the years before 1945 would have meant producing a very different kind of book.' Here, in applying a non-literary criterion ('becoming established'), O'Brien admits more than he realises: namely, that epochal swells overflow small pools. If poems by Graves and Co would change the contour of 'poetry after 1945', so be it.

    To frame the relation between aesthetics and history another way: as Robin Skelton's retrospective anthology *Poetry of the Thirties* (1964) continues to show, poems are tested by whether contexts accrue to or leech from them: the poetry of Northern Ireland will eventually be another test-case. Yet Schmidt too easily brushes aside 'the age's shifting preferences and concerns' as if the age were wholly mindless, criticism and poetry disembodied, word and image evacuated of history. The communing reader is conditioned by communities; artistic distance is a ratio not an absolute. Peter McDonald writes of Helen Vendler's critical premises: 'taking for granted poetry's ability to transcend its circumstances, such an attitude forgets how real poetry also answers to its circumstances'.[4] In any case, 'subject-matter' or 'witness' has largely given way to a more insidious form of critical reductiveness: culturalism. Culturalism is insidious, trickling from criticism into poetic practice, because it mimics the aesthetic more closely than most party-lines ever did. Hulse et al's *New Poetry*, O'Brien's *Firebox* and Armitage/Crawford's *Penguin Book* are, to varying degrees, victims of the culturalist fallacy.

    The New Poetry seems a little divided between old and new vocabularies of relevance. Its editors gamely but lamely applaud 'angry' poetry that attends to class: 'Eighties Britain grieved observers. [Peter] Reading's sequence *Perduta Gente* contrasted have-nots sleeping rough outside the Royal Festival Hall and the haves listening to Sibelius within. His anger was shared by many.' They sound a more rousing note, however, when they affirm the culturalist approach to poetry: 'In the absence of shared moral and religious ideals, common social or sexual *mores* or political ideologies, or any philosophy on the conduct of life, plurality has replaced monocentric totemism.' (This marks a shift from Michael Roberts's belief that such conditions produce or intensify creative 'conflict'.) 'Plurality/pluralism' then becomes a *leitmotif*: 'an anthology of poetry that is fresh in its attitudes, risk-taking in its address, and plural in its forms and voices'; poets 'uncomfortable with authority and orthodoxy, seeking out new models and positions...have discovered a new pluralism and are starting to define a believable role for poetry'. 'New' also works hard to validate this "new" anthology which raises the "new" stakes by imitating Alvarez's title and thereby claiming to be the new *New Poetry*. British culturalism, as applied to poetry, more or less follows the American multicultural line, although it features region/country along with gender and race. All of which makes Jackie Kay the ideal plurally new or newly plural poet: 'Kay's personal circumstances as a black Briton adopted and raised by a white Scottish family may be taken as an extreme example of what Terry Eagleton has called "the marginal becoming central". A multicultural society challenges the very idea of a centre, and produces pluralism of poetic voice.' These factors may *condition* (a useful verb and noun with which Louis MacNeice combated the 1930s brand of critical determinism) Kay's moving poem 'Brendon Gallacher', but they hardly explain it. The poem is "about" an imaginary childhood friend, imagination, consonantal rhyme:

'...There never have been any Gallachers next door.'
And he died then, my Brendon Gallacher,
Flat out on my bedroom floor, his spiky hair,
His impish grin, his funny flapping ear.
Oh Brendon. Oh my Brendon Gallacher.

James Fenton's 'An Amazing Dialogue' is the best definition of pluralism as an *aesthetic* principle:

'But this poem is not like that poem!'
'Yes, you are right, it's not.'

Sean O'Brien prefers 'diversity' and 'variety' to 'pluralism', and stresses his own multicultural roots ('of mixed Irish and English parentage') as a prelude to both claiming and urging English 'openness to other literary cultures – Scots, Welsh, Caribbean' as well as Irish. He also singles out 'black poetry' and 'women's poetry' as vital to a 'rich' period which 'has seen the melting of familiar categories and the establishment of unexpected connections, the emergence of new poetries from formerly unsuspected sources'. To pluralism and diversity Armitage/Crawford add 'democracy': heading their introduction 'The Democratic Voice'. This, it appears, arrived (less symbolically than human nature changed) on a particular date: '[Its] emergence was heralded and later schooled by the Butler Education Act of 1944'. (So much for earlier schools like the

trenches or 1930s demotic.) Armitage/Crawford define the demo-
cratic voice, rather bloodlessly, as follows: 'The democratic voice
may speak Gaelic or English. It may be gendered as male or female.
It is unhieratic, belonging to a culture of pluralism, where its auth-
ority is both challenging and challenged.' They at least take a longer
historical view than the other anthologists' rather unspecified sense
that radical change (as distinct from previous twentieth-century
radical changes) has recently overwhelmed poetic authority, ortho-
doxy or categories.

A stress on democracy/pluralism/diversity certainly provides a
basis for aesthetic observation when it removes blinkers, as when
Armitage-Crawford say: 'If poems are linguistic distillations then
this anthology will remind readers of how complex and rich remains
the mixture of tongues and linguistic possibilities present in these
north-west European islands.' Yet awful poetry can be written in
Gaelic or Glaswegian too, and (patronisingly) sometimes allowed
to get away with it. Much confusion arises from the word 'voice'
('pluralism of poetic voice') which elides the difference between,
on the one hand, distinctive poetics and the complexities of voice
in poetry; and, on the other, socio-political self-articulation or
devolved power. The political sexiness of both "language" and
"voice" also conspire to downgrade other structural elements. Poetry
by women has been particularly subject to such confusion in that
"writing" becomes less a metaphor than a surrogate for feminism.
Although the politically "unsaid" may indeed *condition* the imagi-
natively "unsaid", it does not determine it. The centre/margin
paradigm – undermined less by multiculturalism than by so many
margins crowding to the centre shouting 'me too' – further con-
fuses the aesthetic issue. Considerable metropolitan careers have
been built upon perpetual marginality. Once noticed, the margin
shifts, while the finer print of poetry remains unread. *The New
Poetry* construes marginality in entirely political terms ('a culture
which persistently ignores or marginalises the voices and achieve-
ments of a significant number of its people'), whereas O'Brien's
'emergence…from formerly unsuspected sources' hints at a more
mysterious state. In fact, any true poem by definition emerges
from 'unsuspected sources', brings some new planet into our ken.
The expected is hardly poetry, not even when it presents impeccable
marginal or multicultural credentials. Similarly, the only true poetic
metropolis is the shifting locus of creative and critical life. The
reception of Northern Irish poetry affords some useful warnings
against the effect of culturalism on literary criticism. In *Mistaken
Identities: Poetry and Northern Ireland* Peter McDonald shows how

'identity-discourse' has determined and narrowed readings. He asks: 'Is criticism able to imagine a liberation from "identity" which will move into the spaces opened up by different kinds of poetic achievement? Perhaps a kind of criticism responsive to questions like these might make the transformation of culture into "cultural beliefs" less easy, and have applications beyond Northern Ireland.'[5]

To say that poetry comes from 'unsuspected sources' contradicts another current notion: that there is nothing new under the postmodernist sun. Here confusion between cultural and aesthetic terminology beckons once more – for instance, between the multicultural and the multivocal. The poetics of multivocality have no necessary connection with pluralist politics (multivocality in Eliot and Pound laments the death of authority), although Armitage/Crawford's definition of the 'democratic voice' suggests an androgynous figure who writes extremely tolerant macaronic poems. Most contemporary anthologists scent 'postmodernism' somewhere in the atmosphere, but are unsure whether to inhale. Hulse et al suspect its 'cultural spoofery' and failure to 'see causal connections between larger cultural ideas and the facts of everyday life', but are resigned to the idea that postmodernist poetry asks questions like 'Which world is this? What is to be done in it? Which of my selves is to do it?' This is postmodernism as voiced by the doomed whale falling through space in *The Hitch Hiker's Guide to the Galaxy*. O'Brien gives a defter account of various 'playful' devices, rightly pointing out that 'these are not wholly novel practices', but his metaphors also characterise the postmodernist advent in more violent terms: James Fenton's 'exploded, labyrinthine readings of the class system', Michael Hofmann's 'shellshocked ironies', Selima Hill's 'crazed erotic monologues', Jo Shapcott's 'comically vertiginous projections'. No wonder that only the Irish (Paul Muldoon, Ciaran Carson) can really hack it: 'For the most confident and expansive postmodernist poetry…we should look…to Ireland'. But 'confident and expansive' postmodernism sounds odder still. Perhaps what we should really do is expose overweening categories to literary and cultural specifics. Armitage/Crawford wisely say: 'An alertness to the often tricksy grain of words may be the product of a late twentieth-century sensibility educated in a kind of after-world (post-modern, post-Christian, post-war, post-Hiroshima, post-structuralist), but it may owe as much to a sense of choice between languages…' Which might indeed bring us back to Joycean Ireland – or Shakespearean England – or Ovidian Rome.

These anthologies themselves belong to a devolutionary context. One of their positive achievements is to represent the dynamics of

poetry in the British Isles (which need not imply the non-existence
of European or American horizons). But if this makes a refreshing
change from the sealed-off worlds of "national" anthologies, Michael
Schmidt again speaks too disembodiedly of 'landscape and nation,
like gender and ethnicity, becoming language'.[6] In fact, this is a
shot in an old war (discussed below) between an Anglo-American
"modernist" axis, with concealed national biases, and a different
reading of how modern poetry in English came – or still comes –
into being. The point is that we need to dig deeper for "nationality"
as well as for "culture" and "relevance", while keeping intertextuality
in view. A later essay returns to a topic I have aired elsewhere: [7]
how some versions of "Irish poetry" allow 'Irish' to usurp or sub-
ordinate 'poetry'. A glance at most anthologies (with the exception of
Patrick Crotty's judicious *Modern Irish Poetry*, 1995) would disclose
clan-warfare which few editors bother to 'dignify as disagreements
between schools of verse'. Similarly, anthologies of Scottish poetry
plait its linguistic and cultural strands gingerly in the context of
an emergent literary nationalism. Roderick Watson introduces *The
Poetry of Scotland: Gaelic, Scots and English* (1995) with the cry
'Anthologists beware', and continues: 'The only agenda-free anth-
ology of Scottish poetry would be a project worthy of Borges's
notion of the universal library.' National or regional anthologies
inevitably set out to 'sustain, imply, construct or seek a version of
ourselves' (Watson). Lacking such a dimension, poetry would
deny its communal origins. But what national anthologies gain in
cultural definition, they may lose in aesthetic precision (which cul-
tural definition needs) and the ramifications it introduces.

In the days of Alvarez, Ian Hamilton's *Review* and *Penguin
Modern Poets* London provided a vigorous critical forum for poetry.
As a refuge from local commissars it was – up to a point – excused
its south-eastern bias and unconscious English nationalism. While
the devolution of poetry publishing has created a pragmatic plural-
ism, a pluralism of opportunity, criticism (for the most part) has
been less devolved than diluted. It has retreated before the rise of
culturalism – which yet urges its own canon – and allied forces (see
pp.238-41). John Tusa recently called for a revival of 'evaluative
language' in arts journalism.[8] Yet, with the unarticulated English
question on the literary as well as political agenda, morbid symp-
toms of hegemonic anxiety lurk beneath the pluralistic surface.
O'Brien, for instance, reverts to the plangent mode of the "con-
temporary" anthologist when he notices a Celtic 'cultural assur-
ance which their English neighbours may in fact envy', and over-
works the word 'confidence': Ireland's 'confident' postmodernism,

'the current confidence of Scots poetry', 'the confidence of women poets'. To index the state of poetry to the state of the nation or Union, or to gender-morale, has superficial appeal – Larkin pondered the link between two 'primitive' phenomena: 'poetry and sovereignty'[9] – but poetry hardly stems from or promotes 'confidence' in the vulgar sense, as if it were *Riverdance* or *Braveheart*. What may be lacking, as English culture turns its fickle attention to other matters, is less confidence than *belief* – belief in poetry. Consider the passionate sense of vocation disclosed by Larkin's letters. Northern Ireland offers few grounds for confidence; it may offer grounds for belief. And belief is what generates argument about value. In his collection of essays and reviews *The Deregulated Muse* (1998) O'Brien hankers more persuasively for what, he concedes, may be a 'fiction': a 'previous age of cultural coherence, when questions of literary meaning and value could be argued on more-or-less common ground, in more-or-less common language'.[10] 'Coherence' or authority matters less than that a lively agora should persist. Without 'common language', indeed, pluralism becomes solipsism. To illustrate the point, I will briefly review some anthological dialectics that belong to an earlier period when British, American and Irish poetry were peculiarly and fruitfully intimate even at their most quarrelsome. If this "marginalises" other English-language poetry, these dialectics constitute a model, perhaps an origin, not a limit.

Yeats's *Oxford Book of Modern Verse* and Roberts's *Faber Book of Modern Verse* appeared in the same year: 1936. Yeats outraged Ireland by excluding Austin Clarke, England by excluding Wilfred Owen, and America by excluding America – except for two poets of 'long residence in Europe'. (Babette Deutsch wondered 'why H.D. does not fit into this category'.)[11] Yeats distances America, as Larkin via Thwaite distances the young, to put some of the competition beyond any reckoning: 'A distinguished American poet urged me not to to attempt a representative selection of American poetry; he pointed out that I could not hope to acquire the necessary knowledge.' Yet Yeats's mischievous political strategy serves some of his deepest aesthetic convictions. On the national front Irish poets do well (bad personal relations with Yeats explain Clarke's exclusion).[12] Stephen Spender called the anthology 'that Irish fen'.[13] In *Left Review* Cecil Day Lewis, perhaps included for Ireland, bemoaned for England:

> The omission of the war poets, together with the inadequate representation of some of the post-war writers – notably Auden and Spender – detracts very seriously from the value of Mr Yeats's anthology. A

reader of fifty years hence...would receive an erroneous idea of what
has happened in English poetry. The extracts from Eliot and MacNeice
would give him the impression of a disintegrating age hardening into
fragmentary fatalism.[14]

Day Lewis then praises some execrable communist verse from *The
Year's Poetry 1936*. In fact, Yeats's line on the trench poets may
have less to do with his theory about 'passive suffering' than with
restoring his battered Irish nationalist credibility (he had been a
covert war poet himself). As for 'what has happened in English
poetry' since 1930: although a too-skimpy selection from Auden
puts down the young English pretender, Yeats's finale is more
open to difference than Larkin's. Indeed, he plays Auden, MacNeice,
Spender and Day Lewis for Ireland against America; or, more
specifically, against the rival aesthetics of T.S. Eliot and Ezra
Pound. F.O. Mathiessen, reviewing the anthology in *Southern
Review*, knew what Yeats was up to when he omitted *The Waste
Land*: he was 'skilfully represent[ing Eliot] by a selection that
keeps him in a minor key'.[15] In *The Origins of Free Verse* (1996)
H.T. Kirby-Smith comes to the same conclusion when he describes
Yeats as seeking 'to diminish Eliot's reputation and influence', and
to show 'that modernism was a monstrous mistake'.[16]

Here serious formal disagreements, as well as amusing rivalries,
are at issue. Yeats implicitly claims the "new" poets of the 1930s
(with their mixed English and Irish origins) for his own aesthetic
on the grounds that they 'handle the traditional metres with a new
freedom – *vers libre* lost much of its vogue some five years ago'.
Eliot, in contrast, 'produces his effects by a rejection of all rhythms
and metaphors used by the more popular romantics rather than the
discovery of his own, this rejection giving his work an unexagger-
ated plainness that has the effect of novelty'. Yeats gets round
subject-matter and ideology by calling the thirties poets' intensity
of belief 'not political', and by managing to detect a subtextual
quest for Yeatsian transcendence: 'beyond the flux something un-
changing, inviolate'. Yet, *pace* Day Lewis, he may have identified
deeper tendencies of the 'disintegrating age'. As for Pound, Yeats
continues an aesthetic argument begun in *A Packet for Ezra Pound*
(1925) and inflamed by a recent literary quarrel which had led him
to call Pound a 'sexless American professor'.[17] His doubts about
the *Cantos* always turn on what he regards as their spatial and
theoretical, as opposed to sequential and rhythmic, organisation:

There is no transmission through time, we pass without comment from
ancient Greece to modern England to medieval China; the symphony,
the pattern, is timeless, flux eternal and therefore without movement...

He hopes to give the impression that all is living, that there are no edges,
no convexities, nothing to check the flow; but can such a poem have a
mathematical structure? Can impressions that are in part visual, in part
metrical, be related like the notes of a symphony...Style and its opposite
can alternate, but form must be full, sphere-like, single.

Warwick Gould sees Yeats as diagnosing a case of 'form...negated'.[18]
Eliot, with his sins of omission ('rejection'), his passive as opposed
to active vandalism, seemingly suffers from a less terminal strain of
the same disease.

In *The Faber Book of Modern Verse* the new generation inhabits
the different context created by starting with Hopkins rather than
with Pater, and by Roberts's American contingent: not only Pound
and Eliot, but Aiken, H.D., Moore, Stevens, Ransom, Tate, Crane,
Cummings. In fact, Roberts includes good selections from Owen,
Rosenberg and Graves, and distinguishes between 'European'
(mostly expatriate American) and 'English' poetry on the basis that
the former depends more on 'existing cultural values' and 'memories
of other poetry', the latter on 'first order...intensification of qualities
inherent in the English language itself'. Perhaps this obliquely
reclaims ownership of the language from across the Atlantic – Yeats
being placed in both camps. Roberts excludes some poets, such as
de la Mare and Muir, who 'have written good poems without having
been compelled to make any notable development of poetic tech-
nique'. Once again, he sees technical development as inseparable
from negotiating psychological, political or philosophical 'crisis'. (For
Yeats, the crisis – modernity – has already occurred, and he watches
from a lofty distance his struggling juniors.) Roberts opens with
'The Wreck of the Deutschland' because 'working in subterranean
fashion [Hopkins] moulded a style which expressed the tension and
disorder that he found inside himself'. Yet his comprehensive review
of current techniques is not biased towards modernist effects, and he
knows that poetry eludes the critic's categories: 'if for the moment
I have classified poets, it is merely as a shop-window arrangement,
a tactful use of contrast to focus attention on certain qualities'. What
eludes Roberts's own categories is how disorder and technical dev-
elopment might be found in Thomas Hardy and Edward Thomas.

Two decades later, Conquest and Alvarez came along to upset
the *Faber Book*'s English-European or, rather, Anglo-American
balance. Conquest's opening sentences make no bones about the
politics of anthologies:

> In the late 1920s a group of poets were starting to write who were to
> be the typical poets of the 1930s. Towards the end of the 1930s a
> group of writers with quite different attitudes began to emerge, who

were to dominate the 1940s. Each of these groups was, if not launched, at least presented to public fire by anthologies which took up definite positions.

Louis MacNeice, reviewing Fraser's *Poetry Now*, exempts *New Lines* from his remark that 'There have been too many anthologies of contemporary verse and much in their introductions has been either dull or ridiculous.' Nonetheless, what he says of Fraser might also apply to Conquest: 'This game of pigeonholing literary generations has gone too far...Posterity may find our generations closer to each other than we care to think.'[19] But, bent upon domination (that word again), Conquest exaggerates difference by caricaturing the 1930s and 1940s: 'great systems of theoretical constructs... agglomerations of unconscious commands'. This very refusal of politics and psychology, of course, calls attention to the anthologist's own political and psychic subtexts. On the aesthetic surface Conquest makes a plea for 'intellect', for 'a rational structure and comprehensible language, even when the verse is most highly charged with sensuous or emotional intent'. However, one subtext may be English centrality: 'Lallans-mongers', as well as the supposedly 'Celtic' Dylan Thomas (important to Larkin and Wain), are put in their place. Defending *New Lines* in *New Lines 2*, Conquest merges centrality and tradition: 'the cardinal traditions of English verse', 'the main tradition of English poetry', 'the central current of English verse', 'the central principle of English poetry'. A second subtext in the introduction to *New Lines* is physical and mental 'health': 'a genuine and healthy poetry', 'the sort of corruption which has affected the general attitude to poetry in the last decade', 'other types of vicious taste', 'a new and healthy general standpoint'. Thus Conquest proposes a kind of centralised poetic vice-squad.

A deeper subtext may be the war. Whereas writers of 1930s admitted their irrational guilt about missing the test of 1914–1918, Alvarez is surely right to notice repression, cultural confusion and aesthetic hiatus here. (In *New Lines 2* Conquest gets revealingly tetchy about 'the impudent assertion that English poets were unaware of the existence of the darker elements in the human personality, and of large-scale suffering, until psychoanalysts and world wars drew attention to them'.) Among its other qualities, poetry in the 1940s was structurally influenced by diverse war-zones. Conquest declares Orwell's 'honesty' (a complicated matter) exemplary, without reference to its contexts. Similarly, he does traditional forms some service – singling out Graves, playing Yeats for England against America as 'the great poet of the century' – except where he implies that forms and meanings are wholly under the poet's

control. The Movement aesthetic, as theorised by Conquest, turns
more on control and authority, united as 'lucidity', than on what
Alvarez terms 'gentility...a belief that life is always more or less
orderly'. The difference suggests a more interesting, less passive
form of denial.

Conquest also renews in a different tone, and from a different
cultural angle, Yeats's anti-modernist polemic. In *New Lines 2*
Conquest, like Yeats before him, puts modernism in the past tense:
'the innovations of that time are [now] seen to be peripheral addi-
tions to the main tradition of English poetry'. And, less interroga-
tively than Yeats and less precisely than MacNeice (see p.158), he
targets Pound: 'an absurdly inflated search for novelty through an
attempted blend of the flashier and more irrelevant features of past
schools'. He continues: 'It might be thought paradoxical that this
wilful, self-conscious insistence on "tradition" of a sort should com-
bine with an equally self-conscious insistence on "experiment". But
the key word is "self-conscious"...' Whereas Yeats's judgment of the
Cantos illuminates the century's pivotal formal dispute, and brings
to a climax his long engagement with Pound, Conquest's *de haut
en bas* language puts Pound down as *nouveau* or yankee.

Larkin's *Oxford Book* is a more empirical if self-interested attempt
to assert or retrieve an English national line, most successfully in
its installation of Hardy alongside Yeats – the poles of his own
Anglo-Irish dialectic – and Eliot. It's strange that he does not
make more of Edward Thomas, but gives him the same space as
de la Mare, Gibson (who '*never wrote a good poem in his life*'),[20]
Hodgson and Masefield. This dissipates what might emerge from
the collision between so-called Georgians and the Great War, as
does far too little from Owen and Rosenberg, nothing from Sorley.
Larkin's strict definition of 'twentieth-century English verse' as
'verse written in English by writers born in these islands (or resi-
dent here for an appreciable time)' now officially, rather than acci-
dentally-on-purpose, distances America (as it does Scots 'poems
requiring a glossary'). It may be Larkin's own complicated relation
to the Second World War that gives Eliot too easy a run in the
period 1914-1922 and allows the main burden of "Englishness" to
be carried by Kipling, Betjeman and Auden, as well as Hardy.
Certainly, in a weird English counterpoint to Yeats's Irish bias,
neither war disturbs the anthology as Alvarez would desire. The
less tangible parallels between Yeats and Larkin confirm that if
younger poets anthologise to advance their careers, older poets do
so to secure their posterity.

In *New Lines 2* Conquest again answers *The New Poetry* when he objects to the 'not uncommon insistence that British poets have a duty to be influenced by American poetry [though] only a particular type...long notorious for obliquity of grammar, vocabulary, structure, and sense'. Alvarez is hardly a Poundian; but, in a famous provocation, he nominates American leaders (Lowell, Berryman) to jolt English poetry out of 'a series of negative feedbacks'. By expatriating the 'experimental techniques' which issued from 'attempts to forge a distinctively American language for poetry', he considers that English poetry has simultaneously excluded 'new areas of experience'. (Interestingly, he accuses Auden of diverting his 'deep neurotic disturbances into light verse', while calling MacNeice's 'socio-political verse...more effective and certainly more deeply felt'.) How does Alvarez's 'negative feedback' look now? He lists successive phases – anti-modernism, anti-intellectualism, refusal of psycho-analytical insights – which culminate in the 1950s. The first feedback depends on where you put Yeats, who, as we have seen, wanders all over the anthological map. It also depends on how you regard the renewed formalism of the 1930s: whatever Auden's apostasies, that poetic decade thoroughly sifted Eliot's impact on this side of the Atlantic – which partly explains why the *Faber Book* wears so well. Second, intellect or intelligence, functioning in/as poetry, permeates the whole fabric (where Conquest confines intelligence to rationality, Alvarez confines it to ideas). Although I sympathise with Alvarez's third point, he may require the unconscious as conscious theme (Hughes) rather than as protean actor or metaphorical resource. Yet Alvarez was right even when he was wrong, even when he reads Larkin and Hughes too literally, or when, as he later admits, his anthology does not bear out its 'inflammatory introduction'. He was right in linking poetry's scope and ambition to a sense of being challenged by its own history, which includes being challenged by history.

Alvarez's modernism of 1962 is not Schmidt's of 1999. There have been as many American modernisms as there have been English anthologists caught up in aesthetic polemics with their own compatriots. (Irish and Scottish instances of the same syndrome lie outside my present scope.) Modernism serves as an admonitory index of what England lacks. Hence Conquest's legitimate complaint about 'duty'. But the dialectics of the Conquest-Alvarez argument are still alive. Without the literary penetration of a Roberts or Alvarez, English neo-modernism and preaching of American poetics sometimes runs into a cul-de-sac, as in Michael Horovitz's *Children of Albion* and Crozier/Longville's *A Various Art*. The former's anarchism, the latter's academicism, are founded on extreme versions of American revolution. Thus Horovitz berates 'Alvarez and his readership' for being 'slaves of bad habit, stuck in the stocks, the stock-in-trade clichés and categories of urban literary sniping – incapable of hitting anywhere near Ginsberg, whose head is deep down in the lion's mouth of madness – bringing death to life again, regenerating the womb of his own creation'. Horovitz's utopian image of "new" (Liverpool) poetry in 1968 as a 'street urchin rolling in moss that presses up sharp shoots between the pavement-blocks' may seem a long way from Crozier's pedagogic abstraction in 1987: 'a poetry deployed towards the complex and multiple experience in language of all of us'. Nonetheless, both anthologists display that half-wounded, half-smug avant-gardeism alibied by "America" for not being honoured in its own country. *A Various Art* appeals to history, but has failed to absorb the dialectics of the 1930s and 1940s (in America, too) even as it accuses the 1950s of the same failing. This self-sanctifying passage further illustrates how partial accounts of poetry after Yeats, Eliot and Pound can erode a historical sense of the modern movement:

> the redefinition of taste in the 1950s had had to be enacted by means of a wholesale rewriting of and reorientation towards the history of modern poetry, and this included the virtual suppression of parts of it. When they began to write, therefore, many of the poets in this anthology, confronted with such a depthless version of the past, found that as English poets the ground had been pretty well cut from beneath their feet...one of the means by which [they]...were identifiable to each other was an interest in a particular aspect of post-war American poetry, and the tradition that lay behind it – not that of Pound and Eliot but that of Pound and Williams...American examples [also] indicat[ed] how poets might take matters of publication and the definition of a readership into their own hands by establishing their own publishing houses and journals.

A Various Art also shares some "modernist" premises with Schmidt's *Twentieth-Century Poetry*, such as allergy to being considered 'an anthology of English, let alone British, poetry'. Yet Schmidt has more central ambitions than to run a cult or a British sideshow to American 'Language poetry'. Thus he questions any critical eye 'made partisan by a sense of perceived neglect' of the poets it singles out. He takes his bearings from the metropolitan Eliot-Pound axis, not the Pound-Williams wandering star. And his chief 'purpose' is to 'insist that there is a continuity between the radical experimental poets and those who are usually presented as mainstream'. But 'continuity' (as if 'radical experiment' filled the early twentieth-century scene) is a literary-historical lapse that produces the following muddle of modernisms: 'It is possible to make too much of Pound and Eliot. But we cannot make too much

of the various Modernisms they helped to generate – Wallace
Stevens, Williams, Lawrence, Marianne Moore, H.D., Hugh Mac-
Diarmid, Robert Graves...The impact of the Modernist Yeats –
and of French symbolist poetry – on that curmudgeonly stick-in-the-
mud Philip Larkin is a matter of record.' (Perhaps 'the Modernist
Yeats' will vengefully reincarnate himself in Manchester.) Crozier
and Schmidt subscribe to different types of collusive Anglo-American
narrative, each of which gives England a role, even if it has lost the
poetic empire that Conquest implicitly mourns. Both narratives
pretend to transcend nationality (that very transcendentalism being
culturally and imperially specific), yet ignore Yeats's dialectic with
modernist forms. According to the first narrative, modernism is
hegemonic in the US, a marginalised but potent cell in Britain.
According to the second narrative, it bestrides the Atlantic/globe.
But the term "international modernism" is riddled with academy-
led fallacies where English-language poetry is concerned. First, if
we look back to the 1920s and 1930s, 'inter' functions as an active
preposition and proposition. It does not signify a globally agreed
aesthetic, either within or between "national" traditions. A second
fallacy is that Berkeley must always be less insular or provincial
than Brighton or Belfast. A third fallacy is that we can readily dis-
cern whether a poem or poet is alert to other literatures: the best-
advertised debts may be the slightest. A final fallacy is that one
poet will always excite another – and poets get excited by poetry
in ways that defy classification – to imitation rather than to self-
defining difference.

Schmidt was first to use the plural 'poetries' to name an anthology
published in the UK. This was *New Poetries* (1994) which intro-
duced eight young poets, mostly from Ireland and Britain, but
editorially situated in a mobile 'unboundaried' context. Having
quoted Derek Walcott's true statement that 'Herrick and Herbert
belong to him every bit as much as they belong to Larkin', Schmidt
then celebrates 'the vigour of a literature which, in despite of
geography, remains English'. With respect to tradition and the
individual talent, it is not a question of what Walcott or Larkin
may absorb as readers but as writers. Larkin's intense selectivity
suggests the importance of finding those precursors that sound the
right notes at the right time, and taking it from there. And poets
are located historically and culturally as well as geographically.
(Hence the reinvention of the war elegy in Northern Ireland.)
When Schmidt speaks of 'enabling continuities', or praises his new
poets' 'abundance of technical and linguistic resources', he conjures
up (*contra* modernist revolution) some well-stocked Platonic super-

market. What counts is the chemistry between life, tradition and history at that rare moment when somebody does 'make it new'. While I welcome Schmidt's suspicion of culturalist pluralism (although there is some right-wing *hauteur* in his disdain for those who 'politicise taste and judgment'), he substitutes a watery formalist pluralism. In any case, 'poetries' sells the pass of 'taste and judgment'. Earlier I quoted Sean O'Brien's phrase 'the emergence of new poetries'. Does this implicitly condescend to a multicultural poetry as not quite up to scratch? And does Schmidt's usage in *New Poetries* conversely talk up the distinctiveness of his protégés? He may not, as he fears, be trying 'to assimilate diversity into a factitious unity' but announcing a factitious diversity.

In fact, 'poetries' arrives as critical nerve weakens. This is the kind of nerve shown by Falck and Hamilton, who also speak of 'an overweighting of the intellectual component in poetry and a widespread withering of – or withering of confidence in – intuitive response'. The post-1945 anthologies offer many pleasures. They also offer far too many poets. The *Penguin Book* contains 141 poets, 55 being represented by a single poem. In *The Firebox* the proportions are 126/62. MacNeice observes that '*Poetry Now*...includes seventy-four poets, not one of them represented by more than two poems – oh, the inevitable bittiness of it!'[21] When Armitage/Crawford refer to 'a proliferation of poetries', the ugly wording – which evokes pustules or franchises – confirms this abject relativism as a pluralism too far. What Shelley would bother to write *A Defence of Poetries*? What Shelley does the very idea silence?

Tom Paulin: Wild Irish Critic

'Never begin with immediate undiluted praise of a subject', advises Tom Paulin in one of the 'Critic at the Breakfast Table' columns he reprints in *Writing to the Moment: Critical Essays 1980-1996*. He might think this paragraph unlikely to need the advice, since I have questioned some of his critical ideas and their effect on his poetry. Even a polemicist who relishes 'a terrible tragic disgust' will hardly care for lesser shafts directed towards himself. Yet any contributor to the debate about literature and Ireland (apart from his interest in 'Northern Protestant Oratory', Paulin says little about "culture" in a wider sense) should regard opposition as recognition. More often, however, it is put down to predictable politics – a reflex which itself becomes predictable. Always given to reductionist flourishes, as when he identified Ted Hughes with Thatcherism, Paulin too often labels uncongenial voices and aesthetics 'unionist' or 'loyalist'. This is how Irish debates become polarised and repetitive, mix party politics with literary politics, and confuse non-Irish readers.

Yet in some ways Paulin's criticism does not play the expatriate game. Witness his willingness both to lay himself open and to castigate his English host society. Whereas this can make him unpopular as well as noticed, other literary visitants from Ireland, more sparing of such rebukes or more diplomatic in framing them, enjoy a reciprocal immunity. Seamus Heaney, like the Queen Mother, has been called 'gracious' by metropolitan scribes; and, as a *Guardian* reviewer once observed, English critics who attack Heaney's poetry end up sounding mad. Paulin, in contrast, seems disarmingly keen to sound mad himself, as if acting out some counter-stereotype of the graceless Ulster Prod. But there's method in it, too. Justifying his critical prose in the introduction to *Writing to the Moment*, he says: 'As an occasional subscriber to the loose-cannon school of literary criticism, I don't at all mind the roller-coaster, even at times loopy, effect of [the] uncontrolled searching for an idea.' Mandarin cautions, anxious qualifications, prudential cop-outs, 'Yet, on the other hand' and 'To be fair, Woolf...' belong to the culture of his anathema – 'evasive Anglican compromise'. According to Paulin, 'the critic who is truly a critic is almost never consensual, never balanced or judicious, but always trying to break away from the orthodox and the generally accepted'. The critic is 'a daredevil, an existentialist, a risk-taker, a header', 'Icarus, the impatient son'.

Patrick Kavanagh thought likewise: 'A true creative critic is a sweeping critic, who violently hates certain things because they are weeds which choke the field against the crop which he wants to sow.'[1]

In *Writing to the Moment* Paulin's violent hates are Eliot, Arnold, Conor Cruise O'Brien (the 'essential frivolity of his historical aestheticism'); his violent loves – better not call them touchstones – Milton, Clare, Hopkins, Hughes, Hardy, Lawrence, Dickinson, Bishop. Paulin has helped us to see that the literary dynamic of the dissenting tradition continues into the twentieth century, and that the theological dimension of literature and criticism (he might add "theory") should always be reckoned with. These insights, which inspired Paulin's monograph *The Day-Star of Liberty: William Hazlitt's Radical Style* (1998), is or could be one of Northern Ireland's contributions to literary and cultural criticism; just as Ulster's residues of European ethno-religious war inform 'British Isles history'. Paulin's own evangelical persona reinforces the point. His 'terrible tragic disgust' is most powerful (whether you agree or not) in 'The Making of a Loyalist' (1980), his assault on O'Brien. His visionary advocacy of Clare and Bishop makes you reach for the poems. Praising Clare, he sounds like Edward Thomas when he says: 'if an anthology piece is like an over-cultivated flower, Clare's poems are like wild flowers or wild creatures on whom we have laid almost no percepts, no critical judgements'; more like himself when he comes up with such phrases as 'marvellously clattery', 'whapping intensity', 'echo-less eerie intensity and yukkiness of the noise made by soaked wet shoes and clothes'.

To writing he admires, in whatever genre, Paulin attaches a significant cluster of terms: 'eager, volatile, intense', 'instant, excited, spontaneous', 'something provisional, offhand, spontaneous, risky …volatile', 'all-off-the-top-of-the-head spontaneity', 'the beautiful extemporised bulging precipitate sense of emergency', 'meltfresh, newpainted, all-in-the-moment living quality', 'active, bristling openness', 'apparently formless, often iconoclastic', 'naked, gritty, direct plainness', 'the now of utterance', 'taut nowness', 'direct, here-and-now immediacy', 'rapid, extempore, jazz-like and funky', 'bloody and engaged directness', 'hurtling creativity', 'unpremeditated song'. His quintessential and self-referential phrase of praise might be 'spontaneous, volatile, direct all-now intensity', his quintessential metaphor that of the roller-coaster: 'The critic is compelled to ride the roller-coaster of the *Zeitgeist*'.

The opposite of all this excitement is damned by terms like Parnassian, eirenic, 'Burkean or High Anglican', blandness, civility. Paulin's positive critical language derives from what attracts him in Presbyterianism: the preacher reaching deep for the inspiration of the moment – a model he transfers, perhaps aggrandisingly, to the reviewer on a deadline: 'all that helterskelter wildness running with the sense of social connectedness and communication now'. Certainly there is precedent in Lawrence's debt, as poet and critic, to nonconformism: his distinction between 'instantaneous' utterance and the 'exquisite finality, perfection' that characterises the 'poetry of the beginning and the poetry of the end'. Milton, Hopkins and Hughes, however, are more dubious cases when it comes to an aesthetic of make-it-now. Moreover, Paulin's essays and his advocacy of Hazlitt depend on polemical calculation (those adjectival crescendos) as well as on freewheeling *hwyl*.

Hazlitt's style and writings about style serve to validate Paulin's own practice and theory: 'Anyone who practises literary journalism, with its rapid, heated bursts of energetically assembled quotations, interpretative paraphrase, and related commentary...must recognise that [in Hazlitt's 'Milton and Shakespeare'] the related images of furnace, cento, new-minted coins, and Homeric originality are a means of both praising Milton and drawing attention to critical writing as it is practised by the supreme master of the reviewer's art.' It is for Hazlitt scholars to decide whether *The Day-Star of Liberty* makes Hazlitt sound too much like a contemporary Northern Irish writer who founds his creative and critical project on those Ulster Presbyterians whom the French Revolution turned into United Irishmen. Paulin stresses that Hazlitt's father was 'an Irish Unitarian from Co. Tipperary' (originally from Ulster) who emigrated to England, and that he 'belonged to a particular Dissenting counter-culture'. He sees Hazlitt's 'republican poetics' as stemming from 'the expressive plasticity of the free individual conscience', and as fusing prose and politics into the phenomenon that Paulin calls 'radical style'.

Underlying Paulin's idea of writing-as-politics, however, is perhaps too mimetic an approach to the means whereby language becomes 'style', too formalist an approach to the means whereby style becomes politics. He valuably highlights Hazlitt's sense of prose-rhythm as bodily movement; the vivid physicality of his verbal portraits; his desire to combine the 'liveliness of conversation with the concentrated focus of connected prose'. Yet these are the foundations, not the building. By dwelling excessively on Hazlitt's sensory energy, Paulin turns what Hazlitt (writing on Titian) dubbed 'Gusto' into a closed circuit between critic and artwork, a mutual admiration society, an erotic charge. Thus Hazlitt's delight in the 'tingling sensation' that Titian gives to the eye

becomes Paulin's delight in Hazlitt's 'concentrated zing'. Such
formalism can restrict the political meanings that Paulin presumes
style of itself to carry – as though passion or intensity were enough,
as though nothing said in 'Parnassian' could ever be politically
significant. Besides problematising his equation between style and
politics – Paulin always praises the same qualities in different
writers and misses different qualities in the same writers – this
restriction points to the limits as well as ambitions of Paulin's own
prose style. 'Expressive plasticity' needs to be expressive as well as
plastic; 'helterskelter wildness' must occasionally stop to think. His
tendency to substitute adjectives for argument can induce stylistic
sameness even if the adjectives vary. Hazlitt's 'embodied prose' is
a metaphor for varying movements of mind, not a licence for con-
stant impressionism. Similarly, when Paulin says: 'By dramatising
criticism as conversation, Hazlitt allows the provisional, contradic-
tory nature of critical judgment to fissure in front of our eyes', he
might be describing not an ethic but a template – or a deadline.

   If the structures of Paulin's prose sometimes invoke rather than
exemplify his critical principles, so too with subject-matter. His
focus largely remains the more or less canonical Eng. Lit. text.
Even his *Faber Book of Political Verse* (1986) excludes the (stylisti-
cally) cruder type of political ballad. In *Literature and Culture in
Northern Ireland since 1965* Richard Kirkland makes a case for
Paulin as a more genuinely radical critic. Kirkland argues that
Paulin's role in the *Re-Reading English* controversy of the early 1980s
merely served 'to establish [his] reputation as a dissident voice
within the corridors of the British institution', and regrets that his
opponents failed to grasp that 'it was Paulin's interest in and ten-
tative affiliation to, an unformed Irish culture which led to his
polemic against *Re-Reading English*'. (*Re-Reading English* was a
pro-theory manifesto by diverse academic hands.) But, in trying to
reconcile Paulin with theory via Ireland, a reconciliation that Paulin
himself still finds difficult (and which goes against his Leavisite
regard for 'embodiment'), Kirkland must admit: 'it is part of [his]
dilemma that even on withdrawal from the British institutional
arena he may find that…Irish citizenship, in actuality, has a culture
less unformed than he would like'.[2] Nor has Paulin's idea of
nationality or culture absorbed, even to reject as premature in the
Irish case, the critique of essentialism. Thus he suggests in *The
Day-Star of Liberty* that Hazlitt knew 'the complex self-disgust
which can exist on the interface between two cultural identities'.
However autobiographically revealing, this also shows Paulin's
imperviousness to the theoretical and practical work on 'identities'

and 'interfaces' – not only Irish-British ones. His 'dilemma' might be resolved, his dissidence become less solipsistic and more critically fruitful, if he paid broader attention to English, Irish (and Scottish) culture, to internal differences as well as interpenetrations. As it is, he risks becoming a 'minotaur' lost within the labyrinth of English systems or a literary exile who depends on the polarities of a fixed universe. Either way, he ceases to challenge readers.

There are dangers in perpetual dissidence. Louis MacNeice writes of himself and Anthony Blunt at Marlborough: '[we] were spending too much time in being *enfant terribles*; it is so easy merely to do the opposite'. MacNeice understood, too, the transaction involved in playing the 'Wild Irish Boy' at an English public school.[3] Paulin plays the wild Irish critic. Seamus Deane's argument that to be thought wild or exotic is to be tamed may be more pertinent to the English reception of contemporary Irish literature, or to Oxbridge and Ireland, than to English views of Irish "terrorism". Today, it may also cover Catholic patronage of the culturally barbarous Ulster Protestant (see 'The Poetics of Celt and Saxon', p.70). Thus Paulin has to fly by mutually entangled nets of licensed wildness. On *Late Review* he can be a sheep in wolf's clothing: he will advance a bold proposition only to retreat into charm. Similarly, the opinions of the *Independent on Sunday*'s Critic at the Breakfast Table were not all that unreceived. It takes rather more work to establish a serious Irish perspective on or in Britain. Admittedly, for various historical reasons, this can be a formidable task. The essayist Hubert Butler lamented in 1952 that the salutary Anglo-Irish critique of England (from Ireland) had ceased to operate after 'Anglo-Irish writers [were] starved out by the Gael so that they had to sell themselves to the English for porridge'.[4] To invoke Butler is also to realise Paulin's inability, owing to his romance with nonconformism, to appreciate the differences between the Irish and English Anglican traditions.

If Paulin has challenged 'the orthodox and the generally accepted', he has not done so consistently. I recall Paulin among the women, 'pinned and wriggling on the wall', as he tried (on TV) to defend the *Field Day Anthology*'s treatment of women's writing. Tennyson's 'silvery angst and trim melody' are, after all, an old target; 'savage vernacular energies' a perennial rediscovery. Perhaps Paulin's 'loose-cannon' mode over-compensates for a certain orthodoxy elsewhere. When attacking Philip Larkin, along with Anthony Thwaite's editing of Larkin's *Selected Letters,* he did not pause to wrestle with his own expressed view (see *Minotaur*) that the letters already cited in Janice Rossen's study 'extend our understanding of the

very cunning and very wounded personality of a poet whose some-
times rancid prejudices are part of his condition, part of the wound'.
Paulin prefers *volte-face* to reappraisal. *Writing to the Moment* con-
tains his review of Anthony Julius's *T.S. Eliot, Anti-Semitism and
Literary Form*. Paulin supports Julius's charges not only against
Eliot but against critics and academics who have ensured that there
is 'no other modern writer whose prejudices have been treated with
such tolerance'. I happen to agree with most of this; but then I
have never been one of those who, like Paulin, subscribed to the
orthodoxy that Eliot's poetry is 'endlessly subtle and intelligent'.
Karl Shapiro cried in the wilderness 30 years ago about what
Paulin now terms 'the overwhelming, stifling cultural authority
which Eliot's oeuvre has acquired'. Nor is it exactly news that
murky romanticism lurks in the 'supposedly classical Eliot'. Like
Larkin, Eliot belongs in spirit to the Decadence, and male/national
anxieties about impurity can be part of that picture. But the task
is to read, not censor, their poetry for what it reveals (voluntarily
and involuntarily) about human wounds. Extremes of denunciation,
like extremes of praise, usually miss the literary point.

Perhaps Paulin devotes his critical energies to the sick metropolis,
because at heart he knows that the actually-existing Republic makes
Irish culture 'less unformed than [he] would like'. If, to a citizen of
that state such as myself, his interests seem unduly circumscribed
by the Union, some intellectuals from northern Catholic back-
grounds also disdain the south. Bernard O'Donoghue emphasises
that no one should think Paulin 'well-disposed to the Irish Republic
or to the possibility of its subsuming Ulster as a political unity
centred on the Dáil'.[5] This is because, as for other writers from the
Protestant north, a literary republicanism based on the Presbyterian
United Irishmen does not necessarily endorse the premises or per-
formance of the southern state.[6] Paulin has even called the latter a
'statelet' – more commonly a nationalist jeer at Northern Ireland.
On *Late Review* (September 1999) Paulin strongly attacked Roddy
Doyle's novel of the Republic's origins, *A Star Called Henry*. His
critique identified the novel's failings with those of the state.

This was again form read as politics, politics read as form. In
Ireland & the English Crisis (1984) Paulin announced a 'critical
position…founded on an idea of identity which has as yet no for-
mal or institutional existence'. Although this may seem an unreal
cultural politics, it has been co-opted for the politically more coher-
ent hegemonic drive spearheaded by Seamus Deane. Paulin's 'dil-
emma' occupies the gap between foundation and absence. Scorning
liberalism, intermediate states, the slog of cultural preparation, he

swings between contrary symbols. The intense epiphanies of his literary essays transfer to politics. For example, in the introduction to *Writing to the Moment* he celebrates the late Belfast newspaperman, Ralph Bossence, as 'a lonely working journalist' whose 'powerless decency and exasperation [with unionism] shone through his writing', and who 'became almost a talismanic figure for me'. The wake for Bossence raised the rafters, and this particular glass might be half full rather than half empty.

Paulin thinks about politics in Platonic, iconic, ultimately literary terms: 'historical aestheticism' has many mansions. His own remark about Ted Hughes's *Shakespeare and the Goddess of Complete Being* seems to the point: 'Because Hughes feels…history intensely as myth, he is not much interested in detailing events, and this partly explains the narrow, tunnelled quality of his critical vision.' Paulin's essays on O'Brien and Ian Paisley are reprinted in *Writing to the Moment*. Their focus is personality and mentality rather than context, and they draw ideological conclusions from stylistic 'manner'. Thus 'The Making of a Loyalist' conflates O'Brien's politics with Dublin 'irony': 'that ironical manner which is so characteristic of Dublin culture'; '[Northerners] are beyond the Pale and threaten the ironical civilities of Dublin'; O'Brien's later style is 'broguishly ironical'. Even if some Dubliner gave Paulin a hard time, this is extreme prejudice. In fact, I share Paulin's view that *Maria Cross* and the study of Camus are O'Brien's most interesting critical works, and also his feeling that O'Brien has carried 'political rationalism' too far – currently, indeed, towards a determinism that eliminates hope and inhibits action. However, Paulin fails to understand that O'Brien's attitudes, with their complex roots in the Easter Rising and the Civil War, express real fear that the fascistic elements in northern republicanism threaten the whole island.

Oddly, Paulin has updated neither of these political essays, even though 'Paisley's Progress' ends with speculations about the future of Northern Ireland, and despite the fact that O'Brien's current support for UK Unionist Robert McCartney gives him a splendid chance to say 'I told you so'. Paulin's silence may denote his lack of interest in 'detailing events' or his refusal to betray the 'melt-fresh' moment or perhaps both. He says: 'I wanted to call back the occasions [these essays] represent and to chuck a few stones back in the pond.' Where revising poetry is concerned, I agree that poets can rarely adapt to one historical moment what was conceived in and for another, but a "political" poet might have had something new to say in his prose. Paulin's take on the political also falters in the *Faber Book of Political Verse*. (*Writing to the Moment*

chucks his introduction to this, and to *Vernacular Verse* (1990), back
into the pond.) While warning that 'sometimes a political poem does
not make an obviously ideological statement – "To Penshurst", for
example', he does not add that even radical poems can harbour
hidden agendas. Nor does he notice that his formulation, the 'poet
who elects to write about political reality', may be problematic,
that it lays his own political unconscious on the line. Once again,
Paulin appears most alive to English verse-traditions – although
he inexplicably excludes James Fenton. As regards Ireland, he should
blame history rather than New Criticism for the disposition to hold
poetry at a certain distance from party. He categorises crudely
when he terms Derek Mahon's 'A Disused Shed in Co. Wexford'
'anti-political'; when he sees Paul Muldoon's 'Anseo' as influenced
by the 'revisionist school of history – a school hostile to Irish
nationalism'. Both poems get down to the psycho-cultural roots of
– not only Irish – political behaviour. Paulin's readings collapse
distinctions, and hence bridges, between culture and politics.

A strange feature of Paulin's essay on Conor Cruise O'Brien is
his belief that O'Brien's changing politics manifest an insecurity
about the self, 'a continuing uncertainty about his identity': 'It is
as though his identity is a figment of public opinion.' Turning the
public sphere into a correlative for problems of identity, for inner
conflict, more plausibly characterises Paulin's own speculations
and his writings in general: 'Because he possesses a theological
temperament, Paisley is as opposed to liberalism as any Marxist...
It's a temperament dipped in icy, not lukewarm, water...' Further,
Paulin's interest in Protestantism, like John Hewitt's earlier in
Ulster regionalism, is clearly bound up with forging a strong liter-
ary identity for himself. Thus his poem 'The Other England' (in
Walking a Line, 1994) uses Milton as mask for a voice which puts
would-be-radical butch language to declarative purposes:

> now the shade of John Milton
> asks how long will the loyal
> citizens of Britain
> go on bending the knee
> to a scraggy vulture
> that feasts on a spent tampon
> and a dead dick?

Such projections, however, repress as much as express the psycho-
logical strata of Paulin's imagination. Crossing over between poetry
and criticism, his diction manifests, but does not fully dramatise, a
tension between something macho, at once admired and repudiated,
and softer qualities. Similarly, the fact that he takes Celt-Saxonism

half-seriously suggests psychic transference rather than engagement with a genuine cultural interface. Thus he describes Hopkins as 'imagining a Celtic and Catholic pre-imperial Britain, but...in a language still laced with a colonising fire and stress'. Hence, too, his fondness for adjectives which combine a consonantal, onomatopoeic noun with the tenderising 'y' suffix: buzzy, quartzy, squitchy. Paulin attaches all these to language itself, and we might again diagnose a wish to make the style the man and the politics.

Nevertheless, Paulin's obsession with language produces his most exhilarating criticism. The obsession began when he wrote a book on Hardy's poetry (1986), whose preface he reprints in *Writing to the Moment.* Here Paulin enjoys 'a fricative, spiky, spoken texture', 'the lovely acoustic texture of Hardy's verse'. The *Faber Book of Vernacular Verse* complements and extends *Political Verse* by pleading for 'an alternative community that is mostly powerless and invisible [and] voices itself in gestural, tactile language'. This community is subjugated by the 'Parnassian official order'. Yet Paulin's anthology includes Parnassian as well as 'dialect' poets, and again he seems primarily interested in a linguistic *body*, one that will save the lyric poem from new kinds of abstraction. The subtextual aesthetic tension between blood and intellect, perhaps between poet and academic, is more compelling than Paulin's translation of linguistic phenomena into political parables: the enemies of 'ecstatic tribal innocence' (as exhibited by a Belfast children's song) are print, grammar, standard English, 'polished speech', 'an imposed, normative, official voice'. As with his ideological pigeonholing of writers, and with some of his responses to Hazlitt's style, these utopian conceits simplify the relation between language and politics. Paulin sentimentalises orality and regional speech, while his stress on diction, 'texture' and (onomatopoeic) sound underplays other things that language does. After his long-expressed wish for such a work, his review of C.I. Macafee's *Concise Ulster Dictionary* is disappointingly impressionistic ('Just running through those phrases makes me long for the crack and buzz of Ulster speech.') And is it really the case that 'the word *boke* for "puke" has a richness and a humour which is missing from estuary English'? It's probably all one to the boker or puker.

Writing to the Moment is a cheeky bit of book-making, a taster for *The Day-Star of Liberty.* Yet the exercise, together with his work on Hazlitt, made Paulin reflect – too briefly – on the increasingly strained relations between literary journalism, writing a full-length critical study, literary theory, and (implicitly) poetry. The accessibility of his essays should be cherished, even if publishing in this manner lets him too easily off the boring hooks of academic apparatus, detailed engagement with other critical positions and with "theory". He says: 'Brushed – scratched even – by theory, I'm unable to theorise or apply many of the highly sophisticated concepts and technical terms that have evolved from this type of critical practice.' I sympathise with this, as with a review-article on Lawrence's short stories, daringly called 'Formal Pleasure', which concludes: 'it is only by combining formalism with the historical sense that literary studies can survive [their] deep-seated crisis of confidence'. Yet the article was first printed in 1981, and Paulin also subscribes, when it suits him, to the continuing assault on the category of the aesthetic. In his deployment of theoretical concepts he is still more opportunist and inconsistent than most Irish critics. His conclusion to *The Day-Star of Liberty* is even brushed by post-modernism, together with a touch of special pleading, when he makes a virtue of Hazlitt's 'unfinished, promising quality' as a critic: 'Perhaps what we need is an anthology of his writings that breaks open individual essays and books in order to present fragmentary passages that point to the entire Parthenon frieze on which he worked all his life.'

Paulin's deepest dilemma may be a dilemma about form. His discussions of prose-style are disguised reflections on poetry. While celebrating and practising 'spontaneity' or 'provisionality' he remains haunted by the formality he resists. Hence his aestheticising of culture and politics, his Oedipal problem with the Parnassian, his Parthenon frieze that will finally order the fragments. Yet in any artist's creative process, where does provisionality stop and pattern-making begin? How does Hazlitt get from lively conversation to 'connected prose'? Is 'spontaneity' identifiable on the page? Yeats says: 'Yet if it does not seem a moment's thought,/ Our stitching and unstitching has been naught'. Discussing his Protestant orators, Paulin does observe that the preacher's 'appearance of directness and informality…is a carefully calculated illusion'. But then he re-emphasises 'this vocal aesthetic'. In *The Day-Star of Liberty* he gets confused as to whether a line from D.H. Lawrence's 'Bare Fig Trees' – 'I say untarnished, but I mean opaque' – constitutes 'all-off-the-top-of-the-head spontaneity' or 'a perfect iambic pentameter disguised as a sudden second-thought revision'. Even if we suspect that Yeats would have taken longer over such a line, we can only know it as a brilliant rhetorical stroke. As *Vernacular Verse* splendidly proves, to split the oral from the written is a false dichotomy where poetry is concerned. Moreover, the oral-written or vernacular-standard opposition simplifies the intricacies of rhythm, syntax and cadence.

Tom Paulin's critical roller-coasting can make him dizzy. At such moments, rather than wildly improvising, he overrides analysis by clinging to formula (Hughes's 'entrepreneurial imagination'). The insistent adjectives are wearing a little thin, while more elaborate exegesis would keep his critical and creative processes further apart. As it is, his criticism depends on poetic licence being infinitely renewable. The all-purpose impressionism that has come to govern the theory, method and style of Paulin's prose may be intrinsic to the genre – the short essay – that he favours. It undoubtedly makes for striking insights and zingy effects. Nonetheless, Daedalus, the patient artificer, should have a word with Icarus.

Irish Bards and American Audiences

1

To begin with a parable. In July 1996 the US aircraft-carrier *John F. Kennedy* ('*JFK*') anchored off Dún Laoghaire, Co. Dublin. The *JFK* had been prominent in the Gulf War. The Republic of Ireland is a neutral state. Parties for the great and good took place on board the ship. Ordinary citizens toured its facilities. Sailors came ashore in glamorous uniforms. The women of Dún Laoghaire made up for missing the Second World War. A few hundred people protested on the quay. Several days later two British naval mine-sweepers paid a goodwill visit to Cork. A Sinn Féin councillor objected. In June 1999 a British warship (the frigate *HMS Monmouth* paying a similar visit to Dublin) 'headed up the River Liffey...for the first time since the establishment of the independent Irish state'.[1] A Sinn Féin councillor objected.

I am not making a point about Irish neutrality but about the difference between an American beam and a British mote in Irish eyes. Whereas the *JFK* was hugely invisible, the merest sighting of British forces was picked up by nationalist radar. If the Sinn Féin councillors probably spoke *for* no more people than did the Dún Laoghaire protestors, they also spoke *against* nothing like the public excitement about the *JFK*, the public blindness as to its function and implication. The ship's visit was orchestrated by the actual JFK's sister Jean Kennedy Smith, then US ambassador to the Republic. In November 1996 she facilitated the first 'foreign game' ever played at Croke Park: a soil sacred to Gaelic games, hostile to heretical soccer, but apparently receptive to an exhibition match of American football. History, of course, explains why American power might occupy an Irish blind spot. The name and sponsor of the *JFK* virtually made it 'part of what we are', to cite a patriotic cliché. In contrast, any expression of the British state, even flying the union jack from a Dublin hotel alongside other international flags, remains a touchy issue. I want to argue that within the broader question (how groups in Ireland receive American "colonialism" as compared with the more familiar British brand) lurks an invisibility principle that also affects the reception of Irish poetry.

In 'The Poetics of Celt and Saxon' I suggested that English audiences are attracted to 'Irish' qualities in poetry, 'poetic' qualities in Ireland. English critics, especially from the Left, also carry burdens of guilt and apology. In the US a corporate merger between Celticism and Irish-American Catholic sentiment (the numerous 'Scotch Irish' descendants of Ulster Protestant settlers have been more or less absorbed into WASP America) removes guilt as it disguises power. Even when they lack ethnic credentials, Americans who 'work on' Irish literature *ipso facto* revoke their complicity in anything "Anglo". It's like being able to watch *Braveheart* with a clear conscience. More generally, "Ireland" offers a way of being politically correct without sacrificing white cultural authority, as it does a way of being spiritual without sacrificing capitalism. Thus American Hibernicism resembles platonic Euro-Celticism and recalls the origins of Ossianism in eighteenth-century Sentiment – a cultural mode which pretended to transcend commerce. The Irish-American politician, Tom Hayden, 'dedicating' an anthology of 'Personal Reflections on the Legacy of the Famine' (by reputable Irish writers), says: 'The Irish were in many ways the Indians of Europe...They believed in the spirits of nature. They lived in clans and tribes'.[2] Here St Patrick loses out to Oisín in an ethnic context produced by Catholicism. American versions of the prelapsarian Celt encourage "Ireland" to usurp 'poetry' still more than it does in England, where a disconcerting neighbour occasionally swims into view. Further, the downside of ethnic status, however high, is ghettoisation. Since old tensions with Anglo/Protestant America have not wholly evaporated, "Ireland" sometimes obstructs the actively international view of English-language poetry for which I argue in 'The Millennial Muse'. All of which means that criticism (unlike the *JFK*) is disarmed.

This polemic, about systems rather than individuals, does not deny the huge American contribution to Irish literary studies (which includes the role of Wake Forest University Press in publishing Irish poetry across the Atlantic). It is a plea for greater self-con-sciousness all round, for the ever-incomplete effort to bring premises and perspectives to the surface. On the one hand, excessive proto-cols govern multi-culturalism in America itself; on the other, dif-ferences dissolve into the ocean. Just as it could be hard to tell whether Jean Kennedy Smith was US Ambassador to the Republic or Irish Ambassador to the US, so American exponents of Irish studies see themselves, and are seen, as disinterested ambassadors. At a recent conference in Dublin ('New Voices in Irish Criticism', 1999) an American postgraduate objected to any hint of fewer than a hundred thousand welcomes. She was right to do so; but the counter-assurances that ensued are not the whole answer. First, she should think her innocence well lost. The credentials of *Irish*

exponents of Irish studies come under scrutiny in a highly politi-
cised field where exclusion/inclusion is itself an issue, and where a
warm welcome may seek to co-opt as a chill-factor to deter. Secondly,
when foreign critics' cultural and intellectual dispositions explicitly
enter their dialogue with Irish literature, the results are more
interesting than when they think no barriers exist. Going native,
the usual result of unexamined premises, is no use to the natives
as they struggle with their own partial viewpoints. When Yeats
wanted criticism to be 'as international...as possible', he did not
ask us to recruit a global fan-club for the national literature.[3]

Yeats's project is set back by a work such as Gregory A. Schirmer's
Out of What Began: A History of Irish Poetry in English (1998).
Whereas Helen Vendler's recent study of Seamus Heaney, some
critics would argue, takes an overly transcendental line,[4] Schirmer
goes to the opposite extreme. That is, he saturates his book with
"Ireland". Vendler's readings are at least true to the tenets of New
Criticism; but Schirmer loses one perspective without gaining
another because his sense of Irish contexts does not go beyond the
obvious politics. Having laid out an ambitious proposal – 'to estab-
lish the distinctive aesthetic and cultural qualities of the genre, to
consider its complex relationship to the traditions of English poetry
and of poetry written in Irish, and to make clear the ways in which
it both reflected and contributed to the social, political, and cultural
history of Ireland' – he allows his third aim to overwhelm the first
two. 'Social, political, and cultural history', however, amounts to
confusing the story of Irish poetry with the story of Ireland and
its supposed climax in 1921. A typical sentence runs: '[Thomas
Moore's] setting of traditional Irish airs to English lyrics looked
ahead to efforts to translate Ireland's Gaelic culture into English'.
It is not that Schirmer signs up for Romantic nationalism, but
that he commits the historiographical heresy of letting 'looking
ahead' dictate his narrative.[5] Nor does he map 'Irish poetry in
English' (not a 'genre', by the way) with reference to its changing
conditions. Rather, he derives from nationalist politics an Anglo-
Irish antithesis which he applies trans-historically to poetry. He
would be lost without the word 'ambiguity'.[6] And while his heart
may be in the right (culturally diverse) place, he says with question-
begging naivety: 'this book is as interested in an Ulster Protestant
like Louis MacNeice whose work on the whole belongs more to
English poetry than to Irish but who wrote seriously about Irish
issues and conditions, as it is in a Dublin Catholic like James
Clarence Mangan, whose work is thoroughly and intimately bound
up with Irish culture'.[7] In the modern period, Schirmer reads the

problematic landscape of 'post-Revival' poetry through socio-polit-
ical conditions and through poetic manifestos whose contradictions
(in both senses) he fails to register. For example, he sees the later
Yeats as Austin Clarke saw him, without recognising the cultural
biases involved, the aesthetic issues evaded:

> Yeats effectively wrote himself out of the mainstream of Irish poetry
> that his earlier work had done so much to enrich and broaden. For
> many of the poets who came after him, Yeats's often aggressively
> exclusivist celebration of Anglo-Ireland as the only available environ-
> ment for the preservation of art was a cultural dead end, and Yeats's
> position of cultural isolation meant, finally, that his work had little to
> say about life in postindependence Ireland. The experience of Irish
> Catholicism, for example, that so preoccupied Austin Clarke's work
> was almost unimaginable to Yeats...[8]

Out of What Began, as a work published in the US, is not excep-
tional. Despite the example given by Dillon Johnston's *Irish Poetry
after Joyce* (1985), Schirmer allows "Ireland" to override aesthetics,
mechanisms of tradition, and the critical *caveat* that poems and
poets should not be taken at their word.

  Out of What Began also marks an intersection between Irish literary
studies and the American academy's broader dealings with poetry,
currently a cause for anxiety. Hence Dana Gioia's crusade in *Can
Poetry Matter?* (1992) to rescue poetry from the introverted 'sub-
culture' of the creative writing programme. This American domestic
quarrel, as I hope to show, implicates Ireland. A review by Stephen
Yenser in *Southern Review* gives credence to Gioia's central points
by the very nature of its resistance. Gioia is distressed by the inter-
connected decline of imaginative scope, cultural influence, critical
rigour. By simply listing examples of what Gioia finds lacking –
long poems, politics, 'formal diversity' – Yenser seems to take the
will for the deed. It remains to identify that awkward, shy, rare
and unpredictable animal, a poem. Again, Gioia hardly 'contra-
dicts' himself when he desires poets to write more directly about
poetry, yet asks teacher-poets to stop reviewing their colleagues so
uncritically. Disputing Gioia's accuracy on the first count, Yenser
mainly cites *academic* books by poets – not the same thing.[9] The
second charge, whose thrust Yenser half-accepts but minimises, is
surely very serious. For Gioia, 'the traditional machinery of trans-
mission – the reliable reviewing, honest criticism, and selective
anthologies – has broken down'; while 'by abandoning the hard work
of evaluation the poetry subculture demeans its own art'. Economic
and institutional factors have made poetry 'a modestly upwardly
mobile, middle-class profession'.[10] Thus, like all professions, it

conspires against the public even if it no longer has one. Gioia says: 'Most book reviews are blandly approving, and poetry criticism has become rife with euphemism and empty compliments. Consequently, the average reader no longer trusts poetry reviews. They are almost indistinguishable from dust-jacket blurbs.' [11] Perhaps the intellect of American poetry is forced to choose perfection of the CV or of the work.

A decade earlier Donald Hall had already attacked 'poebusiness', the 'McPoem' which 'validates itself on voice and on emotion', and collapsing critical standards ('the quality control of the least common denominator'). He also lamented a notional golden age in the American university when writers could 'play gadfly to scholars, and scholars help writers connect to the body of past literature'.[12] But even then Randall Jarrell was worrying about an academicised 'age of criticism', although he hardly foresaw the still more iron age of theory that lay ahead. In 1996 Brad Leithauser, a disciple of Jarrell's, looked back to the already declining function of the 'critic in 1975': 'the virtual absence of spirited but cool-headed, of passionate but respectful debate among poetry critics, all too often replaced by acrimonious exchanges between enemies or a soft-headed passing of valentines between friends'.[13] Meanwhile the academic critic, in Britain as in the US, was reaffirming his/her status as a distinct, often unliterary species. Al Alvarez, reviewing his experience of the British academy and poetry since the 1960s, said recently:

> My feeling is that the academic world is full of very clever people, but what most of them seem to lack is instinctive taste. It's second-hand taste. If you meet…some clever don at a cocktail party and you say to him, 'Shakespeare is the greatest poet in the English language', he will then produce a series of very good articles explaining why Shakespeare is the greatest poet in the English language. So you run into him six months later and you say, 'Actually, I think I got it wrong: the really great poet is John Gower'. And then he will produce another series of equally brilliant articles explaining why Gower is better than Shakespeare. Basically, I think a lot of these guys don't know shit from Shinola.[14]

But this complaint (as Alvarez also recognised) is out of date. In the UK the culture of 'research assessment', together with the cult of Theory, has made taste still more beside the academic point; even if poetry, even contemporary poetry, may be grist to the ratings mill. Hence the compensatory rise of 'creative writing' there, too. That most Anglo-American English departments have become uncongenial habitats for the poet-critic is certainly a loss to criticism, possibly a loss to poetry. Yet hard theory and soft or dishonest criticism do not merely co-exist: they obliquely collude. While writing-programmes at least keep literature on the syllabus, would-be poets need to breathe the sharp air of aesthetic debate. Theory, acting in its own political interests, has expropriated Jarrell's 'real critic [who] *must* stick his neck out just as the artist does, if he is to be any real use to art'.[15] Here comes a logic-chopper to chop off both their heads: "literature" has been discredited as an élitist category; the theoretical taboo on value-judgments feeds the swelling subculture. Whatever your wary walk across the PC minefield, it must be recognised as a site where such collusion can occur.

One unconscious reason why America may welcome foreign poets (it's obvious why foreign poets welcome America) is that they, at least, will have gone through some sort of filtering process back home. Yet these islands are not immune from the forces that gave the US 26,000 'registered poets' by the mid-1990s. Geoffrey Grigson, veteran of fierce aesthetic arguments as editor of *New Verse*, wrote in *The Private Art* (1982):

> A form sent by *Who's Who in Poetry* says that the new edition will give information about more than eight thousand poets. I was reading Ben Jonson's *Discoveries* at the time – 'A *Rymer*, and a *Poet*, are two things' – and I thought I would count up not simply the 'best men', as Jonson calls them, but the good and the occasionally good poets listed in the *Cambridge Bibliography* for the two centuries to Jonson's day and the three centuries after. I made the total...about two hundred and sixty in those five hundred years.[16]

The pseudo-democracy spreading along the literary trade routes to Britain and Ireland does not only affect anthologies. Reviews in *Poetry Review*, once again mostly by poets of poets, have gone through cosy phases (cosy is England's bland), with the magazine cheering on rather thin work by media-friendly young poets. Here too, there is a stress on numbers and on keeping them in good heart. An editorial in 1997 anxiously recovers 'a missing generation ...poets who published first books in the last four years and are now winning prizes'.[17] Generations used to take longer than that. So did prizes. More metaphorically, in the words of the nicely-named Harvey Porlock: 'Reading reviews of modern poetry is like attending prize-giving in a small, caring primary school: everyone has done terribly well, it's all absolutely marvellous.'[18] Two American critics, writing in the *Southern Review*, differ on the new British/Irish poetic 'pluralism'. Mark Jarman welcomes 'poetry that reflects diversity, American-style. Whether it likes it or not, Britain is enjoying a healthy dose of here-comes-everybody'.[19] John Matthias, however, has reservations about the claims and aims of *The New Poetry*: 'it prints some remarkable poems and puts forward a confident agenda for poetry...It also prints a significant number of indifferent poems and in its introduction gets perilously close to a kind of politically-correct lingo larded with phrases plucked from the postmodern, feminist, multicultural air'.[20] Where does positive discrimination (e.g. to keep good work by women in circulation and bad work by men out of circulation) end and critical discrimination begin?

Besides scaring off criticism, pseudo-democracy may disguise the politics really at work. Gerald Dawe writes of the Irish Republic in the 1980s:

> Political patronage, commercial sponsorship and public relations seemed to move hand-in-glove with the promotion of 'the Arts'...Consequently, poetry is everywhere...It is important...that we nail all this cant about accessibility and so forth on the door of the last decade since, more often than not, what was at stake was a masked form of American-style self-promotion and careerism...It has precious little to do with art if one considers when the last book by an English, Scottish, Caribbean or Australian poet was reviewed in an Irish newspaper?[21]

This brings me back to the *JFK* factor. The Introduction to *The Penguin Book of Contemporary Irish Poetry* (1990) is partly a pro-motional exercise in that it highlights Ireland's 'transatlantic neighbourhood' with the US. Thus we are told: 'Eamon Grennan, a poet born in Dublin but who teaches in New York State, returning each year to Ireland, has written of his *migrations*. You might say these writers *commute*.'[22] You might indeed. A small country like the Irish Republic invests heavily in the international status of its writers, pop-stars, film-actors and footballers. Clan-loyalty (say nothing in front of outsiders) is the Irish version of cosiness and blandness. Pernickety criticism, like scruples about colonialism, would be bad for literary trade and literary tourism. For example, in the American journal *Éire-Ireland* an emigré Irish poet-academic gives a remarkably uncritical fifteen-page review/ advertisement to the *Selected Poems* of an Irish poet-publisher. The review concludes: 'The good news is that *News of the World* should bring [Peter] Fallon's warm, wry, heartening poems, and the particular corner of Ireland and the Irish psyche from which they spring, to the attention of the wide American audience they deserve.'[23] While not discounting generous motives, one might raise some contextual questions. Has the reviewer unconsciously succumbed to the American virus diagnosed by Gioia? Or is Irish clan-loyalty part of the baggage he has brought to the States? Or has a hybrid form of Hiberno-American blandness evolved? On the whole, I doubt that it is a straightforward case of Irish innocence lost, the 'Irish psyche' found, in America. We are witnessing a literary form of chain-migration and its feedback into the home country.

2

From a historical perspective, Ireland's size and Anglophone status have made inevitable the diaspora of interpretive communities. And there is diaspora within diaspora. Thus the American academic reception of Irish literature fragments into higher Joycean and Yeatsian circles (these generally ignore contemporary Ireland); the mainly traditionalist approaches of the American Conference for Irish Studies (ACIS), a body which spans history and literature; and a newer phenomenon called Irish Cultural Studies. The latter, as contrasted with the mellow old-style Hibernianism of ACIS, is influenced by liaisons between literary theory and Irish republican ideology. Whereas the heartland of ACIS is Boston College, the power-centre of Irish Cultural Studies in the US is another Catholic foundation, Notre Dame. Both universities are currently competing in their 'outreach' relations to Ireland itself, and have large funds to do so. Since this affects the role and influence of Irish universities in the field, it denotes a new twist in the colonial tale. The point is that the boundaries between intellectual interests and ethnic or political affiliations may be subjected to an unusually high degree of stress. The late Dennis Clark spoke against Irish critics of Irish America, and for elements in the founding ethos of ACIS (elements now challenged), when he urged in 1993: 'We as Irish Americans, and you Irish visitors happily among us, are inheritors of a torrent of beauty and cultural brilliance...We are children of a magnificent begetting.'[24]

To date, the bulk of American academic writing on contemporary Irish literature has taken place around ACIS: in journals (*Éire/Ireland*, the *Recorder, New Hibernia*) and a twice-yearly review, the *Irish Literary Supplement*. The *ILS* is not all puffery, but prints some particularly fulsome poetry reviews; for instance, one headed 'Celebrating Eavan Boland's Genius'. And Ireland is, as they say, "foregrounded": 'he [Peter Fallon again] honours the rituals and rhythms of an Ireland that is at once as solid and as permeable as a bog'.[25] Mediocre talents receive earnest attention and even Irish reviewers, perhaps fearful of injuring the export trade, pull their punches in ways they might not do nearer home. Such is the generally cloying atmosphere, that the following sentences (from a critic based in Ireland) come as a relief: 'The failure of The Dedalus Press to produce, even in these three collections, anything approaching a uniform "alternative" voice reflects back on the whole project of attempting to re-form conceptions of "Irish poetry" in the first place. Proclaiming one's productions as "alternative" has often been a procedure for glossing over the unevenness and mediocrity of those productions...'[26] The *ILS* also features lengthy, admiring interviews with writers: a stout refusal to abolish the Irish author which consorts with most contributors' deference (in letter rather than spirit) to the older traditions of American criticism. American graduate-students, indeed, can be dedicated to theory yet determined to interrogate the producer of the contemporary texts that interest them. Other academics are doubly traditionalist. They conceive a lifelong devotion to some Irish writer and receive all his/her utterances as authoritative. Eavan Boland's reception in America (where the bulk of critical writing on her poetry takes place)[27] illustrates the systems at work. At its slackest, it combines the critical permissiveness licensed by literary Irishness with the permissiveness licensed by literary feminism. Thus the *ILS* review of her latest collection, *The Lost Land,* is wholly descriptive: 'This anthology amasses several of Boland's thematic interests: tradition, identity, inheritance, estrangement, individuality, language, voice, silence, ancestry, and polity, among others.' The reviewer calls *The Lost Land* possibly 'her most outstanding work to date', but offers no argument to back up this claim.[28]

American critics have done Boland no service in so readily allowing her to set the terms of her own reception. These terms include insertion of 'the woman poet' into 'the national tradition' and into 'the Irish poem' – which presumes that both have clear or singular identities. Boland further simplifies the historical variables of Irish poetry, when she condemns the 'very stubborn and privileged perspective which would see male poets as Irish poets and women poets as women poets'. In the same interview, she says more subtly that women poets everywhere may be 'internalising the stresses and truths of poetry' at a particular historical moment.[29] Yet she has put the words 'Irish' and 'woman' prominently before 'poet' and before her own work. In fact, where Ireland meets America, feminist criticism often seems magnetised by nationalist tropes despite rhetorics to the contrary. For example, a dialogue between Medbh McGuckian and Nuala Ní Dhomhnaill, designed for an American audience, is framed by its facilitator, Laura O'Connor, in ways that misread the poets' text, subtexts and contexts. O'Connor over-interprets some remarks by McGuckian (whose glosses on her poetry are rarely straightforward) about Irishness and the English language: '[McGuckian] feels buried alive under the Augean muck of enforced anglicisation and ideology'.[30] There are pressures on poets to emphasise their Irishness in America, and according to pre-existing categories. At the same time, Boland may have been more widely recognisable there than the difficult McGuckian, because she signals her debts to Dickinson, Plath and Rich. One American critic, perhaps naively, describes Boland's poems as 'resembling what Rich has done in the US so closely'. Another says: 'Boland identifies her precursors...as Emily Brontë, Emily Dickinson and Sylvia Plath.'[31] That, surely, is for the critic to establish with reference to specific effects in the poems. Will anyone be more impressed by this essay if I identify my precursor as Aristotle?

Consider how three American critics respond to Boland's poem 'The Journey', which has been taken as paradigmatic of her enterprise. The first is Jody Allen-Randolph:

> Perhaps the greatest achievement of [*The Journey and Other Poems*, 1987] is its long central poem...a classic example of what Alicia Ostriker has called feminist myth revision. Usurping and revising both the medieval dream vision and the Irish *aisling*, Boland takes a marginal comment from the *Aeneid* about women and children and makes it the centre of her poem...The poet makes her descent with Sappho as her guide into an 'oppressive suburb of the dawn' where she is shown the suffered, silent histories of mothers and children. Here...Boland is reconciling the ordinary and the mythic to illuminate parts of experience which are absent from tradition.[32]

Here are some extracts from 'The Journey':

> And then the dark fell and 'there has never'
> I said 'been a poem to an antibiotic:
> never a word to compare with the odes on
> the flower of the raw sloe for fever
>
> 'or the devious Africa-seeking tern
> or the protein treasures of the sea-bed.
> Depend on it, somewhere a poet is wasting
> his sweet uncluttered metres on the obvious
>
> 'emblem instead of the real thing...
>
> I finished speaking and the anger faded
> and dark fell and the book beside me
> lay open at the page Aphrodite
>
> comforts Sappho in her love's duress.
> The poplars shifted their music in the garden,
> a child startled in a dream,
> my room was a mess —
>
> the usual hardcovers, half-finished cups,
> clothes piled up on an old chair —
> and I was listening out but in my head was
> a loosening and sweetening heaviness...

and I would have known her anywhere
and I would have gone with her anywhere
and she came wordlessly
and without a word I went with her...

until we came to a sudden rest
beside a river in what seemed to be
an oppressive suburb of the dawn...

'Cholera, typhus, croup, diphtheria'
she said, 'in those days they racketed
in every backstreet and alley of old Europe.
'Behold the children of the plague'...

I whispered, 'let me be
let me at least be their witness', but she said
'what you have seen is beyond speech,
beyond song, only not beyond love...'

While Allen-Randoph accurately summarises the poem's ambition, including its identification of Sappho as precursor, 'The Journey' seems a programmatic inversion, rather than creative subversion, of male poetic myth-making. Thus 'wasting...sweet uncluttered metres on the obvious' is itself obvious. Little inner drama or metaphorical dynamic connects 'Sappho' (portrayed as a kind of health-visitor), the speaker's poetry books and sleeping children, and a female underworld where the mothers of plague-victims lament. Hence some rather forced language: 'dark fell' (twice), 'wordlessly'/'without a word', 'let me at least be their witness'. On the one hand, undifferentiated female victims of history are hazily figured 'suckling darknesses'; on the other, the contemporary world appears in socially restricted terms: women 'stooping, picking up/ teddy bears and rag dolls'. The would-be bridging phrase 'oppressive suburb of the dawn' marks the poem's failure to upset 'traditional' male/Irish norms in a conceptually or aesthetically radical way.

Another commentator, Victor Luftig, argues that in Boland's work 'the intimacy between the poet and the women she depicts remains very much problematised...moments of identification include difficult slippages'. He says of 'The Journey': 'when Boland has looked upon a netherworld of women and children, her "let me be/ let me at least be their witness" seems to be denied by Sappho, who accepts Boland as a poetic "daughter" but insists that the vision is "beyond speech"'.[33] Yet the effect looks more like simple contrast than difficult slippage. All the poem's voices and silences are noticeably orchestrated by the author, who does not mutually complicate (unlike McGuckian in some of her best work) various speaking positions: speaking as poet, speaking as mother, speaking in relation to women's history. Luftig finds *écriture féminine* where none exists. A third critic, Patricia Boyle Haberstroh, resembles Allen-Randolph in assuming the poem's successful access to Sappho (as American-style 'mentor'), to 'Ireland's past' and to 'mythic woman'. She writes: 'the speaker here follows Sappho, her female literary mentor...the contemporary woman speaker, whose children may be safe because of antibiotics, still understands the fear and the loss her female ancestors had to face. Although describing mythic woman, Boland explains that she also had in mind the women in Ireland's past: "the woman I imagined...must have lost her children in that underworld, just as I came to possess mine through the seasons of my neighbourhood".'[34] But to fuse classical allusions, historical cameos and contemporary images into myth requires more parabolic and linguistic inventiveness than Boland shows on this occasion. Haberstroh also rebukes, without refuting, the criticism of one American reviewer (William Logan) who observes that 'New mythologies are rarely less sentimental than the old' and judges: 'The featureless prose and aimless, airless philosophising of...Boland's work are transformed only by a love of pure detail, of the incandescence of the visual.' To Logan's comment that Boland is too often 'the bard of fabric (in one stretch of ten pages we find silk, lace, crêpe de Chine, cotton, linen, damask, gaberdine, synthetics, calico and dimity, some of them two or three times)',[35] Haberstroh replies: 'An enlightened critic would do more than count images of fabric and might see these as a pattern of imagery, as metaphors drawn from and expressing a woman's experience.'[36] But, of course, no imagery is *ipso facto* significant. It depends on the *poetic* fabric.

All three critics recycle Boland's own statements about her work. Convergence between the idioms of interview, review, article and artefact is a trap for every poet and critic in these media-dominated times: a result, too, of ever-more academics chasing ever-fewer uncolonised modern texts. An interdependence is created which can make poets self-conscious – I have seen one or two actually attending papers on their stuff – and keep academics celebratory: Vendler's *Seamus Heaney* simply dismisses the poet's 'negative' or 'adversary' critics as unworthy of counter-argument.[37] The special issues which the *Irish University Review* (edited in Ireland but circulated internationally) devotes to particular writers have a *festschrift* atmosphere, as do other collections of "critical" essays on contemporary Irish writing. Irish writers may also have benefited from the anti-critical shift that Gerald Graff notices in traditional American scholarship after 1960: 'Why force anyone to choose between

Tennyson and Yeats...when so much work still "needed to be done" in advancing both fields? To be sure, curmudgeons like Winters and Leavis intensified their rude challenges to major reputations, but there was no point even dignifying these with counterargument (though it seems symptomatic that Leavis's work became a public issue in England in a way that Winters's did not in the United States).' [38] Curmudgeonly critics have always fought permissive tides. In 1908 Edward Thomas complained: 'An imbecile with ten pounds in his pocket can easily add one to the number of the volumes from which the lover of poetry has to choose.' [39] However, we live in an era when the tides amount to global warming.

Research into the American reception of Irish literature is one means of promoting cooler appraisal, more self-conscious critical intercourse. Two valuable new studies complement one another in anatomising the Irish-American audience and the Joycean sector. John P. Harrington's *The Irish Play on the New York Stage 1874-1966* (1997) uncovers 'an evolving but consistent set of expectations for an "Irish play"' which has 'come to imply a specific kind of Irish subject-matter, invariably rural and Catholic'. At the same time, 'there is in New York a history of Irish Irish plays and non-Irish Irish plays, or plays by Irish playwrights outside the form and content of the narrowest expectations'.[40] The same playwright, such as Shaw, can be known separately in both contexts. Harrington charts complex dynamics involving playwrights, productions and audiences, which issue in conflicts between a desire (variously located) to change the horizon of expectation, and resistance to this project. In *Our Joyce* (1998), a 'reputation-history', Joseph Kelly analyses the relationship between Joyce's writing and a succession of readerships. These include the educated Dublin Catholics whose attitudes he wished to influence; Ezra Pound and T.S. Eliot who (partly with Joyce's sanction) 'changed Joyce from an an Irish writer into an avant-garde, cosmopolitan writer, shucking off his parochial husk to make him serve their literary movement'; the American 'Joyce industry', which followed Richard Ellmann's biography, as well as New Criticism, in 'tending to remove literature from the historical contexts of its publication'. But with Irish critics becoming more vocal in Joyce criticism, there has developed what Kelly terms 'a debate over who gets authority over Joyce'.[41] The Irish repatriation of Joyce can be found, for instance, in Emer Nolan's salutary *James Joyce and Nationalism* (1995) and in the Penguin edition of Joyce's works for which the general editor is Seamus Deane. Perhaps, as with the scenario delineated by Harrington, the debate should hinge not on a "parochial" v. an "international"

Joyce but on a search for readings that thematise neither supposed pole.

And what of the 'Irish poem' (Boland), or perhaps the 'Irish Irish poem' as contrasted with the 'non-Irish Irish poem' (Harrington) or international-Irish poem, in the American critical article? Would this reception-history yield such binary results? Writing about Heaney two decades ago (and employing an imperial first-person plural), Helen Vendler was clearly anxious that his poetry should not be ghettoised as Irish (i.e., presumably, as 'rural and Catholic'): 'In England and the United States, Heaney is usually discussed, understandably enough, as an Irish poet...but that emphasis distorts the beauty and significance of his work...the history of his consciousness is as germane to our lives as that of any other poet'.[42] 'Beauty and significance', it would seem, bypass small countries. Guinn Batten, however, has usefully questioned the stability of perspective available not only to herself as an American, but also to Irish critics, when she writes: 'If the best Irish poets now write about Estonia and reach Japan, Irish scholars of such poetry, more modestly but similarly, may find it increasingly difficult to identify and appraise both the poets they write about and the readers to and for whom scholarship is written.'[43]

Yet Batten's cautionary vista of the worldwide poem caught in a worldwide web of variant readings is too dizzying for this Irish critic to contemplate for long, especially if home-work still needs to be done – we could end up with another Joycean Babel. To return to a more finite point of reference or at least departure: the literary-critical traffic between Irish bards and American audiences is notable for roads not taken; particularly roads, like those travelled by Harrington and Kelly, that face into America itself. For example, New Criticism, despite its significance for Northern Irish poetry, has been a relatively unnoticed locus of American-Irish literary interaction. New Criticism or formalist criticism gets a bad press from Irish critics, as from American theorists, for its "universalist" evasion of history. But the bond between New Criticism and poetry goes deeper. Donald Hall captures its provenance when he says: 'The poet and the critic have been almost continuous, as if writing poetry and thinking about it were not discrete activities.'[44] The post-structuralist attack on New Criticism, as allegedly fetishising the intricate autonomous text, is also a strike against critical values that placed poetry at the centre of their theory and practice: values that made poetry matter. Leah Marcus, discussing shifts in Renaissance studies, notes the loss of interest in the lyric poem 'thirty years ago...generally regarded by scholars of seventeenth-century

English as the most distinguished and intellectually intriguing achievement of the age'.[45] This is further evidence that poetry should not trust the academy's volatile fashions.

But back in late 1950s and early 1960s Ireland, if anything seeped from English departments into the environment of poetry it would have borne traces of New Criticism/Leavisism. Literary exchange acquired a currency that valued the concentrated lyric, verbal complexity, fusion of form and content. This applies to the academic context in which Seamus Heaney began writing poetry at Queen's University, Belfast; Derek Mahon and Michael Longley in Trinity College, Dublin. After 1950 New Criticism or its English counterpart came to Ireland, in a belated and piecemeal way, by various agencies. These included Denis Donoghue[46] at University College, Dublin; Donald Davie at Trinity; and academic members of the Belfast 'Group' run by Philip Hobsbaum in the early 1960s. The Group's meetings (attended by Heaney and Longley) subjected new writing to close reading, practical criticism and vigorously contested value-judgments. Of course, poets could read concentrated lyrics by Yeats or Graves in Dublin or Belfast, just as they could read and criticise one other, without academic mediation. Nonetheless, Michael Allen is right to stress 'the Anglo-American "New Criticism" which had governed the young Heaney's notions of poetic technique and schooled him as a critic in the early 1960s'.[47] Thus when Vendler "discovered" Heaney, and introduced his poetry to 'non-Irish' American audiences, the ground for reciprocities was well-laid. Yet, as Northern Irish poetry negotiated its political context after 1969, insofar as a New Critical ethos persisted, it was translated into new kinds of concentration, verbal complexity, formal reflexiveness, close reading, arguments about value. Poetry began to matter in additional ways. From one angle, this restored the historical-political dimension of Yeats – invisible to the American poet-critics, Allen Tate and John Crowe Ransom, who had built New Critical doctrines on his work and tended to confuse him with Wallace Stevens. Perhaps New Criticism, in the context of Northern Irish poetry, evolved in a direction that cannot be seen as simply antithetical to the theory-derived approaches now (whether aptly or not) linked with the work of younger poets such as Paul Muldoon. And that is why Vendler misreads or manipulates Heaney's career when she over-stresses his poetry's 'symbolic *plane*' (my italics), and claims him for a restrictive version of New Critical aesthetics, let alone one unmodified by Ireland: 'the only thing to which the genre of lyric obliges its poet is to represent his own situation and his responses to it in adequate imaginative language'.[48]

If New Criticism stressed the autonomous poem, it also stressed tradition. Donald Hall again defines, and seeks to preserve, a key principle:

> Most poets need the conversation of other poets. They do not need mentors; they need friends, critics, people to argue with...There have been some lone wolves but not many. The history of poetry is a history of friendships and rivalries, not only with the dead great ones but with the living young.[49]

Conversation with 'the dead great ones', of which Northern Irish poetry shows abundant evidence, owes something to New Criticism, as well as to a society which is traditional, communal, genealogically obsessed – not so far, indeed, from the original stamping-ground of the southern 'Agrarian' poet-critics. But any genuine literary movement critically rewrites the past, and not just in the short term. Thus when Dana Gioia observes that while Americans 'celebrate Seamus Heaney, we ignore Derek Mahon who seems to me one of the best living poets in English' that ignorance connects with his other observation that Louis MacNeice 'is virtually unread in America'.[50] It does so, not only because MacNeice influenced Mahon, but because the intertextual 'conversations' that make up tradition (what do they know of Heaney who only Heaney know?) stretch simultaneously into the past and across the present. Of course, Auden's sojourn in the US, like Heaney's, contributes to such biases. More generally, the latterday atomisation that Hall and Gioia deplore, including its (un)critical consequences, is produced by a characteristically American mix of a-historicism, individualism and celebrity-culture. This obscures the dynamic between tradition, with its loops and back-formations, and the individual talent.

3

What happens to tradition, audience and community when Irish poets 'commute' to America or become more permanent 'writers in residence'? There is certainly no single or constant answer, although negotiating Irish-American and American-American audiences is part of the question. On the professional front, these poets will bring their own values to working with the young, and their exoticism may allow them institutional space. As for the public aesthetic arena, just as American commentators on Irish poetry incline to hyper-enthusiasm, so any literary immigrant must judge whether his/her acid critique will be welcome in the host country. Acclimatising oneself abroad, like extricating oneself from home (or re-entry there), can be a prolonged enterprise – not only for a writer. On a deeper level, poetry seems sensitive to transplantation in a way that proves its holistic nature. Certainly poetic migration involves more than writing "about" America – or Estonia – or writing "to" Japan. A poem's "address" in two senses – its implied cultural environment and its implied reader – affects the chemistry of composition. However, a dialectic between origins and mobility, together with an awareness of multiple or conflicting audiences, has always been a deep structure in Irish poetry. Poets from Northern Ireland are particularly liable to maximise its potential.

For snapshots of this dialectic and awareness, I will look at three poems from three recent collections – Derek Mahon's *The Yellow Book* (1997), Seamus Heaney's *The Spirit Level* (1996) and Paul Muldoon's *Hay* (1998). The poems have explicitly American themes, or make America a theme, and they take out various kinds of insurance against colonial co-option. *The Yellow Book*, a sequence of soliloquies and epistles spoken as from Dublin, has roots in Mahon's earlier epistolary long poem 'The Hudson Letter', spoken as from New York. Canto XVI of *The Yellow Book* is given the title 'America Deserta', subtitled 'postscript to "The Hudson Letter"', and epigraphed by Zelda Fitzgerald: 'High in the air float green-blue copper roofs like the tips of castles rising from the clouds in fairy tales and cigarette advertisements' (*Harper's Bazaar*, 1929). The letter addresses an American woman with whom its author has shared 'restful evening walks/to the West Side pierheads and the desolate docks'. This strategy enables Mahon to speak from an explicitly European angle ('An alien among aliens during my New York time/spying for the old world in the new'), and in a tone that resists America's contagious blend of imperialism and decadence. Speaking also as an Irishman, and to contemporary Ireland, he attacks the country for losing its critical faculty and letting itself be colonised by American values:

> Imitative in all things, we mimic now,
> as nature art, the general new-age weather,
> a smiley-face of glib promotional blather...
> who were known once for witty independence
> and valued things beyond the world of sense...
>
> Back home, I surf the bright box for world news
> and watch with sanctimonious European eyes
> the continuing slave narrative, people in chains,
> the limp ship firing into the vegetation...
> Not long from barbarism to decadence, not far
> from liberal republic to defoliant empire
> and thence to entropy...

Despite 'sanctimonious', some of this too easily blames an "America" constituted by the commercial-military-industrial complex ('McPeace and Mickey Mao', 'mergers and acquisitions, leveraged buy-outs, corporate raiding'). In finer-grained close-up, however, America becomes an atmospherically evoked New York of 'desolate docks' and 'diner mornings in ice and thaw'. Mahon's America is also haunted by its former selves; i.e., by his longstanding attraction to American literature and culture:

> those retro scenes beloved of Sam Menashe
> and the hard-drinking, chain-smoking Eurotrash –
> an older America of the abrasive spirit,
> *film noir*, real jazz and grown-up literate wit...

As critic and artist, the speaker places himself spectatorially outside the "America" he presents, whether it appears alienating in its bourgeois modernity or still faintly exotic in its aesthetic seductions. His cultural bearings are signalled by quotation from anti-imperial Conrad ('firing into the vegetation') and Neruda ('corruption and fatigue'), anti-totalitarian Orwell ('thought-crime/grown secretly like a window box of cannabis'). Also, dawn has become neon-rather than rosy-fingered. America's own media provide a graph of decline: sophisticated *film noir* yielding to images dictated by Spielberg sci-fi: 'a sunset close-encounter blaze'. Meanwhile, the American poet Samuel Menashe also appears disaffected from a country that has finally lost touch with Europe. Yet Mahon's *vale* pays ironical homage to the Gatsby-Fitzgerald dream and to Hart Crane's New York: 'You wildly decadent in forbidden furs...the skyline at your back, the pearl-rope bridges/and a nation singing its heart out in the business pages'. 'America Deserta' apocalyptically updates an old European view of the New World. Nonetheless, in appealing to an implied "civilised" reader, it concedes that Europe and Ireland are also responsible for a global desert from which the spirit has withdrawn. Thus the poet's own absence from New York becomes the ground of questions about poetry at the millennium, as well as about America and poetry ('a nation singing its heart out').

Generically, 'America Deserta' is a (Horatian) satire; Seamus Heaney's 'The Flight Path' an autobiographical meditation. Heaney's six-part sequence takes the poet – and he speaks as poet – from his childhood country, back and forth between Dublin, Wicklow and America; back to Northern Ireland; finally to Rocamadour, a place of pilgrimage in southern France. This is one of the few poems ('Alphabets' is another) in which Heaney directly defines his life and career in terms of transatlantic mobility. The poem features several images of transport: paper boats made by the

poet's father which were first 'taut' then 'soggy'; symbolic planes
(*pace* Vendler) including 'a late jet out of Dublin' seen quasi-reli-
giously as 'a risen light' and 'the red-eye special from New York';
'the train for Belfast'; cars in a nightmare about being forced to
assist an IRA bombing; even space-travel: the 'spacewalk of Man-
hattan' and a lizard at Rocamadour 'its front legs set/ Like the
jointed front struts of a moon vehicle'. Vehicles, including space-
ships, appear more dispersedly elsewhere in Heaney's poetry. The
way in which they come together to structure this retrospect bears
out Michael Allen's argument in 'The Parish and the Dream: Heaney
and America, 1969-1987', an essay written before 'The Flight Path'
was published:

> The concept of the 'American Dream' exemplified – for a teacher in
> Belfast in those days – by texts like *The Great Gatsby* and *Death of a
> Salesman* takes on a triple redolence in Heaney's work: the phrase is
> redolent of the emigrant experience (travelling west to the land of
> opportunity is a powerful idea for the Irish imagination); it accommo-
> dates the frontier experience ('Go West, young man') that was rejuve-
> nated in the 60s when space became the New Frontier (the moon
> landing occurred in the same year as the publication of Heaney's sec-
> ond book); and finally, these locational and spatial metaphors shade
> into the dream of upward mobility, of rags to riches, whereby every
> Irish-American boy can become president.[51]

Fintan O'Toole suggests that President Kennedy, when he visited
the Republic in 1963, 'personified the flowering ambitions of a
new Ireland [and] embodied the lure of America…our own America'.[52]
'The Flight Path' is undeniably less sceptical about the Dream
than is 'America Deserta', although with a sense, so to speak, of
diminishing returns:

> Across and across and across.
> Westering, eastering, the jumbo a school bus,
> 'The Yard' a cross between the farm and campus…

Regular commuting dispels the strangeness of destination ('The
Yard' signifies Harvard) and vehicle ('the jumbo a school bus'),
initially expressed in a contrast between Irish 'stay-at-homes' and
travellers. Heaney's speaker lays claim to both identifications, just
as the poem girdles his imaginative globe in a typically circular
movement. In the first section, a rising dove symbolises his father's
craft; in the last, his own art: 'And somewhere the dove rose. And
kept on rising.' The poem's cultural bearings, however, remain
primarily Irish, Ireland being the (not only symbolic) point of
departure and return. "America" first comes on the scene as release,
opportunity, excitement ('Up and away. The buzz from duty free').

It introduces exotic food, drink and life-styles: ('Bourbon...Laid-back Tiburon./ Burgers at Sam's, deck-tables and champagne') before farm and campus, Harvard and Ireland, routinely merge. Meanwhile, allusions to Horace ('skies change, not cares') and to 'Dante's scurfy hell' anchor Irish 'home truths' to European literary tradition. The latter allusion characterises the 'dirty protest' by republican prisoners. It is here that a Heaney-reader turns up in the flesh: a republican who asks: 'When, for fuck's sake, are you going to write/ Something for us?' To which the poet replies: 'If I do write something,/ Whatever it is, I'll be writing for myself.'

This resistance to a dissatisfied (or unimplied) reader indicates that audience is on Heaney's mind. 'The Flight Path' begins with the poet as his father's audience, and ends by putting the reader in a similar position relative to the dove of poetry. 'Farm' (Irish community) and (American not Irish) 'campus' are invoked as places from/to which the poet has spoken. Whom, then, does the poem address? Achieving an American presence is central to its trajectory and theme. Yet there is a simultaneous sense that America has served the poet's own dream or vision, that he is 'writing for himself' in that, as in the Irish, context. The American differences that remain significant in 'America Deserta' vanish here since, to quote 'Alphabets', 'The globe has spun'. Although 'The Flight Path' finally touches down in Europe, symbols of imaginative mobility persist: the dove, the moon-vehicle lizard, 'a lime-green butterfly/ Crossing the pilgrims' sunstruck *via crucis*'. Nonetheless, and despite writing 'for myself', Ireland and America are the implied poles of the poem's global orbit and address to its global reader.

For Mahon (a visitor), America and Europe are dialectically conceived from an Irish vantage-point. For Heaney (a commuter), they contribute to a circulation, 'both where I have been living/ And where I left', that centres on the poet's subjectivity. For Muldoon (a settler), now an American citizen, some boats are burned, some planes not taken. Heaney, in one classic mode of emigrant behaviour, packed his 'original townland' in his trunk and staged an internal 'American wake'. Muldoon problematised both departure and arrival by writing a series of passages to America: '7 Middagh Street' (1987), *Madoc* (1990) and *The Prince of the Quotidian* (1994) which emulates the Frank O'Hara 'lunch poem'. Muldoon wrote a poem every day for a month to produce a sequence whose American edition calls its author a 'picaro of the information highway'. Perhaps not quite. Nor is the sequence quite as existentially *vers libre* or fast food as O'Hara's. It suggests a trend, advanced in *Hay*, whereby Muldoon's voyage-tale structure coexists or mingles with multiplying versions of 'frontier experience' (to quote Michael Allen). The former is exemplified by 'The Bangle (Slight Return)'; the latter by the autobiographical sequence 'Hopewell Haiku' – autobiography has become a more prominent or explicit connective tissue in the 'American' Muldoon. Hopewell was a neatly emblematic domicile for him when he first went to teach creative writing at Princeton University. As for haiku: in making this miniature unit sustain a larger edifice, Muldoon plays smallness against scope. The effect ironises suburban New Jersey as a reduced version of frontier life; but it simultaneously raises questions about poetic scope, about lyric and epic. Ninety haiku take us from one winter into another while the speaker and his family cope with snow, leaking boots, burst pipes, a dead cat, dying trees, visiting deer and bees. They tap maple syrup, make 'a pot of broth…from a pig's cheek' (all three poets mention American food), pick fruit, set fire to straw, watch the seasons change. Generically, then, 'Hopewell Haiku' is a mock-epic frontier-narrative, an inversion of Whitman set between domestic and wild, in which the pioneering, or perhaps colonising, effort is to make sense of the phenomena that present themselves:

LXXXV
On the road to town
a raccoon in party mask.
Gray shawl. Gray ballgown.

LXXXVI
Winter time, my sweet.
The puppy under our bed
licking salt-raw feet.

LXXXVII
Not a golden carp
but a dog turd under ice.
Not a golden carp.

LXXXVIII
That wavering flame
is the burn-off from a mill.
Star of Bethlehem.

Humans interact with animals, imposing anthropomorphic perceptions or affecting their lives; a vision turns into mundane winter detail; conversely, mundane detail turns into a cosmic sign.

'Hopewell Haiku' falls between the Mahon negatives and the Heaney positives, being in its very title a self-aware contribution to the literature of the Dream. Further American literary points of reference include Robert Frost (already much-invoked by Muldoon) whose poetry contributes to the strangeness of neighbouring deer, to an axe that splits its chopping-block and to a 'two-pointed ladder' on whose highest rung is 'a splash of bird dung'. Frost thus adds a characteristic mix of mystery and scepticism to the homesteading saga. *Moby Dick* represents a more dubious aspect of pioneer energy and creativity *vis à vis* the natural world: 'A hammock at dusk./ I scrimshaw a narwhal hunt/ on a narwhal tusk.' This miniaturises an American voyage-tale. But there are just as many references to Irish authors and genres. Yeats's 'changeless sword' mock-heroically becomes a 'changeless penknife'; the cat is called Pangur Ban after the cat in a well-known ninth-century Gaelic poem; and John Hewitt and Patrick Kavanagh figure in a way that infiltrates the Parish into the Dream. Thus the third haiku returns to Belfast:

> From whin-bright Cave Hill
> a blackbird might...*will* give thanks
> with its whin-bright bill.

Here Muldoon refers both to a ninth-century Gaelic 'gloss' (printed on the opposite page to 'Pangur Ban' in *Celtic Miscellany*) and to Hewitt's 'Gloss, on the Difficulties of Translation' which begins:

> Across Loch Laig
> the yellow-billed blackbird
> whistles from the blossomed whin.
>
> Not, as you might expect,
> a Japanese poem, although
> it has the seventeen
> syllables of the haiku...

As for Kavanagh, the allusion to Bethlehem relates 'Hopewell Haiku', as does the close focus, to his well-known parish-and-universe poem 'A Christmas Childhood'. Muldoon's frontier-pastoral thus keeps microcosmic Irish parish-pastoral in play. The latter (about structural parameters rather than geographical perimeters) both settles and unsettles a poem whose settler-protagonist speaks from a still unfixed abode. 'Hopewell', like '7, Middagh Street', does not imply a permanent address. As for address in its second sense: several haiku involve conversation with the protagonist's wife or child; but people, as opposed to animals, do not otherwise enter the sequence. This reinforces the frontier impression as if there might be Indians beyond the horizon of consciousness so cautiously advancing. (At the same time, 'Hopewell Haiku' seems invisibly subtitled for eavesdropping afficionados, 'Muldoon in America'.) Muldoon's brand of circularity – really a perpetual oscillation – insofar as it turns on America and Ireland, contrasts

with Heaney's. It does so both in its refusal of cultural and liter-
ary boundaries and in the implication that not sameness but either
difference or a weird doubleness defines the relation between 'where
I have been living/ And where I left':

> Snow up to my shanks.
> I glance back. The path I've hacked
> is a white turf-bank.

Ultimately, such ambiguous path-clearing, like the broader Irish
dialectic between home and away, constitutes a locus for poetry
itself. Where a poem comes from haunts what it pioneers. This is
where rhyme and assonance (shanks/glance/bank) come in.

All three poems both comment on cultural encounters and engage
in cultural manoeuvres while yet insisting (through pattern and
persona) on the distinctive styles they crystallise from the flux.
Muldoon is less inclined than Mahon or Heaney to put Americanisms
in notional inverted commas. At the level of vocabulary and image,
the data of his world are – perhaps gradually, perhaps strategically
– becoming more American (plow, airplane, yard – not Heaney's
'the Yard'). In the long run this process might domesticate New
Jersey and defamiliarise Ireland, except that Muldoonian strange-
ness is an imaginative rather than literal matter. When the speaker
'sets a match to straw' he conjures Irish rural arsonists: 'Caravats
and Shanavests'. But these names are exotic in Ireland itself.
Evidently, none of the poems makes an Irish-Irish poetic pitch to
America. Equally, none polarises the American *qua* "international"
against the "Irish". Mahon's satire renders contemporary America
provincial. Heaney has his place and eats it. Muldoon mixes forms
and genres (Gaelic gloss, haiku, strong rhyme, lyric sequence, parish-
pastoral, frontier-pastoral) in a way that manifests not so much
postmodern picaresque as how mechanisms of tradition can be
combined and recombined to make a poem. The mixing may be
eclectic, but it is neither atomised nor arbitrary. It was, however,
too much for one practitioner of haiku. In the *Journal of the British
Haiku Society* David Cobb praises parts of 'Hopewell Haiku', but
complains that 'other "Muldoones" have all the features which...
we struggle to avoid, with generalisations and anthropomorphisms
...full-in-your-face [rhymes] (like *Pangur-banger*)...an excess of
imagery'.[53] Cobb's criticism casts incidental light on 'Hopewell
Haiku' in Irish and American formal contexts, since his version of
haiku harks back to Ezra Pound and Imagism. Muldoon loads haiku
with structures, such as pronounced rhythm and rhyme, that Imagism
sought to expel from poetry (and about which Pound disagreed with

Yeats). His intricate patterns – haiku on facing pages rhyme ABA/
BAB, and the central rhyme-sounds from the last five haiku become
the enclosing rhyme-sounds for the first five – orient the sequence
in continuing transatlantic dialectics about "modern poetry". 'America
Deserta' and 'The Flight Path' belong there, too.

As for the implied reader: the poems assume or promote an
educated literary awareness, including familiarity with the poet's
earlier work. Clearly this does not preclude a nod, a smile or a
wink in the direction of the academic reader (like me in this essay)
wherever that reader may be situated. But the poems also speak in
everyday idioms of everyone's experience: city-strolling, travelling,
home-coming, home-making. While they sometimes catch their
authors tightrope-walking rather riskily between university and
community, they do not give up on the latter. America and its
poets have stimulated Irish poetry in many ways. Perhaps one of
the things that Irish poetry offers in return is its greater collective
resistance to atomisation, its residually holistic ambition, its con-
viction – whether well-founded or not – that poetry matters.

'Atlantic's Premises': American Influences on Northern Irish Poetry in the 1960s

Poetic traffic, it seems, is rarely one-way. Changing tack, I want to consider the impact of American poetry on three poets from Northern Ireland when they were writing their early poems. I should say that my sources and perspectives include personal recollection. The long shadow cast by "poetry and the Troubles" has obscured the literary history of the decade before 1969. Not that this history (as will appear) lacks cultural and political contexts. Hence 'Atlantic's premises' – a phrase taken from the first line of Michael Longley's 'The Hebrides'. Like the poem, I intend the ambiguity whereby 'premises' can mean either bounded space or underlying concepts:

> The winds' enclosure, Atlantic's premises,
>   Last balconies
> Above the waves, The Hebrides –
>   Too long did I postpone
> Presbyterian granite and the lack of trees,
>   This orphaned stone
>
> Day in, day out colliding with the sea...

The American horizons of contemporary Northern Irish poetry have been unevenly explored. Critics mostly confine themselves to poems that have made America a theme, to poets who have made it a home from home, or to links suggested by the critical writings of individual poets. My own focus – on the early work of Seamus Heaney, Derek Mahon and Michael Longley – will be selective, too. As a generational study, it excludes John Montague and Paul Muldoon; as a study of *juvenilia*, it excludes the more deliberate or knowing ways in which mature poets refer and defer to other poets. Thus when Michael Parker analyses the combined effect of Gary Snyder and Berkeley student protest on Heaney's *Wintering Out* (1972), when Michael O'Neill discusses Mahon's direct allusions to Hart Crane in *The Hudson Letter* (1995), or when Neil Corcoran examines 'America in the Poetry of Derek Mahon' with reference to 'Hiberno-American relations in the 1970s and 1980s', different issues seem to emerge.[1] My concern is with that stage of poets' development at which they most unselfconsciously soak up the images, sounds and rhythms that beckon them along their own distinctive paths, or that indicate roads unlikely to be taken. This unselfconsciousness, in its chemistry with life and culture, allows new aesthetic clusters to form. Northern Irish poetry of the 1960s, I would argue, initiated such a cluster in the tradition of the English lyric, and these American poets (not an exhaustive list) influenced its formation: Robert Frost, Wallace Stevens, Hart Crane, Robert Lowell, Richard Wilbur, Theodore Roethke.

It is not, of course, a case of baggage-free pioneers discovering native woodnotes. In America itself, as Terence Diggory shows in *Yeats & American Poetry* (1983), debates about poetry and tradition have often pivoted on W.B. Yeats. Yet even an American poet like Richard Wilbur, who insists on the inexhaustibility of traditional forms, who points out that '"artlessness"...is just another style', who 'tries to play the whole instrument' and who defines tradition as the 'courteous conversing of one poem with another', states: 'the American writer, both with regret and with attraction, acknowledges the fact of a great diversity of culture, of considerable anarchy in this country, and the presence...of the wilderness still amongst us'. Wilbur is inclined to envy a closer-knit *'live'* culture [in which] people understand each other by looks, by gestures, by postures'.[2] The grass or prairie is always greener. Allen Tate and John Crowe Ransom saw Yeats's access to 'Traditional sanctity and loveliness' as a more literal, less rhetorical, affair than it actually was.[3] Conversely, Irish (like British) poets have been drawn to what they may sometimes over-interpret as American 'mere anarchy'. Even so, Irish poetic and cultural intertextuality is usually a tauter if snarled weave. Verbal gestures and postures are liable to become too dense rather than too loose, too coded to communicate more widely. Also few Irish poets have departed as far from traditional forms as have many American poets. Such biases are reflected in the transatlantic conversations that I propose to trace.

Behind these conversations, bestriding the Atlantic, stands the dialectical relationship between Yeats and American modernism (see pp.215-17). Yet modernist poetics were tested and revised in the US as in 1930s Britain. Hart Crane wrote in 1929: 'to the serious artist, revolution as an all-engrossing programme no longer exists...The poet's concern must be, as always, self-discipline towards a formal integration of experience'.[4] Nonetheless, as Wilbur remarked in 1975: 'For years anybody writing an imitation of William Carlos Williams has felt that he was in the avant-garde'.[5] Consistent with attacking Pound's 'offence[s] against Aristotelian truth' (see pp.157-58), the young Louis MacNeice thought that

E.E. Cummings 'by and in disintegrating, aims at new integrities', and preferred Cummings to Williams because 'Cummings chops off his lines with a sense of rhythmical or dramatic fitness, where- as in a writer like…Williams the arrangement into lines is entirely indifferent'. Later, MacNeice would enthuse about Frost on the same grounds: 'he has that underlying *dramatic* quality which makes a lyric more lyrical'.[6] The point is that MacNeice engaged with American poetry in terms of the aesthetic he was working out between Yeats, Eliot and the socio-political pressures of the British and European 1930s. W.H. Auden, writing retrospectively (and, it should be noted, as an outsider) in the introduction to his *Faber Book of American Poetry* (1956), highlights the centrifugal tendency of American tradition, rather than form: 'The first thing that strikes a reader about the best American poets is how utterly unlike each other they are. Where else in the world, for example, could one find several poets of approximately the same generation so different as Ezra Pound, W.C. Williams, Vachel Lindsay, Marianne Moore, Wallace Stevens, E.E. Cummings and Laura Riding?' Auden diagnoses the American poet's occupational disease as not that 'of writing like everybody else, but of crankiness and a parody of his own manner'.[7]

   The American poets I have cited as influencing the apprentice Heaney, Mahon and Longley do not (apart from Lowell up to a point) belong to the wilder frontier of American poetics. John Crowe Ransom was more popular than Williams; the Berryman of *Homage to Mistress Bradstreet* more so than the Berryman of *Dream Songs*. Mahon has said that Allen Ginsberg and Lawrence Ferlinghetti excited him when he lived in the US and Canada from 1965 to 1967.[8] Yet any mark of the Beats on his work must be their anar- chism of spirit not of form, as when he begins *Lives* (1972) with a poem of 'Homecoming':

> Has bath and shave
> clean shirt etcetera,
> full of potat-
> oes, rested, yet
> badly distraught
> by six-hour flight
> (Boston to Dublin)
> drunk all night
> with crashing bore
> from Houston, Tex.,
> who spoke at length
> on guns and sex.

   What kind of textual presence did American poetry have for these young poets between 1960 and 1970? What were the significant anthologies and collections that they read? In addition to Auden's *Faber Book*, which ends with Lowell and Anthony Hecht, there were Geoffrey Moore's historical (Emily Dickinson to W.S. Merwin) *Penguin Book of Modern American Verse* (1954, 1959); *Five American Poets* (Edgar Bowers, Howard Nemerov, Hyam Plutzik, Louis Simpson, William Stafford) edited by Thom Gunn and Ted Hughes in 1963; and especially Donald Hall's opinionated *Penguin Book of Contemporary American Poetry* (1962, 1972). Hall (1962) begins with Stafford and Robert Lowell; includes Robert Creeley, Robert Bly, John Ashbery and Adrienne Rich; and situates his anthology in the post-war context:

> Immediately after the war, two books were published which were cul-minations of the twin strains of density and delicacy. Robert Lowell's *Lord Weary's Castle* is a monument of the line of tough rhetoricians; beyond this it was impossible to go…The effect of tremendous power under tremendous pressure was a result of a constricted subject matter and a tense line in which the strict decasyllable was counterbalanced by eccentric caesura and violent enjambment. In contrast was Richard Wilbur's *The Beautiful Changes*, which was the peak of skilful elegance. Here was the abllity to shape an analogy, to perceive and develop comparisons, to display etymological wit, and to pun six ways at once.[9]

Hall observes that 'the typical *ghastly* poem of the fifties was a Wilbur poem not written by Wilbur'. In 1972 he emends this: 'You can tell the dominance of a school by the prevalence of bad versions of it. Fifteen years ago, as I have said, it was bad Wilbur. Ten years ago it was bad *Life Studies*. Five years ago it was bad Robert Creeley.'[10] (Aesthetic gyres run on.) Hall's view of Lowell and Wilbur as, seemingly, the Donne and Herbert of American poetry, is relevant to differences between Mahon and Longley (discussed below). As for relations between English and American poetry: Alvarez's critique of *English* 'gentility' was absorbed, but implicitly raised the question of where *Irish* poets who looked back to Yeats and MacNeice – both full of history and libido – belonged in this Anglo-American scenario.

The presence of T.S. Eliot at Faber ensured regular if selective access to American collected poems and individual volumes in a way that ceased to be the case during the 1970s or until Carcanet and Bloodaxe took up the torch. The dustjackets of those beautiful hardbacks list Stevens, Moore, Cummings, Berryman, Jarrell, Lowell, Wilbur. William Snodgrass's *Heart's Needle* was published by the Marvell Press in 1960. Besides Lowell's new collections – *Life Studies* (1959), *Imitations* (1961), *For the Union Dead* (1964) and *Near the Ocean* (1967) – his *Poems 1938-1949* (reprinted in 1960) was also current, as was Wilbur's *Poems 1943-1956* (1957).

America impinged in three other ways that should be noted. First, Jack Sweeney (an Irish American), who then presided over the Poetry Room at Harvard, took a detailed interest in the work of Mahon, Heaney and Longley. He recorded them before they had published collections. Conversely, a Caedmon record of American poets reading their work was endlessly played by Mahon and Longley at Trinity College, Dublin in the early 1960s. Top of the pops was Wallace Stevens reading 'The Idea of Order at Key West'. The recording also featured Cummings (' "Sweet spring is your/ time is my time..." '), Lowell ('The Quaker Graveyard in Nantucket') and Wilbur ('Love Calls Us to the Things of This World'). An influential factor in Belfast was the appointment (in 1963) of Michael Allen, friend and mentor of poets, to teach American literature at Queen's University – a number of such posts having been created to promote American studies throughout Europe.[11]

Two of the poems mentioned above ('Idea of Order', 'The Quaker Graveyard') introduce 'Atlantic's premises'. Hart Crane's 'Voyages' sequence also struck deep chords. I will speculate about the effect of these (inter-related) Atlantic works on Mahon and Longley, and compare it with Heaney's early response to the Atlantic, to American *terra firma*, and to Frost and Roethke.

Stevens, Crane and Lowell represent the Atlantic Ocean in linked but contrasting ways. In 'Idea of Order' the relation between the singer and the sea enacts that of the Creator – God or poet – to formless waters. In 'Voyages' the voyager-lover-poet experiences the sea as Eros and Thanatos, the inextricable rhythms of flesh and spirit: 'The seal's wide spindrift gaze toward paradise'. In 'The Quaker Graveyard' history and literary history conspire to make the sea a psychic arena where the mastery and morality of man, the benevolence of God, are 'violently' tested. Part II ends:

> The winds' wings beat upon the stones,
> Cousin, and scream for you and the claws rush
> At the sea's throat and wring it in the slush
> Of this old Quaker graveyard where the bones
> Cry out in the long night for the hurt beast
> Bobbing by Ahab's whaleboats in the East.

The motifs outlined above can be recognised in Mahon's 'Day Trip to Donegal' and his verse-letter 'Beyond Howth Head' (1970), in Longley's 'The Hebrides' and 'Circe', and in other poems which these poets wrote during the 1960s. Yet they also view the Atlantic from the shore where it constitutes Europe's wild terminus rather than an often populous coast: 'Last balconies/ Above the waves'. 'Beyond Howth Head' begins:

264   'ATLANTIC'S PREMISES'

The wind that blows these words to you
bangs nightly off the black-and-blue
Atlantic, hammering in its haste
dark doors of the declining west...

This stormy sense of the Atlantic pulls the poems towards the
bleaker American perspectives – while simultaneously remaking
Irish western tropes. Longley's Hebridean landscape figures what
is beyond human control: 'This orphaned stone'. Lowell says of a
drowned sailor: '[His] open, staring eyes/ Were lustreless dead-
lights'. Longley extends this image to poetic perception: 'My dead-
lights latched by whelk and barnacle'. At the same time, Mahon
and Longley seem less inclined to go all the way with one Atlantic
trajectory. Their structures are more continuously dialectical and self-
referential. Thus 'The Hebrides', a poem about a poet's setting-
forth, dramatises an effort to make its own 'original idea' include
both elemental flux ('The total effect/Of air and ocean') and the
debris of history ('these are my sailors, these my drowned'). Tension
between the sea as flux or chaos and the poem as pattern takes a
more psychological turn in Mahon's 'Day Trip to Donegal':

Give me a ring, goodnight, and so to bed...
That night the slow sea washed against my head,
Performing its immeasurable erosions –
Spilling into the skull, marbling the stones
That spine the very harbour wall,
Uttering its threat to villages of landfall.

Here the speaker has returned to the suburbs, implicitly of Belfast,
after an Atlantic visit. The mundane 'Give me a ring' played against
the sensuous polysyllables of 'immeasurable erosions' recalls Crane.
As in 'The Hebrides', the human body, in a layered metaphysical
conceit, is identified with threatened land and with systems of
rational and artistic control. After 1969 Mahon more radically
questioned ideas of poetic order. His 'Rage for Order' – neither
an opportunistic nor merely ironical return to Stevens – reduces
the latter's 'Words of the fragrant portals, dimly-starred' to 'An
eddy of semantic scruple/ In an unstructurable sea'.

'Day Trip to Donegal' appears in Mahon's sea-named *Night-
Crossing* (1968); 'The Hebrides' in Longley's also fluidly entitled
No Continuing City (1969). If both first collections abound in sea-
imagery (and they do), this is not wholly due to the effects of
reading Crane, Lowell and Stevens. Nonetheless, these American
voices reverberate at moments of oceanic intensity, moments close
to the poetry's Romantic reach, its visionary and mythic ambition,
its symbolic pitch. This is the pitch at which it burns up anything
that could be termed descriptive or journalistic. (Stevens and Lowell

help to explain the marked difference between Longley's 'Hebrides' and Louis MacNeice's poem of the same name.) If Stevens reasserted poetry's cosmic confidence, Crane added erotic flesh, and bequeathed more functional visionary templates. Thus a set of Odysseyan love poems in *No Continuing City* takes some compass-bearings from 'Voyages'.[12] 'Circe', for instance, adapts love's 'spindrift gaze' to heterosexual desire:

> Out of the night husband after husband
> – Eyes wide as oysters, arms full of driftwood –
> Wades ashore and puts in at my island.
> My necklaces of sea shells and seaweed,
>
> My skirts of spindrift, sandals of flotsam
> Catch the eye of each bridegroom for ever...

Crane also helped to rescue the coastal city of Belfast from the drably factual, anti-poetic role in which it had often been cast. Of Crane's 'To Brooklyn Bridge' Mahon wrote in 1970: 'Reading Hart Crane's – "All afternoon the cloud-flown derricks turn;/ Thy cables breathe the North Atlantic still" – it was possible to endow the shipyards of Belfast with an immanence of poetic life they had never had before.'[13] Quoting from Crane, Mahon actually substituted the more usual Belfast word 'gantries' for Crane's 'derricks' (perhaps punning subliminally on 'Crane' and 'Derek'...). In the ageing mind of Mahon's 'Grandfather', 'Boiler-rooms, row upon row of gantries roll/ Away to reveal the landscape of a childhood/ Only he can recapture'; in 'The Hebrides' the speaker says: 'Dry dock, gantries,//Dykes of apparatus educate my bones/ To track the buoys/ Up sea lanes love emblazons...' Both effects explicitly look beyond superficial industrial appearances.

So what is going on here? First, Mahon and Longley seem drawn to American poets whose thrust is cosmic, spiritual, archetypal; whose structures are symbolic and rhetorical. In these poets, indeed, they may have found aspects of the Yeatsian aesthetic remade across the Atlantic. But, more particularly and instinctively, they may have recognised religious (and hence metaphysical) dimensions that reflected their own ambivalent relation to Ulster Protestantism. (Yeats's 'Protestant magic', to use R.F. Foster's term, transmutes a more High Church religious sensibility.)[14] Such ambivalence appears in Longley's wariness of 'Presbyterian granite', Mahon's desire for 'immanence'. But the poetry of Stevens, Lowell and Crane is conditioned in positive as well as negative ways by nonconformism and the transcendentalist philosophy it engendered. Crane and Stevens, in particular, write "poems about poetry" that reassert the *vates*. Yeats, for all his vatic aspirations, primarily reasserts the *makar*.

Discussing 'The Letters of Hart Crane', and Crane's proposal to 'take [T.S.] Eliot as a point of departure toward an almost complete reversal of direction', Langdon Hammer comments:

> Like Wallace Stevens, Crane viewed the decay of Christian belief as an opportunity for poetry, not a crisis, as it is in *The Waste Land*. In particular, it was an opportunity for poetry to 'lend a myth to God', as Crane proposes in the proem to *The Bridge*. 'The great mythologies of the past (including the Church) are deprived of enough facade to even launch good raillery against', he argued in 'General Aims and Theories'. But this did not mean that tradition was defunct; rather, it was 'operative still – in millions of chance combinations of related and unrelated detail, psychological reference, figures of speech, precepts, etc.' Poetry's task was to activate those mythological resources – to bring them to consciousness – through its access to the 'logic of metaphor'.[15]

To return to Stevens's cosmic confidence: 'Sunday Morning', with its text 'Death is the mother of beauty', might be interpreted as an Old Testament version of Crane's mission-statements. Here all creation affirms the metaphorical opportunities afforded by spilt religion. I quote the poem's famous conclusion:

> We live in an old chaos of the sun,
> Or old dependency of day and night,
> Or island solitude, unsponsored, free,
> Of that wide water, inescapable.
> Deer walk upon our mountains, and the quail
> Whistle about us their spontaneous cries;
> Sweet berries ripen in the wilderness;
> And, in the isolation of the sky,
> At evening, casual flocks of pigeons make
> Ambiguous undulations as they sink,
> Downward to darkness, on extended wings.

I suspect that 'Sunday Morning', like 'Idea of Order' and Stevens's work in general, made it less likely that Mahon's and Longley's poetry would ever perceive the natural world in a wholly material light. 'Thirteen Ways of Looking at a Blackbird', so to speak, added a new theological strand to Irish pastoral. Their uncollected *juvenilia* suggest this,[16] as do two other symbolic songs of the sea in the poets' first collections: Mahon's 'Bird Sanctuary' and Longley's 'Leaving Inishmore'. Each poem presents a vocal sea-and-island microcosm in which natural superabundance acts as the threshold for revelation:

> I expect great things
> Of these angels of wind,
> Females, males, and fledgelings.
> The sudden whirring of their wings
> Disturbs the noon, and midnight rings
> With echoes from their island.   (Mahon)

Miles from the brimming enclave of the bay
I hear again the Atlantic's voices,
The gulls above us as we pulled away –
So munificent their final noises
These are the broadcasts from our holiday.

Oh, the crooked walkers on that tilting floor!
And the girls singing on the upper deck
Whose hair took the light like a downpour...   (Longley)

A second (and related) cultural factor is the historical connection between Belfast and the east coast of North America within the Atlantic world. The Scottish intellectual Christopher Harvie has evoked the powerful heyday of 'Atlantic cities' – from Boston to Belfast – whose trading and industrial role was diminishing by the mid twentieth century. Discussing the geography of the Ulster novelist Joyce Cary, Harvie says: 'over the Western horizon was Walt Whitman, preceptor of [Irish and Scottish] autodidacts...At Paumanok in the 1870s Whitman was American nationalist *and* universalist, in his "Sea-Drift" poems and the technology which they projected'. As they identify, through Stevens and Crane, with what Crane calls in *The Bridge* Whitman's 'Sea eyes and tidal, un-denying, bright with myth', Mahon and Longley simultaneously catch what Harvie terms 'the Atlantic community in collapse'.[17] Mahon, son of a shipyards family, is supreme elegist of the *Titanic* and the culture that produced it. But 'As God is my Judge', a soliloquy spoken by Bruce Ismay (head of the White Star line), also exemplifies how both poets criticise the hubris, the literal and moral pollutions, of Belfast's commercial history: 'I sank as far that night as any/ Hero'. 'Those homewaters petroleum hurts' is Longley's phrase in 'The Hebrides'. Their critique, however, introduces new pan-Atlantic vistas, post-industrial and artistic. For instance, Longley in 'To Bessie Smith' responds to her Blues by 'think[ing] of Tra-na-rossan, Inisheer,/ Of Harris drenched by horizontal rain'.[18] And Mahon's mid-60s stay in North America produced a counterpoint between transatlantic capitalism and Irish western islands which links five consecutive poems in *Night-Crossing* : 'Canadian Pacific' (to be discussed later), 'Recalling Aran', 'Epitaph for Robert Flaherty', 'April on Toronto Island', 'As God is my Judge'.

When 'Recalling Aran' and 'Epitaph' make the Aran Islands symbolise spiritual-aesthetic perfection, it is as desired *from* America ('Four thousand miles away tonight')[19] or *by* an American (Flaherty's 'islands of dark ore'). In 'April on Toronto Island' Mahon represents the local landscape and culture as requiring a more than physical release from winter:

Nothing along the lakeshore but bird-bones and fish-bones
Greasy with diesel oil, and the clapboard
Church of Saint Andrew-by-the-Lake.

There is not even a bird, although there are bird noises
And the growl of commerce...

No wonder that the returning people, in another visionary transla-
tion of the sea and Nature, 'dream of other islands,/ Clear cliffs
and salt water,// Fields brighter than paradise in the first week of
creation'. It is as though the Irish Atlantic coast might evangelically
redeem the Canadian, although the poem's informing theology
belongs to both shores. (The ethos of Toronto, until the 1970s,
was largely shaped by emigration from Protestant Ulster and
Protestant Scotland.) Mahon's verse-letter 'Beyond Howth Head',
the last poem in *Lives,* is a work of post-industrial *bricolage* which
raises questions about the condition of the Atlantic world. The poem
moves with wind and tide from 'Long Island or Cape Cod' to the
west of Ireland to Wales and Lancashire. Its political references
include US intervention in Cambodia and bombs in Belfast; and its
cultural commerce includes both the poetically sublime – Spenser,
Milton's 'Lycidas', 'Thoreau like ice among the trees', Mahon's
considerable debt to the Marvellian octosyllabics of Lowell's *Near
the Ocean* – and the materially ridiculous: 'contraceptives deftly tied/
with best regards from Merseyside'.

Seamus Heaney's youthful attraction to America and American
poetry took rather different turns. In 'Irish Bards and American
Audiences' I quoted from Michael Allen's article 'The Parish and
the Dream: Heaney and America'. Impressed by the 'powerful and
distinctive subculture' of 'Catholic Irish Americans', Allen suggests
that Northern Irish poets from a Protestant background have less
'prospect of a symbiotic relationship with American readers'. He
also finds that 'apart from some stylistic indebtedness to Hart Crane,
there is little American presence in the early poetry of Longley
and Mahon'.[20] Evidently I dissent from this view. The 1960s were
a more innocent time when questions of Northern Irish poetry,
politics and cultural diaspora were less articulated than in Allen's
retrospect. Nor was Catholic Irish America so conspicuous a lobby
either outside or inside the academy. Indeed, the Protestant dimen-
sion of "Irish America" is currently being recuperated (in its narrower
aspect, this simply renews a unionist pre-JFK rhetoric of the Ulster
"Scotch Irish" as American pioneers and Presidents).[21] I would
argue, alternatively, that all three poets, during their apprenticeships
in Dublin and Belfast, reacted to a mix of aesthetic and cultural
elements in the American poetry they read. Moreover, this reaction

intersected with their reaction to one another. And here, in certain respects, Heaney's Catholic background makes a difference, rendering his artistic relation to Robert Frost all the more complex. Writing on Frost, Auden observes: 'In New England, Protestants of Anglo-Scotch stock consider themselves a cut above Roman Catholics' – so *plus ça change* across the Atlantic: Belfast and Boston have similar sectarian histories. Yet there are internal gradations, as Auden also notes: 'the most respectable Protestant denominations are the Congregationalists and the Unitarians'.[22] Nor is poetry immune from these prejudices. Elizabeth Bishop takes a somewhat Yankee attitude to Marianne Moore's 'extremes of Protestant, Presbyterian, Scotch-Irish literalness'.[23]

Critics have picked up the echoes of Frost in Heaney's early poetry,[24] but what counts is again conversation – not imitation or even "affinity". In 'Dividing Lines: Robert Frost and Seamus Heaney' (a valuable article to which I will return) Stephen James sets an example by looking beneath surface parallels. He points out, for instance, that the persona of Heaney's 'Personal Helicon' is more willing 'to explain' than is the speaker of its Frostian source, 'For Once, Then, Something'.[25]

Whether as geography, culture or symbol, the sea figures much less prominently in the two collections that Heaney published during the 1960s: *Death of a Naturalist* (1966) and *Door into the Dark* (1969). The inland, rural co-ordinates of his poetry do not register the urban-Atlantic history, not to mention the post-Protestant metaphysical turmoil, that seems so present to Mahon and Longley. Thus, when the Atlantic enters *Death of a Naturalist,* it does so in a more exclusively personal or literary way: the 'timeless waves…sifting from the Americas' in 'Lovers on Aran'; the 'nib filed on a salt wind/ and dipped in the keening sea' of 'Synge on Aran'. Allen argues that a transatlantic voyage begins for Heaney in *Door into the Dark.* The structures that he sees as corresponding to Irish emigrant visions and the literature of the American dream differ from the Atlantic circulations in early Mahon and Longley. For instance, the eel of Heaney's 'Lough Neagh Sequence' passes beyond the western Irish coast on an independent oceanic journey that dramatises the poet's discovery of new artistic bearings. Yet Heaney has already, so to speak, travelled to America in that his land-poems have absorbed Frostian New England. Among its other concerns, 'Bogland' (the last poem in *Door into the Dark*) asserts, what Heaney and others have proved: Ireland's potential to compete with the 'pioneers' and 'prairies' that constitute the poem's image of relations between American writers and America. Here national literatures are being obliquely compared. The speaker's claims that 'Our unfenced country/ Is bog that keeps crusting/ Between the sights of the sun', and 'Our pioneers keep striking/ Inwards and downwards' recall Yeats's rivalry with Whitman.[26] If, to quote 'Bogland', Irish 'bogholes might be Atlantic seepage', this implies a relation between two poetic lands of opportunity – and perhaps also the greater historical depths that an Irish poet can plumb: 'The wet centre is bottomless'.

During the 1940s John Hewitt developed a concept of Ulster literary regionalism. Although Hewitt's ideas have been criticised,[27] one of his speculations (already mentioned in 'The Poetics of Celt and Saxon', p.66) may have hit an unexpected mark. He proposed Protestant New England in general, and Frost's poetry in particular, as exemplars for Northern Irish writing. Hewitt cites the historical and theological ties between the two areas, and concludes: 'The careful rejection of the rhetorical and flamboyant, the stubborn concreteness of imagery, the conscientious cleaving to the objects of sense which, not at all paradoxically, provides the best basis and launching ground for the lonely ascents of practical mysticism lie close to the heart of Ulster's best intellectual activity, and make us bold enough to claim Concord as a townland of our own.'[28] But, of course, relations between culture and aesthetics do not always go according to plan. As we have seen, Mahon and Longley (like Lowell) were greatly drawn to 'the rhetorical and flamboyant'. And it was Heaney who claimed Frost's 'concreteness of imagery' for his own 'original townland'.[29]

In 'Above the Brim' (1990) Heaney celebrates a 'lifetime of pleasure in Frost's poems as events in language, flaunts and vaunts full of projective force and deliquescent backwash, the crestings of a tide that lifts all spirits'. I will return to the terms of this overview. Here I would stress what Heaney recalls as his initial attraction to 'the inner evidence of Frost's credentials as a farmer poet', his admiration for 'the way he could describe (in "The Code") how forkfuls of hay were built upon a waggonload for easy unloading later'. Heaney also mentions two other Frost poems that feature rural skills: 'Mowing' and 'The Axe-Helve'.[30] The influences on Heaney's early pastoral exemplify the remaking of traditions in this Northern Irish aesthetic cluster. One might construct, for instance, an Irish-English-American diagram whereby the Heaney farm-poem filters its local materials through Kavanagh, Hughes and Frost on its way to becoming utterly distinctive. But what is Frost's input? Heaney's term 'farmer poet' places Frost between Kavanagh, more genuinely a farmer, and Hughes, then more

exclusively a poet. This fits Heaney's own inside/outside relation
to the environment he evokes or constructs. Auden stresses the
dialectic, in 'the Frost pastoral', between rural people and 'the lit-
erary city dweller, often a college student'.[31] There is no equivalent
in Kavanagh or Hughes to this dialectic, or to its aesthetic corollary:
that the traditional country skills developed by the interplay between
tool and task parallel the poetic skills developed by the interplay
between technique and subject matter.[32] For Heaney, more than
Frost, this seems an artistic validation.

Certainly, he takes the analogy further – in early poems such as
'The Diviner', 'The Forge' and 'Thatcher' – by attaching greater
mystique to technique, to the rural craftsman and hence to the
poet. His blacksmith, diviner and thatcher transmit a numinous
aura (the anvil is an 'altar'). The expertise that distinguishes them
from the impressed 'bystanders' or spectators seems akin to priest-
ly intercession – a structure absent in Frost. In 'The Axe-Helve'
Baptiste, who shows the Yankee speaker 'that the lines of a good
helve/Were native to the grain before the knife/Expressed them',
has his superior skill recognised, but this allows different kinds of
'knowledge' to be exchanged and pondered on an equal basis.
Alternatively, the difference can be read as Heaney asserting the
power of, and his power over, lyric form: an assertion to which
Frost's practice less continuously lends itself. Like Edward Thomas,
Heaney does not follow Frost into his narrative mode, and only
occasionally into his dramatic mode. Michael Parker is right to
suggest that a few monologue or dialogue poems by Heaney, such
as 'The Wife's Tale' (in *Door into the Dark*) derive from the Frostian
eclogue.[33] Here Heaney pushes the conversational register of his
lyric voice towards fuller characterisation. Yet in 'The Wife's Tale'
the dialogue between male and female turns less on psychological
or gender tensions than, once again, on rural skills and roles as a
metaphor for poetry. The wife who brings food to her husband
and his co-workers threshing corn is another impressed, if more
ironical, spectator: 'Always this inspection has to be made/ Even
when I don't know what to look for'.

Heaney's poetry thus seems more centred than Frost's on lyric
craft and the lyric first-person voice. Both 'For Once, Then, Some-
thing' and 'Personal Helicon', of course, are concentrated lyrics.
Both deal with poetry, the self, and mysteries beyond the self. Yet
Heaney's poem takes shape as autobiography, Frost's as dialectic:

> Others taunt me with having knelt at well-curbs
> Always wrong to the light, so never seeing
> Deeper down in the well than where the water

Gives me back in a shining surface picture
Me myself in the summer heaven godlike
Looking out of a wreath of fern and cloud puffs.
Once, when trying with chin against a well-curb,
I discerned, as I thought, beyond the picture,
Through the picture, a something white, uncertain,
Something more of the depths – and then I lost it.
Water came to rebuke the too clear water.
One drop fell from a fern, and lo, a ripple
Shook whatever it was lay there at bottom,
Blurred it, blotted it out. What was that whiteness?
Truth? A pebble of quartz? For once, then, something.

'For Once, Then, Something' (which never quite falls into sonnet-form or concealed stanzaic units) proceeds by clashes between voices and between tones of voice: what 'others' say, the speaker's implied attitude to that, water rebuking 'the too clear water', the mock-heroic Apollonian self-image 'in the summer heaven', the mock-poetic 'lo, a ripple', the mock-philosophical thesis, antithesis and false synthesis of the last line. In adapting Frost's symbolic-satirical well/Helicon, Heaney does not destabilise perception to the same extent. The Frost-speaker answers his taunters or inner doubts by implying that there may be nothing outside subjectivity since objectivity is itself a shaky premise. At the same time, he suggests less ironically, though still relativistically, that the difficult effort of the subjective poet to produce the objective poem creates 'something' which may convey 'more of the depths'. For Heaney (in what is, of course, a young poet's poem) subjective and objective 'seeing' remain at once separately feasible and capable of an imaginatively productive interaction:

As a child, they could not keep me from wells
And old pumps with buckets and windlasses.
I loved the dark drop, the trapped sky, the smells
Of waterweed, fungus and dank moss.

One, in a brickyard, with a rotted board top.
I savoured the rich crash when a bucket
Plummeted down at the end of a rope.
So deep you saw no reflection in it.

A shallow one under a dry stone ditch
Fructified like any aquarium.
When you dragged out long roots from the soft mulch
A white face hovered over the bottom...

Now, to pry into roots, to finger slime,
To stare, big-eyed Narcissus, into some spring
Is beneath all adult dignity. I rhyme
To see myself, to set the darkness echoing.

Here the main tonal switch is from a voice inflected by childhood to a voice that assumes the literary 'adult dignity' already implicit in words like 'fructified'. The poem also assumes – and 'explains', to quote Stephen James – Wordsworthian continuity between these voices. 'Personal Helicon' is not tension-free. Heaney transmutes the critique of Frost's 'godlike' persona into a self-accusation of Narcissism, a hint of self-alienation in the 'white face hover[ing] over the bottom'. Yet, overall, his Helicon resists the relativism, the problematics of seeing and saying, that issue in the dialectical twists of Frost's sentence-sounds. And this distinction appears all the more significant when a young poet engages with a precursor poem about the sources of poetry.

Conversely, Heaney's poetry may bring something fresh to Frostian scenarios: a kind of sensory real presence. James argues that in 'Above the Brim' Heaney's metaphor of overbrimming ('overbrimming…invention', 'overbrimming technical joys') seems inappropriate when applied to 'formal principles'. Further, its

> emphasis on affirmation (quite apart from exercising an homogenising force on Frost's poetry) is too easeful: in recruiting Frost as an ally in his defence of the poem as a joyously autonomous world, Heaney undervalues the scepticism and distrust, the pessimism even, of Frost's poetic vision.[34]

If Heaney's critical language sometimes violates the native Frostian grain, we might connect this with cultural factors, including Catholicism, that shaped his original creative response to Frost's poetry. In 'Personal Helicon' Image takes on greater power relative to Word. The wells are more elaborately realised as sense-impressions, while sentence-sounds ('they could not keep me', 'I loved', 'I savoured', 'Now, to pry into roots') play a more declarative but thereby less various and more supportive role. And the image crystallises in contrast with the Frost-speaker's stabs at a wavering 'picture'. The 'rich crash' of Heaney's language ultimately overrides all tensions in the visual-verbal fusions of 'rhyme to see' and 'darkness echoing'. Auden's verdict on Frost's style as 'Good Drab' (itself possibly tinged with anti-puritan condescension) does not fit Heaney, whose attraction to the richly loaded lines of Keats is again partly inflected by cultural Catholicism. And Frost rarely lets a sensory image rest without prying further, without worrying it into metaphysical shape. His Protestant cognitive work-ethic will not allow the woods merely to be 'lovely, dark and deep'. Heaney significantly favours poems such as 'A Hillside Thaw'[35] or 'Mowing', in which Frost allows 'sensuous music' to emerge more continuously from the image and give a poem its characteristic sound: 'the day

the sun lets go/Ten million silver lizards out of snow'; 'My long
scythe whispered and left the hay to make'. Heaney says of 'Mowing':
'the heart of the poetic matter is the whisper of the scythe'. 'A
Hillside Thaw' includes an image of negative capability, of the poet's
self-immersion, self-baptism, in the image: 'And threw myself wet-
elbowed and wet-kneed/In front of twenty others' wriggling speed'.
In 'Above the Brim' Heaney is prepared only to 'salute...dutifully'
the conceptual strata of Frost's poetry, before 'pass[ing] on to my
own particular area of interest'. His selective focus, indeed, brilliantly
exposes unsuspected grain. Yet linguistic events cannot really be
divorced from 'Frost's dimensions as a philosophical writer'. When
Heaney concretises all Frost's poetry as 'flaunts and vaunts', and
stresses his 'unpremeditated rush of inspiration' at the expense of
his meditations in language, he represses Frost's dialectical music,
fills his 'desert places' with consolatory presences, and thus brings
him a little further than '*Toward* heaven': 'I shall be concerned to
show that his specifically poetic achievement is profoundly guar-
anteed and resilient because it is genuinely rescued from negative
recognitions, squarely faced, and abidingly registered'.[36]

Conversation with Frost (or conversion of him) evidently still
helps Heaney to locate his own Helicon. A more truly kindred
American spirit in the 1960s was Theodore Roethke whose 'green-
house poems' show him to be a notable pryer into roots, fingerer
of slime, adept of watery ground. In 1968 Heaney empathetically
reviewed Roethke's *Collected Poems*. He quotes 'Cuttings' – 'I can
hear, underground, that sucking and sobbing' – and describes
Roethke's 'repossession of the childhood Eden' as 'issuing in a sense
of unity with cosmic energies...acts of faith made in some state of
grace'. He adds the still more expressly Catholic language of 'a
divine unity working through' the poems and through Nature.[37]
Other Roethke poems with which early poems by Heaney seem at
home are: 'Root Cellar' ('dank as a ditch...Shoots dangled and
drooped,/ Lolling obscenely') and 'Moss-Gathering': 'But some-
thing always went out of me when I dug loose those carpets/ Of
green...And afterwards I always felt mean...'

My argument thus far is, first: that all three poets from Northern
Ireland have picked up echoes of familiar religious and cultural
dynamics in the American poetry that seems most important to them
at this period. These echoes they adopt, adapt, or resist. Second,
they all prefer more concentrated and formal kinds of American
poetry. And they go further; they pull American tendencies to
prophecy (Stevens, Crane) or discursiveness (Frost) back towards a
tighter lyrical structure, one that is highly aware of its own patterns.

In Mahon and Longley this structure often has a dialectical character that reflects their sense of Yeats (and Graves), and connects with Mac-Neice's admiration for the 'dramatic' qualities of Frost's lyric. Even though none of these three Irish "Protestant" poets follows Frost much in practice, they are theoretically more in sympathy with some of his structures than is Heaney. But Heaney distils what he takes from Frost – perhaps primarily a fusion between craft and mystery – into poems that also stress their own forms in Yeatsian style.

Finally, I want to glance at form in early Mahon and Longley with reference to Lowell and Wilbur. Earlier I quoted Donald Hall on the polarity between Lowell's 'tense line', 'tremendous power under tremendous pressure', and Wilbur's skilful elegance, his 'ability to develop an analogy' and 'etymological wit'. Mahon was never a Wilbur man; although Wilbur's 'Objects' and 'A Dutch Courtyard' must have partly inspired his later poem 'Courtyards in Delft'; and his verse-translations of Molière (*High Time*, *A School for Wives*) seem conscious of Wilbur's precedent. There are even traces of Wilbur in *Death of a Naturalist*.[38] Longley's concern with form (as practice and theory) in *No Continuing City*, however, shows more pervasive signs of commonality and influence. This is epitomised by the way in which his 'Emily Dickinson' – New England strikes again – takes off from Wilbur's 'Altitudes' (as well as Crane's 'To Emily Dickinson'). Wilbur writes of Dickinson: 'Think of her climbing a spiral stair/Up to the little cupola with its clear// Small panes, its room for one.' Longley's poem begins: 'Emily Dickinson, I think of you/ Wakening early each morning to write,/ Dressing with care for the act of poetry…' Precise care for the poetic act characterises the work of another poet admired by both – George Herbert. Longley's 'Hebrides' and 'A Personal Statement' borrow stanza-shapes from Herbert. As for form as theme: Longley has assimilated those Wilbur poems that frame or poise Nature, especially birds, only to expose the tableau to forces of life and disintegration.[39] 'A Glance from the Bridge' is one of Wilbur's variations on this theme:

> Letting the eye descend from reeking stack
> And black facade to where the river goes,
> You see the freeze has started in to crack
> (As if the city squeezed it in a vice),
> And here and there the limbering water shows,
> And gulls colonial on the sullied ice.
>
> Some rise and braid their glidings, white and spare,
> Or sweep the hemmed-in river up and down,
> Making a litheness in the barriered air,

And through the town the freshening water swirls
As if an ancient whore undid her gown
And showed a body almost like a girl's.

Wilbur celebrates thaw in a self-referential movement whereby the poem becomes more limber and lithe as it proceeds, especially in the bravura of its closing simile. Longley's 'Freeze-up' seems to call on New England for help with weather less usual in Ireland:

The freeze-up annexes the sea even,
Putting out over the waves its platform.
Let skies fall, the fox's belly cave in –
This catastrophic, shortlived reform
Directs to our homes the birds of heaven.
They come on farfetched winds to keep us warm.

Bribing these with bounty, we would rather
Forget our hopes of thaw when spring will clean
The boughs, dust from our sills snow and feather,
Release to its decay and true decline
The bittern whom this different weather
Cupboarded in ice like a specimen.

Apart from the six-line stanza often favoured by Wilbur (who may partly account for its prominence in *No Continuing City* and *Night-Crossing*), technical similarities include rhetorical assonance: Wilbur's reeking-stack-freeze-squeeze, Longley's freeze-up-annexes-fox's. Wilbur often exploits assonance to ground abstract words in physical conditions: 'Freeze-up annexes' and 'bittern…different' resemble 'gulls colonial on the sullied ice'. Wilbur's punning awareness of etymology underpins his liaisons between abstract and concrete, and a similar awareness shapes Longley's oxymoronic (and Greek-Anglo/Saxon-Latin) phrase 'catastrophic, shortlived reform'. There are, of course, differences too. Perhaps 'Freeze-up' is again more dialectical in syntax and structure: the relation between its stanzas a shade less narrative, the relation between its sounds a shade less mellifluously iambic. The rhymes are more varied, not only in the alternation of monosyllables and dissyllables, but in the nature of the rhyme-words. All this serves thematic complication. Longley's poem, also self-referential, represents thaw as a paradoxically un-welcome condition, allying this with an implied critique of how form can become formalism. Wilbur himself pursues such a critique in other poems,[40] but possibly not as far as the bittern 'Cupboarded in ice like a specimen'. If 'Freeze-up' converses with 'A Glance from the Bridge', Longley may seek to fend off the daintiness that can soften Wilbur's effects. Hence, too, the counter-influences of Lowell and Crane.

Mahon was undoubtedly a Lowell man in the 1960s, although the freer forms in *Life Studies* may have been less significant than the subject-matter. Mahon's poems of the neurotic *vie de Bohème*, such as 'De Quincey in Later Life' or 'Death of a Film-Star', share some psychic territory with Lowell's 'Words for Hart Crane' and 'Man and Wife'. 'My Wicked Uncle', however, more fully emulates Lowell's 'My Last Afternoon with Uncle Devereux Winslow':

> While I sat on the tiles,
> And dug at the anchor on my sailor blouse,
> Uncle Devereux stood behind me.
> He was brushed as Bayard, our riding horse.
> His face was putty.
> His blue coat and white trousers
> grew sharper and straighter.
> His coat was a blue jay's tail,
> his trousers were solid cream from the top of the bottle.
> He was animated, hierarchical,
> like a ginger snap man in a clothes-press.
> He was dying of the incurable Hodgkin's disease...

Mahon-as-nephew contemplates a dead rather than dying body to similar distancing yet disturbing effect:

> I found him closeted with living souls –
> Coffined to perfection in the bedroom.
> Death had deprived him of his mustache,
> His thick horn-rimmed spectacles,
> The easy corners of his salesman dash
> (Those things by which I had remembered him)
> And sundered him behind unnatural gauze.
> His hair was badly parted on the right
> As if for Sunday school. That night
> I saw my uncle as he really was.

'My Wicked Uncle' is parody as well as imitation. The Belfast counterpart of Lowell's upmarket relative has been not only a salesman but also 'The crookedest chief steward in the Head Line'. His appearance is less classy, his death taken with less consistent seriousness, despite the pathos of 'unnatural gauze' and the hair parted 'As if for Sunday school'. It may be a subversive comment on New England poetic dynasties when 'the gradual graph of my uncle's life and/ Times dip[s] precipitately/ Into the bowels of Carnmoney Cemetery'. That 'life and times', however, makes this another maritime poem, another elegy for Atlantic decline: 'the empty freighters/Sailing for ever down Belfast Lough'. Religion also appears empty: seemingly neither Sunday school nor the 'Rumpled and windy' Presbyterian minister who conducts the funeral can do much about 'wickedness'. Thus Mahon subverts,

too, Protestant orthodoxies and respectabilities – clearly one of his
touchdowns with Lowell. Mahon's critique of Ulster Protestantism
in poems such as 'Ecclesiastes' resembles, and may have absorbed,
Lowell's critique of puritan New England.

The thematic and formal parallels between Lowell's 'Children
of Light' (in *Poems 1938-1949*) and Mahon's 'Canadian Pacific' go
beyond coincidence or imitation into deep affinity. The poems
also complement each other from different sides of the Atlantic:

Children of Light

Our fathers wrung their bread from stocks and stones
And fenced their gardens with the Redman's bones;
Embarking from the Nether Land of Holland,
Pilgrims unhouseled by Geneva's night,
They planted here the Serpent's seeds of light;
And here the pivoting searchlights probe to shock
The riotous glass houses built on rock,
And candles gutter by an empty altar,
And light is where the landless blood of Cain
Is burning, burning the unburied grain.

Canadian Pacific

From famine, pestilence and persecution
Those gaunt forefathers shipped abroad to find
Rough stone of heaven beyond the western ocean,
And staked their claim, and pinned their faith.
Tonight their children whistle through the dark,
Frost chokes the windows. They will not have heard
The wild geese flying south over the lakes
While the lakes harden beyond grief and anger –
The eyes fanatical, rigid the soft necks,
The great wings sighing with a nameless hunger.

Although Mahon speaks from a Canadian train, his imaginative
attraction is to the original setting-forth of Scots and Ulster Scots
'gaunt forefathers'. Lowell's concern, rather, is with what the pil-
grim fathers have made of New York and America. His poem, with
its ironical title, furiously apologises for the sins of fathers who
'fenced their gardens with the Redman's bones', and ultimately
denied their own founding principles by turning from God to
Mammon. Mahon, in developing a similar contrast between then
and now, takes a more nuanced attitude to the mixture of spiritual
and material motives that sought 'Rough stone of heaven beyond the
western ocean'. He registers positive as well as negative qualities –
balancing doctrinal 'fanaticism' and 'rigidity' against an absolute
'faith' (suggested by the absence of a preposition after 'pinned')

and spiritual 'hunger'. He also represents their modern descendants as having lost something ('They will not have heard') rather than as having proved the bad faith of the whole enterprise.

Once again we have a transatlantic poetic dialogue, once again conducted through the tones and rhythms of similar-looking stanzas. Lowell's powerfully 'tense' polemic begins and stays in top rhetorical gear even to the point of strain – as does much of his early poetry. In fact, his rhetoric transposes Calvinist anathema. 'Children of Light' is built largely on accumulation – four 'ands' at the beginning of lines, the repetition of 'here' – and on a narrative constructed by metonymic phrases that fuse Biblical texts with agricultural colonisation: 'Serpent's seeds of light', 'landless blood of Cain'. Mahon's three sentences are more tonally various, less metaphorically predictable in their movement between flesh and spirit, critique and empathy. Besides setting up a Yeatsian interplay between syntax, stanza and assonance, Mahon attaches fresh theological and cultural meaning to Yeats's symbolic wild geese. The cadences of desire that convey their flight also identify poetry itself with spiritual 'hunger'. Lowell's anguished display of spilt religion implicitly makes the same identification – he saw himself as 'a sort of gospeller'[41] – though not according to quite the same cultural codes. Yet 'Canadian Pacific', 'Personal Helicon' and 'Freeze-up' all suggest that the first collections in which they appear would have been aesthetically different if 'Those gaunt forefathers' had never 'shipped abroad'.

Northern Irish Poetry
and the End of History

1

This essay has itself become historical. Its title was conceived after the ceasefires of 1994 – the IRA ceasefire in August, the Loyalist ceasefire in October – but before other events in Ireland and Britain, for instance: the Canary Wharf bombing (February 1996); the Manchester bombing (June 1996); the murder of Garda Jerry McCabe in Co. Limerick – by the IRA (June 1996); the murder of a Catholic student and taxi-driver, Michael McGoldrick – by Loyalists (July 1996); the murder of Lance-Bombadier Stephen Restorick – by the IRA (February 1997); the murder of a Catholic, John Slane – by Loyalists (March 1997); the murder of two Reserve policemen, David Johnston and John Graham – by the IRA (June 1997); the second IRA ceasefire (July 1997); the murder of Catholic and Protestant friends Damien Trainor and Philip Allen in Poyntz-pass – by Loyalists (March 1998); the murder of the three Quinn brothers in Ballymoney – by a Loyalist petrol-bomb (July 1998); the 'Real IRA' bomb that killed 29 people and unborn twins in Omagh (August 1998); the assassination of the lawyer Rosemary Nelson – by Loyalists (March 1999). Add: five years of the Orange Order's dangerous obstinacy in seeking to hold a July parade at Drumcree, Co. Armagh; optimism created by the Good Friday Agreement (April 1998) giving way to pessimism as mistrust and arguments about decommissioning produced political stalemate (July 1999); the brutal punishment-attacks and expulsions that maintain paramilitary control over working-class communities: here there has never been a ceasefire. Comparisons with the ethos of the Weimar Republic (which notably failed to end history) are being made as I finally update this essay in autumn 1999.

But, of course, its title was always ironical, although a reaction less to shallow optimism than to shallow analysis – which, in a minor way, affected the literary sphere too. For months after the first IRA ceasefire, arts journalists from abroad would visit Belfast to ask writers 'What are you going to write about now?' and occasionally to ask critics 'What will post-ceasefire literature be like?' One reply was that it might be less a matter of writing differently than of reading differently; and that poetry, the most prominent

genre, had never depended either on one theme or on one orches-
tration of that theme. As for history ending when the headlines
change, Tommy Patton, a working-class unionist Mayor of Belfast,
makes a useful counter-theorist to Francis Fukuyama. During his
period of office, Patton was invited to launch Jonathan Bardon's
Belfast: An Illustrated History (1982). Responding to the book with
great enthusiasm, he said he could 'see that Belfast had had a lot
of history in the past', and he was 'sure it was going to have a lot
of history in the future'.

In Tommy Patton's sense there is also a lot of history in con-
temporary Northern Irish poetry, not just what is conventionally
understood as "Irish history" or the "Troubles". Poems allude to
the world wars, the Holocaust, Korea, the Spanish Civil War,
North American colonial history, the Trojan war. This is not only
because one war or its associated literature provides analogies,
structures or images for interpreting another (although the traffic
may be two-way), but also because odds and ends of battles long
ago are still active within communal mentalities. For instance, the
status of the world wars remains sensitive.[1] The Free State's neu-
trality during the Second World War (like that of other neutral
countries) has only slowly come into scholarly as well as public
focus; as have the many Irish Catholics who fought in that war,
the 250,000 who fought in the Great War. Not until July 1994
was the Irish National War Memorial opened at Islandbridge, Co.
Dublin. In April 1995 a VE commemoration took place there during
which the then Taoiseach John Bruton (Fine Gael) broke a taboo
when he commended Irish participation in the Second World War.
These occasions, attended by politicians from North and South
and from both Northern camps, belong to the 'ceasefire' dynamic.
So does the Island of Ireland Peace Park established by cross-border
initiative at Messines, Belgium, and inaugurated jointly by Queen
Elizabeth and President Mary McAleese (11 November 1998). As
for the North internally: the only Northern Irish combatant who
won a VC in the Second World War was 'Mick' Magennis, a
Catholic from the Falls Road. This suited neither nationalist nor
unionist prejudices. Thanks to a disinterested local historian, a
Magennis memorial has now been erected at Belfast City Hall
(October 1999).[2] Yet despite increasing historical ecumenism with
regard to the world wars, most Ulster Catholics still see the poppy
as an Orange symbol. Meanwhile, the Orange Order, which has
put up its own memorial at Thiepval, dubiously claims the Ulster
Protestants who died in the Battle of the Somme.

Commemorations of all kinds, including commemorations of

commemorations, ceaselessly remake history into present-day Irish
politics. A recent case in point was the bicentenary of the 1798
rebellion(s). Enfolded into this was 1898: the highly politicised cen-
tenary which had triggered 'a new era in Irish nationalist politics'.[3]
"1798" activated a range of contemporary agendas, especially those
surrounding the Northern Ireland "peace process". An exhibition at
the Ulster Museum encouraged Protestants and Catholics to ponder
a Northern rebellion in which their ancestors did not occupy the
expected niches (its leaders being Presbyterian United Irishmen);
in which they also promiscuously occupied all the niches, both pro-
and anti-rebellion; and in which motives were often ideologically
mixed. Whereas the Belfast exhibition broadly manifested a Northern
'community relations'/'cultural diversity' agenda,[4] 'Comóradh '98'
was a differently constituted commemoration of the differently con-
stituted Wexford rebellion. It aligned itself with a view of the "peace
process" conditioned by politics in the Republic, and by broadly
nationalist perceptions. The current (Fianna Fáil) Taoiseach Bertie
Ahern read from this script when he thought that the process
would 'fulfil some of the ideals of the United Irishmen'. Given the
determining role of relations between Britain and revolutionary
France (as most historians agree), and antagonism between the
Catholic Church and the Revolution, 1798 (like 1914 and 1939)
opens up European horizons which can be nuanced in further topical
ways. Overall, historians (sometimes fighting each another) were
drawn into a symptomatic *Kulturkampf* on the volatile Irish interface
between historiography and politics. For example, what Kevin
Whelan called a 'window of opportunity which opened and was
forcibly closed in the 1790s, a window which beckoned to the still
unattained prospect of a non-sectarian, democratic and inclusive
politics, adequately representing the Irish people in all their inher-
ited complexities', Tom Dunne called a 'vicious, chaotic civil war'.[5]

As recent conflicts suggest, however, Northern Ireland is not
the only European region that keeps residues of old wars available
for toxic precipitation. Elsewhere in these islands such residues
persist more benignly at the ideological level. Murray G.H. Pittock
concludes *Poetry and Jacobite Politics in Eighteenth-Century Britain
and Ireland* (1994) by proposing:

> Jacobitism is, in its varied forms, the prime root and the first fruits of
> opposition to the British state...Jacobitism is most centrally our con-
> temporary as we are most centrally the inheritors of its enemies, of the
> Revolution settlement and its associated legislation, of the unwritten
> constitution ratified by Victorian apologists. At the margin, in a Scotland
> torn between sentimental and meaningful belief in its own nationality,

Jacobitism is a typology invoked in explanation of the national tendency always to retreat from Derby, while in more sinister media the Lambeg drums of Ulster beat out the message of the siege of Derry.[6]

In 'Protestants', the first chapter of *Britons* (1992), Linda Colley shows how eighteenth-century "Britishness"' was defined against a European (especially French) Catholic "Other":

> Protestantism was the dominant component of British religious life. Protestantism coloured the way that Britons approached and interpreted their material life. Protestantism determined how most Britons viewed their politics...
>
> Protestantism meant much more in this society than just bombast, intolerance and chauvinism. It gave the majority of men and women a sense of their place in history and a sense of worth. It allowed them to feel pride in such advantages as they genuinely did enjoy, and helped them endure when hardship and danger threatened. It gave them identity.[7]

Pittock contends that Colley's thesis underplays Anglican-dissenter differences and Catholic-High Anglican affinities before 1789 (she omits Ireland and may not fully reckon with Scotland). Yet this actually supports Ian McBride's argument that Northern Ireland makes a central, rather than remote, vantage-point from which to examine ' "the British nation" itself'.[8] The 'identity' portrayed by Colley, to which accrued pride in nineteenth-century industry and empire, lingered among Ulster Protestants when it had passed its metropolitan sell-by date. Thus Northern Ireland provides a laboratory where the British nineteenth century, together with the Irish nineteenth century, may be conveniently studied. Since Northern Irish politics depend on narratives and ideologies of history, change is the enemy. The self-understanding of Ulster unionism has been particularly vulnerable (though similar forces have affected 'Old Labour' South Wales, for instance) to post-imperial politics, post-industrial economic shifts, separatist or devolutionary pressures: in sum, to the breakdown of the UK meta-narrative whose creation Colley charts, and to which Irish contexts added subplots of internal cultural defence. Irish nationalist ideology, although currently in better or more adaptable shape, has been eroded by the EU, the diminished authority of the institutional Catholic Church, the Republic's general modernisation, its wariness of northern absolutisms. Yet history (as the 1798 affair showed) remains a political actor in the Republic, too. Patrick O'Mahony and Gerard Delanty, noting an emergent culture-based, critique-resistant neo-nationalism in the 1990s, comment: 'The argument between revisionists and the new nationalists is not simply an intellectual controversy about interpretations of history; it is also anchored in everyday consciousness and in political parties.'[9]

I have illustrated the impossibility of circumscribing historical memory and historical relevance in order to underline the point that the notional 'end' of Northern Irish history would require other endings too. History reaches (into) Northern Irish poetry as a mass of contexts that ramify in time, space and mental space beyond the immediate crucible. It conditions the poet who works on it and in it. Poems may contract the historical field – sometimes to challenge grander narratives – taking on shapes analogous to local or micro history, to family history or autobiography, to oral history, to 'thick description'; or they may change the field, figuring as women's history or natural history. Of course, historiographical genres are not mutually exclusive; and, to return Hayden White's scheme in *Metahistory* (1973) to its literary origins (one purpose of this essay), poets' engagement with history involves other structural choices: in their own way, they practise the explanatory modes that White terms 'emplotment', 'argument' and 'ideological implication'. Later I will consider how White's 'poetics of history' fit some poems written at a historical moment torn between endings, beginnings and a fearful repetition.

Yet such a project, as will appear, is again entangled in distant battles that have come closer, and not only to home – battles in mental space. All late twentieth-century argument about history and historiography stems from an argument about the Enlightenment which has particular resonances in Irish contexts. Hence Conor Cruise O'Brien's extreme 'endist' gloom in *On the Eve of the Millennium* (1995), subtitled *The Future of Democracy Through an Age of Unreason*. (O'Brien begins by quoting the whole of Yeats's 'The Second Coming'.) The Enlightenment values that inspired some Ulster Presbyterians in the 1790s were, in their civic-political aspect, defeated by the *ancien régime* imperatives of Irish Protestants and Catholics as well as of the British state. Although this defeat has often prompted elegy or accusation, as in Tom Paulin's *Liberty Tree* (1983), deeper ideological and epistemological (as well as historical) questions are at issue. Frank Wright has influentially attributed the weakness of nineteenth-century Liberal Ulster to 'the primacy of the deterrence relationship between the sectarian subsocieties' in a frontier-zone.[10] This also explains the difficulties of twentieth-century socialist Ulster, exemplified by the career of the Northern Irish politician Paddy Devlin who died in August 1999.[11] Paul Muldoon's elaborate parable *Madoc* (1990) pivots on the crux whereby the Enlightenment must admit the forces that power sectarian subsocieties. Here Pantisocracy, the utopia projected by Coleridge and Southey, comes to grief, violence and internal contradiction.

The poem ends with the bloody 'slime' of history having pre-empted the 'iridescent Dome' of philosophy and poetry. And as Muldoon's poets initially move along the Susquehanna river from 'Athens' to 'Ulster', they reach a watershed where

> the Way of Reason
> narrows to the Way of Faith.

In what follows I will discuss, first, some aspects of the argument about history and historiography, then some 'end of history' scenarios that occupy Irish imaginations. The actual endings of various texts will be relevant here, and I will end with ends and endings in poems from several collections published since August 1994. These are Ciaran Carson's *Opera Et Cetera* (1996), Seamus Heaney's *The Spirit Level* (1996), Michael Longley's *The Ghost Orchid* (1995), Medbh McGuckian's *Captain Lavender* (1994), Derek Mahon's *The Hudson Letter* (1995), and Paul Muldoon's verse-play *Six Honest Serving Men* (1995).

2

Two broad propositions underlie my thinking about history and Northern Irish poetry. The first is that poets have long been in a similar situation to poets during the 1930s – a surprisingly neglected comparison. Whatever their aesthetic and other differences, they have shared a raised consciousness of history. This, in requiring formulation – in requiring form – has acted upon aesthetics. Secondly, historical self-consciousness, together with its unconscious undertow, has tightened the intertextuality between poems, and between poetry and other written and unwritten texts. A kind of instant New Historicism implicates Northern Irish poetry in a mass of cultural materials involving representations of history. To keep to the printed word, poetry enters a crowded arena where the textual gladiators include every newspaper's 'first draft of history'; the Sinn Féin mouthpiece *An Phoblacht*; Loyalist news-sheets and pamphlets; the works of local historians and other 'heritage'-producers; reflective exercises like the Ulster Society's symposia (in which some non-unionists speak) *The Twelfth: What it Means to Me* (1997) and *Remembrance* (of the world wars) (1997) or the studies published by the Dublin Forum for Peace and Reconciliation; political speeches such as those made by John Major and John Bruton when fraught talks began at Stormont in June 1996. Major then said that 'history in Northern Ireland has poisoned the present and threatened the future'; Bruton, with even less metaphorical originality, that 'we must overcome the legacy of history'. In the literary sphere, poetry interacts with fiction and drama, or perhaps competes with them: two novels that comment on the last thirty years, Robert McLiam Wilson's *Eureka Street* (1996) and Michael Foley's *The Road to Notown* (1996), satirise the pretensions of poets, the tropes of poetry. As for the academic sector: some books that bear on poetry and history in the post-ceasefire period are (from Irish historians) R.F. Foster's inaugural lecture at Oxford, *The Story of Ireland* (delivered in December 1994); *The Making of Modern Irish History: Revisionism and the Revisionist Controversy*, edited by D. George Boyce and Alan O'Day (1996); Tom Garvin's *1922: The Birth of Irish Democracy* (1996); and (from Irish literary/cultural critics): Declan Kiberd's *Inventing Ireland* (1995); Seamus Deane's *Strange Country* (the 1995 Clarendon Lectures); Seamus Heaney's *The Redress of Poetry* (1995); Luke Gibbons's *Transformations in Irish Culture* (1996). This is only the tip of the iceberg in a country gripped by historiographical mania.

International debate about theory, history and historiography intersects with a local Irish debate which intersects with the politics of Northern Ireland. I want, first, to pick out a theme in the wider debate: the conjoined theme of *Posthistoire* and postmodernism. In English the word 'end' has an often fruitful ambiguity. For Francis Fukuyama, in *The End of History and the Last Man* (1992) 'end' implies 'goal' more than terminus, but goal in the sense of revealed destination as opposed to desired or predicted destiny. Nonetheless, he takes the same teleological view as do other philosophers of history. Thus he proposes that 'at the end of the twentieth century, it makes sense for us once again to speak of a coherent and directional History of mankind that will eventually lead the greater part of humanity to liberal democracy'. This does not mean that history will make nothing happen or that 'new nationalisms' in eastern Europe or the Third World will be 'politically neutralised' either today or tomorrow. It *does* mean (following the Hegelian and Marxist model) that there will 'be no further progress in the development of underlying principles and institutions because all of the really big questions [will have been] settled'.[12]

History may already have refuted Fukuyama, even to himself, but Alex Callinicos's critique in *Theories and Narratives* (1995) remains useful. First, he questions Fukuyama's rehabilitation of the grand narrative, the philosophy of history, and his paradoxical appeal to bereft Marxists on that account. (Hence also the appeal of Irish nationalism.) Second, he questions Fukuyama's claim to be in the intellectual tradition of Hegel and Marx, since Hegel's absolute was situated beyond history, while for Marx the conditions for history to begin had not yet been fulfilled. Third, he sees Fukuyama's ideas as originating in the elitist pessimism of the right-wing German cultural theorists who developed the concept of *Posthistoire*, and for whom, obsessed with 'the spiritlessness of capitalist modernity', the 'problematic of posthistory is not the end of the world but the end of meaning'.[13] Thus, with Nietzsche, and up to a point with Yeats, Fukuyama does not really relish the unheroic 'last man' produced by liberal democracy. He writes: 'The last man at the end of history *knows* better than to risk his life for a cause because he recognises that history was full of pointless battles in which men fought over whether they should be Christian or Moslem, Protestant or Catholic, German or French. The loyalties that drove men to desperate acts of courage and sacrifice were proven by subsequent history to be silly prejudices.'[14]

That passage holds obvious ironies not only for the Middle East or central and eastern Europe, but also for a corner of western Europe where old nationalisms and liberal democracy grate against each other. Their contradiction was registered by Derek Mahon in an early poem, 'Suburban Walk', which may now have resumed a prophetic, end-of-history status that it appeared to lose after 1969. Later called 'Glengormley', the poem part welcomes, part regrets the post-war recovery of liberal civilisation. It ends:

> Only words hurt us now. No saint or hero,
> Landing at night from the conspiring seas,
> Brings dangerous tokens to the new era –
> Their sad names linger in the histories.
> The unreconciled, in their metaphysical pain,
> Strangle on lamp-posts in the dawn rain
>
> And much dies with them. I should rather praise
> A worldly time under this worldly sky –
> The terrier-taming, garden-watering days
> Those heroes pictured as they struggled through
> The quick noose of their finite being. By
> Necessity, if not choice, I live here too.

Today there is tension between 'unreconciled' paramilitarism and the desire for international investment in Northern Irish working-class communities. A member of a group working for the Economic Regeneration of Lisburn, helped to man a roadblock erected when the Drumcree parade was banned in 1998. He explained that economic regeneration was 'business', but Drumcree was 'principles'. In August 1999 Derry republicans destroyed commercial property in their prosperous, refurbished, mainly Catholic city, after the independent Parades Commission had allowed a Protestant parade.

So, in Northern Ireland, would liberal posthistory be dawn or decadence?

And what of postmodernism – which Fukuyama attaches to his endist wagon-trail? The pages of *New Left Review* have long groaned with 'metaphysical pain' about history's transformation into a pick 'n' mix of representations without referents let alone ends. In an article on Derrida, Fredric Jameson even embraces a version of Messianism that 'brings the whole feeling of dashed hopes and impossibility along with it', locating a spectral Marx in 'a new kind of trembling or shimmering of the present in which new ghosts now seem on the point of walking'.[15] Yeats's millennial veil trembles again. Perry Anderson in *The Origins of Postmodernity* (1998) takes Jameson himself for the Messiah: 'In the dominion over the term post-modernism won by Jameson, we witness…a concept whose visionary origins were all but completely effaced in usages complicit with the established order, wrested away by a prodigious display of theoretical intelligence and energy for the cause of a revolutionary Left.' Anderson also calls the poet Charles Olson 'prophetic' in combining 'poetic innovation with political revolution' (he does not take into account mixed views as to the quality of Olson's verse).[16] At this *fin de siècle*, strange rational gloom on the intellectual Right faces strange religious hope on the Left. A related case is Richard Rorty's casting of himself as a 'tragic liberal', for whom, 'if there is hope it lies in the imagination of the Third World'.[17] This echo of Orwell's Winston Smith has itself been echoed by Terry Eagleton.[18]

Two further dispatches from the political-theoretical debate seem more specifically relevant to the Irish debate about history and historiography; or at least to the proposition that the indigenous argument takes the shape it does because Ireland's intellectual and political culture has only patchily undergone the Enlightenment. The first is a suggestion by Christopher Norris that more attention should be paid to the theological sources of anti-referential theory. He traces current efforts to relativise scientific discourse to a French Catholic tradition of thought that tried to ringfence faith and 'modes of metaphoric or creative reverie' from assault by the truth-claims of science.[19] The second is Alex Callinicos's argument that socio-logically grounded *theories* of history, as opposed to totalising *philosophies*, have a crucial explanatory function if we want to go on 'asking whether human reason can comprehend the historical process in whose making it is entangled'. Callinicos says: 'A theory of history which rejects the idea of inevitability…needs narrative historiography to gain insight into the situations in which events decisively took one course rather than another.'[20]

Meanwhile historians are still coming to terms with the disciplinary consequences of 'theory', especially the cats that Hayden White let out of the bag when he set out to 'classify the deep structural forms of the historical imagination'. Since I will be trying on his scheme for size, a summary seems in order. I quote from the conclusion to *Metahistory*:

> I have maintained that the style of a given historiographer can be characterised in terms of the linguistic protocol he used to prefigure the historical field prior to bringing to bear on it the various 'explanatory' strategies he used to fashion a "story" out of the "chronicle" of events contained in the historical record. These linguistic protocols, I have maintained, can be further characterised in terms of the four principal modes of poetic discourse. Using the tropes of Metaphor, Metonymy, Synecdoche and Irony as the basic types of linguistic prefiguration, I have discussed the modes in which historians can explicitly or implicitly justify commitment to different explanatory strategies on the levels of argument, emplotment, and ideological implication respectively.[21]

White identifies three interacting kinds of 'explanatory strategy' in the nineteenth-century historians he studies: 'four different theories of truth' and hence 'modes of argument' (Formism, Mechanism, Organicism, and Contextualism); 'four different archetypal plot structures' which he takes from Northrop Frye (Romance, Tragedy, Comedy and Satire); and 'four different strategies of ideological implication by which historians can suggest to their readers the import of their studies of the past for the comprehension of the present: Anarchism, Radicalism, Conservatism and Liberalism'.[22] Argument, plot and ideology should line up according to their position on each list. In practice, however, certain combinations of tropes or modes potentially vary the scheme, and this can create productive dialectical tension. White, along with Rorty, is picked out by Keith Jenkins in *On 'What is History'* (1995) as – successful – antagonists for the older thinking of Edward Carr and Geoffrey Elton. For Jenkins now,

> History is arguably a verbal artifact, a narrative prose discourse of which, *après* White, the content is as much invented as found, and which is constructed by present-minded, ideologically positioned workers (historians and those acting as if they were historians) operating at various levels of reflexivity...[The] past, appropriated by historians, is never the past itself...the cogency of historical work can be admitted without the past *per se* ever entering into it – except rhetorically. In this way histories are fabricated without 'real' foundations beyond the textual, and in this way one learns always to always ask of such discursive and ideological regimes that hold in their orderings suasive intentions – *cui bono* – in whose interests?[23]

The readings of history implied or urged by Irish commemorations might seem to support Jenkins's last point. I am aware, too, that this essay organises historical narrative in an 'ideologically positioned' way. Yet "1798", for instance, may not really lend itself to such clearcut contemporary interests as those of one historian who rejoiced that it had been liberated from 'passé revisionist debunkery'.[24] Nonetheless, many historians acknowledge the challenge presented by the theorists who have recast 'history' as 'a verbal artifact'. For example, in *In Defence of History* (1997) Richard J. Evans admits that 'Postmodernism in its more constructive modes has encouraged historians to look more closely at documents...to think about texts and narratives in new ways...to interrogate their own methods and procedures as never before'. Besides forcing historians to become more 'self-critical', it 'has led to a greater emphasis on open acknowledgement of the historian's own subjectivity'. Yet Evans also defends the historian's goal of '*probable* truth':

> In the end, it simply is not the case that two historical arguments which contradict one another are equally valid, that there is no means of deciding between them as history because they are necessarily based on different political and historical philosophies. It is one thing to say that different historians use the same sources to ask different questions, quite another to say that they use them for the same question and come up with diametrically opposed answers. If one historian argues that big business put the Nazis into power in Germany in 1933 and another argues that it did not, these arguments cannot both be correct...In a number of cases, political commitment, freed by postmodernist relativism from the shackles that normally bind historians to the facts, has produced deeply flawed work which clearly distorts or misinterprets the source material in the service of present-day ideology.[25]

Such freedom, not only when taken to its logical conclusion, interferes with the fine-tuning of Callinicos's 'theories of history' which require 'narrative historiography' to 'gain insight into the situations in which events decisively took one course rather than another'. By inviting historians to overcome the inhibitions of the detached Ironic trope 'as the *necessary* perspective from which to view the historical process', White may actually restrict 'the import of their studies of the past for comprehension of the present'. This applies to excessively partisan (re)constructions of "1798".

In *Thinking with History* (1998) Carl E. Schorske makes even more concessions to the theoretical revolution which has shaken the 'hierarchical order of disciplines', and freed history to 'proliferate a variety of subcultures', to choose intellectual partners at will, and hence to 'erupt with new creations at the frontiers of system and convention'. Nonetheless, Schorske insists: 'Virtually

the only stable centre of the historian's armamentarium is the simple
calendar that determines what came before something, what came
after.' Worried lest the synchronic orientation of anthropology has
destabilised this final redoubt, too, and thus weakened historians'
commitment 'to chart not only continuity but change', he concludes:
'the model of Herodotus, with his interactive dynamic between
culture and politics, and between the diochronic and synchronic
dimensions of history, can still serve us well'.[26] In *Virtual History:
Alternatives and Counterfactuals* (1998), Niall Ferguson makes the
same point about the effects of anthropology, and maintains that
'post-modernists are merely rehashing old idealist nostrums when
they declare history "an interpretative practice, not an objective
neutral science"'. Yet Ferguson also argues against the inevitabilism
induced by 'what actually happened', preferring to see any historical
moment as a set of forking paths, and quoting Robert Musil's *The
Man Without Qualities*: 'The course of history was…not that of a
billiard-ball, which, once it has been hit, ran along a definite course;
on the contrary, it was like the passage of clouds, like the way of a
man sauntering through the streets – diverted here by a shadow,
there by a little crowd of people…finally arriving at a place that
he had neither known of nor meant to reach'.[27]

3

Irish historians have sometimes been charged with lacking 'philo-
sophical resource' in a manner that implies a straightforward dis-
tinction between the theoretically sophisticated and the theoretically
illiterate. However, even in this brief sketch, it can be seen that,
on a wider front, debates about history and historiography are
precisely that – debates – in which a range of theoretical positions
are taken both by Marxist theorists and by historians. (Schorske
discovered that the 'striking feature of the articles in *History and
Theory*' since its foundation in 1961 was 'the continuously even
distribution of the various positions represented in it'.)[28] Several
Irish historians have taken the '*après* White' point. Thus at the
start of his Oxford lecture R.F. Foster emphasises his familiarity
with White, Jameson, Paul Ricoeur and Vladimir Propp, and says:
'one is struck again and again by the importance of the narrative
mode: the idea that Irish history *is* a "story", and the implications
that this carries about a beginning, a middle, and the sense of an
ending. Not to mention heroes, villains, donors, helpers, guests,
plots, revelations, and all the other elements of the story form.'
Two of Foster's comments on 'the sense of an ending' have (no

doubt deliberate) contemporary relevance. First, he notes how, in A.M. Sullivan's influential *The Story of Ireland* (1867), the language of religion fixes an ending in the future: namely, resurrection 'after such a crucifixion and burial'. Second, he stresses that the 'end of the story [in 1916 or 1921] was not what had been expected [in 1900]'.[29]

Some contributors to *The Making of Modern Irish History* exploit the ambiguities in its title which covers something (being) written as well as something (that goes on) happening. For instance, Alvin Jackson analyses the reflexive 'story of Unionism': 'A schismatic and fissile Unionism is reflected in a scholarship which, itself divided by political and methodological sympathy, focuses on analyses of Unionist division'.[30] S.J. Connolly, in an (unpublished) inaugural lecture given at Queen's University (1997), 'Catastrophe, Normality and the Irish Historian', looked at narrative coding from another angle. He outlined the grounds for alternative readings of Irish history first as 'normal', then as 'catastrophic', that is, 'as unusually violent, tragic and conflict ridden'. Nevertheless, in opting for neither reading, Connolly claimed that his 'inconclusiveness' was objective rather than subjective. He did not espouse postmodernist indeterminacy, but argued that indeterminacy, in this case, *refers*:

> Ireland's past is indeed inconclusive: more violent and disturbed than that of the larger geographical and political unit, the British Isles, with which it is inextricably entangled, yet not so much so as to be wholly outside the realm of West European or even British experience. What I would like to stress is that this ambivalence is in fact the key to a proper understanding of Irish history.

If we were to accept Connolly's ultimately positivistic argument, we might see ambivalence (rather than 'abnormality' or 'anomaly') as underlying, together with post-1798, post-Enlightenment political and intellectual tensions, the shape of Irish academic debates about historical shaping. Hence such statements as the opening sentence of Luke Gibbons's *Transformations in Irish Culture*: 'Ireland is a First World Country, but with a Third World memory.'[31]

To point towards underlying conditions is hardly to take the relativist position in any debate. But, perhaps, neither does Gibbons when, writing as a cultural theorist, he approves a critique of the 'clinical...value-free' style of academic history, and subsequently urges:

> the very existence of a *symbolic* dimension in human action requires a historical method that goes beyond literalist assumptions, and scientific norms of causality and certainty. For this reason, it is important not only to re-think but to *re-figure* Irish identity, to attend to those recalcitrant areas of experience which simply do not lend themselves to certainty,

and which impel societies themselves towards indirect and figurative discourse – narratives, generic conventions, rhetorical tropes, allegory, and other 'literary' modes of composition.

Gibbons contends that Foster's account of A.M. Sullivan ignores 'the precise nature of Sullivan's conservative political project, and in particular, his sustained opposition to Fenianism and popular insurgency'. This he sees as of a piece with how Foster himself confines historical narrative 'to *books* and the *writing* of history as against the lived experience of popular memory'. Later Gibbons suggests that the 'most telling [nineteenth-century] expressions of inchoate structures lie not in the tightly controlled "Stories of Ireland" discussed by Foster, but rather in the proto-modernist tales of terror which haunted the gothic fiction of Charles Maturin, Lady Morgan, William Carleton and others'.[32] Here the emphasis on facts ('precise nature') ignored by Foster and on 'experience' does not entirely consort with Gibbons's recruitment of Hayden White. The latter's categories are not so much invoked to relativise 'historical method' or returned to their literary origins, as used to give literary structures more power over the historical scene. They serve 'identity' and chime with 'popular memory' – and 'popular insurgency'. Gibbons's thinking is in line with postmodernist neo-Romanticism – that imaginary where the Third World meets a folkloric and spectral underworld. But it also reinstates or restates the traditionally literary character of Irish historical narratives, if with a new bias towards the Gothic (witness the amazing academic popularity of *Dracula*). The proposition that 'recalcitrant areas of experience...do not lend themselves to certainty' confuses two kinds of 'certainty': a historian might be certain about the existence of uncertainties or mysteries. It is itself finally a kind of 'literalism' to claim that the '*symbolic* dimension in human actions' demands symbolic treatment to guarantee empathy – if empathy is what must be guaranteed.

Evans, a British historian, is pleased (up to a point) that postmodernism 'has shifted the emphasis in historical writing...back from social-scientific to literary models'.[33] Foster, however, complains that 'Irish historical interpretation has too often been cramped into a strictly literary mode; the narrative drive has ruthlessly eroded awkward elisions'.[34] Similarly, he might view as premature, in the Irish case, White's deliverance of historical writing from the professional Ironic perspective. Gibbons's dismissal of 'scientific norms of causality' recalls Norris's point, and arguably simplifies the terminologies, methodologies, and relations between them, currently to be found even in the more conventional sector of historiography.

Nor, from a theoretical angle, do his proposals for historical narra-
tive necessarily improve on Foster's. Perhaps Foster looks for a
story of Ireland that accommodates counterfactuals and re-conceives
narrative ends; whereas Gibbons looks for a story that accommo-
dates antifactuals and reconceives narrative means. In *Rethinking
Irish History* (1998) Patrick O'Mahony and Gerard Delanty single
out Gibbons's book as exemplifying a trend. They note 'the rela-
tive absence of theoretically informed critical social science' in the
Irish Republic (lingering Catholic resistance to the Enlightenment
influenced not only the state's ideology but its intellectual make-up);
and regret that 'Reflection upon identity has been dominated by
the humanities with a new "soft" cultural nationalism inspired
more by literature and literary criticism than by history or social
science emerging to contest revisionist historical writing.'[35]

What about the 'narratives, generic conventions, rhetorical tropes'
that might emerge if we took the liberty of applying Hayden White
to recent works of Irish cultural history? It is not surprising that, as
compared with most economic, social and political historiography,
such works should appear less governed by what White terms 'the
condition of irony into which historical consciousness was plunged
at the end of the nineteenth century';[36] and that they should incline
more to Organicism and Mechanism – 'integrative' modes of
argument – than to Formism (occupied with particularities) and
Contextualism (occupied with 'functional interrelationships'). The
Irish nation gives Declan Kiberd's *Inventing Ireland* its integrative
dynamic. And his title, like Gibbons's, links Ireland with a word
that suggests the imagination at work – he does not opt for *Con-
structing* or *Rethinking*. All the literary data that Kiberd presents
conduce in some way to the national story, this shape (as with other
national(ist) narratives) being prefigured by the synecdochic trope:
i.e., the part represents 'some *quality* presumed to inhere in the
totality'. White also says: 'The *mythos* of Synecdoche is the dream
of Comedy, the apprehension of a world in which all struggle, strife,
and conflict are dissolved in the realisation of a perfect harmony,
in the attainment of a condition in which all crime, vice, and folly
are finally revealed as the *means* to the establishment of the social
order which is finally achieved at the end of the play.'[37] That
applies to Kiberd's happy "ending", with its climactic re-figuring
of Cathleen ní Houlihan as Synecdoche rather than Metaphor:

> If the notion of 'Ireland' seemed to have become problematic, that was
> only because the seamless garment once wrapped like a green flag
> around Cathleen ní Houlihan had given way to a quilt of many patches
> and colours, all beautiful, all distinct, yet all connected too. No one

element should subordinate or assimilate the others: Irish or English,
rural or urban, Gaelic or Anglo, each has its part in the pattern.[38]

This is also a highly *literary* conclusion to a book in which litera-
ture has seized from historians the narrative of modern Irish his-
tory. 'Comedy', in another sense, fits the importance of Oscar
Wilde as hero, Kiberd's style of witty paradox, and the prominence
of dramatic texts. In White's scheme, Comedy belongs with an
Organicist mode of argument, whose thrust towards a whole greater
than the sum of its parts characterises the nationalistic historiography
of nineteenth-century Europe. Yet Kiberd's 'mode of ideological
implication' (which should be Conservative) diverges in the way
that White sees as giving historiography its productive tension.
Kiberd handles the Comic plot summarised by White as the prota-
gonist's triumph 'over the society which blocks his progression to
his goal' ('colonial' Britain as villain, if sometimes in comic whiskers),
in the Radical spirit that welcomes structural change. Nonetheless,
his textual unconscious may be more Conservative than appears
on the surface.[39]

In contrast, the ideological implication of Seamus Deane's *Strange
Country* is thoroughly Radical (though with Anarchist moments),
just as the emplotment seems Tragic (no quasi-Comic villains here),
and the mode of argument largely Mechanistic (Marxist). All literary
and cultural data are referred to the 'crisis' produced by British
colonial involvement in Ireland, and to an unresolved dialectic
between the 'failed' project of the Union and 'the competing pro-
ject of nationalism'.[40] At the same time, Deane is more consistent
than Kiberd in treating "Ireland" as a discursive and textual phe-
nomenon. Thus, while *Strange Country* involves historical narrative,
it comes closer to philosophy of history. White's relativism, how-
ever, dissolves the distinction between the two; and Deane accepts
this licence 'to conceptualise history...and to construct narrative
accounts of its processes in whatever modality of consciousness is
most consistent with [his] own moral and aesthetic aspirations'.
Tragedy, Mechanism and Radicalism again belong together in
White's scheme. White, of course, warns that his ideological modes
signify 'general ideological preference' rather than 'specific political
parties'.[41] But if one were to identify Deane's prefiguring trope as
Metonymy (that is, he conceives the historical field in terms of
fracture and disjunction) it would seem plausible that structural
differences between his and Kiberd's texts are conditioned by the
dispositions of a northern and southern Irish intellectual as, in the
mid 1990s, they write forms of nationalist cultural history which
renew nineteenth-century historiographical paradigms. The conclusion

of *Strange Country*, as contrasted with that of *Inventing Ireland*, suggests Metonymy in search of Synecdoche or even Metaphor. Its immediate trigger is a critique of the historian F.S.L. Lyons:

> Within this series of sliding prevarications, there is no doubt that the key to all the mythologies is to be found in Ireland while the British, although prone to infirmity and error, are nevertheless safely within the precincts of the rational. This is nothing more than the rhetoric of Yeatsian cultural nationalism, masquerading as analysis in virtue of the claim that it is being written from a subject-position free of that rhetoric's rational or anti-rational sources. The paradigm prevails; in order to be understood, Ireland must be split between the rational and the national. It is a strange country, resistant to the normalisation that is offered to it by the historian who has been emancipated from the strangeness that his version of normality constitutes. Monotonously, the choice remains – apocalypse or boredom…The country remains strange in its failure to be normal; the normal remains strange in its failure to be defined as anything other than the negative of strange. Normality is an economic condition, strangeness a cultural one. Since Burke there have been strenuous efforts to effect the convergence of the twain, even though the very premiss of their separation has been powerful in ensuring that the twain will never meet.[42]

To quote from White on Marx: 'Marx's thought moved between Metonymical apprehensions of the severed condition of mankind in its social state and Synecdochic intimations of the unity he spied at the end of the whole historical process'. And to quote from White's definition of Tragedy: 'states of division', which never approach Comic 'reconciliation' (or Marxist synthesis) are felt in every aspect of this paragraph, although the speaker's/Ireland's 'tragic agon' may stimulate 'a gain in consciousness for the spectators of the contest'.[43] The allusion to Hardy's *Titanic* elegy introduces tragedy from another angle, perhaps unconsciously casting 'convergence' as apocalypse. Other features here, which relate to my earlier argument, are: the representation of historians as untheoretical; the question as to whether their self-proclaimed rationalism (like that of the British state) stands up to scrutiny; the corollary that a literary-theoretical model might make more sense of Irish data than do the models offered by historiography or social science. *Strange Country*, then, in a different way from *Inventing Ireland*, uses literature to write history. Deane's distastefully viewed 'historian' also resembles the liberal 'last man' since he has caused a teleological impasse, and may threaten a teleological collapse.

Despite the smallness of my sample, one might speculate that disciplinary biases, as well as Irish locations, politics and intellectual history, influence tropes and modes. Hence both the commonalities and divergences between *Inventing Ireland* and Tom Garvin's *1922*.

Garvin also inclines to Comic reconciliation in that he tells a story of the Irish Republic whose tendency amounts to 'Look, we have come through!', a direction signalled by his metaphorical subtitle *The Birth of Irish Democracy.* I quote from another last paragraph, which, more directly than Deane's or Kiberd's, refers to Northern Ireland since 1994:

> Democracy in Ireland was the child of strange parents: Anglo-American political culture and the Catholic Church. Its crucial moment came in 1922-23, when force was used to prevent it being forcibly disestablished by insurrectionist 'republicans' who mouthed democratic slogans but whose violent actions belied their words. Since the Free State victory of 1923, no alternative regime has been taken seriously in Ireland. No all-Ireland polity, were one to emerge in the future, could ever be established without the clear consent of the Northern majority…The North of 1922 set a severe test for the democratic credentials of the Southerners; some of them failed that test at the time, but their successors, under the Fianna Fáil Taoiseach Albert Reynolds, passed it with flying colours in 1994. The Treaty settlement of 1921-22, much fought over at the time, is now complete, and Ireland can finally move on.[44]

Nevertheless, like most orthodox historiography, *1922* is Contextualist in mode of argument and Liberal in ideological implication; even if Irish conditions and themes qualify Garvin's Irony, producing the positive inclination to Comedy rather than Satire. To take the disciplinary point further: a more recent work of cultural history, Gerry Smyth's *Decolonisation and Criticism* (1998), 'investigates the role played by the discourse of literary criticism in the process of Irish decolonisation since the late eighteenth century, with special emphasis on the 1950s'. Although again written by an academic from the Republic, the book ends on a downbeat note, with some familiar resonances, that points to tension between its focus and its disciplinary locus (post-colonial theory on an extra-European model). Smyth finds that 'Irish book-length literary criticism' conforms to the 'unbroken' 'circle of colonial domination' that he detects in other literary-critical quarters during his chosen period:

> Whether its impetus was state-affiliated aggrandisement…whether adhering to the codes and practices of professional scholarship and its drive towards truth; or whether reacting to the increasing international critical interest in Irish literature and the growth in the number of monographs, Irish literary criticism effectively failed to imagine a new agenda, or construct a new language, for its debates.[45]

To summarise the dialectics between these stories of Ireland: for Garvin as for Kiberd, 'Irish history' in the old sense has ended: there is an achieved 'pattern', 'completion' – and Garvin explicitly inserts the Northern Irish "peace process" into his reconciliatory conclusion; for Smyth as for Deane, both discursively oriented, there has been neither end nor birth but a continuing circle or unfertile set of oppositions. Luke Gibbons's final pages, too, attribute 'the *absence* of the sense of an ending which has characterised the national narratives of Irish history...the lack of historical closure' to the ineradicable marks of a colonial power on Irish experience. He is another teleological tourist who finds hope in Third World vistas down 'unapproved roads' unpatrolled by 'global powers'.[46]

So far I have alluded to heterogeneous forms and images of historical ending – often hard to distinguish from a historical beginning: ceasefire and its cessation, the inglorious last man, Yeats's and O'Brien's rough beast of the millennium, Sullivan's resurrection realised by Patrick Pearse's 'unexpected' apotheosis, Kiberd's quilted Cathleen, the differently inconclusive readings of S.J. Connolly and Seamus Deane, Garvin's elephant-long gestation and birth. There are also, always, alternative universes with alternative endings – including what had been 'expected' to happen. For Ferguson, the value of counterfactual history (defined as '*only those alternatives which we can show on the basis of contemporary evidence that contemporaries actually considered*') is that it serves 'judgments about probability', illuminates the role of 'determinist theories' in history, and thereby provides 'a necessary antidote to determinism' and its political effects.[47] *Virtual History* contains a counterfactual essay by Alvin Jackson: 'British Ireland: *What if Home Rule had been enacted in 1912?*' Jackson plausibly shows that

> there was certainly nothing inevitable about the failure of the third Home Rule Bill as a piece of legislation...Nor was partition inevitable, at least in the form of a permanent exclusion of the six northern counties from the Home Rule scheme. It has been suggested that there was a chance that Ulster Unionists might have at least temporarily reconciled themselves to a Dublin administration, particularly in the context of a united Irish commitment to the Allied war effort in 1914.[48]

Yet he also points out that 'the political risks involved were great, and might well have been realised...[there being] every possibility that a short-term political triumph for Liberal statesmanship might have been bought at the price of a delayed apocalypse'. Jackson's own perspectives, however, may be conditioned by more recent events. He ends: 'Northern Ireland under the Union has been likened to Bosnia; but Ireland under Home Rule might well have proved to be not so much Britain's settled, democratic partner as her Yugoslavia.'[49] So *plus ça change.*

Teleological narratives of history combine with the commemorative recycling of 'what actually happened' to produce the inevitabilism that is so powerful in Irish historical consciousness. The impasse between Protestants and Catholics in Northern Ireland seems insoluble because it is proleptic. Each group's politics vault to the desired or dreaded finale. The end paralyses the beginning. For republicans, the end is a goal: 'Our day will come': the day of British withdrawal when history can at last begin. For unionists, that same day figures the end of history as a terrible terminus. Some years before he became leader of the Ulster Unionist Party David Trimble spoke of 'the fear that the people might cease to be, at least culturally'.[50] The unionist political scientist Arthur Aughey points out that unionists distrust all language of movement and 'process' because they read it as propelling them in one direction only – towards a United Ireland. Therefore, analysing the Frameworks Documents (1995) which succeeded the ceasefires, Aughey desiderates: 'first, a framework for a settlement which can be accepted as a settlement and not as a stepping stone to something else; second, an end to "endism", the unionist politics of the apocalypse and nationalist politics of destiny'.[51]

Apocalypse and utopian nativity alternate in some literary texts that respond to the period between the first IRA ceasefire and Canary Wharf. On the positive side, there is an outbreak of comedy, sex and babies. In Robert McLiam Wilson's *Eureka Street* (1996) the iconoclastic, revisionist narrator ends up in love and bed with a republican woman whom he has detested (and who appears to have changed her tune). He simultaneously makes a kind of love to the city of Belfast: 'Sometimes, this frail cityful of organs makes me seethe and boil with tenderness. They seem so unmurderable...' [52] The female, mothering quality of his emotion (Comic reconciliation) connects with the motif of pregnancy in other 'condition of Ulster' fiction. Deirdre Madden's *One by One in the Darkness* (1996) and Colin Bateman's comedy-thriller *Of Wee Sweetie Mice and Men* (1996) both have babies in the womb. Frank Ormsby's poem for his daughter Helen, born on 12 August 1994, the last poem in *The Ghost Train* (1995), epitomises this complex of ending, love, birth and new beginning:

The war will soon be over, or so they say.
Five floors below the Friday rush-hour starts.
You're out and breathing. We smile to hear you cry.
Your long fingers curl around our hearts.

The place knows nothing of you and is home.
Indifferent skies look on while August warms
the middle air. We wrap you in your name.
Peace is the way you settle in our arms.

Yet most of these texts entertain the apocalyptic possibility too. In a kind of double indemnity they insure themselves against false prophecy. Thus Bateman's novel begins: 'Peace had settled over the city like the skin on a rancid custard. Everyone wanted it, just not in that form. The forecast remained for rain, with widespread terrorism.'[53] The IRA ceasefire occurs in the time-frame of *Eureka Street*, but the novel makes a point of refusing to repress a violent past. There is graphic detail of a murderous explosion and the lives it ended or changed. In *One by One in the Darkness*, whereas one sister expects a baby, another cannot forget her father's murder. Such contrasts are more than an insurance policy where they lay out political options along with historical possibilities.

4

Philosophical and political 'ends of history' were, of course, envisaged or implied by Irish poetry before August 1994 or August 1969. Breandán Ó Buachalla summarises the 'millennial message' of the Jacobite Gaelic *aisling*, which influenced nineteenth-century nationalist ballads in English, and which still shapes Irish configurations of destiny and doom: 'the prophetic message foretold the re-establishment of the natural order: the rightful King on his throne, the native aristocracy restored to their ancestral lands, the intelligentsia re-established in office and esteem...it also foretold more universal changes: the triumph of the Irish language, the demise of English; the expulsion of the followers of Calvin and Luther, the triumph of the Church of Rome...in short, that the respective roles of the "in" and "out" categories of Irish society...would eventually be reversed'.[54] More immediately, Yeats and MacNeice seem as significant for poetic 'ends of history' as they are in other respects; one reason being that, like the *aisling*, their work acts as a conduit for the structural influence of stories of Christianity on stories of Ireland. Yeats's millenarianism returned centre-stage as the millennium drew nearer and everybody quoted 'The Second Coming'. Between the 1890s and 1920s Yeats switched from the positive millenarianism of 'The Secret Rose' ('Surely thine hour has come, thy great wind blows') to the negative apocalypse of 'Nineteen Hundred and Nineteen': 'Violence upon the roads, violence of horses/...Herodias' daughters have returned again,/ A sudden blast of dusty wind...' In the 1930s Yeats's writings sometimes embodied a 'sense of an ending' which connects with today's unionist 'politics of the apocalypse'. One factor behind his symbolic ruined houses, his rhetoric of 'Heroic reverie mocked by clown and knave', was the changing, dwindling southern Protestant world.[55] For MacNeice, Yeats's historical gyres (which he saw as more positive than Eliot's 'dissolution' because their cyclical scheme made room for birth as well as death)[56] interacted with the British 1930s literary theme of 'waiting for the end'. This, too, moved from the eagerly messianic to the darkly apocalyptic. The Marxian 'Saviour's birth', anticipated by C. Day Lewis and others, lost out to the ominous images in which MacNeice specialised: 'Salome comes in, bearing/ The head of God knows whom' ('Night Club', 1939) – perhaps an echo of 'Herodias' daughters'. The broader relation between poetry and history in 1930s Britain is a case-study in the dynamics between language, literary tropes and changing referents. These dynamics culminate in the historically self-conscious, and historically open-ended, *Autumn Journal*.

Autumn Journal spans images of apocalypse and images of utopia; scenarios in which the protagonist's situation seems determined by the 'bloody frontier/Converg[ing] on our beds' and scenarios in which he may have free will. The poems considered below display similar antinomies in varying ratios – not necessarily because they are directly influenced by MacNeice, but because *Autumn Journal* seems a paradigmatic twentieth-century "historical poem". For Mac-Neice, the Munich crisis opened up those 'forking paths' which provide special insights into history, especially if still in the making. The poem's trajectory encompasses various known, expected, un-expected and unknowable ends of history. If, then, Northern Irish poetry has come to a similar juncture, *Autumn Journal* may help with some parameters. Is there a fundamental difference between applying Hayden White (tentatively, I would stress) to historiography, to the literary forms of cultural history noticed above, and to literary forms themselves? Although theorists might not endorse Sir Philip Sidney's statement that poetry 'nothing affirmeth', we hardly receive it as pretending to "fact" in the vulgar sense. Perhaps, then, poetry belongs with philosophy or theory of history. Without need-ing White's permission, poets follow their own 'moral and aesthetic aspirations' in order to create historical meanings. These meanings are liable to be extremely concentrated so that narrative (which may not point at identifiable "events") is subsumed by the modes of its explanation. And all White's classifications become subject to the more complex structural shading, the deeper dialectical ten-sion, that poetry can command. Any genuine poem in some sense explains its own historical moment to the reader. Raised historical consciousness, however, introduces into that moment more freight from various pasts, more anxiety about various futures. The final section of *Autumn Journal* makes this explicit. MacNeice defines the poem's historical aesthetic in terms of the historical process itself: 'Time is a country, the present moment/A spotlight roving round the scene...'

Michael Longley's sonnet 'The Vision of Theoclymenus' (July 1995) presents alternative outcomes, forking paths, choices, at a moment characterised as 'like midnight here'. He counterpoints an apocalyptic octet with a sestet that proposes the power of rational ("enlightened") human will to prevent a catastrophic ending. The poem is based on a seer's unheeded warning to the suitors in the *Odyssey*. Longley's way of introducing ('As you say') the Ulster Scots word 'peerie-heedit' (with a head like a top) suggests that his prophetic speaker mainly addresses Ulster Protestants:

> What class of a nightmare are you living through,
> Poor bastards, your faces, knees shrouded in darkness,
> The atmosphere electric with keening – for it all
> Ends in tears – the walls bloody, and the crossbeams
> Like branches after a cloudburst drippling blood,
> The porch full of zombies, likewise the haggard
> Where they jostle to go underground, and no
> Sun while deadly marsh-gas envelops the globe?
>
> Though it feels to me like midnight here, I'm not,
> As you say, peerie-heedit, in need of help –
> With my eyes, ears and two feet, with unimpaired
> Intelligence I shall make it through those doors
> To the real world, and leave hanging over you
> Catastrophe, richly deserved, inescapable.

Longley's earlier Homeric sonnet 'Ceasefire' (August 1994), which conflates several passages in the *Iliad*, takes shape as historical narrative in its epic key. Questions of choice recede into the narrative tone as the poem tells the story of Priam's visit to Achilles to beg for the body of Hector:

> I
> Put in mind of his own father and moved to tears
> Achilles took him by the hand and pushed the old king
> Gently away, but Priam curled up at his feet and
> Wept with him until their sadness filled the building.
>
> II
> Taking Hector's corpse into his own hands Achilles
> Made sure it was washed and, for the old king's sake,
> Laid out in uniform, ready for Priam to carry
> Wrapped like a present home to Troy at daybreak...

In the next quatrain, Priam and Achilles eat and talk together, while 'it pleased them both/To stare at each other's beauty as lovers might'. The Homeric context ensures that 'ceasefire' does not mark a definitive ending (the Trojan war will resume). But the poem explores the moment and meaning of ceasefire in a way which speculates about the *mutual* conditions for an end to war. The sonnet itself ends with a couplet that goes back to the beginning, because it recapitulates Priam's 'earlier' submission to Achilles in order to win his son's body: '"I get down on my knees and do what must be done/ And kiss Achilles' hand, the killer of my son."'

These differently constructed sonnets (in their formal aspect too) suggest that, considered as historiography, as reflections on history, poems by the same poet need not opt for the same modes. Although the 'ideological implication' is Liberal in both cases, 'The Vision of Theoclymenus' has been plotted as Satire while 'Ceasefire' appears poised between Comedy and Tragedy. Eating, talk, familial and erotic love belong to the festive spirit of Comedy, but they are placed as a remission in the violence and grief of Tragedy. This highlights the compromises and surrenders necessary ('what must be done') to turn ceasefire into armistice. The differences between the sonnets may stem from their initial troping: 'The Vision of Theoclymenus' being primarily Ironic, while 'Ceasefire' hovers somewhere in the zone of Metonymy and Synecdoche. I have suggested that the conceptual 'prefiguring' of poetic 'history' is less clearcut. It also shows itself as actual verbal figures or the local balance of relations between them. Metonymy and Synecdoche, less fully realised forms of Metaphor, the one signifying fracture, the other mending, are tropes to which the poets discussed here seem particularly drawn. They move between them, both conceptually and locally, as their roving spotlights take up new positions. In Longley's symbolic scenarios parts of the body, their relations with, and figuring of, mind and emotion are central to how he perceives mankind in history. But whereas 'The Vision of Theoclymenus' alternates fractured and 'unimpaired' human images, the ambivalent poise of 'Ceasefire' pivots on 'hand': used for caring and killing. Motifs of the split body and of doubles (which in 'Ceasefire' splice epic with war elegy by echoing Wilfred Owen's 'Strange Meeting' and Keith Douglas's 'How to Kill') occur in other poems that explore an end to Northern Ireland's recent history.

Derek Mahon's 'Hudson Letter' has an overtly philosophical protagonist who works more directly on history and with a broader brush. He processes events from his New York apartment, ('this autistic slammer') after the manner of *Autumn Journal*. 'Events' include the news, noises and voices of New York and the Global Village, and some historical echoes from Ireland (one section is spoken by an immigrant servant-maid). This eighteen-part poem is dated New York, Dublin, January-September 1995. Although it barely alludes to Northern Irish affairs, its historical – sometimes millennial – meditation encompasses their wider context. Irish politics briefly appear when J.B. Yeats, to whom a section is addressed, prompts the exile, 'A recovering Ulster Protestant' (which implies recovery from more than alcohol) to imagine his return. Here Mahon revives the MacNeicean tactic of landscape panorama as critique: 'I can see a united Ireland from the air,/ its meteorological gaiety and despair'. Nonetheless,'The Hudson Letter' marks an upbeat twist in Mahon's narrative of history, which has hitherto been principally Tragic in plot and Anarchist-Conservative (like Evelyn Waugh's) in ideological implication: other poems besides 'Suburban Walk' take a dim view of the Last Man. In 'Lives' we 'know too much/To be anything any more'. On Mahon's usual reading, history has become simply humanity's rubbish defacing the globe. Because his historical vision is teleological (millennarian/ apocalyptic), his mode of argument tends to be Mechanistic – the problem being original historical sin – whereas in 'Ceasefire', for example, the narrated events are Contextually interpreted as conflicts and reciprocities. But in 'The Hudson Letter' Mahon's blueprint for redemption achieves greater presence than usual, as in the baptismal 'formal dance' of 'Waterfront' where the speaker almost casts himself as born again:

> Chaste convalescents from an exigent world,
> we come to rivers when we are young or old;
> stir-crazy, driven by cabin-fever, I choose
> the 10th St. Pier and toddle into the cold.
> Where once the waters spun to your fierce screws
> – *Nieuw Amsterdam, Caronia, Île de France!* –
> ice inches seaward in a formal dance...
>
> This morning, though, the throes of a warm snap
> so ice cracks far off like a thunderclap
> somewhere along Bohemia's desert coast
> and puffs drift in the harsh riparian light,
> gun-cotton against storm-clouds in the west
> that rain infection and industrial waste,
> though now we emerge from the industrial night;
> and I recall my ten-year-old delight
> at the launch of a P&O liner in Belfast,
> all howling 'O God Our Help in Ages Past'.
> I hear no Jersey blackbird serenade
> this rapt friar on the Big Apple side;
> yet, having come so far from home,
> I try to imagine our millennium
> where, in the thaw-water of an oil-drum,

the hot genes of the future seethe. The sun
shines on the dump, not on the *cote d'azur*
and not on the cloistered murals, to be sure.
– QUESTION REALITY. DEATH IS BACK. MIGUEL 141.

The section is headed by a pessimistic end-of-history epigraph
from MacNeice's 'Eclogue for Christmas': 'We shall go down like
palaeolithic man/ Before some new Ice Age or Ghengiz Khan';
and 'sun/shines on the dump' quotes *Autumn Journal* VIII: 'We
lived in Birmingham through the slump –/ Line your boots with a
piece of paper –/ Sunlight dancing on the rubbish dump'. The
MacNeice quotations and (as in some poems discussed in the pre-
vious essay) the death of the Atlantic shipping tradition allude to
modern endings, or evoke what modernity has ended. But a more
optimistic (Comic) ending also comes into view since 'now we
emerge from the industrial night' – which includes the latter's
effect on benighted Belfast. When the poem fast-forwards to the
millennium Mahon's post-historical, post-industrial nirvana has a
social contour, although the concluding enigmatic New York graffito
hints that 'the hot genes of the future' could produce something
more interesting than 'the last man'. 'Home' and the homeless of
New York haunt 'The Hudson Letter' which itself (continuing the
metaphor of ice and thaw) ends on a rhetorical question that anti-
cipates Comic reconciliation: 'When does the thaw begin?/ We have
been too long in the cold. – Take us in; take us in!' The collective
'we' of the poem speaks for all our lost souls – a reprise of the mush-
rooms' mute desire in Mahon's 'A Disused Shed in Co. Wexford'
– in their need and quest for a redeemed history.

Too much has been made, and too literally, of the different ways
in which Derek Mahon and Seamus Heaney figure home and his-
tory. Not only politics condition the fact that in some poems one
is attracted to the apocalyptic – though also redemptive – strain in
Protestant theology, the other to the transcendental mode of spilt
Catholicism. The point is that both structures are among those
culturally available. Thus the differences in historical imagination
between *The Hudson Letter* and *The Spirit Level* may be more
significant as regards form than content. Here I want to focus on
Heaney's ceasefire poem 'Tollund' dated September 1994, but con-
cepts and forms elsewhere in *The Spirit Level* help to interpret it.
Some poems roughly accord with White's definition of writing
history as Romance, that is, as 'a drama of self-identification sym-
bolised by the hero's transcendence of the world of experience, his
victory over it'.[57] The 'hero' may be individuals or groups or nations.
Where the Mahon voice desires the spirit to re-enter history, the

Heaney voice celebrates victories of the spirit over history: survival, being changed, the way or heart 'opening', the dove after the flood. A related structure (discussed elsewhere in this book as a 'pastoral' structure) is Heaney's tendency to bracket off history while reaffirming origins. Because his religious teleology finds its end in the beginning, his cycles differ from Yeats's. The gyre returns to an integrated and integrative starting-point, its circular movement sometimes explicated as the poem being 'foreknown' in the event. Similarly, one way in which Heaney nuances the word 'self' parallels – without necessarily invoking – the nationalist selfhood that precedes and overcomes history: 'deeper in themselves for having been there' ('Mycenae Lookout'), 'we sailed/Beyond ourselves' ('The Swing').

'Tollund', however, returns with a difference to the ground ('the old man-killing parishes') of Heaney's well-known poem 'The Tollund Man' which dates from the early 1970s. Written in a post-Catholic rather than post-Protestant religious idiom, the poem betokened another quest to redeem violent history. 'Tollund' begins with a sense of time and space travelled since that earlier powerful epiphany:

> That Sunday morning we had travelled far.
> We stood a long time out in Tollund Moss:
> The low ground, the swart water, the thick grass
> Hallucinatory and familiar.
>
> A path through Jutland fields. Light traffic sound.
> Willow bushes; rushes; bog-fir grags
> In a swept and gated farmyard; dormant quags.
> And silage under wraps in its silent mound.
>
> It could have been a still out of the bright
> 'Townland of Peace', that poem of dream farms
> Outside all contention. The scarecrow's arms
> Stood open opposite the satellite
>
> Dish in the paddock, where a standing stone
> Had been resituated and landscaped,
> With tourist signs in *futhark* runic script
> In Danish and in English. Things had moved on...

'Tollund', so aware of history 'moving on' and of its own history, revisits literary history in both contexts. Heaney alludes to poems by other Northern Irish poets; and perhaps, later, to the sculptor Carolyn Mulholland in his choice of the Ulster place-name 'Mulhollandstown' along with the writerly name 'Scribe' (although internal rhyme must have been a factor too). By explicitly invoking one poem, 'Townland of Peace', he signals the cross-cultural negotiations that 'Tollund' registers or sets in motion. 'Townland of Peace' is section III of John Hewitt's utopian sequence 'Freehold', written during the 1940s as an Ulster regionalist manifesto. The poem begins with its poet-speaker escaping from wartime Belfast and 'stepping...into' a timeless idyll:

> Once in a showery summer, sick of war,
> I strode the roads that slanted to Kilmore,
> that church-topped mound where half the tombstones wear
> my people's name...
> Thus walking dry or sheltered under trees,
> I stepped clean out of Europe into peace...
> The crooked apple trees beside the gate
> that almost touched the roadside with the weight
> of their clenched fruit, the dappled calves that browsed
> free in the netted sunlight...
> the farm unseen but loud with bucket and dog
> and voices moving in a leafy fog,
> gave neither hint nor prophecy of change...

'Townland of Peace' may have come into Heaney's mind because its images distinguish peace from war so simply and clearly, and because it explains how wartime circumstances stimulated the visionary new history for 'Ulster...my region' that emerges later in 'Freehold'. Heaney has been in dialogue with John Hewitt before, as in the Catholic-Protestant dialectic of 'The Other Side'.[58] Now he calls up Hewitt's ghost to help him review their shared literary-political conundrum of the North, its Janus-faces as territorial 'contention' and 'dream farms' (here Heaney encodes his own poems). Pastoral modes are also at issue: Heaney's manner of referring to 'Townland of Peace' places 'Tollund' itself as eclogue in time of war. A darker intertextual allusion lurks in 'silage under wraps in its silent mound'. Paul Muldoon's poem 'Christo's' (from *Meeting the British*, 1987) links 'unbiodegradable' – a metaphor for historical memory – black flags in the Irish countryside, at the time of the hunger strikes by IRA prisoners, with a deathly image of polythene-sheeted silage. The speaker prophesies that 'By the time we got to Belfast/the whole of Ireland would be under wraps'. The polarity between Muldoon's use of the wrap-artist Christo and Hewitt's Constable-like refuge (Heaney punningly applies the visual term 'still'), as well as Hewitt's own juxtaposition of war and peace, serves Heaney's reflection on ambiguous prospects.

This self-aware poem has an unusually ironical tone for Heaney as it seemingly tries to reconcile his most characteristic imagery with a contingent, urban, historical world that his imagination has often held at bay. 'Light traffic sound' is admitted, and the speaker acknowledges the taming of the wild, the translation of mythic history into heritage, into folk museum: the standing stone 'resituated and landscaped'. The next quatrain says: 'it was user-friendly outback'. To similar effect, Heaney revisits (implicitly Irish) linguistic politics and his own poetic politics of the English language, when he notices '*futhark* runic script' recruited for 'tourist signs… In Danish and in English'. Irony shades into ambivalence where both sets of images acquire a particularly parodic contour, as in Heaney's version of body–doubles. And while the arms of the scarecrow may be 'open' to 'the satellite//Dish in the paddock', they are 'opposite' as well. The last man or liberal man is being quizzed from a different perspective to Mahon's: from that of prehistory not post-history.

   I would argue that 'Tollund' also takes a semi-Ironic attitude to history in Hayden White's sense. Its structures contrast, for instance, with the Metaphorical trope that governs Heaney's (related) lecture 'Frontiers of Writing', and which issues in a Romantic emplotment and Organicist mode of argument. Here Heaney presents a symbolically integrated vision of "Ireland" as a quincunx of poetic towers (Spenser, Yeats, Joyce, MacNeice, and the round tower of 'prior Irelandness'). Conscious that 'there is not yet a political structure to reflect this poetic diagram' he effectively "ends" with a plea to unionists 'to make their imagination press back against the pressure of reality and re-enter the whole country of Ireland imaginatively, if not constitutionally, through the northern point of the quincunx'.[59] This is another literary (and nationalist) way of writing Irish history. 'Tollund' may be literary too, but it is also literature. Other poets are much more subtly inscribed into a potential settlement, and the tensions within its modes and troping make it more complex (and exemplify poetry's capacities) as historical explanation and theory. The poem locates itself on the verge of Comic reconciliation, Contextual argument, Liberal ideological implication. It is as if Heaney substitutes *realpolitik* for the *aisling* 'politics of destiny' and the nationalist imperative of 'the whole country'. In so doing, he introduces into his parabolic landscape not only the nationalist/unionist quarrel but also the two-hundred year old epistemological quarrel between the Enlightenment and Romanticism. 'Tollund' is at once conditioned by, and alert to, the impact of these quarrels on historical consciousness and historical narratives (in their poetic guises, too). Hence the sense that it constitutes a more secular vision than does 'The Tollund Man', although one still haunted by 'hallucinatory' mystery, by the possibility of remaking Metaphor in different terms.

The last two quatrains may not resolve all ambiguities and ambivalences:

It could have been Mulhollandstown or Scribe.
The byroads had their names on them in black
And white; it was user-friendly outback
Where we stood footloose, at home beyond the tribe,

More scouts than strangers, ghosts who'd walked abroad
Unfazed by light, to make a new beginning
And make a go of it, alive and sinning,
Ourselves again, free-willed again, not bad.

The positive elements here are the coincidence between name and place ('right names' have been politically significant in Heaney's work), the rhetorically persuasive 'new beginning', the atmosphere of dawn after dark, the substitution of 'at home beyond the tribe' for 'lost,/ Unhappy and at home' in 'The Tollund Man', the speaker's commitment to 'making a go of it', perhaps simply to 'making'. At the same time, the more the poem generalises, the more elusive its horizon becomes: in what sense do the 'we' who stand 'footloose, at home beyond the tribe' represent the advance-guard for a post-tribal future? And how has the ceasefire placed them in this position? But perhaps the imprecision as to what or which 'self' has achieved 'free will' is deliberate – an invitation or a choice once again, rather than an arrival. Nonetheless, Heaney's ending leaves some earlier images in a state of Metonymic suspension. Transcendence is more asserted than symbolically realised, and this affects the language of the last line where a slippage into nationalist vocabulary (conscious or unconscious?) precedes the throwaway conclusion (bathos or understatement?) The phrase 'Ourselves again' appears to conflate Ourselves Alone and 'A Nation Once Again'. Perhaps it is fitting that subtextual irresolution should characterise an "end" that cannot yet generate the language, the tropes and modes, for 'a new beginning': for Northern Ireland as a townland of peace rather than a centre for conflict studies.

The way in which women are written into endings and beginnings would be a large topic in itself. I have already mentioned the emblematic mother and child; *Eureka Street* includes a lesbian love-affair as well as a baby and male maternal surrogacy. Correspondingly, perhaps, Medbh McGuckian's *Captain Lavender* arrives late on this stage where history and poetry meet. Some of the poems, indeed, were provoked by her omission from Frank Ormsby's anthology, *A Rage for Order: Poetry of the Northern Ireland Troubles* (1992). Hence *Captain Lavender* 's pointed epigraph, Picasso's remark in 1944: 'I have not painted the war...but I have no doubt

310 POETRY AND THE END OF HISTORY

that the war is in these paintings I have done'. Although *Captain Lavender* was completed before the first IRA ceasefire – the book appeared in November 1994 – the poems respond to the escalating violence of 1993 together with the hopes for peace raised by the Hume-Adams rapprochement and by the Downing Street Declaration (December 1993). Either of the latter might be 'the treaty that moves all tongues' in 'The War Degree':

> You smell of time as a Bible smells of thumbs,
> a bank of earth alive with mahogany-coloured
> flowers – not time elaborately thrown away,
> (you wound yourself so thoroughly into life),
> but time outside of time, new pain, new secret,
> that I must re-fall in love with the shadow
> of your soul, drumming at the back of my skull.
>
> Tonight, when the treaty moves all tongues,
> I want to take the night out of you,
> the sweet Irish tongue in which
> death spoke and happiness wrote...

If McGuckian's poetry has been read by Ormsby and others as detached from contemporary history, it has equally been read as encoding a hidden 'women's history' in its half-sexual, half-aesthetic dialectic between male and female principles. Although the blurb of *Captain Lavender* promises that Part Two 'addresses the politics of the author's native province', McGuckian aficionados will not have expected upfront bulletins. What we get, to quote the blurb again, are 'extended metaphors of personal relations'. These offer a more erotic form of historical Romance than Heaney's. The mutual Otherness of Protestant and Catholic, North and South, is translated into a complex of desire, estrangement and lovemaking. The allusions to the Bible and 'drumming' and to 'the sweet Irish tongue' suggest that a Catholic woman (poet) may be addressing a Protestant male (poet) – perhaps a Protestant male "Ulster". This transgressive *aisling* begins in a temporal context which hints at a productive suspension or transcendence of history; although its spatial context rather disturbingly mingles indoor and outdoor, natural and unnatural features ('mahogany-coloured flowers'). The poem continues:

> a wartime, heart-stained autumn drove
> fierce half-bricks into the hedges; tree-muffled
> streets vanished in the lack of news.
> Like a transfusion made direct from arm
> to arm, birds call uselessly to each other
> in the sub-acid, wintry present. The pursed-up
> fragrances of self-fertile herbs
> hug defeat like a very future lover.

Now it is my name and not my number
that is nobody now, walking on a demolished
floor, where dreams have no moral.
And the door-kiss is night meeting night.

The concluding 'kiss' does not figure resolution (or even ceasefire) but ominously meshes love and death. Nor does 'night' go away but intensifies. It engulfs the 'life' evoked earlier in the poem to produce a ghostly limbo-world: an ethos of unbearably prolonged winter, blighted suburbs, the organic and inorganic at odds. Time has now become unproductively frozen in malign space. As for the reflexive theme of language, the movement of 'tongues' towards a mingling in sex or political dialogue or poetry is blocked by solipsism and sterility. Similarly, as regards the body there is doubleness ('arm to arm', a kiss as 'night meeting night') but no 'meeting', no life-giving exchange of blood, no birth. This absence of reciprocity immobilises history: a 'sub-acid wintry *present*' cannot reach 'a very *future* lover' (my italics). So Romance seems cheated of fulfilment by Tragedy (*Romeo and Juliet*). Here, too, McGuckian may question the historical optimism that informs a benedictory cadence in the last section of *Autumn Journal*: 'The future is the bride of what has been'. The phrase 'where dreams have no moral' more definitely shadows an earlier text – Yeats's 'In dreams begin responsibilities' – a precept that the locus of 'The War Degree' negates or denies.

As in other poems, McGuckian's syntax of images – which tropes 'The War Degree' as (frustrated) Metaphor – does not let the Enlightenment off lightly. She conceives history, and perhaps some poetry of history, as an impervious logocentric patriarch. The speaker of 'Credenza', a poem about the widow of a murder-victim says: 'war-talk sentences/act as if they had never been shot at' – although this echoes *Autumn Journal* XVI: 'my own/ Countrymen who shoot to kill and never/ See the victim's face become their own'. At the same time, McGuckian scrambles White's alignments to an unusual extent: the argument of 'The War Degree' inclines to Mechanism (as sin explains history for Mahon, failure of emotion explains it for McGuckian) and its ideological implication is Liberal. Despite all the bleakness, these apparent contradictions may create room for manoeuvre. Like Luke Gibbons, for example, McGuckian favours the '*symbolic* dimension in human action' – indeed, she may recognise no other. Yet her poetry's resistance to cognitive certainty (on the part of author or reader) includes resistance to clearcut politics. Here poetic history seems rather more consistent than history written poetically. Accordingly, the influence of cultural Catholicism on McGuckian's anti-Enlightenment aesthetic

need not determine the vision of her historical narratives, though
it may condition their structure.

Paul Muldoon takes the writing of poetic history furthest into
Irony. His poems also air the question, and are cited for the ques-
tion, as to whether history is constituted by narrative and narra-
tive by language: 'The trope of Irony...provides a linguistic
paradigm of a mode of thought which is radically self-critical with
respect not only to a given characterisation of the world of experi-
ence, but also to the very effort to capture adequately the truth of
things in language'.[60] Muldoon's verse-play *Six Honest Serving Men*
concerns a group of IRA volunteers who are not only at war with
the British, but mistrust each other to such an extent that, in a
typical grisly pun, 'The point must be driven home' with a Black
and Decker. The six volunteers double up until they coalesce into
a single mutilated and mutilating figure. Like 'The War Degree',
the play "narrates" the status quo *ante* the ceasefires (a poem in
Hay, 'Third Epistle to Timothy', may be Muldoon's mature
reflection on the "peace process") as a condition of neurotic stasis.
However, Muldoon's Ironical troping, Satirical emplotment and
Contextualist mode of argument differ from McGuckian's, although
his implied ideology also appears Liberal. What makes the play's
argument Contextualist is that Muldoon both focuses on the internal
dynamics of a political group and connects these with off-stage
political players and forces.

Muldoon is another poet who takes a cyclical view of history,
except that here its cycles denote entrapment rather than alterna-
tion or a return to origins. Kate, a Cathleen ní Houlihan persona
fought over by men, endlessly plays a record of 'I'll Take You Home
Again, Kathleen'. On one level this refrain ironically figures the
unfulfilled nationalist politics of destiny; on another, refrain itself
as circularity figures the structure of nationalist historical con-
sciousness. One character, 'Joe Ward', continues to act out the para-
military destiny already determined for him in 'Anseo', Muldoon's
poem of the late 1970s. 'Anseo' is a parable of how narratives of
history combine with other social forces to make history repeat
itself. Thus the patriotically memorial name 'Joseph Mary Plunkett
Ward' proves predictive. Scene XXX of *Six Honest Serving Men*,
set in 'the safe house', is an acrimonious exchange about versions
of recent and longer-term history. It seems no accident that the
language makes connections, not always intended by its speakers,
between the mutilated body, the impaired mind, and the desire to
silence unacceptable narratives:

CLERY   Is your head cut? You let *both* Mugabe
             and Taggart go? Is your head bloody cut?
MCANESPIE   You listen to me, Clery, you hoor's git.
             Mugabe spent two years in the same kip
             as The Chief. They were both on the blanket.
CLERY   And once Mugabe got out of the Kesh
             he was *under* the blanket...
MCANESPIE   Hold your wheesht...
CLERY   Along with Pearse, Joseph Mary Plunkett,
             Connolly, Clarke, Ceannt – and maybe Clark Kent
             and Lois Lane – as well as Kiss Me Kate.
MCANESPIE   That's sacrilege, Clery. I swear to God
             I'll personally cut off your gonads
             and stuff them down your throat.
CLERY   I'll have to hum
             along to the tune of 'I'll Take You Home...'

Through Clery, Muldoon parodies Yeats's 'Easter 1916', with its
concluding litany of leaders of the Easter Rising executed by the
British. 'Connolly, Clarke, Ceannt' modulates by way of assonance
into quite another frame of reference. Rather than a postmodernist
doodle, this (to judge by McAnespie's reaction) seems as pointed as
a Black and Decker. Hayden White's view of Romance and Satire
as antitheses fits certain dialectics between Heaney and Muldoon,
Satire being 'a drama of diremption, a drama dominated by the
apprehension that man is ultimately a captive of the world rather
than its master'.[61] Yet if Muldoonian history has usually been troped
as Irony, it may be what Kenneth Burke terms 'dialectical irony',
irony as a dynamic of analysis, which 'derives from each term's
failure to see its part in the "total development"' rather than rela-
tivistic irony.[62] To put it another way, while Muldoon rejects a
teleology of history in general, and of Irish history in particular, he
does not lack a *theory* of history, which his narrative-parables serve
to support and explain. They also, as here, decode the political
unconscious of other historical texts. Thus Muldoon might be the
Marxist theorist rather than postmodernist playboy among Northern
Ireland's poet-historians. The *Honest Serving Men* of his title involve
another kind of irony given their origins in the proverbial rhyme: 'I
keep six honest serving men/ (They taught me all I knew);/ Their
names are What and Why and When/ And How and Where and
Who.' Since in Muldoon's play these agents of empirical enquiry
are kept busy and bewildered working out who has betrayed whom,
they hardly give cheer to positivist historiography. Nonetheless, the
inability of the play's characters to 'capture adequately the truth of
things in language' provides its own clarifications. In quasi-Brechtian
style, the dialogic sonnets of *Six Honest Serving Men* provoke its

audience to ask deeper questions about the mechanism of traps. Ciaran Carson's historical enquiry is less systematic than Muldoon's, more inclined to relish narrative for its own sake. He presents history not as one damned thing after another, but as one blessed story after another, always different, always fluid. To quote his 'Hamlet', 'time/ Is conversation'. Thus Carson's sequence 'Opera', based on the radio-operator's alphabet, promises order only to deliver its opposite. The speaker/writer of 'Romeo' does not really lament the appalling difficulty of imposing textual coherence on Irish history:

> Romeo was not built in a day, not to speak of Romulus or Remus –
> Cain and Abel – why Protestants are called Billy – and Catholics are
>   Seamus.

> It took a school lab labyrinth of history to produce these garbled notes
> In careful fountain-pen. The arrowed maps of North and South, the
>   essays filled with quotes...

> It's all a tangled tagliatelle linguini Veronese that I'm trying to unravel
> From its strands of DNA and language. Perhaps I need a spirit level.

Carson's method, more truly "narrative" than that of the other poets, parallels what White terms a Formist mode of explanation: one that magnifies the trees at the wood's expense (or the words at the line's?). Formist historiography 'depicts...the variety, colour, and vividness of the historical field', 'the uniqueness of...different agents, agencies, and acts'. Being 'dispersive rather than integrative', it may lack 'conceptual "precision"'.[63] Carson's joke against Heaney ('spirit level') jokes about conceptual precision too. That an Anarchist ideological implication belongs with Formism in White's scheme also seems to fit. However, Carson's emplotment breaks productively with the scheme by being more often Comic or Satirical than Romantic (though there may be Romance in his implied attitude to his materials). 'Jacta Est Alea' plays Northern Irish history as Comedy, or perhaps farce, since reconciliation takes the paradoxical and ludicrous shape of continuing impasse, the latter being regarded with less gravity than in the other poems I have discussed:

> It was one of those puzzling necks of the wood where the South was
>   in the North, the way
> The double cross in a jigsaw loops into its matrix, like the border was
>   a *clef*

> With arbitrary teeth indented in it. Here, it cut clean across the plastic
> Lounge of The Half-Way House; my heart lay in the Republic

> While my head was in the Six, or so I was inclined. You know that
>   drinker's
> Angle, elbow-propped, knuckles to his brow like one of the Great
>   Thinkers?

He's staring at my throat in the Power's mirror, debating whether
He should open up a lexicon with me: the price of beer or steers, the
    weather.
We end up talking about talk. We stagger on the frontier. He is pro.
    I am con.
Siamese-like, drunken, inextricable, we wade into the Rubicon.

Once again, a doubled and fragmented body is dispersed through
a poem. The narrative's references to 'neck', 'teeth', 'throat' and
mirror insinuate a subtextual vampire-narrative, a hint of Gothic
horror. Underlying violence bubbles up into the euphemistic
'debating whether/ He should open up a lexicon with me'. Festively,
however, drink and talk avert open conflict and hence Tragedy,
even if they do not precipitate a full Comic resolution. Different
kinds of 'talk', spoken and literary, contribute to Carson's 'tangled'
data, although this does posit the integrative concept that language
is an arena, rather than a reflection, of Northern Irish contention.
However, if Carson's puns put 'lexicon' in the foreground of the
poem, this does not detach the combat between 'pro' and 'con'
from referentiality; rather, it designates a symbolic domain consti-
tuted by language, by different cultural codes, as that to which the
combat 'refers'. Here Irony again functions dialectically and con-
structively, and hardly requires Romance to rescue it from the
prison-house of language. 'Talks about talks', like other clichés in
the poem, comes alive to provide a historical theory and, if not an
ending, a contingent 'ending up'. 'Jacta Est Alea', of course, repeats
as farce a famous historical and textual moment of decision. Carson's
gloss on the Latin tag contrasts with the solemner sense of forking
historical paths at the end of *Autumn Journal*: 'Tonight we sleep/
On the banks of Rubicon – the die is cast'. Similarly, he lightens
up the imagined negotiation between Catholic and Protestant in
Heaney's 'The Other Side', which ends with the former's symbolic
proposal to 'talk about the weather//or the price of grass-seed'. Yet
Comic emplotment, as of a novel such as *Eureka Street*, can function
as historical critique in Northern Irish contexts. Rather than being
Tragically or Romantically posed/opposed, our familiar doubled pair
become 'Siamese-like, inextricable' – Self and Other identical and
interdependent in their obdurate differences. Whether some histor-
ical narratives take themselves too seriously is a serious question.
    Wading into the Rubicon seems a suitably open-ended image to
end on. When compiling *A Rage for Order*, Frank Ormsby had an
intuition that all the Troubles poems had been written. As with the
end of history, this does not mean there will be no more Troubles
poems. It does mean that the collective script might be changing in

response to some mysterious referent out there. Hence the accentuated tendency for poets to quote and revise not only earlier poets and each other but also their former textual selves. Yet, even when the ceasefires influence their formulations of the historical moment, none of them rules out apocalypse. We still splash about in the Rubicon. It may be significant that the poems I have cited bring all White's classifications into play, and that their emplotment should be finely poised between Tragedy and Satire (which anticipate 'an eternal return of the Same in the Different') and Romance and Comedy (which 'stress the emergence of new forces or conditions').[64] The variety of ways in which history is narrated and its end conceived – whether popularly, academically, or poetically – suggests the complexity of the story or stories of Northern Ireland. And poetry's special ability not just to deploy, but to explore and mutually complicate, tropes/modes, illuminates the neglected area of "mentalities". Poetry penetrates to those zones where, as regards Ireland, the epistemology of history and the history of epistemology are peculiarly intertwined. Some people read Irish history as poetry. I prefer to read poetry as history. As such, it neither excludes nor favours Enlightenment cognitive structures. Perhaps poetry's counterpart to the historian's 'dialogue with evidence' is the intertextual dialogue between poems. Perhaps, too, poetry's historical acumen is deeply tested by time since all its structural elements are on the line. Mysteriously, how history judges poetry depends on how poetry judges history.

NOTES

Preface: A Note on Posterity *(pp.9-22)*

1. Barbara Herrnstein Smith, *Contingencies of Value* (Cambridge, Mass. & London, 1991), p.15.
2. *Contingencies of Value*, p.15.
3. In ' "Take Down this Book": Yeats's Early Volumes, 1895-99', lecture given at the Yeats Summer School, Sligo, August 1996.
4. Louis MacNeice, 'Poetry Today', in (ed.) Alan Heuser, *Selected Literary Criticism of Louis MacNeice* (Oxford, 1987), pp.10-44 (13).
5. W.H. Auden, *The Dyer's Hand and Other Essays* (London, 1963), p.52.
6. Donald Hall, *Poetry and Ambition* (Ann Arbor, Michigan, 1988), p.4.
7. John Ashbery, Introduction to (ed.) Donald Allen, *The Collected Poems of Frank O'Hara* (New York, 1971), p.ix.
8. (Ed.) Donald Allen, *The Selected Poems of Frank O'Hara* (New York, 1974), p.v.
9. *Selected Poems of Frank O'Hara*, p.xiii.
10. W.B. Yeats, 'A General Introduction for My Work', *Essays and Introductions* (London, 1961), pp.509-26 (522).
11. Kenneth Koch, *The Art of Poetry* (New York, 1996), p.192.
12. Paul Muldoon, 'The Point of Poetry' (a BBC Radio script for Northern Ireland schools in the late 1980s), *Princeton University Library Chronicle*, 59/3 (Spring 1998), pp.503-16 (505).
13. Geoff Ward, *Language Poetry and the American Avant-garde* (Keele, 1993), p.17.
14. Sean O'Brien, *The Deregulated Muse: Essays on Contemporary British and Irish Poetry* (Newcastle upon Tyne, 1998), p.12.
15. Peter Childs, *The Twentieth Century in Poetry: A critical survey* (London, 1999), p.180.
16. Sven Birkerts, *The Gutenberg Elegies: The Fate of Reading in an Electronic Age* (London, 1994), p.191.
17. Peter McDonald, 'Louis MacNeice's Posterity', *Princeton University Library Chronicle*, 59/3 (Spring 1998), pp.376-97 (376-7, 97).
18. Donald Hall, *Their Ancient Glittering Eyes: Remembering Poets and More Poets* (New York, 1992), pp.5-7.
19. See Dana Gioia, *Can Poetry Matter? Essays on Poetry and American Culture* (Saint Paul, Minnesota, 1992), pp.1-24.
20. Fredric Jameson, ' "End of Art or End of History"?', in Jameson, *The Cultural Turn: Selected Writings on the Postmodern 1983-1998* (London, 1998), pp.73-92 (87).
21. Quoted by Hall, *Their Ancient Glittering Eyes*, p.26.
22. See Edward Thomas's First World War poem, 'This is no case of petty right or wrong': 'Dinned/ With war and argument I read no more/ Than in the storm smoking along the wind/ Athwart the wood.'

The Business of the Earth *(pp.23-51)*

1. Raymond Williams, *The Country and the City* (London, 1973), p.240.
2. *The Country and the City*, pp.245-6, 256, 261.

3. Citations of Edward Thomas's poetry are from (ed.) R. George Thomas, *The Collected Poems of Edward Thomas* (Oxford, 1978).

4. Williams, *The Country and the City*, p.260.

5. Robyn Eckersley, *Environmentalism and Political Theory: Toward an Ecocentric Approach* (London and New York, 1992), p.49.

6. *Environmentalism and Political Theory*, pp.182, 86.

7. Jonathan Bate, *Romantic Ecology: Wordsworth and the Environmental Tradition* (London, 1991), p.9.

8. *Romantic Ecology*, pp.10-11.

9. *Poetry Review*, 80/1 (Spring 1990), pp.3, 41.

10. Anne Buttimer, *Geography and the Human Spirit* (Baltimore and London, 1993), pp.8, 2-3.

11. Edward Thomas, *The South Country* (London, 1909, 1993), p.65.

12. Jose Harris, *Private Lives, Public Spirit: Britain 1870-1914* (London, 1993; rpt. 1994), p.42.

13. Edward Thomas, review of (ed.) Edward Marsh, *Georgian Poetry 1911-1912*, *Daily Chronicle*, 14 January 1913; reprinted in (ed.) Edna Longley, *A Language Not To Be Betrayed: Selected Prose of Edward Thomas* (Manchester, 1981), pp.112-13.

14. Samuel Hynes, *The Edwardian Turn of Mind* (New Jersey, 1968, 1991), pp.5, 63.

15. Harris, *Private Lives, Public Spirit*, p.252.

16. *Daily Chronicle*, 14 August 1905 and 30 August 1905; the second passage is excerpted in (ed.) Longley, *A Language Not To Be Betrayed*, pp.201-02.

17. Helen Thomas, *As It Was and World Without End* (London, 1956), p.115.

18. Hynes, *The Edwardian Turn of Mind*, p.126.

19. Thomas, *The South Country*, p.43.

20. Letter, 9 August 1908, in (ed.) R. George Thomas, *Letters from Edward Thomas to Gordon Bottomley* (London, 1968), p.167.

21. See Introduction to (ed.) Longley, *A Language Not To Be Betrayed*.

22. Edward Thomas, *Richard Jefferies* (London, 1909, 1978), p.294.

23. Edward Thomas, 'Some Country Books', from (ed.) Edward Thomas, *British Country Life in Autumn and Winter: The Book of the Open Air* (London, 1908); reprinted in (ed.) Longley, *A Language Not To Be Betrayed*, pp.162-65 (164).

24. Harris, *Private Lives, Public Spirit*, pp.5, 36.

25. Edward Thomas, *The Country* (London, 1913), p.21.

26. Thomas, *The South Country*, p.71.

27. Stan Smith, *Edward Thomas* (London, 1986), pp.18-19.

28. Smith, *Edward Thomas*, p.19.

29. Chapter 12 of *The South Country* is called 'Children of Earth'; see also p.161 and pp.18, 131-34, 148.

30. Thomas, *The South Country*, p.164.

31. *The South Country*, pp.121-22, 50.

32. 'Chalk Pits', *The Last Sheaf* (London, 1928), pp.27-28; and see Peter Coates: *Nature: Western Attitudes since Ancient Times* (London, 1998), p.176.

33. Thomas, *The South Country*, p.26, 19.

34. Edward O. Wilson, *The Diversity of Life* (London, 1993, 1994), p.330.

35. Thomas, *The South Country*, p.20.

36. Wilson, *The Diversity of Life*, pp.332-33.

37. Thomas, *The South Country*, pp.116, 110.

38. (Ed.) Andrew Dobson, *The Green Reader* (London, 1991), p.8.
39. Thomas, *The South Country*, p.115.
40. Robert Wells, 'Edward Thomas and England', in (ed.) Jonathan Barker, *The Art of Edward Thomas* (Bridgend, 1987), p.71.
41. Edward Thomas, 'Tipperary', in *The Last Sheaf* (London, 1928); reprinted in (ed.) Longley, *A Language Not To Be Betrayed*, pp.231-40 (232).
42. Wells, 'Edward Thomas and England', pp.72, 66.
43. 'Diary of Edward Thomas' 1 January – 8 April 1917, Appendix C, *The Collected Poems of Edward Thomas*, pp.481, 472.
44. David Gervais, *Literary Englands: Versions of 'Englishness' in Modern Writing* (Cambridge, 1993), p.41.
45. John Barrell, *The Dark Side of the Landscape: The Rural Poor in English Painting 1730-1840* (Cambridge, 1980).
46. (Ed.) W.J.T. Mitchell, *Landscape and Power* (Chicago & London, 1994), p.17.
47. Thomas, *The South Country*, p.55.
48. John Barrell, 'Being is Perceiving', in (ed.) Barrell, *Poetry, Language and Politics* (Manchester, 1988), pp.126-27.
49. Smith, *Edward Thomas*, p.67.
50. Smith, *Edward Thomas*, p.44.
51. Williams, *The Country and the City*, p.259.
52. Entry of 23 March 1917, 'Diary of Edward Thomas', *Collected Poems of Edward Thomas*, p.478.
53. Edward Thomas, *The Heart of England* (London, 1906), p.4.
54. Smith, *Edward Thomas*, p.84.
55. Gervais, *Literary Englands*, p.43.
56. John Lucas, *England and Englishness* (London, 1990), p.6.
57. Harris, *Private Lives, Public Spirit*, pp.18-19.
58. Edward Thomas, review of (ed.) John Cooke, *The Dublin Book of Irish Verse*, in *Morning Post*, 6 January 1910.
59. 'That he could himself embrace his Welshness and yet at the same time not feel the strain of reconciling it with his idea of England testifies to the power of ideology to contain contradictions.' Smith, *Edward Thomas*, p.15.
60. Thomas, *The South Country*, p.19.
61. Edward Thomas, 'England', in *The Last Sheaf* (London, 1928); reprinted in (ed.) Longley, *A Language Not To Be Betrayed*, pp.222-31 (231).
62. Letter, 11 February 1916, *Letters to Gordon Bottomley*, p.259.
63. Smith, *Edward Thomas*, p.66 *ff.*
64. Eckersley, *Environmentalism and Political Theory*, pp.97-117.
65. Edward Thomas, 'George Meredith', *A Literary Pilgrim in England* (London, 1917); excerpted in (ed.) Longley, *A Language Not To Be Betrayed*, pp.36-37 (37).

The Poetics of Celt and Saxon *(pp.52-89)*

1. Tom Paulin, 'Laureate of the Free Market? Ted Hughes', in Paulin, *Minotaur: Poetry and the Nation State* (London, 1992), pp.252-75 (252).
2. Michael Parker, *Seamus Heaney: The Making of a Poet* (London, 1993), pp.44-45.
3. See Hildegard L.C. Tristram, 'Celtic in Linguistic Taxonomy in the Nineteenth Century', in (ed.) Terence Brown, *Celticism* (Amsterdam, 1996), pp.35-60 (60).

4. See (ed.) Howard Gaskill, James Macpherson, *The Poems of Ossian and Related Works* (Edinburgh, 1996).

5. Clare O'Halloran, 'Irish Re-creations of the Gaelic Past: The Challenge of Macpherson's Ossian', in *Past and Present*, 124 (August 1989), p.70, p.95.

6. Joep Leerssen, 'Celticism', (ed.) Brown, *Celticism*, p.3. Leerssen used the expression 'impervious to paradigm-shifts' in a lecture at Queen's University, Belfast, March 1999.

7. For the history and definition of the term see Leerssen, (ed.) Brown, *Celticism*, pp.6-7; Chapter 6, 'The Question of Celticism', W.J. Mc Cormack, *Ascendancy and Tradition in Anglo-Irish Literary History from 1789 to 1939* (Oxford, 1985), pp.219-38.

8. See (eds.) Mark Thornton Burnett and Ramona Wray, *Shakespeare and Ireland: History, Politics, Culture* (Houndmills, Basingstoke, 1997), *passim*.

9 See Hugh Kearney, 'Contested Ideas of Nationhood 1800-1995', *Irish Review*, 20 (Winter/Spring 1997), pp.1-22 (18).

10. Frederic E. Faverty, *Matthew Arnold the Ethnologist* (reprinted New York, 1968), pp.38-40.

11. Tristram, (ed.) Brown, *Celticism*, p.58.

12. Lloyd and Jennifer Laing, *Celtic Britain and Ireland: The Myth of the Dark Ages* (Blackrock, Co. Dublin, 1990), pp.95, 179, 154. And see (eds.) Paul Graves-Brown, Sian Jones, Clive Gamble, *Cultural Identity and Archaeology: The Construction of European Communities* (London, 1996) *passim*.

13. *The Guardian*, Friday 13 March 1998, p.6. James has since published *The Atlantic Celts: Ancient People or Modern Invention?* (London, 1999).

14. Andrew P. Fitzpatrick, '"Celtic" Iron Age Europe: The theoretical basis', *Cultural Identity and Archaeology*, pp.236-55 (251).

15. Timothy Champion, 'The Celt in Archaeology', (ed.) Brown, *Celticism*, pp.61-78 (74-75).

16. See (ed.) R.H. Soper, *The Complete Works of Matthew Arnold*, 3 (Michigan, 1962), pp.291-395.

17. See Faverty, *Matthew Arnold*, Chapter 3, 'The Saxon Philistine', pp.41-75.

18. Patrick Sims-Williams, 'The Invention of Celtic Poetry', (ed.) Brown, *Celticism*, pp.87-124 (106-10).

19. See Ernest Renan, *Oeuvres Complètes*, 3 (Paris, 1948), pp.252-301.

20. Joep Leerssen, *Remembrance and Imagination: Patterns in the Historical and Literary Representation of Ireland in the Nineteenth Century* (Cork, 1996), pp.189-91.

21. Benedict Anderson, *Imagined Communities: Reflections on the Origin and spread of Nationalism* (London, 1983), p.19.

22. Leerssen, *Remembrance and Imagination*, pp.35-38; 'Celticism', *Celticism*, (ed.) Brown, pp.16, 20; Malcolm Chapman, *The Celts: The Construction of a Myth* (London, 1992), p.3.

23. John Collis, 'Celts and Politics', *Cultural Identity and Archaeology*, pp.167-78 (176).

24. Gil Jouanard, 'L'Imaginaire, c'est l'Irlande', *L'Imaginaire, c'est l'Irlande* (Montpellier, 1996), p.8. Quoted by Wesley Hutchinson, work in progress, 'Espaces de l'imaginaire unioniste'.

25. Gerhard Heimler, 'Germany's Land of Desire', *Books Ireland*, 197 (September 1996), p.203; Robert O'Byrne. 'Land of Poetry and Purity?', *Irish Times*, 13 November 1996, p.17.

26. John Lichfield, 'Lost in France', *Independent on Sunday*, 30 November

1997, Review, p.13.
27. L.P. Curtis Jr., *Anglo-Saxons and Celts: A Study of Anti-Irish Prejudice in Victorian England* (Bridgeport, Connecticut, 1968), p.64.
28. Sheridan Gilley, 'English Attitudes to the Irish in Britain, 1789-1900', in (ed.) Colin Holmes, *Immigrants and Minorities in British Society* (London, 1978), pp.81-110 (96-98); and see R.F. Foster, 'Paddy and Mr Punch', in Foster, *Paddy and Mr Punch* (London, 1993), pp.171-94.
29. Christopher Harvie, 'Anglo-Saxons into Celts: The Scottish Intellectuals 1760-1930', (ed.) Brown, *Celticism,* pp.231-56 (240-1, 256).
30. Chris Morash, 'Celticism: Between Race and Culture', *Irish Review,* 20 (Winter/Spring 1997), pp.29-36 (33-5).
31. See Aodán MacPóilin, ' "Spiritual Beyond the Ways of Men": Images of the Gael', *Irish Review,* 16 (Autumn/Winter 1994), pp.1-22.
32. Morash, 'Celticism: Between Race and Culture', p.36.
33. Robert Fisk, *In Time of War: Ireland, Ulster and the Price of Neutrality 1939-45* (London, 1983), p.332.
34. See Edward A. Hagan, 'The Aryan Myth: A Nineteenth-Century Anglo-Irish Will to Power', (eds.) Tadgh Foley and Seán Ryder, *Ideology and Ireland in the Nineteenth Century* (Dublin, 1998), pp.197-205.
35. See Reiner Luyken, 'Celtic as a Secret Weapon', *Irish Literary Supplement,* Spring 1998, p.5 (first printed in *Die Zeit,* 26 July 1996).
36. Gonzalo Ruiz Zapatero, 'Celts and Iberians', *Cultural Identity and Archaeology,* pp.179-95 (187).
37. See John O'Donohue, *Anam Cara: Spiritual Wisdom from the Celtic World* (London, 1997), *passim.*
38. Donald E. Meek, 'Modern Celtic Christianity', (ed.) Brown, *Celticism,* pp.143-57 (148).
39. John Mackinnon Robertson, *The Celt and the Saxon: A Study in Sociology* (London, 1897), p.xiii.
40. See Dennis Kennedy, *The Widening Gulf: Northern Attitudes to the Independent Irish State 1919-49* (Belfast, 1988), p.36.
41. John Hewitt, 'Planter's Gothic' and 'The Bitter Gourd: Some Problems of the Ulster Writer', in (ed.) Tom Clyde, *Ancestral Voices: The Selected Prose of John Hewitt* (Belfast, 1987), pp.1-33 (8-9); pp.108-21 (109, 120).
42. Terence Brown, *Ireland's Literature: Selected Essays* (Mullingar, 1988), pp.9-10.
43. James Barkley Woodburn, *The Ulster Scot: His History and Religion* (London, 1914), pp.17, 397, 396.
44. 'Bitter Gourd', *Ancestral Voices,* p.111, pp.113-14.
45. See R.F. Foster, 'Protestant Magic: W.B. Yeats and the Spell of Irish History', *Paddy and Mr Punch,* pp.212-32; (ed.) W.J. Mc Cormack, 'Irish Gothic and After', in (ed.) Seamus Deane, *Field Day Anthology of Irish Writing* (Derry, 1991), pp.831-949.
46. 'Planter's Gothic', *Ancestral Voices,* p.15.
47. Harvie, (ed.) Brown, *Celticism,* p.243.
48. Louis MacNeice, *The Poetry of W.B. Yeats* (Oxford, 1941; London, 1967), p.52.
49. Murray G.H. Pittock, *Poetry and Jacobite Politics in Eighteenth-Century Britain and Ireland* (Cambridge, 1994), p.184.
50. Colin Graham, *Ideologies of Epic: Nation, Empire and Victorian Poetry* (Manchester, 1998), pp.113-14.

322 NOTES

51. Roy Hattersley, 'The terrible beauty born of doom and gloom', *The Guardian*, 17 July 1995.
52. Sam Hanna Bell, *Erin's Orange Lily and Summer Loanen and Other Stories* (Belfast, 1996), p.125.
53. See Edna Longley, 'What do Protestants Want?', *Irish Review*, 20 (Winter/Spring 1997), pp.104-20.
54. Robert McLiam Wilson, *Eureka Street* (London, 1996), p.176.
55. In 'Espaces de l'imaginaire unioniste'.
56. Pittock, *Poetry and Jacobite Politics*, p.182; Pittock, *Spectrum of Decadence: The Literature of the 1890s* (London, 1993), p.86.
57. John Hewitt, '"The Northern Athens" and after' in J.C. Beckett et al, *Belfast: The Making of the City 1800-1914* (Belfast, 1983), pp.71-82 (79).
58. See Edna Longley, 'Defending Ireland's Soul: Protestant Writers and Irish Nationalism after Independence', Longley, *The Living Stream: Literature and Revisionism in Ireland* (Newcastle upon Tyne, 1994), pp.130-49; (ed.) Frank Ormsby, *The Collected Poems of John Hewitt* (Belfast, 1991), p.581n.
59. See Hewitt's bitter memoir, 'From Chairmen and Committee Men, Good Lord Deliver us', (ed.) Clyde, *Ancestral Voices*, pp.48-55.
60. (Ed.) Ormsby, *Collected Poems*, p.590n.
61. (Ed.) Ormsby, *Collected Poems*, p.590n.
62. See Samuel Beckett, 'Recent Irish Poetry', first published in *The Bookman* (August, 1934), reprinted (ed.) Seamus Deane, *Field Day Anthology of Irish Writing* (Derry, 1991), 3, pp.244-48 (244).
63. John Wilson Foster, 'Getting the North: Yeats and Northern Nationalism', (eds.) Warwick Gould & Edna Longley, *Yeats Annual*, 12 (London, 1996), pp.180-212 (184).
64. See Edna Longley, ' "It is time that I wrote my will"': Anxieties of Influence and Succession', *Yeats Annual*, 12, pp.138-39.
65. D.P. Moran writing on 'The Future of the Irish Nation', *New Ireland Review* (February 1899), quoted by Deirdre Toomey, 'Moran's Collar: Yeats and Irish Ireland', *Yeats Annual*, 12, p.51.
66. W.B. Yeats, letter to *The Leader* (edited by Moran), 26 August 1900, (eds.) Warwick Gould, John Kelly & Deirdre Toomey, *Collected Letters of W.B. Yeats*, 2 (Oxford, 1997), pp.564, 568.
67. See W.B. Yeats, 'The Celtic Element in Literature', *Essays and Introductions* (London, 1961), pp.173-88.
68. Declan Kiberd, *Inventing Ireland* (London, 1996), pp.316-26.
69. See Kiberd's Field Day pamphlet, *Anglo-Irish Attitudes* (Derry, 1984).
70. Letter to George Russell, ?April 1904, (ed.) Allan Wade, *The Letters of W.B. Yeats* (London, 1954), p.434.
71. Seamus Deane, *Celtic Revivals: Essays in Modern Irish Literature 1880-1980* (London, 1985), p.27; Deane, *Strange Country* (London, 1997), pp.19, 88.
72. *Strange Country*, pp.53, 110, 181.
73. *Strange Country*, p.171.
74. Seamus Deane, *Reading in the Dark* (London, 1996), p.57.
75. Review of *Reading in the Dark*, *Independent on Sunday*, 1 September 1996.
76. George Boyce, '"They Have Got Yeats"': Asking some more of the right questions about Literature and Politics in Ireland', *Text and Context*, 3 (Autumn 1988), p.48.
77. Neil Rhodes, 'Bridegrooms to the Goddess', (eds.) Burnett and Wray, *Shakespeare and Ireland*, pp.152-72 (153, 161, 167, 160).

78. Paulin, *Minotaur*, pp.252, 266.

79. Ted Hughes, 'Notes on Shakespeare', in Hughes, *Winter Pollen: Occasional Prose* (London, 1994), p.110.

80. Seamus Heaney, 'Feeling into Words', *Preoccupations: Selected Prose 1968-1978* (London, 1980), p.57.

81. Robert Graves, *The White Goddess* (London, 1961 edn), pp.14, 476.

82. *The White Goddess*, pp.151, 156, 153, 157.

83. 'On a New Work in the English Tongue'/After reading *Birthday Letters*, Seamus Heaney dedicates this personal tribute to the poet laureate, *Sunday Times* Books section, 11 October 1998, p.7.

84. Heaney, *Preoccupations*, pp.159-60, 164-65, 150-51, 159.

85. *Preoccupations*, pp.154, 158-59.

86. Quoted by Rhodes, 'Bridegrooms to the Goddess', *Shakespeare and Ireland*, p.157.

87. 'Bridegrooms to the Goddess', p.152.

88. Heaney, *Preoccupations*, pp.207-10 (209).

89. Hughes, *Winter Pollen*, pp.368-71.

90. (Eds.) Seamus Heaney & Ted Hughes, *The School Bag* (London, 1997), pp.568-9.

91. Rhodes, 'Bridegrooms to the Goddess', *Shakespeare and Ireland*, pp. 167-68.

92. Heaney, Hughes, *The School Bag*, p.xvii.

93. Pittock, preface to *Poetry and Jacobite Politics*.

94. Rhodes, 'Bridegrooms to the Goddess', *Shakespeare and Ireland*, p.167.

95. W.B. Yeats, 'The Hosting of the Sidhe', *The Wind Among the Reeds*.

Pastoral Theologies *(pp.90-133)*

1. See Jonathan Bate, *Romantic Ecology* (London & New York, 1991), p.19; Lawrence Buell, *The Environmental Imagination: Thoreau, Nature Writing and the Formation of American Culture* (Cambridge, Mass. & London, 1995), p.33.

2. E.g. comparisons with early Christian poetry in Irish or with *Dinnseanchas*, the lore of prominent places, whose names are explained by legends linked to them by pseudo-etymological techniques.

3. See Seamus Heaney, 'In the Country of Convention', *Preoccupations: Selected Prose 1968-1978* (London, 1980), pp.173-80.

4. It is remarkable how many Irish as well as English poets have paid tribute to Clare: e.g., Patrick Kavanagh's 'Mary' ('I think of poor John Clare's beloved'); Michael Longley's poem 'Journey out of Essex'; various writings by Tom Paulin, such as 'John Clare in Babylon', *Minotaur: Poetry and the Nation State* (London, 1992), pp.47-55; and Seamus Heaney's lecture 'John Clare's Prog', *The Redress of Poetry* (London, 1995), pp.63-82.

5. See (eds.) John Wilson Foster and Helen C.G. Chesney, *Nature in Ireland: A Scientific and Cultural History* (Dublin, 1997), p.40.

6. *Nature in Ireland*, pp.401-3.

7. Dorinda Outram, 'The History of Natural History: Grand Narrative or Local Lore?', *Nature in Ireland*, p.469.

8. See Greta Jones, 'Catholicism, Nationalism and Science', *Irish Review*, 20 (Winter/Spring 1997), pp.47-61.

9. Outram, *Nature in Ireland*, p.465.

10. See Antoinette Quinn's valuable edition, *Patrick Kavanagh, Selected Poems* (Harmondsworth, 1996), p.113.

11. Patrick Kavanagh, *Catholic Standard*, 8 May 1942.

12. Antoinette Quinn, *Patrick Kavanagh: Born-Again Romantic* (Dublin, 1991), p.38.

13. Samuel Johnson, 'On Pastoral and Country Life' (1750), reprinted in (ed.) Bryan Loughrey, *The Pastoral Mode* (London and Basingstoke, 1984), pp.67-71.

14. Louis MacNeice, 'Experiences with Images', reprinted in (ed.) Alan Heuser, *Selected Literary Criticism of Louis MacNeice* (Oxford, 1987), p.155.

15. James H. Murphy, *Catholic Fiction and Social Reality in Ireland, 1873-1922* (Westport, Connecticut, 1997), p.3.

16. See Kevin Whelan, 'Town and Village in Ireland: a socio-cultural perspective', *Irish Review*, 5 (Autumn, 1988), pp.34-43.

17. Eamonn Hughes, ' "Town of Shadows": Representations of Belfast in Recent Fiction', *Religion and Literature*, 28/2-3 (Summer-Autumn 1996), p.151.

18. Fintan O'Toole, *Irish Times*, 12 January 1998, p.16.

19. Luke Gibbons, 'Coming out of Hibernation? The Myth of Modernisation in Irish Culture', in Gibbons, *Transformations in Irish Culture* (Cork, 1996), pp.92-93.

20. See Patrick Maume, *'Life that Exile': Daniel Corkery and the Search for Irish Ireland* (Belfast, 1993).

21. Daniel Corkery, *The Hidden Ireland: A Study of Gaelic Munster in the Eighteenth Century* (Dublin, 1924), pp.23, 125, 67.

22. Eg., Roddy Doyle, Dermot Bolger, Colm Tóibín, Robert McLiam Wilson. In *Eureka Street* (London, 1996) Wilson satirises 'pale-faced city boys [who] most obviously had never seen any of the hedges, berries or spades about which they wrote so passionately' (p.175).

23. See Michael Parker, *Seamus Heaney: The Making of a Poet* (London, 1993), p.39.

24. Seamus Heaney, 'Forked Tongues, Céilís and Incubators', in (eds.) Robert Bell, Robert Johnstone and Robin Wilson, *Troubled Times: Fortnight Magazine and the Troubles in Northern Ireland 1970-91* (Belfast, 1991), pp.113-16 (114).

25. Seamus Heaney, *Opened Ground: Selected Poems 1966-1996* (London, 1998), p.415.

26. Nicholas Roe, 'Wordsworth at the Flaxdam', in (eds.) Michael Allen & Angela Wilcox, *Critical Approaches to Anglo-Irish Literature* (Gerrards Cross, 1989), pp.168-69.

27. See Dietrich von Engelhardt, 'Science, society and culture in the Romantic Naturforschung around 1800', in (eds.) Mikulás Teich, Roy Porter & Bo Gustafsson, *Nature and Society in Historical Context* (Cambridge, 1997), pp.195-208.

28. Heaney, *Preoccupations*, p.145.

29. See Seán Lysaght, 'Heaney vs Praeger: Contrasting Natures', *Irish Review*, 7 (Autumn 1989), pp.68-74.

30. For Praeger's life and work, see Timothy Collins, *Floreat Hibernia: A Bio-bibliography of Robert Lloyd Praeger 1865-1953* (Dublin, 1985); Michael D. Guiry, 'No Stone Unturned: Robert Lloyd Praeger and the Major Surveys', in *Nature in Ireland*, pp.209-307; Seán Lysaght, *Robert Lloyd Praeger: Life of a Naturalist* (Dublin, 1998).

31. Seán Lysaght, 'Contrasting Natures: The Issue of Names', *Nature in Ireland*, p.145.

32. Quoted by Terry Gifford in *Green Voices: Understanding Contemporary*

Nature Poetry (Manchester 1995), p.99.

33. Gifford, *Green Voices*, pp.96, 99, 20.

34. Heaney, *Preoccupations*, p.63.

35. Heaney, *Opened Ground*, p.417.

36. Peter Coates, *Nature: Western Attitudes since Ancient Times* (London, 1998), p, 58.

37. Gifford, *Green Voices*, p.98.

38. Heaney, *Preoccupations*, p.65.

39. Heaney, *Preoccupations*, pp.132-33.

40. Keith Thomas, *Man and the Natural World: Changing Attitudes in England 1500-1800* (London, 1983), p.89.

41. John Feehan, 'Threat and Conservation: Attitudes to Nature in Ireland', *Nature in Ireland*, p.593.

42. Buell, *The Environmental Imagination*, p.52.

43. Heaney, *Preoccupations*, p.19; *The Government of the Tongue* (London, 1988), pp.106-07.

44. Edward Picot, *Outcasts from Eden: Ideas of Landscape in British Poetry since 1945* (Liverpool, 1997), pp.264, 205.

45. W.H. Auden, 'Dingley Dell & The Fleet', *The Dyer's Hand and Other Essays* (London, 1963), pp.410-11.

46. Tim Robinson, *Stones of Aran: Pilgrimage* (Mullingar, 1986), p.8.

47. Declan Kiberd, 'Contemporary Irish Poetry', in (ed.) Seamus Deane, *Field Day Anthology of Irish Writing*, 3 (Derry, 1991), p.1315.

48. See John Wilson Foster, 'Certain Set Apart: The Romantic Strategy – John Millington Synge', in Foster, *A Changeling Art: Fictions of the Irish Literary Revival* (Syracuse, NY, 1987), pp.94-113.

49. Terence Brown, 'Poets and Patrimony', in Brown, *Ireland's Literature* (Mullingar, 1988), p.189-202 (189).

50. Among pastoral authors native to the west of Ireland are Liam O'Flaherty, Máirtín Ó Direáin and the Blasket Island story-tellers Tomás Ó Criomhthain and Peig Sayers. For the latter, and for the complications introduced by literary interest from outside the islands, see Foster, *A Changeling Art*, pp.323-40.

51. Wayne K. Chapman, *Yeats and English Renaissance Literature* (London, 1991), p.133.

52. Auden, *The Dyer's Hand*, p.409.

53. Yeats, *Autobiographies* (London, 1955), pp.115-16.

54. Foster, 'The Culture of Nature', *Nature in Ireland*, p.606.

55. (Eds.) John Kelly & Eric Domville, *The Collected Letters of W.B. Yeats*, 1 (Oxford, 1986), p.8; W.B. Yeats, *Essays and Introductions* (London, 1961), p.444.

56. Yeats, *Essays and Introductions*, pp.201-02, quoted in 'Poetry and Science', in Holub, *The Dimension of the Present Moment* (London, 1990), p.130.

57. Michael Baron, 'Yeats, Wordsworth and the Communal Sense: The Case of "If I were Four and Twenty"', *Yeats Annual*, 5 (London, 1987), pp. 62-82 (62). And see Yeats's remarks to his father, who disliked Wordsworth, (ed.) Allan Wade, *The Letters of W.B. Yeats* (London, 1954), p.590: 'He strikes me as always destroying his poetic experience, which was of course of incomparable value, by his reflective power. His intellect was commonplace, and unfortunately he has been taught to respect nothing else. He thinks of his poetic experience not as incomparable in itself but as an engine that may be yoked to his intellect. He is full of a sort of utilitarianism and that is perhaps the reason why in later life he is always looking back on a lost vision, a lost happiness.'

58. Yeats, *Essays and Introductions*, p.520.
59. See Baron, *Yeats Annual*, 5, pp.62-82.
60. Maneck H. Daruwala, 'Yeats and the Ghost of Wordsworth', *Yeats Annual*, 13 (London, 1998), pp.197-220 (205, 209).
61. Patrick Sheeran, 'The Narrative Creation of Place: The Example of Yeats', in (ed.) Timothy Collins, *Decoding the Landscape* (Galway, 1994), pp.154, 157.
62. Frank Kinahan, *Yeats, Folklore and Occultism: Contexts of the Early Work and Thought* (Winchester, Mass., 1988), pp.203-4.
63. W.B. Yeats, 'The Poet of Ballyshannon', *Letters to the New Island* (London, 1989), pp.71-78 (72).
64. He asked Lady Dorothy Wellesley, 'Why can't you English poets keep flowers out of your poetry?', *Letters on Poetry from W.B. Yeats to Dorothy Wellesley* (London and New York, 1964), p.190.
65. Yeats, *Letters to the New Island*, p.89.
66. Yeats, *Essays and Introductions*, p.163.
67. For this 'stirring row', see (eds.) Warwick Gould, John Kelly & Deirdre Toomey, *The Collected Letters of W.B. Yeats*, 2 (Oxford, 1997), pp.293-95; and Louis MacNeice, *The Poetry of W.B. Yeats* (Oxford, 1941; London, 1967), pp.84-88; (ed.) Mark Storey, *Poetry and Ireland since 1800: A Source Book* (London, 1988), pp.118-31; (ed.) John Eglinton, *Literary Ideals in Ireland* (1899).
68. See Stan Smith, 'Writing a will: Yeats's ancestral voices', in Smith, *The Origins of Modernism: Eliot, Pound, Yeats and the Rhetorics of Renewal* (Hemel Hempstead, Hertfordshire, 1994), pp.152-76; Edna Longley, 'Helicon and Ni Houlihan: *Michael Robartes and the Dancer*', in (ed.) Jonathan Allison, *Yeats's Political Identities* (Ann Arbor, Michigan, 1996), pp.203-20 (218-9).
69. For MacNeice and the west of Ireland, see Jon Stallworthy, *Louis MacNeice* (London, 1995), Chapter 1, 'The Pre-natal Mountain', pp.1-13; Edna Longley, *Louis MacNeice: A Study* (London, 1988), pp.28-34.
70. For a discussion of his eclogues, see Longley, *Louis MacNeice: A Study*, pp.98, 101-03.
71. See *Louis MacNeice: A Study*, pp.24-27; and Edna Longley, '"It is time that I wrote my will": Anxieties of Influence and Succession', in (eds.) Warwick Gould & Edna Longley, *Yeats Annual*, 12 (London, 1996), pp.117-62 (154-6).
72. (Ed.) Patrick Crotty, *Modern Irish Poetry: An Anthology* (Belfast, 1995), pp.149, 197.
73. Sheeran, *Decoding the Landscape*, p.158.
74. Peter McDonald, 'Michael Longley's Homes', in McDonald, *Mistaken Identities: Poetry and Northern Ireland* (Oxford, 1997), pp.110-44 (119).
75. MacNeice, *Poetry of W.B. Yeats*, p.25.
76. Martin McDonagh, *The Lonesome West* (London, 1997), p.34.
77. Des O'Rawe, review of *Time and the Island*, *Irish Review*, 19 (Spring/Summer 1996), p.120.
78. Michael Viney, Introduction to Robert Lloyd Praeger, *The Way That I Went* (reprinted Cork, 1997), p.xii.
79. Michael Viney, *A Year's Turning* (Belfast, 1996), p.vii.
80. In Thomas's poem 'The Unknown Bird' the speaker says: 'I told/ The naturalists; but neither had they heard/ Anything like the notes that did so haunt me...'
81. Tim Robinson, *Stones of Aran: Pilgrimage*, p.12.
82. Cilian Roden, 'The Burren Flora', in (eds.) J.W. O'Connell & A. Korff,

The Book of the Burren (Kinvara, Co. Galway, 1991), p.36.
83. *Nature in Ireland,* pp.251, 142.
84. Robinson, *Stones of Aran: Pilgrimage,* p.2.

'Something Wrong Somewhere?': Louis MacNeice as Critic
(pp.134-66)
1. 'Subject in Modern Poetry', (ed.) Alan Heuser, *Selected Literary Criticism of Louis MacNeice* (Oxford, 1987), p.58.
2. 'An Alphabet of Literary Prejudices', *Selected Literary Criticism,* p.145.
3. Louis MacNeice, *The Poetry of W.B. Yeats* (Oxford, 1941; London, 1967), p.16.
4. MacNeice, *Poetry of W.B. Yeats,* p.26.
5. Louis MacNeice, *Modern Poetry* (Oxford, 1938, 1968), p.78.
6. MacNeice, *Poetry of W.B. Yeats,* p.18.
7. 'Poetry Today', *Selected Literary Criticism,* p.13.
8. MacNeice, *Poetry of W. B. Yeats,* p.23.
9. 'Poetry, the Public, and the Critic', *Selected Literary Criticism,* p.167.
10. Review of Randall Jarrell, *Poetry and the Age,* and C.M. Bowra, *Inspiration and Poetry,* in *Selected Literary Criticism,* p.203.
11. 'Poetry, the Public and the Critic', *Selected Literary Criticism,* p.168.
12. 'An Alphabet of Literary Prejudices', *Selected Literary Criticism,* p.146.
13. See Edna Longley, *Louis MacNeice: A Study* (London, 1988), pp.98-100; Peter McDonald, *Louis MacNeice: The Poet in his Contexts* (Oxford, 1991), pp.222-29; and Longley, '"It is time that I wrote my will": Anxieties of Influence and Succession', in (eds.) Warwick Gould and Edna Longley, *Yeats Annual,* 12 (London, 1996), pp.117-62.
14. MacNeice, *Poetry of W.B. Yeats,* p.22.
15. MacNeice, *Poetry of W.B. Yeats,* p.26.
16. Foreword to MacNeice, *Poetry of W.B. Yeats,* p.11.
17. 'Pleasure in Reading: Woods to Get Lost in', *Selected Literary Criticism,* p.232.
18. 'Introduction to *The Golden Ass of Apuleius*', *Selected Literary Criticism,* pp.127-28.
19. 'Experiences with Images', *Selected Literary Criticism,* pp.153-54.
20. Stephan Collini, in (eds.) Jeremy Treglown & Bridget Bennet, *Grub Street and the Ivory Tower: Literary Journalism and Literary Scholarship from Fielding to the Internet* (Oxford, 1998), p.153.
21. Review of Patricia Hutchins, *James Joyce's World* and (ed.) Stuart Gilbert, *Letters of James Joyce, Selected Literary Criticism,* p.212.
22. Review of Rosemond Tuve, *A Reading of George Herbert, Selected Literary Criticism,* p.175.
23. 'The Poet in England Today: A Reassessment', *Selected Literary Criticism,* p.114. MacNeice had evidently read Richards's *Principles of Literary Criticism* (1924) and *Practical Criticism: A Study of Literary Judgment* (1929).
24. 'Poetry, the Public and the Critic', *Selected Literary Criticism,* p.167.
25. 'That Chair of Poetry', *Selected Literary Criticism,* pp.228, 225.
26. See Longley, *Louis MacNeice,* pp.53-5, 101-03.
27. Louis MacNeice, *The Strings are False: An Unfinished Autobiography* (London, 1965), p.167.
28. *Modern Poetry,* p.34.

NOTES

29. See Longley, 'The Room Where MacNeice wrote "Snow"', in *The Living Stream: Literature and Revisionism in Ireland* (Newcastle upon Tyne, 1994), pp.252-70.
30. 'Poetry Today', *Selected Literary Criticism*, p.11.
31. *Modern Poetry*, p.197.
32. *Modern Poetry*, p.20.
33. *Modern Poetry*, p.33.
34. *Modern Poetry*, p.33.
35. 'Poetry, the Public and the Critic', *Selected Literary Criticism*, p.166.
36. 'Poetry, the Public and the Critic', *Selected Literary Criticism*, p.169.
37. 'An Alphabet of Literary Prejudices', *Selected Literary Criticism*, p.143.
38. *Modern Poetry*, p.2.
39. *Poetry of W.B. Yeats*, p.28.
40. *Poetry of W.B. Yeats*, pp.29-30.
41. *Poetry of W.B. Yeats*, p.18.
42. Louis MacNeice, *Varieties of Parable* (Cambridge, 1965), p.151.
43. *Varieties of Parable*, p.8.
44. *Varieties of Parable*, p.146.
45. *Modern Poetry*, p.205.
46. 'Broken Windows or Thinking Aloud', (ed.) Alan Heuser, *Selected Prose of Louis MacNeice* (Oxford, 1990), p.141
47. 'Poetry Today', *Selected Literary Criticism*, p.22; review of Honor Tracy, *Mind You, I've Said Nothing!* and Chiang Yee, 'The Silent Traveller in Dublin', *Selected Prose*, p.189; review of Tuve, *A Reading of George Herbert*, *Selected Literary Criticism* p.179; review of Jarrell, *Poetry and the Age*, *Selected Literary Criticism*, p.203. It should be said that in *Poetry and the Age* Jarrell compares Denis Devlin unfavourably to MacNeice: 'after the hundredth mesmeric echo of MacNeice, it is hard not to forsake him for that better and far more sympathetic poet' (p.202).
48. In conversation.
49. *Varieties of Parable*, p.84.
50. 'Poetry Today', *Selected Literary Criticism*, pp.25-26.
51. 'Poetry Today', *Selected Literary Criticism*, p.37.
52. Cecil Day Lewis, *A Hope for Poetry* (London, 1934), p.38.
53. *Modern Poetry*, p.177.
54. *Modern Poetry*, p.148.
55. *Modern Poetry*, pp.204-05.
56. *Poetry of W.B. Yeats*, p.18.
57. See Tom Paulin, 'Letters from Iceland: Going North', in *Renaissance and Modern Studies*, 20 (1976), pp.65-80.
58. *Modern Poetry*, pp.7-8; 'Subject in Modern Poetry', *Selected Literary Criticism*, pp.60-61.
59. (Eds.) Keith Williams & Steven Matthews, *Rewriting the Thirties: Modernism and After*, Introduction, p.1.
60. Stan Smith, 'Remembering Bryden's Bill: Modernism from Eliot to Auden', *Rewriting the Thirties*, pp.53-70 (59-60).
61. See Peter McDonald, 'Believing in the Thirties', *Rewriting the Thirties*, pp.71-90.
62. David Bromwich, review of Perry Anderson, *The Origins of Postmodernity* and Fredric Jameson, *The Cultural Turn*, *London Review of Books*, 21/3 (4 February 1999), pp.16-18 (18).

63. Alex Callinicos, *Against Postmodernism: A Marxist Critique* (London, 1989), p.ix.

64. *Modern Poetry*, p.189.

65. Review of W.H. Auden, *Look, Stranger! Poems, Selected Literary Criticism*, pp.75-76.

66. Review of (ed.) W.H. Auden, *The Oxford Book of Light Verse, Selected Literary Criticism*, pp.99-100.

67. (Ed.) Edward Mendelson, *The English Auden: Poems, Essays and Dramatic Writings 1927-1939* (London, 1977), pp.370, 396.

68. *The English Auden*, p.403.

69. See Longley, *The Living Stream*, pp.264-66.

70. 'The Poet in England Today: A Reassessment', *Selected Literary Criticism*, p.113.

71. Review of Jarrell, *Poetry and the Age, Selected Literary Criticism*, p.205.

72. Also see *Selected Literary Criticism*, p.122.

73. Christopher Caudwell, *Illusion and Reality: A Study of the Sources of Poetry* (1937), pp.155, 28.

74. Caudwell, *Illusion and Reality*, pp.7, 220, 8; MacNeice, *Modern Poetry*, pp.1, 3, 29.

75. *Modern Poetry*, p.2.

76. *Illusion and Reality*, pp.293-94, 29, 219-20.

77. *Varieties of Parable*, pp.27-28.

78. 'Subject in Modern Poetry', *Selected Literary Criticism*, p.57.

79. 'Poetry Today', *Selected Literary Criticism*, p.13.

80. Geoff Ward, *Statutes of Liberty: The New York School of Poets* (London, 1993), p.61.

81. *Folios of New Writing*, 3 (Spring 1941), p.42.

82. *Folios of New Writing*, 3 (Spring 1941), pp.26-27.

83. *Folios of New Writing*, 3 (Spring 1941), p.35.

84. 'The Tower that Once', *Selected Literary Criticism*, p.120.

85. Peter Widdowson, 'Between the Acts? English Fiction in the Thirties', in (eds.), Jon Clark, Margot Heinemann, David Margolies & Carole Snee, *Culture and Crisis in Britain in the Thirties* (London, 1979), pp.133-64 (138).

86. Virginia Woolf, 'The Leaning Tower', *Folios of New Writing*, 2 (Autumn 1940), p.22.

87. 'The Tower that Once', *Selected Literary Criticism*, p.124.

88. 'The Tower that Once', *Selected Literary Criticism*, p.123.

89. 'Poetry Today', *Selected Literary Criticism*, p.12.

90. *Modern Poetry*, p.35.

91. 'The Traditional Aspect of Modern English Poetry', *Selected Literary Criticism*, p.141.

92. 'The Tower that Once', *Selected Literary Criticism*, p.120.

93. Review of (ed.) G.S. Fraser, *Poetry Now* and (eds.) Howard Sergeant & Dannie Abse, *Mavericks, Selected Literary Criticism*, p.207.

94. Review of Jarrell, *Poetry and the Age, Selected Literary Criticism*, p.203.

95. Jon Stallworthy, *Louis MacNeice* (London, 1995), p.470.

96. 'Poetry Today', *Selected Literary Criticism*, p.28.

97. 'Poetry Today', *Selected Literary Criticism*, pp.29-30.

98. 'Poetry Today', *Selected Literary Criticism*, p.27.

99. *Modern Poetry*, p.117.

100. 'Subject in Modern Poetry', *Selected Literary Criticism*, p.70.

101. *Modern Poetry*, p.35.
102. *Modern Poetry*, p.78.
103. Review of Tuve, *A Reading of George Herbert*, *Selected Literary Criticism*, p.177.
104. *Modern Poetry*, p.77.
105. 'Poetry Today', *Selected Literary Criticism*, p.17.
106. *Poetry of W.B. Yeats*, p.146.
107. *Poetry of W.B. Yeats*, p.146.
108. 'Poetry Today', *Selected Literary Criticism*, p.17.
109. *Modern Poetry*, pp.130-31.
110. 'Poetry Today', *Selected Literary Criticism*, p.17.
111. *Varieties of Parable*, p.16.
112. *Varieties of Parable*, p.1.
113. *Varieties of Parable*, pp.13-15.
114. Brian Vickers, *In Defence of Rhetoric* (Oxford, 1988), p.457.
115. See Peter McDonald, ' "With Eyes Turned Down on the Past": Mac-Neice's Classicism', in (eds.) Kathleen Devine and Alan J. Peacock, *Louis MacNeice and his Influence* (Gerrards Cross, 1998), pp.34-52.
116. Matei Calinescu, *Five Faces of Modernity* (Durham, USA, 1987), p.299.
117. Peter McDonald, *Louis MacNeice*, p.156.
118. *Varieties of Parable*, pp.106-07.
119. *Varieties of Parable*, p.78.
120. Stallworthy, *Louis MacNeice*, p.436.
121. See *The Poetry of W.B. Yeats*, pp.145-48.
122. MacNeice writing on *Solstices* for the *Poetry Book Society Bulletin*, *Selected Literary Criticism*, p.224.
123. See 'Poetry, the Public, and the Critic', *Selected Literary Criticism*, pp.164-69 *passim*.
124. Gail McDonald, *Learning to be Modern: Pound, Eliot and the American University* (Oxford, 1993), p.210.
125. See note 13.
126. Review of W.B. Yeats, *Collected Poems*, *Selected Literary Criticism*, p.173.

In Praise of 'In Praise of Limestone' *(pp.167-77)*

1. See Edna Longley on 'Directive', into which Frost may weave Edward Thomas, as Auden weaves MacNeice into 'In Praise of Limestone', *Poetry in the Wars* (Newcastle upon Tyne, 1986, 1996), pp.45-46.
2. See Michael Wood, ' "In Praise of Limestone": A Symposium', ' "In Solitude, for Company": W.H. Auden After 1940', *Auden Studies*, 3 (Oxford, 1995), pp.250-53.
3. Edward Upward, *Auden Studies*, 3, p.246.
4. Auden's 'secret system of caves and conduits', derives from the phrase 'a network of caves and conduits' in Anthony Collett's *The Changing Face of England* (1926, 1932), as do some other details in 'In Praise of Limestone'. Auden also took phrases from Collett in the 1930s. See Lawrence Lipking, *Auden Studies*, 3, p.265; and Edward Mendelson, *Early Auden* (London, 1981, 1999), pp.336-38.
5. See Louis MacNeice, 'Traveller's Return', in (ed.) Alan Heuser, *Selected Prose of Louis MacNeice* (Oxford, 1991), pp.83-91.
6. See 'The Prolific and Devourer', in (ed.) Edward Mendelson, *The English Auden*, (London, 1977), pp.394-406.

7. Lucy McDiarmid, *Auden's Apologies for Poetry* (Princeton, 1990), p.136.

8. *Auden's Apologies for Poetry*, pp.12, 137.

9. Philip Larkin, *Required Writing: Miscellaneous Pieces 1955-1982* (London, 1983), pp.124-28.

10. W.H. Auden, *Collected Shorter Poems* (London, 1966), pp.15-16.

11. (Ed.) Nicholas Jenkins, Alan Ansen, *The Table Talk of W.H. Auden* (London, 1991), p.36.

12. Letter to Lady Elizabeth Pelham, 4 January 1939, in (ed.) Allan Wade, *The Letters of W.B. Yeats* (London, 1954), p.922

Larkin, Decadence and the Lyric Poem *(pp.178-202)*

Abbreviations in text of essay: *Letters*: (ed.) Anthony Thwaite, *Selected Letters of Philip Larkin 1940-1985* (London, 1992); *Girl*: Philip Larkin, *A Girl in Winter* (London, 1947); *RW*: Philip Larkin, *Required Writing: Miscellaneous Pieces 1955-1982* (London, 1983).

1. E.g. in Andrew Swarbrick's *Out of Reach: The Poetry of Philip Larkin* (London, 1995). Swarbrick introduces Mikhail Bakhtin to Larkin criticism.

2. W.B. Yeats, *Essays and Introductions* (London, 1961), p.522.

3. Cyril Connolly, *Enemies of Promise* (London, 1938), p.36.

4. James Booth, 'The Turf-cutter and the Nine-to-Five Man: Heaney, Larkin, and "the spiritual intellect's great work"', *Twentieth Century Literature*, 43/4 (Winter 1997), pp.369-93 (372).

5. M.W. Rowe, 'Unreal Girls: Lesbian Fantasy in Early Larkin', in (ed.) James Booth, *New Larkins for Old: Critical Essays* (Houndmills, Basingstoke, 2000), pp.79-96 (92).

6. Andrew Motion, *Philip Larkin: A Writer's Life* (London, 1993), pp.438, 202.

7. Philip Larkin, New Introduction, Cyril Connolly, *The Condemned Playground: Essays 1927-1941* (reprinted London, 1985).

8. Cyril Connolly, *The Condemned Playground* (London, 1945), p.vi.

9. Motion, *Philip Larkin*, p.43.

10. Connolly, *Enemies of Promise*, p.174.

11. Connolly, *Condemned Playground* (1945), p.266.

12. Connolly, *Condemned Playground*, p.268.

13. Connolly, *Enemies of Promise*, p.173, 108-09.

14. New Introduction, *Condemned Playground*.

15. Keith Douglas's contribution to a symposium 'On the Nature of Poetry', *Augury: An Oxford Miscellany of Verse and Prose* (1940); reprinted in Keith Douglas, *The Complete Poems* (Oxford, 1978), p.123.

16. See Edna Longley, 'Poète Maudit Manqué', in (ed.) George Hartley, *Philip Larkin 1922-1985: A Tribute* (London, 1988), pp.220-31.

17. Philip Larkin, Introduction, *The North Ship* (London, 1966 edn), p.9.

18. Larkin, Introduction, *The North Ship*, p.10.

19. E.g. the end of 'All catches alight' ('And all their buried men/ Stand on the earth again' echoes 'Under Ben Bulben': 'They but thrust their buried men/ Back into the human mind again'; 'The Dancer' is based on the second stanza of 'Long-legged Fly'.

20. Larkin, Introduction to *The North Ship*, p.9.

21. (Ed.) Elaine Showalter, *Daughters of Decadence: Women Writers of the Fin-de-Siècle* (London, 1993), Introduction, p.x; and see Showalter, *Sexual*

Anarchy: Gender and Culture at the 'Fin de Siècle' (London, 1991).

22. Among many echoes and parallels is the relationship between Rossetti's 'Advent' and Larkin's 'First Sight', and see *RW*, pp.55-56.

23. Motion, *Philip Larkin*, pp.86-87.

24. Lisa Jardine, 'Saxon Violence', *The Guardian*, 23 November 1992.

25. See Laurence Lerner, *Philip Larkin* (London, 1997), p.46; Swarbrick, *Poetry of Philip Larkin*, p.31. Both may take their cue from Andrew Motion's tone in *Philip Larkin*, pp.85-101.

26. See C. Fred Alford, *Narcissism: Socrates, the Frankfurt School, and Pschoanalytical Theory* (New Haven, 1988), for a useful summary of the literature. Also, John Russell, *Hamlet and Narcissus* (Newark, 1993); and David Punter, *The Romantic Unconscious: A Study in Narcissism and Patriarchy* (London, 1989).

27. See Alford, *Narcissism*, pp.5-6.

28. Punter, *Romantic Unconscious*, p.19.

29. Alford, *Narcissism*, p.69.

30. Alford, *Narcissism*, pp.47-48.

31. See Alford, *Narcissism*, p.59; Guinn Batten, *The Orphaned Imagination: Melancholy and Commodity Culture in English Romanticism* (Durham, USA & London, 1998), p.122.

32. Longley, 'Poète Maudit Manqué', p.229.

33. See Swarbrick, *Out of Reach*, pp.62-63.

34. Donald Davie, *Thomas Hardy and British Poetry* (London, 1973), p.64.

35. A.T. Tolley, *Larkin at Work* (Hull, 1997), p.55.

36. Tom Paulin, *Minotaur: Poetry and the Nation State* (London, 1992), pp.239-40.

37. David Gervais, *Literary Englands: Versions of 'Englishness' in Modern Writing* (Cambridge, 1993), p.213.

38. See Swarbrick, *Out of Reach*, pp.131-32.

39. James Booth, 'From Here to Bogland: Larkin, Heaney and the Poetry of Place', *New Larkins for Old*, pp.190-212 (204-07).

40. Quoted Swarbrick, *Poetry of Philip Larkin*, p.131.

41. Gervais, *Literary Englands*, p.217.

42. Swarbrick, *Out of Reach*, p.145.

The Millennial Muse *(pp.203-23)*

1. Carol Rumens, 'Anthologising the Archipelago' 1, *Irish Review*, 14 (Autumn 1993), pp.94-99 (97).

2. Douglas's contribution to a symposium 'On the Nature of Poetry', *Augury: An Oxford Miscellany* (1940), reprinted in (ed.) Desmond Graham, *Complete Poems* (1978), p.123.

3. Weekend Review, *The Independent*, 20 March 1999.

4. Peter McDonald, 'Faith and Fidelities: Heaney and Longley in mid-career', *The Tabla Book of New Verse* (Bristol, 1999), pp.63-72 (64).

5. Peter McDonald, *Mistaken Identities: Poetry and Northern Ireland* (Oxford, 1997), p.19.

6. See note 3.

7. See 'Introduction: Revising "Irish Literature"', *The Living Stream* (Newcastle upon Tyne, 1994), pp.9-68 (44-50).

8. John Tusa, 'We do ourselves a disservice by praising the second rate', *The Guardian*, 11 August 1999.

9. Philip Larkin, *Required Writing: Miscellaneous Pieces 1955-1982* (London, 1983), p.75.

10. Sean O'Brien, 'Introduction: Who's in Charge Here?', *The Deregulated Muse* (Newcastle upon Tyne, 1998), pp.13-20 (13).

11. Babette Deutsch, review of *Oxford Book of Modern Verse*, *New York Herald Tribune Books*, 13 December 1936.

12. See Edna Longley, '"It is time that I wrote my will": Anxieties of Influence and Succession', in (eds.) Warwick Gould & Edna Longley, *Yeats Annual*, 12 (London, 1996), pp.117-62 (125-29).

13. Stephen Spender, *Time and Tide*, 19 December 1936, p.1804.

14. See C. Day Lewis, *Left Review*, 5/16, pp.99-100.

15. F.O. Matthiessen, 'W.B. Yeats and Others', *Southern Review*, 2/4 (Spring 1937), pp.815-34 (816).

16. H.T. Kirby-Smith, *The Origins of Free Verse* (Ann Arbor, 1996), p.257.

17. *Letters on Poetry from W.B. Yeats to Dorothy Wellesley* (Oxford, 1940), p.25.

18. See Warwick Gould, 'The Unknown Masterpiece: Yeats and the Design of the Cantos', in (ed.) Andrew Gibson, *Pound in Multiple Perspective* (London, 1993), pp.40-92 (43-45).

19. Louis MacNeice, 'Lost Generations?', in (ed.) Alan Heuser, *Selected Literary Criticism of Louis MacNeice* (Oxford, 1987), pp.206-11 (207).

20. (Ed.) Anthony Thwaite, *Selected Letters of Philip Larkin* (London, 1992), p.401.

21. MacNeice, 'Lost Generations?', p.207.

Tom Paulin: Wild Irish Critic *(pp.224-34)*

All unattributed quotations are from Tom Paulin, *Writing to the Moment: Selected Critical Essays 1980-1996* (London, 1996); or Tom Paulin, *The Day-Star of Liberty: William Hazlitt's Radical Style* (London, 1998).

1. Patrick Kavanagh, 'Critics, Actors and Poets', in Kavanagh, *Collected Pruse* (London, 1967), pp.241-43 (241).

2. See Richard Kirkland, *Literature and Culture in Northern Ireland Since 1965: Moments of Danger* (London, 1996), pp.104-9.

3. Louis MacNeice, *The Strings are False: An Unfinished Autobiography* (London, 1965), pp.100, 222.

4. Hubert Butler, 'Two Critics: E.M. Forster and Edmund Wilson', *Escape from the Anthill* (Mullingar, 1985), pp.182-92 (186).

5. Bernard O'Donoghue, 'Involved Imaginings: Tom Paulin', in (ed.) Neil Corcoran, *The Chosen Ground: Essays on the Contemporary Poetry of Northern Ireland* (Bridgend, 1992), pp.171-88 (176).

6. See Edna Longley, 'Progressive Bookmen', in Longley, *The Living Stream: Literature and Revisionism in Ireland* (Newcastle upon Tyne, 1994), pp.109-29 (114-15).

Irish Bards and American Audiences *(pp.235-58)*

1. *Irish Times*, 24 June 1999.

2. (Ed.) Tom Hayden, *Irish Hunger: Personal Reflections on the Legacy of the Famine* (Boulder, Colorado & Dublin, 1997), p.8.

3. (Eds.) John Kelly & Eric Domville, *The Collected Letters of W. B. Yeats*, 1 (Oxford, 1986), p.409.

4. See, for example, John Kerrigan, 'Hand and Foot', *London Review of Books*, 27 May 1999, pp.20-23 (23).

5. Gregory A. Schirmer, *Out of What Began: A History of Irish Poetry in English* (Ithaca, NY & London, 1998), pp.xi, 73.

6. E.g. the opening sentence of the book proper: 'The very concept of eighteenth-century Irish poetry in English is shrouded in ambiguity' (p.3); Blanaid Salkeld's 'view of her Irishness was always somewhat ambiguous' (p.322).

7. Schirmer, *Out of What Began*, p.xii.

8. Schirmer, *Out of What Began*, pp.280-81.

9. Stephen Yenser, *Southern Review*, 30/1 (January, 1994), p.167.

10. Dana Gioia, *Can Poetry Matter? Essays on Poetry and American Culture* (Saint Paul, Minnesota, 1992), pp.12, 8, 13.

11. Dana Gioia, interviewed by Isabelle Cartwright, *Irish Review*, 16 (Autumn/ Winter 1994), pp.109-22 (111).

12. Donald Hall, *Poetry and Ambition: Essays 1982-88* (Ann Arbor, Michigan, 1988), pp.64, 130, 8, 14.

13. Brad Leithauser, 'The Saving Minutes', in (eds.) Katharine Washburn and John Thornton, *Dumbing Down: Essays on the Strip Mining of American Culture* (New York, 1996), pp.114-25 (122).

14. Al Alvarez, interviewed by Gregory LeStage, *Poetry Review*, 88/1 (Spring 1998), pp.88-94 (88-89).

15. Randall Jarrell, *Poetry and the Age* (London, 1955, 1973), p.85.

16. Geoffrey Grigson, *The Private Art: A Poetry Note-Book* (London & New York, 1982), p.10.

17. Peter Forbes, *Poetry Review*, 86/4 (Winter 1996/97), p.3.

18. Quoted in (ed.) Tony Curtis, *As the Poet Said...: Poetry Pickings and Choosings from Dennis O'Driscoll's Poetry Ireland Review Column* (Dublin, 1997), p.56.

19. Mark Jarman, 'Diversity Comes to British Poetry', *Southern Review*, 30/2 (April 1994), pp.393-408 (393-94).

20. John Matthias, 'The New Poetry', *Southern Review*, 30/2 (April 1994), pp.409-20 (409).

21. Gerald Dawe, 'The Critical Mass: Poetry and Ireland in the 1980s', in Dawe, *False Faces: Poetry, Politics and Place* (Belfast, 1994), pp.81-89 (81-87).

22. (Eds.) Peter Fallon & Derek Mahon, *The Penguin Book of Contemporary Irish Poetry* (London, 1990), Introduction, pp.xxi-ii.

23. Eamon Grennan, 'Chosen Home: The Poetry of Peter Fallon', *Éire-Ireland*, 29/2 (Summer 1994), pp.173-87 (187).

24. *Irish Literary Supplement* (Fall 1993), p.29.

25. *Irish Literary Supplement* (Fall 1994), p.21; Shaun O'Connell, *Irish Literary Supplement* (Spring 1994), p.11.

26. *Irish Literary Supplement* (Spring 1994), p.12.

27. This was certainly the case at the stage when Jody Allen-Randolph compiled 'Eavan Boland: A Checklist', *Irish University Review* (Special Issue: Eavan Boland), 23/1 (Spring/Summer 1993), pp.131-48.

28. Deborah Hunter McWilliams, *Irish Literary Supplement* (Spring 1999), p.15.

29. Jody Allen-Randolph, 'An Interview with Eavan Boland', *Irish University Review*, 23/1 (Spring/Summer 1993), pp.117-30 (124, 130).

30. 'Comhrá, with a Foreword and Afterword by Laura O'Connor, Medbh McGuckian and Nuala ní Dhomhnaill', *Southern Review*, 31/3 (July 1995),

pp.581-614 (613).

31. Victor Luftig, ' "Something Will Happen to You Who Read": Adrienne Rich, Eavan Boland', *Irish University Review*, 23/1 (Spring/Summer 1993), pp.57-66 (57); Jody Allen-Randolph, 'Private Worlds, Public Realities: Eavan Boland's Poetry 1967-1990', pp.5-22 (12).

32. *Irish University Review*, 23/1 (Spring/Summer 1993), p.19.

33. *Irish University Review*, 23/1 (Spring/Summer 1993), pp.63-64.

34. Patricia Boyle Haberstroh, *Women Creating Women: Contemporary Irish Women Poets* (Syracuse, NY and Dublin, 1996), p.75.

35. William Logan, 'Animal Instincts and Natural Powers', *New York Times Book Review*, 21 April 1991, p.22.

36. Haberstroh, *Women Creating Women*, p.88.

37. Helen Vendler, *Seamus Heaney* (London, 1998), pp.6, 9.

38. Gerald Graff, *Professing Literature: An Institutional History* (Chicago, 1987), p.208.

39. Edward Thomas, review of (ed.) Walter Jerrold, *The Book of Living Poets* and (ed.) Alfred H. Miles, *Poets and Poetry of the Nineteenth Century: Christina Rossetti to Katharine Tynan, Daily Chronicle*, 13 January 1908 reprinted in (ed.) Edna Longley, *A Language Not To Be Betrayed: Selected Prose of Edward Thomas* (Manchester, 1981), p.66.

40. John P. Harrington, *The Irish Play on the New York Stage: 1874-1966* (Lexington, Kentucky, 1997), p.7.

41. Joseph Kelly, *Our Joyce: From Outcast to Icon* (Austin, Texas, 1998), pp.9-10, 208.

42. See Helen Vendler, *The Music of What Happens: Poems, Poets, Critics* (Cambridge, Mass, 1988), p.149.

43. Guinn Batten, 'Piece Talk', *Irish Review*, 23 (Winter 1998), p.158.

44. Hall, *Poetry and Ambition*, p.15.

45. Quoted by Margery Sabin, '"The Debate": Seductions and Betrayals in Literary Studies', *Raritan*, 13/3 (Winter 1994), pp.123-46) (140).

46. Denis Donoghue recollects the impact of New Criticism on him, in *The Practice of Reading* (New Haven and London, 1998), pp.5-8.

47. (Ed.) Michael Allen, *Seamus Heaney* (London, 1997), Introduction, p.1.

48. Vendler, *Seamus Heaney*, pp.6, 175.

49. Hall, *Poetry and Ambition*, p.12.

50. Gioia, *Irish Review*, 16, p.120.

51. Michael Allen, 'The Parish and the Dream: Heaney and America, 1969-1987', *Southern Review*, 31/3 (July 1995), pp.726-38 (728).

52. Fintan O'Toole, *A Mass for Jesse James: A Journey through 1980s Ireland* (Dublin, 1990), p.87.

53. David Cobb, *Journal of the British Haiku Society*, 9/1, pp.53-54.

'Atlantic's Premises': American Influences on Northern Irish Poetry in the 1960s *(pp.259-79)*

1. See: Michael Parker, 'Gleanings, Leavings: Irish and American Influences on Seamus Heaney's *Wintering Out, 1972*', *New Hibernia Review*, 2/3 (Autumn 1998), pp.16-35; Michael O'Neill, 'Montague and Mahon: American Dimensions', *Symbiosis*, 3/1 (April 1999), pp.54-62; Neil Corcoran, *Poets of Modern Ireland* (Cardiff, 1999), pp.137-55.

2. Richard Wilbur, *Responses: Prose Pieces 1953-1976* (New York & London,

1976), pp.163, 123, 182; (ed.) William Butts, *Conversations with Richard Wilbur* (Mississippi, 1990), pp.67, 41.

3. See Terence Diggory, *Yeats and American Poetry* (Princeton, 1983), p.136.

4. Hart Crane, 'Modern Poetry', reprinted in *Complete Poems of Hart Crane* (New York, 1933, 1958), pp.179-83 (179).

5. *Conversations with Richard Wilbur*, p.138.

6. (Ed.) Alan Heuser, *Selected Literary Criticism of Louis MacNeice* (London, 1987), pp.2, 21, 244.

7. (Ed.) W.H. Auden, *The Faber Book of Modern American Verse* (London, 1956), pp.18-19.

8. In conversation with me, 1998.

9. (Ed.) Donald Hall, *The Penguin Book of Contemporary American Poetry* (Harmondsworth, 1962), p.20.

10. Hall, *Penguin Book* (1972), p.36.

11. The posts (which included Denis Donoghue's chair at University College, Dublin) were funded by the Rockefeller Foundation and organised by US embassies in Europe.

12. 'Voyages' V ends: 'Draw in your head and sleep the long way home'; Longley's 'Odyssey' ends: 'Your bodies comprising the long way home'; 'Mark how her turning shoulder winds the hours' ('Voyages' II); 'The ocean gathers where her shoulder turns' (Longley, 'Nausicaa'); Crane's 'Carib' has 'Brutal necklaces of shells'. The Longley poems (which also include 'No Continuing City') seem to base their conceit of body/ voyage on Crane's 'Permit me voyage, love, into your hands...' ('Voyages' III).

13. Derek Mahon, 'Poetry in Northern Ireland', *Twentieth Century Studies*, 4 (November 1994), pp.89-93 (91).

14. See R.F. Foster, 'Protestant Magic: W.B. Yeats and the Spell of Irish History', *Paddy and Mr Punch* (London, 1993), pp.212-32.

15. Langdon Hammer, 'The Letters of Hart Crane', *Raritan*, 17/1 (Summer 1997), pp.101-20 (118-19).

16. See the Trinity College, Dublin student-magazine *Icarus* from 1959 to the mid 1960s, and the *Dubliner/Dublin Magazine* between 1964 and 1968.

17. See Christopher Harvie, 'Garron Top to Caer Gybi: Images of the Inland Sea', *Irish Review*, 19 (Spring/Summer 1996), pp.44-61 (48).

18. This is one of a sequence of Jazz poems (which also celebrates Bix Beiderbecke, Bud Freeman and Fats Waller). Fictional American (artist) figures who are the subject of poems in *No Continuing City* are Walter Mitty and Rip Van Winkle.

19. Mahon altered the title of 'Recalling Aran' to emphasise America as the site of recollection. In *Poems 1962-1978* (1979) the poem is called 'Thinking of Inishere in Cambridge, Massachusetts'; in *Selected Poems* (1991) it goes doubly more native as 'Thinking of Inis Óirr in Cambridge, Mass.'

20. Michael Allen, 'The Parish and the Dream: Heaney and America, 1969-1987', *Southern Review*, 31/3 (July 1995), pp.726-38 (726-27).

21. The Ulster-American Folk Park in Omagh, for instance, is a museum which emphasises the Scotch-Irish as well as Catholic Irish-American experience, and which connects with Scotch-Irish heritage groups in the US. Historians have recently been complicating the map of the Irish diaspora in America. Descendants of Ulster Protestant emigrants are probably as numerous as those of Catholic immigrants, because the former emigration (at the end of the 18th century) was earlier if smaller. However, the Catholic Church has ensured that

Catholic Irish America would manifest greater cohesion as a ethnic concept. Irish Protestants have been more fully absorbed into a multifaceted American Protestantism. See Kerby A. Miller, *Emigrants and Exiles: Ireland and the Irish Exodus to North America* (London and New York, 1985).
  22. W.H. Auden, 'Robert Frost', in *The Dyer's Hand* (London, 1963), pp. 337-53 (350).
  23. Elizabeth Bishop, 'Efforts of Affection: a Memoir of Marianne Moore', in *Collected Prose* (London, 1984), pp.121-56 (140).
  24. See Neil Corcoran, *The Poetry of Seamus Heaney: A Critical Study* (London, 1998), and Michael Parker, *Seamus Heaney: The Making of a Poet* (Basingstoke, 1993).
  25. Stephen James, 'Dividing Lines: Frost and Heaney', *Symbiosis*, 3/1 (April 1999), pp.63-76 (66).
  26. Whitman's *Song of Myself*, Emerson and Thoreau exemplified for Yeats an achievement that an Irish national literature should not only emulate but surpass. 'America, with no past to speak of, a mere *parvenu* among the nations, is creating a national literature which in its most characteristic products differs almost as much from English literature as does the literature of France.' Letter to *United Ireland*, 17 December 1892, (eds.) John Kelly & Eric Domville, *Collected Letters of W.B. Yeats*, 1 (Oxford, 1986), p.339.
  27. See John Wilson Foster, 'Radical Regionalism', in Foster, *Colonial Consequences: Essays in Irish Literature and Culture* (Dublin, 1991), pp.278-96; Edna Longley, ' "Defending Ireland's Soul": Protestant Writers and Irish Nationalism after Independence', in Longley, *The Living Stream* (Newcastle upon Tyne, 1994), pp.130-49.
  28. (Ed.) Tom Clyde, *Ancestral Voices: The Selected Prose of John Hewitt* (Belfast, 1987), p.111.
  29. Heaney certainly read Hewitt's essay ('The Bitter Gourd: Some Problems of the Ulster Writer'), which originally appeared in the 1940s literary magazine *Lagan*: 'In 1962, while a student at St Joseph's College of Education, I had done an extended essay on the history of literary magazines in Ulster', Seamus Heaney, *The Government of the Tongue* (London, 1988), pp.6-7.
  30. Seamus Heaney, 'Above the Brim', in Joseph Brodsky, Seamus Heaney & Derek Walcott, *Homage to Robert Frost* (London, 1997), pp.61-88 (66, 86).
  31. Auden, 'Robert Frost', p.350.
  32. In his early poetry Kavanagh identifies the poet with the ploughman; but rural tasks generally belong to a wider scenario as opposed to being highlighted in close-up, and Kavanagh's aesthetic (like Hughes's) emphasises vision more than craft. When Kavanagh compares the farm-world with the literary world, it is in terms of opposition not analogical convergence.
  33. Parker, *Seamus Heaney*, pp.80-81.
  34. James, 'Dividing Lines', pp.70-71.
  35. Michael Allen recalls Heaney singling out 'A Hillside Thaw' in conversation in the 1960s.
  36. Heaney, 'Above the Brim', pp.65, 68, 63.
  37. See Seamus Heaney, 'Canticles to the Earth', *Preoccupations: Selected Prose 1968-1978* (London, 1980), pp.190-94.
  38. Heaney's 'At a Potato Digging' ('They lie scattered/like inflated pebbles. Native/ to the black hutch of clay…these knobbed and slit-eyed tubers seem/ the petrified hearts of drills. Split/ by the spade, they show white as cream.//Good smells exude from crumbled earth…knots of potatoes (a clean

birth)/ whose solid feel, whose wet inside/ promises taste of ground and root')
shows that he has read Wilbur's much-anthologised 'Potato' ('An underground
grower, blind, and a common brown...Cut open raw, it looses a cool, clean
stench...Therein the taste of first stones, the hands of dead slaves...Polishes
yellow, but tears to the plain insides;/ Parching, the white's blue-hearted like
hungry hands'). Heaney's 'Turkeys Observed' may have noted Wilbur's 'A
Black November Turkey'.
  39. Poems that might be compared, for instance, are Wilbur's 'All These
Birds', 'Marché aux Oiseaux' and 'Lamarck Elaborated' with Longley's 'Cam-
ouflage' and 'The Ornithological Section'; Wilbur's 'Flumen Tenebrarum'
with Longley's 'Epithalamium'.
  40. Such as 'Year's-End', 'Beowulf' and 'The Undead'.
  41. Quoted by Jonathan Raban in (ed.) Raban, *Robert Lowell's Poems: A
Selection* (London, 1974), Introduction, p.16.

Northern Irish Poetry and the End of History *(pp.280-316)*

  1. See, for instance, Keith Jeffery, 'The Great War in modern Irish mem-
ory' in (eds.) T.G. Fraser and Keith Jeffery, *Men, Women and War* (Dublin,
1993); Jane Leonard, 'The Twinge of Memory: Armistice Day and Remembrance
Sunday in Dublin since 1919', in (eds.) Richard English and Graham Walker,
Unionism in Modern Ireland: New Perspectives on Politics and Culture (Dublin,
1996); Donal Ó Drisceoil, *Censorship in Ireland, 1939-1945: Neutrality, Politics
and Society* (Cork, 1996); Dermot Keogh, *Jews in Twentieth-Century Ireland:
Refugees, Anti-Semitism and the Holocaust* (Cork, 1998).
  2. See George Fleming (the historian in question), *Magennis VC* (Dublin,
1998).
  3. Senia Paseta, '1798 in 1898: The Politics of Commemoration', *Irish
Review*, 22 (Summer1998), pp.46-53 (52).
  4. See *Up in Arms: The 1798 Rebellion in Ireland: A Bicentenary Exhibition*,
compiled and edited by W.A. Maguire (Belfast, 1998). The Preface says: 'For
everyone involved it was a tragedy'.
  5. Tom Dunne, unpublished paper, '1798: Memory, History, Commemor-
ation'; see Dunne, '1798 and the United Irishmen', *Irish Review*, 22 (Summer
1998), pp.54-66; and Thomas Powell, 'The United Irishmen and the Wexford
Rebellion: The Sources Re-examined', *Irish Review*, 23 (Winter 1998), pp.127-40.
  6. Murray G.H. Pittock, *Poetry and Jacobite Politics in Eighteenth-Century
Britain and Ireland* (Cambridge, 1994), pp.241-42.
  7. Linda Colley, *Britons: Forging the Nation 1707-1837* (London, 1992),
pp.18, 53.
  8. See Pittock, *Inventing and Resisting Britain: Cultural Identities in Britain
and Ireland, 1685-1789* (London, 1997), pp.5-6, 173; Ian McBride, 'Ulster
and the British Problem', *Unionism in Modern Ireland*, pp.1-18 (2).
  9. Patrick O'Mahony & Gerard Delanty, *Rethinking Irish History: Nationalism,
Identity and Ideology* (London, 1998), p.11.
  10. Frank Wright, *Two Lands on One Soil: Ulster Politics before Home Rule*
(Dublin, 1996), p.3.
  11. For Devlin's difficulties between leftwing and nationalist politics, see
his autobiography, *Straight Left* (Belfast, 1993).
  12. Francis Fukuyama, *The End of History and the Last Man* (London, 1992),
p.xii.

13. Alex Callinicos, *Theories and Narratives: Reflections on the Philosophy of History* (London, 1995), pp.35, 38.
14. Fukuyama, *The End of History*, p.307.
15. Fredric Jameson, 'Marx's Purloined Letter', *New Left Review*, 209 (January/February 1995), pp.75-109 (106, 109).
16. Perry Anderson, *The Origins of Post-Modernity* (London, 1998), pp.66, 12.
17. Rorty quoted by Keith Jenkins, in Jenkins, *On 'What is History?'* (London, 1995), pp.129-30.
18. Eagleton envisages a future which will show 'the post-colonial world' to be 'in the van of human development', with the result that 'what now seems the latest thing to some Irish liberal modernisers will be shown up in its true reactionary colours, while the Irish colonial history some of them find so acutely embarrassing can be read as prefiguring the shape of the future.' Terry Eagleton, *Crazy John and the Bishop and Other Essays on Irish Culture* (Cork, 1998), p.327.
19. Christopher Norris, 'Truth, Science, and the Growth of Knowledge', *New Left Review*, 210, pp.105-23 (120-21).
20. Callinicos, *Theories and Narratives*, pp.14, 210.
21. Hayden White, *Metahistory* (Baltimore & London, 1973), pp.31, 426.
22. See White, *Metahistory*, pp.1-42.
23. Jenkins, *On 'What is History?'*, pp.178-79.
24. Jim Smyth, quoted by Powell, *Irish Review*, 23 (Winter 1998), p.138.
25. Richard J. Evans, *In Defence of History* (London, 1997), pp.248, 219-21.
26. Carl E. Schorske, *Thinking with History* (Princeton, 1998), pp.230-31, 16, 231-32.
27. (Ed.) Niall Ferguson, *Virtual History: Alternatives and Counterfactuals* (London, 1997), pp.65-69.
28. Schorske, *Thinking with History*, p.230.
29. R.F. Foster, *The Story of Ireland* (Oxford, 1995), pp.3, 11, 27.
30. (Eds.) George Boyce and Alan O'Day, *The Making of Modern Irish History: Revisionism and the Revisionist Controversy* (London, 1996), p.137.
31. Luke Gibbons, *Transformations in Irish Culture* (Cork, 1996), p.3.
32. Gibbons, *Transformations in Irish Culture*, pp.17-18, 15.
33. Evans, *In Defence of History*, p.248.
34. Foster, *The Story of Ireland*, p.30.
35. O'Mahony and Delanty, *Rethinking Irish History*, pp.14-15.
36. White, *Metahistory*, p.433.
37. White, *Metahistory*, p.190.
38. Declan Kiberd, *Inventing Ireland* (London, 1995), p.653.
39. White, *Metahistory*, p.190.
40. Seamus Deane, *Strange Country: Modernity and Nationhood in Irish Writing since 1790* (London, 1997), p.145.
41. White, *Metahistory*, pp.434, 24.
42. Deane, *Strange Country*, p.197.
43. White, *Metahistory*, pp.285, 9.
44. Tom Garvin, *1922: The Birth of Irish Democracy* (Dublin, 1996), pp.206-07.
45. Gerry Smyth, *Decolonisation and Criticism: The Construction of Irish Literature* (London, 1998), pp.1, 207.
46. Gibbons, *Transformations*, pp.179-80.
47. Ferguson, *Virtual History*, pp.88-89.

48. Ferguson, *Virtual History*, p.226.
49. Ferguson, *Virtual History*, p.227.
50. David Trimble, in (ed.) Maurna Crozier, *Cultural Traditions in Northern Ireland: Varieties of Irishness* (Belfast, 1989), p.50.
51. Arthur Aughey, 'Balance and the Frameworks', *Irish Review*, 17/18 (Winter 1995), pp.160-65 (165).
52. Robert McLiam Wilson, *Eureka Street* (London, 1996), p.396.
53. Colin Bateman, *Of Wee Sweetie Mice and Men* (London, 1996), p.7.
54. Breandán Ó Buachalla, 'Irish Jacobite Poetry', *Irish Review*, 12 (Spring/Summer 1992), pp.40-49 (45).
55. See Edna Longley, ' "Defending Ireland's Soul": Protestant Writers and Irish Nationalism after Independence', in Longley, *The Living Stream* (Newcastle upon Tyne, 1994), pp.130-49.
56. Louis MacNeice, *The Poetry of W.B. Yeats* (Oxford, 1941; London, 1967), p.120.
57. White, *Metahistory*, p.8.
58. 'The Other Side' is a response to Hewitt's poem 'The Hill Farm'.
59. Seamus Heaney, *The Redress of Poetry* (London, 1995), pp.200, 202.
60. White, *Metahistory*, p.37.
61. White, *Metahistory*, p.9.
62. See Callinicos, *Theories and Narratives*, pp.209-11.
63. White, *Metahistory*, pp.14-15.
64. White, *Metahistory*, p.11.

ACKNOWLEDGEMENTS

' "The Business of the Earth": Edward Thomas and Ecocentrism' first appeared in (eds.) Maria DiBattista and Lucy McDiarmid, *High and Low Moderns: Literature and Culture 1889–1939* (New York, 1996). ' "Something Wrong Somewhere?" Louis MacNeice as Critic' is a revised and extended version of the essay that appeared in (eds.) Kathleen Devine and Alan J. Peacock, *Louis MacNeice and His Influence* (Gerrards Cross, 1998). 'In Praise of "In Praise of Limestone"' is a revised and extended version of my contribution to ' "In Praise of Limestone": A Symposium', in (eds.) Katherine Bucknell and Nicholas Jenkins, ' "In Solitude for Company": W.H. Auden after 1940,' *Auden Studies*, 3 (Oxford, 1995). 'Larkin, Decadence and the Lyric Poem' appears in a slightly different form in (ed.) James Booth, *New Larkins for Old: Critical Essays on Philip Larkin* (London, 1999). 'The Millennial Muse' is a revised and extended version of 'Signposting the Century' which appeared in *Poetry Review*, 86/1 (Spring, 1996). 'Tom Paulin: Wild Irish Critic' is a slightly revised version of a review-article which appeared in *Thumbscrew*, 7 (Spring 1997). 'Irish Bards and American Audiences' is a revised and extended version of the essay which appeared in *Southern Review*, 31/3 (July 1995). ' "Atlantic's Premises": American Influences on Northern Irish Poetry in the 1960s' began as a lecture at Princeton University (May 1998), one of several events to mark the gift to Princeton University Library of The Leonard E. Milberg Collection of Irish Poetry. 'Northern Irish Poetry and the End of History' began as a lecture at the conference on Poetry and History, Stirling University (June 1996).

The author and publisher are grateful for permission to print the following copyright material: **W.H. Auden**, extracts from *Collected Poems* (1994) by permission of Faber & Faber Ltd and Random House Inc; **W.H. Auden & Louis MacNeice**, extracts from *Letters from Iceland* (Faber & Faber, 1937, 1967) by permission of David Higham Associates; **Eavan Boland**, extracts from *Collected Poems* (1995) by permission of Carcanet Press Ltd and W.W. Norton & Company, Inc; **Ciaran Carson**, extracts from *Opera Et Cetera* (1996) by permission of the Gallery Press and Wake Forest University Press; **Raymond Carver**, extracts from *All of Us: The Collected Poems* (1989) by permission of The Harvill Press, and Atlantic Monthly Press; **Seán Dunne**, extracts from *Time and the Island* (1996) by permission of the Gallery Press; **Paul Durcan**, extracts from *A Snail in My Prime: New and Selected Poems* (Harvill, 1993) by permission of The Harvill Press; **Robert Frost**, extracts from *The Poetry of Robert Frost*, ed. Edward Connery Lathem (1969) by permission of Jonathan Cape, Henry Holt and Company, and the editor; **Robert Graves**, extracts from *Complete Poems* (1995) by permission of Carcanet Press Ltd; **Seamus Heaney**, extracts from *New Selected Poems* (1998), *Door into the Dark* (1969), *The Haw Lantern* (1987), *Seeing Things* (1991), *The Spirit Level* (1996) by permission of Faber & Faber Ltd and Farrar, Straus & Giroux, Inc.; extracts from 'On a New Work in the English Tongue' by permission of the author and the *Sunday Times*; **Ted Hughes**, extracts from *New Selected Poems 1957-1994* (1995) and *Remains of Elmet* (1979) by permission of Faber & Faber Ltd, and Farrar, Straus & Giroux, Inc; **John Hewitt**, extracts from *The Collected Poems of John Hewitt* (Blackstaff Press, 1991) by permission of the publisher; **Geoffrey Hill**, extract from *The Triumph of Love* (Penguin Books, 1998) by permission of the publisher; **Patrick Kavanagh**, extracts from his poetry by permission of Eiléan Ní Chuilleanáin for the Estate of Patrick Kavanagh; **Philip Larkin**, extracts from *Collected Poems* (1988) by permission of Faber & Faber Ltd and Farrar, Straus & Giroux, Inc.; **Michael Longley**, extracts from *Poems 1963-1983* (Secker and Warburg, 1991) by permission of the author; extracts from *The Ghost Orchid* (1995), *Selected Poems* (1998) and *The Weather in Japan* (2000), by permission of Jonathan Cape, Wake Forest University Press and Lucas Alexander Whitley; **Robert Lowell**, extracts from *Poems 1938-1949* (1950) by permission of Faber & Faber Ltd, and Harcourt Brace & Company, and from *Selected Poems* (1965) by permission of Faber & Faber Ltd and Farrar, Straus & Giroux, Inc.; **Medbh McGuckian**, extracts from *Captain Lavender* (1994), by permission of trhe Gallery Press and Wake Forest University Press; **Louis MacNeice**, extracts from *Collected Poems* (Faber & Faber, 1966), by permission of David Higham Associates; **Derek Mahon**, extracts from *Collected Poems* (Gallery Press, 1999) by permission of the publisher; **Paul Muldoon**, extracts from *Meeting the British* (1987) by permission of Faber & Faber Ltd, and Wake Forest University Press; from *Six Honest Serving Men* (Gallery Books, 1995) by permission of the publisher; from *Hay* (1998) by permission of Faber & Faber Ltd, and Farrar, Straus & Giroux; **Richard Murphy**, extracts from *The Price of Stone* (Faber & Faber, 1985), by permission of the Gallery Press; **Frank O'Hara**, extracts from *Selected Poems* (1991) by permission of Carcanet Press Ltd and Random House, Inc; **Frank Ormsby**, extract from *The Ghost Train* (1995), by permission of the Gallery

Press; **Tom Paulin**, extract from *Walking a Line* (1994) by permission of Faber & Faber Ltd; **Theodore Roethke**, extracts from *Collected Poems* (1995) by permission of Faber & Faber Ltd, and Doubleday; **Wallace Stevens**, extracts from *Collected Poems* (1955) by permission of Faber & Faber Ltd and Alfred A. Knopf, Inc.; **Derek Walcott**, extract from *Omeros* (1990) by permission of Faber & Faber Ltd, and Farrar, Straus & Giroux, Inc.; **Richard Wilbur**, extracts from *New and Collected Poems* (Faber & Faber, 1989) by permission of Faber & Faber Ltd and Harcourt Brace & Company; **W.B. Yeats**, extracts from Yeats's *Poems*, ed. A.N. Jeffares (Macmillan, 1989) by permission of the publisher and A.P. Watt Ltd on behalf of Michael Yeats.

INDEX

350   INDEX

Vendler, Helen, 210, 237, 246, 248, 249, 253
Vickers, Brian, 158
Viney, Michael, 130
Virgil, 119, 122

Wain, John, 218
Walcott, Derek, 86, 222
Ward, Geoff, 17-18, 152
Watson, Roderick, 214
Waugh, Evelyn, 195
Webb, Beatrice, 29
Wells, Robert, 35
Whelan, Kevin, 95, 99, 282
White, Hayden, 283, 289, 291, 293-96, 301, 308, 314
White, T.H., 84
Whitman, Walt, 156, 159, 255, 267
Widdowson, Peter, 153
Wilbur, Richard 11, 21, 260, 262, 263, 275-76
Wilde, Oscar, 117, 179, 185, 295
Williams, Raymond, 23-24, 33, 44, 94
Williams, William Carlos, 83, 221, 260, 261
Wilson, Edward O., 32

Wilson, Robert McLiam, 70, 286, 299, 315
Winters, Yvor, 247
Wood, Michael, 169
Woodburn, James Barkley, 65-66
Woolf, Virginia, 145, 147, 149-50, 153-54
Wordsworth, William, 92, 99, 100-09, 113, 118, 121, 126, 158
Wright, David, 204, 205
Wright, Frank, 284

Yeats, J.B., 304
Yeats, W.B., 13-14, 16-17, 19, 52, 57, 58, 61, 67, 69, 71, 74, 76-80, 83, 86, 111, 112, 113-22, 125-28, 131, 135, 137, 139, 140-41, 156, 157-58, 162, 163-64, 172, 177, 183, 204, 206, 215-16, 218, 219, 221, 222, 233, 237, 258, 261, 265, 300-01, 308, 313
Yenser, Stephen, 238

Index compiled by Stephanie J. Dagg

THE Bloodaxe Book OF
20TH CENTURY POETRY

edited by EDNA LONGLEY

This epoch-marking anthology presents a map of poetry from Britain and Ireland which readers can follow. You will not get lost here as in other anthologies – with their vast lists of poets summoned up to serve a critic's argument or to illustrate a journalistic overview. Instead, Edna Longley shows you the key poets of the century, and through interlinking commentary points up the connections between them as well as their relationship with the continuing poetic traditions of these islands.

Edna Longley draws the poetic line of the century not through culture-defining groups but through the work of the most significant poets of our time. Because her guiding principle is aesthetic precision, the poems themselves answer to their circumstances. Readers will find this book exciting and risk-taking not because her selections are surprising but because of the intensity and critical rigour of her focus, and because the poems themselves are so good.

This is a vital anthology because the selection is so pared down. Edna Longley has omitted showy, noisy, ephemeral writers who drown out their contemporaries but leave later or wiser readers unimpressed. Similarly there is no place here for the poet as entertainer, cultural spokesman, feminist mythmaker or political commentator.

While anthologies survive, the idea of poetic tradition survives. An anthology as rich as Edna Longley's houses intricate conversations between poets and between poems, between the living and the dead, between the present and the future. It is a book which will enrich the reader's experience and understanding of modern poetry.

Paperback: ISBN 1 85224 514 X 352 pages £10.95

Also available by Edna Longley from Bloodaxe:

Poetry in the Wars: A classic work on Ireland, poetry and war, with essays on Yeats, MacNeice, Frost, Edward Thomas, Keith Douglas, Heaney, Larkin, Mahon and Muldoon. 272 pages, £9.95 paper, 0 906427 99 1.

The Living Stream: Literature & Revisionism in Ireland: Longley investigates the links between Irish literature, culture and politics. Questioning the fixed purposes of both nationalism and unionism, she shows in particular where Northern Irish writing fits into this process of change. 304 pages, £10.95 paper, 1 85224 217 5; £25 cloth, 1 85224 216 7.

STRONG WORDS

modern poets on modern poetry

edited by W.N. HERBERT
& MATTHEW HOLLIS

Poetry has never been so rigorous and diverse, nor has its audience been so numerous and engaged. *Strong words?* Not if the poets are right. As Ezra Pound wrote: 'You would think anyone wanting to know about poetry would go to someone who *knew* something about it.' That's exactly what Bloodaxe has done with this judicious and comprehensive selection of British, Irish and American manifestos by some of modern poetry's finest practitioners.

Opening the 20th century account with Ezra Pound, W.B. Yeats and T.S. Eliot, the book moves through key later figures including W.H. Auden, Ted Hughes, Stevie Smith and Dylan Thomas. America is richly represented too, from Robert Frost and William Carlos Williams to the influential New England poets Robert Lowell, Elizabeth Bishop and Sylvia Plath.

Strong Words then brings the issues fully up to date with over 30 specially commissioned statements from contemporary writers including Seamus Heaney, Andrew Motion, Simon Armitage, Selima Hill, Paul Muldoon and Douglas Dunn, amounting to a new overview of the poetry being written at the start of the 21st century.

For poets and readers, for critics, teachers and students of creative writing and contemporary poetry, this is essential reading. As well as representing many of the most important poets of the last hundred years, *Strong Words* also charts many different stances and movements, from Modernism to Postmodernism, from Futurism to the future theories of poetry. This landmark book champions the continuing dialogue of these voices, past and present, exploring the strongest form that words can take: *the poem.*

Paperback: ISBN 1 85224 515 8   320 pages   £10.95

For a complete catalogue of Bloodaxe titles, please write to:
Bloodaxe Books Ltd, Highgreen, Tarset, Northumberland NE48 1RP